Play at the Center of the Curriculum

Play at the Center of the Curriculum

Fourth Edition

Judith Van Hoorn

Mills College and University of the Pacific

Patricia Monighan Nourot

Sonoma State University

Barbara Scales

University of California, Berkeley

Keith Rodriguez Alward

PEARSON

Merrill
Prentice Hall

Upper Saddle River, New Jersey
Columbus, Ohio

KH

Library of Congress Cataloging-in-Publication Data
Play at the center of the curriculum / Judith Van Hoorn . . . [et al.].— 4th ed.
    p. cm.
  Includes bibliographical references and index.
  ISBN 0-13-172082-1
  1. Play. 2. Early childhood education—Curricula. 3. Child development. I. Van Hoorn, Judith Lieberman.
  LB1139.35.P55P57 2007
  155.4'18—dc22   2005036211

Vice President and Executive Publisher: Jeffery W. Johnston
Publisher: Kevin M. Davis
Acquisitions Editor: Julie Peters
Editorial Assistant: Michelle Girgis
Production Editor: Linda Hillis Bayma
Production Coordination: Thistle Hill Publishing Services, LLC
Design Coordinator: Diane C. Lorenzo
Cover Designer: Candace Rowley
Cover image: Fotosearch
Production Manager: Laura Messerly
Director of Marketing: David Gesell
Marketing Manager: Amy Judd
Marketing Coordinator: Brian Mounts

This book was set in Baskerville by Laserwords Private Limited, Chennai. It was printed and bound by R.R. Donnelley & Sons Company. The cover was printed by R.R. Donnelley & Sons Company.

Photo Credits: Pereira Studios, pp. 1, 4, 8, 39, 49, 79, 173, 181, 194, 239, 333; Judith Van Hoorn, p. 16; Ralph Granich, pp. 26, 29, 45, 52, 110, 124, 185, 205, 217, 226, 236, 265, 268, 275, 291, 300, 312, 363, 366, 375, 384; Todd Yarrington/Merrill, pp. 56, 356; Heather Gray, pp. 67, 77, 139; Barbara Schwartz/Merrill, pp. 87, 202; Patricia Nourot, p. 95; Anne Vega/Merrill, pp. 128, 142, 151, 319; Shirley Zeiberg/PH College, p. 135; Tom Watson/Merrill, p. 167; Virginia Quock, p. 246; Scott Cunningham/Merrill, p. 252; Lynn Bradley, p. 302; Ken Karp/PH College, p. 336; Anthony Magnacca/Merrill, p. 341.

PEARSON

**Merrill
Prentice Hall**

10 9 8 7 6 5 4 3 2 1
ISBN: 0-13-172082-1

7/12/06

This book is dedicated to Millie Almy,
beloved mentor to our study of children's play.

Preface

In this fourth edition of *Play at the Center of the Curriculum,* we reaffirm our commitment to play in the early childhood classroom. The natural link between play and development is our blueprint. Developmental theory shows that play is critical to the development of intelligence, personality, competencies, a sense of self, and social awareness. We therefore believe that a developmentally appropriate, holistic, and integrated early childhood curriculum has play at its center.

The old adage that "play is children's work" is re-examined in this book for teachers. We demonstrate how play can be drawn upon to improve developmentally based early childhood education. Early childhood extends into the early primary grades, and we propose that play is a critical dimension to children's learning and development throughout the preschool and primary grade years.

We believe that an ideal early childhood classroom is characterized by an abundance of play. Our experience tells us that teachers can learn to structure the early childhood classroom environment and to sequence classroom routines so that the learning expectations for children are embedded in spontaneous and guided play activity.

In today's climate of academic accountability, parents, teachers, and administrators may worry that a play-centered curriculum cannot meet academic standards. In this edition, we've paid particular attention to the standards issue, demonstrating how developmentally appropriate standards can be met in a play-centered curriculum.

This book carefully blends theory and practice. As seasoned teachers, we demonstrate how to draw both the methods and the content of a successful curriculum from children's play. We interweave anecdotes of children's play, theories of play and development, and instructional strategies that place play at the center of the curriculum.

By combining sound theory with practical illustrations, *Play at the Center of the Curriculum* achieves a solid argument for play in formal education. Teachers and students in the field of early childhood education will find this book to be a valuable resource. This is not merely a "how to" book, nor is it simply a "thought" book. Rather, it is a blending of each, serving the reader in a number of ways.

Play at the Center of the Curriculum is a resource for those who want to engage children in a developmental zone where children and teachers are learning.

Current and future teachers are guided in methods of supporting children's progress through play. The teacher becomes the architect of the environment, using play and development as the blueprint.

NEW TO THIS EDITION

In this edition, we have enriched and expanded the emphasis in a number of areas, drawing upon our own teaching and observations in classrooms, as well as recent research and writing in the field of early childhood curriculum and children's play.

- This edition also includes **a more explicit focus on how a play-centered curriculum addresses curriculum standards and benchmarks.** The chapters on assessment, the arts, science, mathematics, language and literacy, and socialization (chapters 6 through 11) have been expanded to reflect these emphases and to incorporate current work in the field.

- Each chapter provides more discussions, examples, and research that demonstrate how play-centered curricula can be **inclusive,** inviting programs for children and families from all cultural backgrounds and children who are **English language learners.**

- Each chapter provides a more thorough discussion of serving **children with special needs.** New references and additional classroom anecdotes are provided.

- The fourth edition includes a fuller acknowledgment of the importance of **emotions** in the lives of children, both in and outside the classroom.

- Chapter 12 includes an expanded discussion of the **developmentally appropriate use of technology,** the Internet, speech-to-text, and the impact of toy marketing and media.

ORGANIZATION AND STRUCTURE

This text has been written for students with varying experience and knowledge. Chapters 1 through 6 are designed to form foundation concepts and principles. We recommend that these be read first.

Chapters 2 and 3 introduce theory and research that support our understanding of play and development. The reader is introduced to the ideas of major figures in developmental theory—Piaget, Vygotsky, Erikson, and Mead—as well as to the work of contemporary researchers.

Chapters 4 and 5 bring this developmental focus back to the reality of the classroom. We explore the teacher's role in setting the stage, actively guiding, and orchestrating play. The issue of how teachers might respond to violent and aggressive play is addressed through anecdotes and practical strategies.

Chapter 6 looks at how the creation of a successful play-centered curriculum can be used to assess children's developmental progress. Included are many examples of play that embed state and national curriculum standards.

Chapters 7 through 11 explore curriculum areas that are of interest to contemporary early childhood education: mathematics, language and literacy, science, the arts, and socialization. Each chapter begins with an anecdote that focuses on how a potential curriculum is embedded in the children's spontaneous play. The reader will find a rich palette of practical ideas for the articulation of the play-centered curriculum.

Chapter 12 looks at ways in which play, toys, and technology interact to affect the young child's life. We present many ideas and observations useful to teachers and families on the roles of toys and games, media, and technology in the lives of young children.

Depending on the background of students, instructors can vary the order of these chapters and draw upon some of the suggested resources to extend students' understanding. Chapters 7 through 12 can be assigned in an order that is compatible with the instructor's course structure.

Chapter 13 extends your understanding of developmental theory and play, expanding on the constructivist views presented by Piaget and Vygotsky. The role of play in developing intelligence, personality, competency, and sense of self is explored. We pay particular attention to the role of work and autonomy in the early childhood years as they relate to the broader goals of education. This chapter will, we believe, be more meaningful after reading the more experience-focused chapters that have preceded it.

OTHER FEATURES OF THIS TEXT

Anecdotes

Each chapter anchors its focus in the world of children by beginning with an anecdote related to play and education. Numerous additional classroom anecdotes and examples are provided throughout each chapter. These practical observations ground the reader in day-to-day educational experiences.

When Teachers Talk

This section is included in many of the chapters in order to address some of the challenging issues and questions that teachers have raised.

Summary and Conclusion

Each chapter ends with a summary and conclusion, giving the reader a brief review of the main points of the chapter and some practical implications. The student might read this first to get an overview of the focus of the chapter.

Suggested Resources

Each chapter is rich in up-to-date references. All chapters end with several key resources that allow students to pursue key concepts in greater depth or for instructors to enhance course work.

ACKNOWLEDGMENTS

We gratefully acknowledge those who have shared with us their experiences, ideas, critical reviews, exemplary references, and examples from their own practice: Melinda Bachman, Lyda Beardsley, Sara Billingslee, Libby Byers, Greta Campbell, Shirley Cheal, Randi Dingman, Heather Dunlap, Sandra Easley, Johanna Filp-Hanke, Patricia Fluetsch, Buffy Frick, Anita Gensler, Janet Gonzalez-Mena, Suzanne Gray, Cynthia Halewood, Bonnie Hester, Kristin Hope, Jackie Imbimbo, Rochelle Jacobs, Robin Johnson, Richard Karsch, Marjorie Keegan, Susan Kyle, Rose Laugtug, Janet Lederman, Kim Lovsey, Christa McCoy, Gail Mon Pere, Virginia Quock, Margaret Potts, Ada Rappeport, Kitty Ritz, Shane Rojo, Kathy Rosebrook, Ann Siefert, Dorothy Stewart, Lisa Tabachnick, Lia Thompson-Clark, Lea Waters, Maureen Wieser, and Professors Millie Almy, Jennie Cook-Gumperz, Ann Dyson, Celia Genishi, Ageliki Nicopoulou, as well as Vivian Paley. Their contributions have been practical, often inspiring, and have enriched our text.

We acknowledge the special contributions of Leni von Blanckensee, a specialist in educational technology as well as an experienced teacher, who contributed to our understanding of young children and technology for this edition.

We are grateful to Theresa Lozac'h, a gifted kindergarten teacher, who served as a sounding board for our ideas for this edition, provided thoughtful comments on the manuscript, and contributed anecdotes from her extensive experience.

We thank the University of the Pacific for the McDaniel Grant and the Merck Foundation Grant, which provided support for developing chapters 6 and 7. Special thanks to Marcy McGaugh for her excellent work preparing the manuscript.

We are grateful for the continued support and wise counsel we received from our editor, Julie Peters, as well as Carol Sykes, photo department manager. We also wish to thank the following reviewers of the manuscript, who provided valuable comments and suggestions: Jennifer Aldrich, Central Missouri State University; ReGena Booze, Pacific Oaks College; Susan Catapano, University of Missouri-St. Louis; Beverly Brown Dupre, Southern University at New Orleans; and Nancy Wiltz, Towson University. Above all, thanks to the children and their teachers who brought life to our presentation of the play-centered curriculum.

Discover the Companion Website Accompanying This Book

The Prentice Hall Companion Website: A Virtual Learning Environment

Technology is a constantly growing and changing aspect of our field that is creating a need for content and resources. To address this emerging need, Prentice Hall has developed an online learning environment for students and professors alike—Companion Websites—to support our textbooks.

In creating a Companion Website, our goal is to build on and enhance what the textbook already offers. For this reason, the content for each user-friendly website is organized by topic and provides the professor and student with a variety of meaningful resources. Common features of a Companion Website include:

- **Introduction**—General information about the topic and how it is covered in the website.

- **Web Links**—A variety of websites related to topic areas.

- **Timely Articles**—Links to online articles that enable you to become more aware of important issues in early childhood.

- **Learn by Doing**—Put concepts into action, participate in activities, examine strategies, and more.

- **Visit a School**—Visit a school's website to see concepts, theories, and strategies in action.

- **For Teachers/Practitioners**—Access information you will need to know as an educator, including information on materials, activities, and lessons.

- **Observation Tools**—A collection of checklists and forms to print and use when observing and assessing children's development.

- **Current Policies and Standards**—Find out the latest early childhood policies from the government and various organizations, and view state, federal, and curriculum standards.

- **Resources and Organizations**—Discover tools to help you plan your classroom or center and organizations to provide current information and standards for each topic.

- **Electronic Bluebook**—Paperless method of completing homework or essays assigned by a professor. Finished work can be sent to the professor via email.

To take advantage of these and other resources, please visit Merrill Education's **Early Childhood Education Resources Website.** Go to **www.prenhall.com/ vanhoorn**, click on the book cover, and then click on "Enter" at the bottom of the next screen.

TEACHER PREP

MERRILL
PRENTICE HALL

Teacher Preparation Classroom

Your Class. Their Careers. Our Future. Will your students be prepared?

We invite you to explore our new, innovative and engaging website and all that it has to offer you, your course, and tomorrow's educators! Organized around the major courses pre-service teachers take, the Teacher Preparation site provides media, student/teacher artifacts, strategies, research articles, and other resources to equip your students with the quality tools needed to excel in their courses and prepare them for their first classroom.

This ultimate on-line education resource is available at no cost, when packaged with a Merrill text, and will provide you and your students access to:

Online Video Library. More than 150 video clips—each tied to a course topic and framed by learning goals and Praxis-type questions—capture real teachers and students working in real classrooms, as well as in-depth interviews with both students and educators.

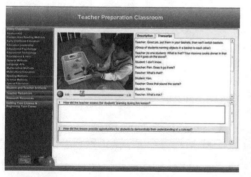

Student and Teacher Artifacts. More than 200 student and teacher classroom artifacts—each tied to a course topic and framed by learning goals and application questions—provide a wealth of materials and experiences to help make your study to become a professional teacher more concrete and hands-on.

Research Articles. Over 500 articles from ASCD's renowned journal *Educational Leadership*. The site also includes Research Navigator, a searchable database of additional educational journals.

Teaching Strategies. Over 500 strategies and lesson plans for you to use when you become a practicing professional.

Licensure and Career Tools. Resources devoted to helping you pass your licensure exam; learn standards, law, and public policies; plan a teaching portfolio; and succeed in your first year of teaching.

How to ORDER *Teacher Prep* for you and your students:

For students to receive a *Teacher Prep* Access Code with this text, instructors **must** provide a special value pack ISBN number on their textbook order form. To receive this special ISBN, please email: **Merrill.marketing@pearsoned.com** and provide the following information:

- Name and Affiliation
- Author/Title/Edition of Merrill text

Upon ordering *Teacher Prep* for their students, instructors will be given a lifetime *Teacher Prep* Access Code.

Brief Contents

Contents

5   Orchestrating Play: Interactions with Children   110

8   Language, Literacy, and Play   202

12   Play, Toys, and Technology   333

13   Conclusion: Integrating Play, Development, and Practice   363

Note: Every effort has been made to provide accurate and current Internet information in this book. However, the Internet and information posted on it are constantly changing, so it is inevitable that some of the Internet addresses listed in this textbook will change.

Looking at Play Through Teachers' Eyes

With dramatic gestures, Brandon loudly sings, "Can you milk my cow?" After he and his kindergarten classmates finish the song with a rousing, "Yes, ma'am!" their teacher, Anna, calls upon Becky and Tino to figure out the date and count the number of days the children have been to school. (This is the 26th day.) As other children join in the counting, Brandon takes a toy car out of his pocket. He spins the wheels, turns around, and shows it to Chris. After a moment, he reaches out to touch Kara's shoelaces, whispering, "I have snaps." Then he opens and refastens the Velcro snaps on his shoes.

Anna announces that it's choice time and calls on children to leave the circle and go to the activities of their choice. Brandon sits up straight, wanting to be called on and ready to start. The moment his name is called, he heads to the housekeeping area where Chris and Andy are opening some cupboards. Brandon announces: "I'll make breakfast." (He picks up the coffeepot.) "Here's coffee." (He pretends to pour a cup and gives it to Chris.)

Mary, a new student in the class, wanders into the housekeeping area holding the pet rat. Brandon interrupts his breakfast preparation and says to Mary, "You can't bring Fluffy in here. You have to keep her near her cage."

Within a few minutes, the theme of the children's play turns from eating to fire fighting. Brandon and Andy go to the block area to get some long block "hoses." They spend a few minutes there pretending to hose down several block construction "fires." Brandon knocks one down, to the angry cries of the builders, Valerie and Paul. He then transforms the block hose into a gun, which he uses to shoot at them.

As he and Andy stomp about the block area, Brandon passes Mary, still holding the rat, and says to her, "That's too tight. See, like this." He takes the rat from her, cradles it, looks it in the eyes, and pats it. "Fluffy was at my house during vacation. I got to feed her. See, she remembers me."

Brandon and Andy spend the next 10 minutes building a house and a maze for Fluffy while Mary looks on. Brandon has chosen to play in the block area each day for more than a month. The boys gather five arches for a roof, partially covering a rectangular enclosure they have made by stacking blocks horizontally, using long blocks and, when none are left, two shorter blocks placed side by side.

When he and Andy have finished building the "roof," Brandon rushes to a nearby table where Rotha and Kai are chatting and drawing. He grabs a piece of paper and hastily scribbles on the middle of it, knocking off a few templates and scissors in the process. "This is my map. This is my map for the maze," he says. Brandon then goes to his teacher for some tape to put on the maze. He points to a figure on the paper where two lines intersect and says, "See my X? That's where Fluffy gets out." ✆

Every observation of children's play illustrates its multidimensional qualities. By observing Brandon's play for just a short time, we can learn about the way he is developing socially. For example, we see that Brandon is able to join Chris and Andy in their play in the housekeeping area by introducing an appropriate topic, offering to make breakfast. This observation also informs us about Brandon's developing cognitive abilities. In his play, he uses a block to symbolically represent first a hose, and then a gun. While building the house for Fluffy, Brandon demonstrates practical knowledge of equivalencies when he uses two short blocks to equal the length of one longer block. Thus, by observing Brandon's play, we witness how he applies his developing abilities in real situations.

This observation also raises some of the many questions that teachers ask about children's play. How should a teacher respond when a child plays during group instruction? How can a teacher balance spontaneous play with teacher-directed activities? Should teachers redirect children when they select the same play materials or themes day after day? Should gun play be allowed? How can play help us understand and assess children's cognitive, linguistic, social, emotional, and physical development? How can we be sure we are creating an inclusive curriculum that promotes equity and school success for all? How can a play-centered curriculum address state standards?

Observing Brandon leads us to the central issue this book addresses: Why should play be at the center of the curriculum in early childhood programs?

PLAY AT THE CENTER OF A DEVELOPMENTALLY BASED CURRICULUM

Developmentally based early childhood programs place the developmental characteristics of the young child—the learner—at the center of the curriculum. This book is based on the premise that play is the central force in young children's development. Consequently, a developmentally based program is a play-centered program. A play-centered curriculum is not a laissez-faire curriculum in which anything goes. It is a curriculum that uses the power of play to foster children's development. It is an emergent curriculum in which teachers take an active role in balancing spontaneous play, guided play, directed play, and teacher-directed activities.

In honoring the child's play, we honor the "whole child." When discussing a play-centered curriculum, we think of the child as a developing "whole" human being in whom the processes of development are integrated. Play fosters all aspects of the child's development: emotional, social, intellectual, linguistic, and physical. It involves the integration of what children have learned. This view contrasts with the idea of development as the linear acquisition of separate skills.

In promoting a play-centered curriculum, we make short- and long-term investments in development. In the short term, play creates a classroom atmosphere of cooperation, initiative, and intellectual challenge. If we look at long-term consequences, we find that play supports children's growth in broad, inclusive competencies such as self-direction and industry. These are

The play-centered curriculum is emergent.

competencies valued by both parents and educators, and ones that children will need to develop in order to function as adults in our society.

Throughout this book, we emphasize how curricula in particular areas such as mathematics, language and literacy, science, art, socialization, and technology can support and enrich young children's play. This idea contrasts with the widespread notion that play serves merely to support subject-matter competencies. Our view also contrasts with the idea of play traditionally found in the intermediate grades—play as a reward for finishing work.

This does not mean that all play is equal in our eyes. Play is fun, but it is more than fun. Play-centered curricula are not opportunities for teachers to stand aside, but require highly competent, involved teachers. The critical dimension is to provide conditions that foster children's development using their own sources of energy. In the following chapters, we articulate the play-based curricula that support children's own developmental forces.

Play as a Fundamental Human Activity

Play is a human phenomenon that occurs across the life span, as well as across cultures. Parents in Mexico teach their babies the clapping game "tortillas," while older children and adults play Loteria. Adolescent East Indians play soccer, while younger children play hopping games accompanied by singing. Chinese toddlers clap to a verse celebrating their grandmothers, "banging the gong merrily to accompany me home," while the grandmothers, in their old age, play Mah-Jongg. As humans, we enjoy not only our own engagement in play, but we often are fascinated by the play of others. The entertainment and sports industries reflect the popularity of observing play.

The Power of Play in Development

What is the specific rationale for making play the central focus of school programs for young children? During early childhood, play is fundamental because it drives young children's development. As we describe in the chapters that follow, play is simultaneously a facet of development and the source of energy for development. It is an expression of the child's developing personality, sense of self, intellect, social capacity, and physicality. At the same time, through their play, children direct their energy to activities of their own choice. These activities stimulate further development.

The fundamental premise of this book is that play is the heart of developmentally appropriate early childhood programs and, therefore, should be at the center of every curriculum. If the young child is at the center of the curriculum, then play should be at the center of the curriculum as well, for play is the basic activity of early childhood.

Play is essential for optimal development and learning in young children. The match between the characteristics of play and the characteristics of the young child provides a synergy that drives development as no teacher-directed activity can.

Grounding Practice in Theory, Research, and the Wisdom of Practitioners

The idea of play at the center of the early childhood curriculum is grounded in work from four early childhood traditions: (1) early childhood practitioners, (2) researchers and theorists who have studied play, (3) researchers and theorists in the area of development and learning, and (4) educational historians. These four traditions inform our ideas of a practice of play.

Play and the Wisdom of Practitioners. Historically, play has been at the center of early childhood programs. Early childhood educators have observed and emphasized that young children bring an energy and enthusiasm to their play that not only seems to drive development, but also seems to be an inseparable part of development. A kindergarten student playing with blocks might spend an hour focused intently on this task, but might squirm when asked to sit down for 10 minutes to practice writing letters of the alphabet. Using a favorite word of young children, we might ask, "Why?"

Play, Theory, and Research.   Theorists and researchers who study play suggest possible reasons for its importance in the development of young children when they describe the characteristics of play. According to theorists, the distinguishing features of play include: (1) intrinsic motivation, (2) active engagement, (3) attention to means rather than ends, (4) nonliteral behavior, and (5) freedom from external rules (Monighan-Nourot, Scales, & Van Hoorn, with Almy, 1987).

When young children are actively engaged and intrinsically motivated, we observe their zest, as well as their focused attention. We see them use language to communicate with others, solve problems, draw, ride trikes, and so on. Children's sense of autonomy, initiative, and industry are rooted in intrinsic motivation and active engagement.

Attention to means rather than ends indicates that children are less involved with achieving a goal than with the process of reaching it. Young children are well aware of the grown-up things they cannot yet do. Even the competencies that are expected of them are often frustrating, such as waiting for a snack, sharing, cutting with scissors, and (in the primary years) learning to read, add and subtract, and carry out simple household chores. In their play, children can change the goals and the ways to achieve the goals.

> This shifting among alternative patterns of means and goals appears to contribute flexibility to the child's thinking and problem solving. These new combinations may be accompanied by a sense of discovery and exhilaration. Miller (1974) borrows "galumphing," a term from Lewis Carroll's poem "Jabberwocky," to describe this. "Galumphing" with ideas lacks the smoothness and efficiency that characterize more goal-specific activity, but it is experimentation that may enhance creative thinking. Opportunities for "galumphing" are lacking in curricula that are programmed to have the child arrive at only "correct" responses. (Monighan-Nourot et al., 1987, p. 17)

Young children's play is often non-literal, pretend play that is not bound by external rules. How is fantasy play useful to a young child who is learning to function in the real world? Children's symbolic development is fostered through the creation and use of symbols in pretend play, as well as in hypothetical, "as if" situations. Through play, children develop boundaries of the real and the imagined, and also visions of the possible, the drive from childhood that turns the wheels of invention.

Play, Development, and Learning.   Support for placing play at the center of the curriculum comes from the work of theorists and researchers who have examined the role of play in development and learning. For more than a century, theorists have explored these links. Today, we draw upon the work of "classical" theorists who reflected particular times and values in their work. We discuss these theories from current viewpoints that reflect today's concerns and understandings of development. In the chapters that follow, we turn to the work of Piaget and Vygotsky for an understanding of the importance of play in cognitive development. We turn to Erikson and Mead for an understanding of the role of play in the child's developing sense of self and ability to establish social relationships, and to Vygotsky and Erikson for an understanding of how play might reflect issues of culture and society. We also include more recent critical thinking on issues of equity, inclusion, the peer culture, violence in the lives of children, and promotion of peaceful classrooms (e.g., Alvarado, Derman-Sparks, & Ramsey, 1999; Levin & Carlsson-Paige, 2006; Cortés, 2000; Giddens, 2000; Gonzales-Mena, 1998).

Play and Traditions of Schooling. Writings on the history of schooling also lead us to place play at the center of the early childhood education curriculum. Historians have examined issues such as "What is worth learning?" and, importantly, "Who should learn?" as well as the ways in which formal schools differ from informal apprenticeship structures found in less industrialized, traditional societies (Dewey, 1915/1971).

Early schools in the Middle East and Europe evolved for specific purposes, such as training scribes. Only select groups of boys in middle childhood and adolescence attended school. Later, as formal schools spread geographically, the number of students attending schools began to grow. During the past century, the rationale for schooling changed. In today's formal schools, many activities have become separate from their real-life applications.

During the late 1800s, a greater number of adults needed to have basic competencies in numeracy and literacy, while a more elite group of adults needed more technical competencies. It was also during this period and the early 1900s that girls and boys younger than 7 or 8 years old entered "school-like" settings. For the children of factory workers, these settings were child-care institutions designed to keep children out of harm's way. For the children of the emerging, more educated middle class, the settings were nursery schools and kindergartens that aimed to support the development of the child. Play often comprised a large part of these programs.

However, in the decades that followed, the gradual blending of the goals of child care, preschool, kindergarten, and the primary grades often has led to increased pressure for teacher-directed curricula and programs that stress learning "academic" skills (Nourot, 2005). We witness this trend today. When curricular models include play, the play is bent to support these skills. Teachers find that young students bring little spontaneous energy and interest to learning addition facts or sight words if only a didactic approach rather than a balanced approach is employed.

Today, pressure for performance is increased in preschool and the primary grades. Increasingly, play is viewed for its instrumental value: "What game will make memorizing these words more fun?" When most play takes this form, the central role of play in children's development is subverted. When children do not repeat such teacher-directed activities in their own play, it usually means that the activities are without interest or perceived value.

These considerations of the history of formal schooling bring us back to our position that play should be at the center of the early childhood curriculum. Play-centered programs promote equity because they are built around the strengths of young children rather than their weaknesses. At a time when our population is becoming increasingly diverse we can not maintain educational practices that fail many students.

Play at the Center of a Balanced Curriculum

To meet the needs of all children, we see a preschool–kindergarten program as firmly play centered and complemented with daily life activities and some teacher-directed activities. We see first grade as a transitional year, with emphasis on both play and daily life activities complemented with teacher-directed activities, and second grade as a time when play and work are merged into children's extended projects, thereby integrating areas of academic learning.

The play-centered curriculum can meet the needs of all children.

In our view, education for children from preschool through second grade should promote the development of both the competent young child and the competent future adult. This is best accomplished by means of a balanced, play-centered program where neither spontaneous play nor teacher-directed activities are the only mode.

As Figure 1.1 illustrates, play is at the center of a balanced curriculum. Daily life activities are the critical second strata. For example, daily life activities include involving preschoolers in setting the table, kindergartners in planting a garden, first graders in mailing their first letters, and second graders in learning to tell time. Teacher-directed activities, including thematic units as well as subject area units, constitute the third strata.

In the play-centered curriculum described in this book, a constant flow occurs among these three levels. We discuss how children repeat daily life and teacher-directed activity in their play, how teachers plan daily life activities so that they draw upon the power of play, how teachers can develop effective assessment strategies, and how teachers can use children's play to promote curricular objectives.

In contrast to the common emphasis on how play can be used to support subject-matter objectives, in this book we also emphasize how curricula in content areas can enrich and support good play. By changing our focus from play to daily life activities to teacher-directed activities (and always back to play), our view becomes the opposite of the traditional view. When children play, we

Figure 1.1
Play at the Center of a
Balanced Curriculum

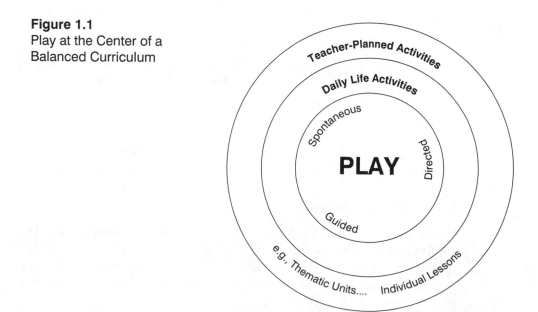

believe they are engrossed in what interests them most. They are also practicing and developing competencies at the edge of their potential. In play, self-directed learning engages and focuses attention, and provides numerous opportunities for children to practice self-control.

When children are involved in such daily life activities as writing a letter, sending an e-mail message, cleaning up, and learning to tie their shoes, they are engaged in what is important in the lives of the adults around them. The purpose of daily life activities is readily apparent, if not always enjoyable. When carrying out daily life activities, there are procedures to learn and rules, that the society determines, to obey. This is not necessarily true of play. For example, when a child like Brandon pretends to make coffee for breakfast, he does not have to adhere to the sequence of how an adult makes coffee and can choose to turn the cup of coffee into a glass of orange juice or a cup of ice cream if he wants to. Play, too, has rules, but children have more power to determine them.

Children's involvement in play, daily life activities, and teacher-directed activities differs when we compare the rationale for children's activity. Children play because of their own interests. In play, no "one task" is imposed upon the child by adults. The child does not need to utilize a sense of will or purposeful intention to meet adult expectations. A sense of will is needed though in order to accomplish tasks or daily life activities that are not of one's choosing; this is self-regulation. Unless teacher-directed activities are developmentally attuned to the children's level, it is difficult for the children to adhere to the task. Prior to middle childhood, children have difficulty marshaling sufficient willpower as they aspire to learn such adult competencies as reading or writing.

During middle childhood, children become increasingly interested and able to master daily life competencies. Historically, children living in more traditional cultures, as well as those attending formal schools, were 7 or 8 years old—the beginning of middle childhood—before such tasks were expected of them. This remains true today in many countries where educators wait until children are 7 or 8 years old before introducing formal reading or mathematics lessons. Up to that point, the emphasis is on creating programs rich in opportunities for the informal development of subject matter competencies.

The Play Continuum

When teachers focus on play at the center of the curriculum, they include spontaneous play, guided play, and teacher-directed play. Although these three terms appear to distinguish three separate domains of play, we view them as points along a continuum that goes from child-initiated to teacher-initiated play, as shown in Figure 1.2.

Figure 1.2
The Play Continuum

Spontaneous Play	Guided Play	Teacher-Directed Play

Child-Initiated ◄- - - - - - - -► Teacher-Initiated

Throughout this book, we emphasize that the balance among three types of play depends on many factors, such as the developmental level and interests of the children, the cultures of the families, and the culture of the school. Children's school curricula also must be seen in the context of their lives. The child who goes from child care to school to an evening at home watching TV has a different need for play than the child who attends nursery school 2 days per week and plays outside most of the time.

Early childhood educators balance play with appropriate teacher-directed strategies as they address the needs of all children. For example, an older first grader who continues to struggle with letter-sound relationships or basic number concepts may need both more direct adult-guided instruction, as well as more opportunities to integrate developing understandings within the context of spontaneous play.

HOW TEACHERS OF YOUNG CHILDREN VIEW PLAY

In the following pages, we return to the vignette of Brandon and his teacher Anna from the beginning of this chapter. We also draw from interviews with other preschool and primary teachers who spoke about the implementation of a play-centered curriculum.

Play Through the Eyes of Brandon's Teacher

We first consider the ways that Anna, Brandon's teacher, uses her observations of his play to gain insight into his growth and development:

Play gives Brandon opportunities to select activities of his own choosing. I am learning a lot about Brandon by watching him play. He tends to visit several areas during this 30- to 40-minute period, but I've noticed that he often sustains a dramatic theme such as fire fighting for a fairly long time or returns to the same theme at several points during the day. He shows much more focused attention during this time than he does when I'm presenting a more structured lesson, like today, for example, in circle time when I introduced counting skills.

He's definitely one of the more verbal children in our group. His social skills are improving, and he often demonstrates a caring attitude toward the other children. I noticed he was also very nurturing toward Fluffy today. He loves to help care for her. I feel this is a wonderful opportunity for him to develop his sense of responsibility, though he has been a bit possessive about her since he took her home. He's really attached to her. He's interested in learning more about rats and brought in a book from the library and copied a picture. Choice time gives him and the other children more of a chance to develop their individual interests.

He generally gets along with the other children, but he can be aggressive at times, for instance, when he knocked down someone's blocks. This year, he rarely gets into direct physical confrontations as he did last year in preschool. I've been keeping anecdotes on this and it seems that these aggressive acts tend to happen when he's rushed or has too many people around him. Today's episode involving using the blocks as guns certainly raised my classic question about war play: "Should I stop it?" I'm often uncertain about what to do, especially when it is such a momentary theme as it was today.

Along with my written anecdotes, I've been trying to decide what else to include in his portfolio. Today I thought about keeping the map. He was so eager to take it home that I decided to make a copy of it to save.

Anna continues:

I'm experimenting a lot with play. It's been a gradual process. Observing the children's behavior, I feel that I'm on the right track. It's hard to believe how different my program is from the way it was only 3 or 4 years ago. I had a desk for each child and all of my "inside" time was teacher-directed, either whole class activities or centers. Now, though my program is definitely play-centered, I include materials to encourage literacy, math, art, and social development. Now we have work tables and a lot more open space. The first thing I did was order blocks. We haven't had blocks in a kindergarten at this school for as long as I've been here and that's 12 years. The kindergarten teacher who has been here the longest said that her old set of blocks was probably still in a district storehouse somewhere.

I also expanded the housekeeping area. In the beginning, I had a very small one, but I never really thought about it as more than a special area where kids could go when they were finished with something else. Now I see how important the playhouse is. I have had a lot of fun making it more attractive to the children who are immigrants. I included more photos of the families, pictures from ethnic calendars showing places and people from different cultures, dolls with ethnically diverse clothing, and objects the children are familiar with from their own backgrounds, like rice bowls and chopsticks. The children seem to feel more at home in my classroom and can play out what they know.

    Anyway, I think my kids are a lot more creative and thoughtful than when my program was more teacher-dominated. For example, I see this in their stories and journals. Half of the students who were in my class last year are in Kristin's class now. She told me last week that she noticed a difference. The children who were in my class are particularly eager to initiate projects, and they tend to stay engrossed longer. She also sees a difference in the way they cooperate with everyone, not just their good friends, and the way they respect each others' work.   * *

Anna mentioned that Sarah's mother noticed a difference, too. Several years ago, Anna used a very structured reading program with prereaders and worksheets. This year the children began their own journals on the first day of school. She put pads of paper and pencils in many places in the classroom to encourage writing. It's also important to note here that Anna still attends to teaching phonic awareness but that she is now using a greater repertoire of strategies.

    Sarah's mother told Anna that she was very happy that Anna was finally teaching reading, and that Sarah was reading and writing a lot at home. Anna remarked that Sarah's sister was in her class 5 years ago when she was presenting formal reading lessons and having her students work in workbooks. Anna realized that this story of the two sisters didn't conclusively prove the point, but she thought that in general her students were now much more self-directed in reading and writing.

    Anna pointed out that during what she calls *choice time* (which she used to call *play time*), probably a third of the children are reading or writing at any given moment.

I've been joking that I want to "up play" rather than "down play" play! I want to show parents how it benefits their children. We had our first open house last week. I put together a slide show with slides from last year and some slides from the first 2 weeks of school. It made a great difference for parents to see "live" examples of how play is important. As I discussed the development of self-esteem, I showed several slides of Jimmy and Andrea building a tower taller than they are. (I wish I had had a video camera for that.)

    The slides also gave me a chance to talk about play and social development. I purposely selected slides that included every student in my class so parents could get a personal message about how important play is to their own child's social development.

    Of course, I also emphasized the ways in which children use what they've learned in academic areas and learn more through play. I showed slides of the children building with blocks, pouring and measuring as they played "making chili" at the sand table, and talked about their development of math concepts. I used slides of children writing in their journals, others scribbling on the chalkboard, and one reading to another as I talked about literacy development. The slides helped parents make the connections between play and their children's development in all areas.

I worked out a way to illustrate developmental progress. Four wonderful slides—if I may say so—show how Genette's block constructions became more complex over a 2-month period last year. ✏️

In this brief conversation, Brandon's teacher mentions issues vital to the play-centered curriculum—issues that we shall return to throughout this book. She discusses the development of her program in terms of carefully observing children to understand their interests and development. She uses play anecdotes as part of her assessment program and puts play-created products, such as Brandon's map, in her students' portfolios. Anna reflects carefully on the effects of her interventions in children's play, questioning, for example, "what to do about war play" and "how to help immigrant children feel more comfortable in the classroom." She also experiments with curricular ideas such as using play to support emerging literacy and conceptual mathematics development.

Across the country, preschool and primary teachers continue to examine the role of play in their programs. Teachers are trying to make programs more empowering for all, that is, embracing the full range of diversity of children and their families and meeting the developmental needs of children. As we wrote this book, we visited and spoke to the teachers and administrators at Brandon's school and numerous other schools to observe the variety of current practices and understandings about children's play. Our conversations with three teachers from Brandon's school exemplify the typical, yet important, ideas and concerns educators raise and that we discuss throughout this text.

Randi, a preschool teacher, emphasizes the role of play in meeting the social and emotional needs of individual children. Pat, a kindergarten teacher, raises the question "What is good play?" and the issue of assessment. Kristin, a first-grade teacher, focuses on the importance of choices in children's development. She also discusses how the play curriculum challenges students to use their developing academic skills in a comfortable environment.

Randi: Meeting the Needs of Individual Children in Preschool

I think that play gives children a chance to make their own choices, their own decisions. The chances it provides for socialization also are very important. As they play, children communicate their feelings and ideas. This is especially important in my program, where almost all my children have special needs. For many, English is a second language. Play gives them a chance to express themselves in a less formal and more comfortable situation than circle time, for example. Play also provides opportunities for children to use their own language fluently and to express ideas in nonverbal ways. It's important for developing their sense of self-worth.

Among the questions I have are: "Am I doing the best I can for my students who are learning English as a second language?" It's hard for me when I can't follow the dialogue of their dramatic play. When I think about children like Brandon, I find I have questions about how to handle aggressive play. ✐

Pat: From Dittos and Desks to Blocks and Bubbles in Kindergarten

I consider play anything children decide to do that's not adult directed, like reading by themselves. If the choice is theirs, logically, they should enjoy it. Play gives young children the time to develop language skills, get along with their peers, make choices, and be responsible. It gives me the chance to learn more about the children, see what they do, and discover what they're really interested in doing. It also gives me time to interact with each child personally.

What I want to happen, what I consider "good play," depends on the child. Yesterday, I observed Marissa in what I consider good play for her. Marissa always seems to follow the other children. Yesterday, however, she was playing by herself with a small playhouse. She had selected what she herself wanted to do. She talked to herself a lot and stayed focused. This is a new behavior for her: selecting her own activity and staying with it.

I've made a commitment to write observations. I need to learn more about what to look for when I'm observing. Also, I want to ask questions to find out what children are really thinking, so they can respond without thinking "What's the right answer?" I feel as though I'm at a new stage in learning how to intervene. ✐

Kristin: Letting Children Develop at Their Own Pace in First Grade

During free-choice time, my children have access to blocks, Legos and other manipulatives, art materials like paint and markers, and the housekeeping corner. It's also a time when they can dictate a story to me or a parent volunteer, or get some help from their peers in inventing the spelling of words.

I think kids need to have time to work on concepts they are developing at their own pace and by their own choice. Right now, there's a lot of writing going on. Some write letters. Others write whole sentences. In language, as in other areas, there is a wide range of abilities. During free-choice time, children work at a level that's comfortable for them. During the past year, I've extended the amount of play time I provide. Now I plan for at least

30 to 40 minutes a day, usually in the early afternoon. When they've had enough time to make their own choices about learning, the children are much more able to focus on the social studies or science activities scheduled at the end of the day.

Another goal of mine is to discuss my program effectively with parents. Play has never been a traditional part of first grade curriculum in our area. Parents often ask me whether we really have time to play if we are to get the children ready for second grade. ⊘

During our visits to schools, we listened to the questions about play, children's development, education practices, and state standards. These visits were fun because teachers shared so many stories, and they were impressive because teachers revealed insights and raised issues. In this book, we address these issues and share stories from some of the teachers we talked to, as well as stories of our own. We create bridges between practice, research, and theory that deal with play in a playful way.

PLAY: THE CORE OF DEVELOPMENTALLY APPROPRIATE PRACTICE

Some teachers with whom we spoke told us that their whole program consists of play. Others, like Kristin, are experimenting with including more play in the curriculum. Some are wondering if play is appropriate, and, if so, what kinds and how much. All are trying to answer questions about the role of play in meeting the needs of the children they teach.

Play includes intrinsic motivation and active engagement.

Developmentally appropriate practice (DAP) is a term used by the National Association for the Education of Young Children (NAEYC) to describe programs grounded in child development theory and research and designed to meet the developmental needs of children (Bredekamp & Copple, 1997). These are programs in which children's development in all areas is fostered through age-appropriate activities congruent with children's growth. Such programs also address the individual developmental needs of each child in the classroom.

Most of the teachers we talked to take these developmental needs into account with regard to their teaching practices. For example, in discussing her program, Rosemarie considers both typical development of 3- and 4-year-olds, as well as the particular needs of children who are English language learners. Neil thinks about the normal growth needs of 6- and 7-year-olds and of special needs children such as Mona, diagnosed with autism and mainstreamed into Neil's class for part of the day.

The growing literature on developmentally appropriate practice emphasizes the need to provide children with a meaningful curriculum that provides choices that interest and challenge them, and to provide adult guidance appropriate to individual needs.

The premise of this book is that play is at the center of a developmentally appropriate curriculum. This follows from our conviction that play provides the integrative context essential to support the growth of the whole child, particularly through the preschool years and during the primary grades. The position that play is at the center of a developmentally appropriate curriculum leads to our position that a play-centered curriculum can effectively address curriculum standards.

ADDRESSING STANDARDS IN THE PLAY-CENTERED CURRICULUM

Play is the heart of developmentally appropriate practice because it is the driving force in young children's development. Therefore, we consider a play-centered curriculum the most developmentally appropriate way of addressing meaningful curriculum content standards in early childhood education programs.

The Purpose of Standards

What do we hope that children will gain from participating in early childhood programs? A central stated goal of curriculum standards is to ensure equity for children, to assure that each child receives a quality education. In the best sense, standards reflect the importance of early childhood and are attempts to specify the features of quality educational programs and the most important learning expectations for children.

Although the standards movement had a growing effect on 1–12 grade programs beginning in the 1980s, it was not until 2000 that many national associations and state departments of education considered standards for preschool and kindergarten children. The implementation of standards and the No Child Left Behind legislation led to widespread discussion within the early childhood education community about the appropriateness of the standards.

Identifying the Most Important Learning Outcomes. The National Association for the Education of Young Children and the national professional organizations in the specific content areas have identified the "big ideas" and important processes they consider developmentally appropriate. All underscore the importance of the kind of in-depth curriculum that we advocate throughout this book, curriculum which provides children with numerous opportunities to revisit these big ideas and processes—in their play as well as in more teacher-directed activities. National associations include the International Reading Association (IRA), the National Council of Teachers of Mathematics (NCTM), the Consortium of the National Arts Education Associations, the National Science Teachers Association (NSTA), and the National Council for the Social Studies (NCSS).

Several of these associations have issued joint position papers with the National Association for the Education of Young Children. The position papers advocate that curriculum content standards must be meaningful to children and recommend that they are based upon children's active, engaged experiences. These associations also advocate that curriculum be developed to reflect the cultures and languages of children and their families, and to meet children's special needs. We agree with these major position statements of the national professional organizations and find most major goals consistent with the type of play-centered early childhood curriculum we describe.

Guidelines for Developing Appropriate Standards for Young Children

The opportunities and challenges that standards provide for promoting effective early childhood programs are discussed in *Early Learning Standards: Creating the Conditions for Success,* the joint position statement from NAEYC and National Association of Early Childhood Specialists in State Departments of Education (NAECS/SDE) (2002). This position statement emphasizes that, to be effective, early learning standards will result in high quality educational experiences and outcomes for young children only if four conditions are met.

1. The content and outcomes of early learning standards are developmentally appropriate to children's current developmental abilities as well as their life situations and experiences. (See pp. 4–5.)

2. Numerous stakeholders are engaged in developing and reviewing early childhood standards. Stakeholders include parents and other community representatives and early childhood educators including early childhood special education specialists. (See p. 6.)

3. "Early learning standards gain their effectiveness through implementation and assessment practices that support all children's development in ethical, appropriate ways" (p. 6). This means that teaching practices promote social interactions and curricula promote engagement and depth of explorations.

   "Tools for assessing young children's progress must be clearly connected to important learning represented in the standards; must be technically, developmentally, and culturally valid; and must yield comprehensive, useful information." (p. 7)

4. Standards are accompanied by strong supports for early childhood programs, including adequate support for professionals and professional development, and respectful support for families as partners in their children's education. (See pp. 7–8.)

We agree with these guiding principles for the development of standards for early learning as well as the guidelines of the national content area associations. Within this context, play-centered curricula optimize children's learning and can effectively address standards.

The Challenges of Standards

In our discussions with early childhood educators, we found that most challenges arise when the four conditions outlined above are not met. Teachers point to state and district content and outcomes that show a lack of understanding of young children's development and learning, including cultural and individual differences. Secondly, teachers explain that neither those with expertise in early childhood development and education nor community members had opportunities to contribute their expertise to the development or review process.

A primary concern many teachers have about standards is that the assessment practices are developmentally inappropriate. Of most concern is the practice of "high stakes testing." Teachers point to the use of one-time assessment instruments that identify a small range of specific skills. The result of this assessment is then used for a "high stakes" decision such as telling parents that their child is not ready for kindergarten. In fact, the position statement *Early Learning Standards: Creating the Conditions for Success* (2002) emphasizes that "such misuses of standards-related assessments violate professional codes of ethical conduct" (p. 7).

Lastly, teachers find that, in trying to address the numerous standards in each area, they rely more on teacher-directed instruction. Some teachers remark that, as a result, their program has not only become less engaging for their students but for them as well. Wien (2004) explores this problem in great detail in her book, *Negotiating Standards in the Primary Classroom: The Teacher's Dilemma*. She presents detailed portraits of eight primary-grade teachers and the ways that they responded to and addressed standards. Wein describes how teachers responded, all struggling with the issues of developmentally appropriate practice, fostering children's interests, and trying to maintain their own engagement in teaching. Wein describes their reflections as well as their classroom practices. Several tried to address the hundreds of standards in an organized, linear manner. Others maintained a greater interest in teaching by integrating standards into an integrated, holistic curriculum that drew upon children's interests.

Similarly, Seefeldt (2005) describes how standards can actually assist teachers in integrating the curriculum more effectively. She points out that if teachers are to implement numerous standards in diverse subject areas, they must identify the "big ideas" and develop a framework identifying the relationships among these major standards. It is through this careful analysis that teachers can create a richer integrated curriculum. This is the approach that we take throughout this book. In the chapters that follow, we describe best practices to address standards in a play-centered curriculum.

THE CRITICAL ROLE OF THE TEACHER IN THE CURRICULUM

If play is at the center of the early childhood curriculum, how is the curriculum developed? How does a teacher foster literacy, mathematical thinking, artistic expression, social development, self-esteem, scientific thinking, and other concepts, dispositions, and skills valued in early education? How does a teacher address and integrate standards in a meaningful way?

We believe that the teacher is the key to the play-centered curriculum. This is a curriculum in constant development—an emergent, evolving curriculum. The knowledgeable teacher uses a wide repertoire of techniques to orchestrate carefully the flow from spontaneous play to guided and directed play, to more subject-oriented instruction, and back to play. This flow is in tune with and arises from the developmental needs of individual children in the class.

Scott introduced himself as a "third-grade teacher just promoted to kindergarten." This was the first year that he had tried to "incorporate any play . . . much less make play the major part of my program." With little opportunity to visit other programs, Scott started the year feeling that he was sinking as much as he was swimming. "In my sinking mode, I went for teacher-structured activities as life rafts. They felt safe. They were like the curriculum I knew."

It took Scott most of the year to set up an environment where his students could have choices and sustained time to play through activities. Scott needed to read enough to convince himself that play was truly the cornerstone of development for young children. Then he could begin to make changes based on that conviction.

He concluded: "This has become the most intellectually challenging year for me. I am learning how to plan for play and how to use play to assess students' growth. I like the concept of an evolving curriculum, but it takes patience as well as creativity to work it out each day. Things don't always work out as I had imagined."

"Because I'm an experienced teacher, I sometimes feel that I should be able to do this right away. But it doesn't work out that way. It involves a major shift in the way I'm thinking as well as in the way I structure the program: a paradigm shift."

Scott also mentioned how he felt at times when his colleagues from the "upper grades" come into his classroom. "I know they're thinking that I'm 'just' playing. I'm finally feeling that I can defend what I do, explain why play is so important." ✆

As the examples throughout this book illustrate, a play-centered curriculum is orchestrated carefully by the teacher. It is not a step-by-step, teacher-proof didactic curriculum. Consequently, this is not a step-by-step curriculum guide. However, the play-centered curriculum we discuss is also very different from laissez-faire play, such as recess time at many schools, in which no one observes or intervenes. A play-centered curriculum involves teachers in careful planning and preparation, both inside and outside the classroom. A play-centered curriculum needs playful teachers who enjoy being spontaneous, involved, and creative, as well as reflective and analytical.

SUMMARY AND CONCLUSION

In this introductory chapter, we discuss the rationale for placing play at the center of early childhood curricula. Chapter 2 examines the development of play, drawing upon major "classical" theories, as well as the work of several current theorists. Chapter 3 provides perspectives on how play supports the development of children's symbolic thought, language and literacy, logical-mathematical thinking, problem solving, imagination, and creativity. Chapters 4 and 5 detail the many levels at which teachers can carefully orchestrate numerous and complex opportunities for children's play in early childhood programs.

These chapters examine the many factors regarding intervention strategies, environments, materials, and timing that educators must consider in program implementation. In each chapter, we discuss general guidelines as well as specific considerations and provide numerous anecdotes as illustrations.

In a play-centered, emergent curriculum, ongoing assessment is needed. Chapter 6, "Play as a Tool for Assessment," provides a multitude of examples and strategies for tracing children's learning and development through play.

Throughout this book, we discuss issues that relate to meeting the special needs of diverse populations of students and their families. An inclusive, play-based curriculum addresses issues of diversity and special needs as integral to the emergent curriculum, not as "add-ons."

Chapters 7 through 10 focus on the relationships between play and traditional subject areas: mathematics (chapter 7), language and literacy (chapter 8), science (chapter 9) and the arts (chapter 10). Each subject area provides a particular lens through which we examine play. In each of these chapters, we discuss how play relates to the development of competencies in that area of the curriculum.

We discuss how play-centered curricula can meet the challenge of addressing standards in a developmentally appropriate manner. In addition, we have added a primary grade focus to highlight the continuum of children's development and to remove the traditional distinctions among preschool, kindergarten, first-grade, and second-grade programs.

In these subject-oriented chapters, we emphasize the important question: "How do activities in academic areas support good play?" This complements the traditional question of how play fosters development in a particular area, for example, "How does play support development in math?" Each chapter emphasizes that play always remains an integrated whole—greater and far more significant than the sum of its parts.

Chapter 11 considers relationships between play and children's socialization. Chapter 12 focuses on considerations of toys and technology in the context of young children's play. Each of these chapters concludes with a section that addresses some of the pressing questions that teachers are asking in our conversations with them. Although each chapter focuses on a separate subject area, play is central to the curriculum because it integrates *all* aspects of development.

Lastly, chapter 13, "Conclusion: Integrating Play, Development, and Practice," provides a more detailed perspective of the central role of the play-centered curriculum in children's development, drawing upon and expanding on issues discussed throughout the book.

Although each chapter in this book has a different focus, play is central to the entire curriculum because it integrates *all* aspects of development, as the following example illustrates. Lisa and Peter are working in the "post office," wrapping packages and sending them "to the Philippines." By reading this anecdote, what can you learn about Lisa's and Peter's language and social abilities, as well as their development of mathematical concepts?

Lisa: "Do we have enough paper to wrap this package (three books)? They're for my Grandma Venecia from Cebu."
Peter picks up two sheets of newspaper.

Peter: "We're going to have to tape these together. Wait, here's the tape. I'll hold this."
They tape the two sheets together by cutting and sticking two short pieces of tape horizontally from one newspaper sheet to the other. They then try to cut a long piece, but the tape gets twisted. Lisa cuts four short pieces and tapes the paper together.

Lisa: "OK, put the books down here." They wrap the books, trying to make the package smooth around the edges, a difficult task because the books are not the same size. "This is going to be expensive! I bet it weighs a ton."
They put the package on the scale. It has numbers to indicate ounces, and a teacher-made, nonstandard measurement chart with three different colors indicating three different degrees of heaviness.

Peter: "See. It's green. That's heavy. It's going to be 3 dollars!" He takes the star stamps and pad and stamps three green stars at the top left of the package. "Wait. You need to put her address on it."
Lisa picks up a thin blue marker and slowly writes GRUM VNSESSA 632 SEEBOO. Then she carefully selects a thick red marker and draws a heart with a butterfly to the left of the address.

In this episode, Lisa and Peter demonstrate that they know some basic information about the applications of mathematics to everyday situations. They know that one weighs a package before sending it, and they have some beginning understandings of the concept of weight. Furthermore, both Lisa and Peter demonstrate that they understand that the weight of the package relates to the price of mailing it. Lisa also demonstrates that she is aware that numerals are used to write an address. Lisa and Peter were also learning about geometry and spatial relationships as they estimated how much paper they needed and wrapped their parcel. At the post office, they were able to take information about weight, prices, addresses, and area; coordinate the information; and apply it.

Observations of Lisa's play also inform us about her dramatic gains in speaking English. At the beginning of the year, Lisa spoke comfortably and fluently with her family members in her native Visayan but was hesitant to speak English with the other children. This observation indicates that Lisa has gained considerable mastery of English, with dramatic gains in sentence length and complexity, as well as vocabulary. She is now comfortable initiating and developing conversations in English with her peers.

As we watch Lisa and Peter, we notice that they are able to sustain their cooperative play for more than 20 minutes. During this time, they encounter several problems. For example, Peter notices that one piece of paper is not large enough to wrap the package. Each time, one or the other or both come up with a solution that the other accepts. For example, Lisa solves the problem with the tape. Their play is goal-oriented, good-natured, and without conflict.

Throughout this book, we examine numerous anecdotes. In the preceding episodes, we see how Lisa and Peter's play-centered activities provide opportunities for socialization and their development of language as well as logical mathematical thinking. Each time we view this vignette from a different perspective, we become more certain that the children's play contributes to their development in that particular domain. We look at the complex, integrated whole of the children's dramatic and creative interactions and creations, and feel a certainty about the value of play in the development of these young human beings.

SUGGESTED RESOURCES

Bruner, J. S., Jolly, A., & Sylva, K. (Eds.). (1976). *Play: Its role in development and evolution*. New York: Basic Books.

These inspiring essays examine the learning processes of adults as well as children from a constructivist perspective. Duckworth's work captures the relationships among playfulness, curiosity, and problem solving. Readers might be particularly interested in several chapters that describe teachers as learners and their "having of wonderful ideas."

A classic book edited by one of America's most influential psychologists. This work consists of 71 essays and studies examining play within a number of disciplines, including psychology, anthropology, biology, and sociology.

Duckworth, E. (1996). *"The having of wonderful ideas" and other essays on teaching and learning* (2nd ed.). New York: Teachers College Press.

These inspiring essays examine the learning processes of adults as well as children from a constructivist perspective. Duckworth's work captures the relationships among playfulness, curiosity, and problem solving. Readers might be particularly interested in several chapters that describe teachers as learners and their "having of wonderful ideas."

Nourot, P. (1990). The legacy of play in American early childhood education. In E. Klugman & S. Smilansky (Eds.), *Children's play and learning: Perspectives and policy implications* (pp. 59–85). New York: Teachers College Press.

This historical account of play in early childhood programs reviews ancient as well as contemporary influences on American early childhood curricula, from the eighteenth to the twentieth century.

Paley, V. G. (1986). *Mollie is three.* Chicago: University of Chicago Press.

Paley, V. G. (1997). *The girl with the brown crayon.* Cambridge, MA: Harvard University Press.

Paley, V. G. (2004). *A child's work: The importance of fantasy play.* Chicago: University of Chicago Press.

Mollie Is Three and *The Girl with the Brown Crayon* are wonderful introductions to this gifted teacher-researcher's work. Each presents Paley's careful observations of young children's play over many months and her insights into their development. Primary-grade teachers as well as preschool teachers will find these books informative and engrossing. In *A Child's Work: The Importance of Fantasy Play,* Paley challenges the widespread educational practices that increase academic pressures on young children. She shows that time for sustained, rich fantasy play is critical to children's development. Vivian Paley is the recipient of a MacArthur Award and the John Dewey's Outstanding Achievement Award.

Play, Policy, and Practice Connections. Newsletter of the Play, Policy, and Practice Interest Forum of the National Association for the Education of Young Children.

This newsletter, published twice yearly, includes a wide range of articles on practice, reviews of current books, and research-related articles. Also included are discussions of current issues related to play and policy (e.g., play and curriculum guidelines).

Seefeldt, C. (2005). *How to work with standards in the early childhood classroom.* New York: Teachers College Press.

Seefeldt presents a summary of the history and implementation of standards as well as a concise explanation of standards and benchmarks in early childhood education. She includes an extensive discussion of implementation of standards, with separate chapters on science, language and literacy, the arts, mathematics, and social studies.

Wien, C. A. (2004). *Negotiating standards in the primary classroom: The teacher's dilemma.* New York: Teachers College Press.

Wien examines how the implementation of standards affects teachers' educational practices as well as their feelings about being teachers. Using lively, highly personalized case studies, she shows how some teachers used standards to integrate their curriculum and other teachers experienced challenges in seeking balanced practice.

The Development of Play

Five-year-old Sophie brings home a large painted butterfly with her own writing "B T R F Y" carefully drawn in the corner. Her parents approach her teacher concerned that allowing her to spell words incorrectly will hinder her success when she begins kindergarten in the fall. ✆

The children in Roseanna's multiage primary class are deep into the third week of their project on restaurants. They've made paper and playdough pizzas, menus, uniforms for the waiters, and paper money for their transactions. A group of children have finished making placemats and ads for the "Don't Forget the Olives" Pizza Parlor and are contemplating adding sushi to the menu. The school principal questions the value of this play-centered project during their social studies hour, and how it encompasses the district's academic standards. ✆

What answers can teachers give to questions about play in the classroom? Perhaps the most frequently quoted clichés are "Play is the child's way of learning" or "Play is the child's work." How does play contribute to learning? Is play related to work in some systematic manner, or is play simply evidence of the flights of fancy and freedom we associate with childhood?

In order to answer these and other questions related to the role of play in curriculum for young children, we as teachers first need to formulate our ideas about the nature of play and how it develops. Although other species engage in physical or sensorimotor play, the range of play from motor play to pretend play to games with rules is a uniquely human capacity (Ackerman, 1999; Singer, 1973). The development of play through these stages forms the foundation for the development of intellect, creativity and imagination, a sense of self, the resolution of feelings, and the capacity to interact with others in positive and morally sound ways. In this chapter and those that follow we view play through each of these various developmental lenses, discussing how play contributes to each in turn and to the integration of physical, social-emotional, and cognitive competencies for the whole child (Bergen, 2002; Fromberg, 1999).

Play is more than a means to an end, however, even though these ends may be highly valued by educators and some parents. Play is the source of laughter and humor, of inventiveness and beauty. It allows us to entertain possibilities and to envision the future. It helps us to persevere in our efforts and to explore the full range of our emotions. It fosters the spontaneity and joy that make us truly human. Keeping this in mind, we also invite you to consider how each lens reflects the ways development contributes to play itself as an essential aspect of human existence.

In this chapter we look at major theories that address the development of play in childhood, and explore the levels and stages suggested by these theories. In developing a theory of practice that is based in the daily lives of children and their teachers, we begin by discussing the more "classic" theorists in developmental psychology whose general theories are well articulated. Then we discuss research focused on play and development that we find particularly useful for teachers. We first consider Jean Piaget (1896–1980), a Swiss psychologist and biologist who set forth a comprehensive stage theory of the development of play in childhood. We then examine the work of Lev Vygotsky (1896–1934), a Russian psychologist and contemporary of Piaget whose writings were unavailable in English until relatively recently. Vygotsky and Piaget's theories share many of the same basic principles regarding play and complement one another by their differences in emphasis. George Herbert Mead (1863–1931), a sociologist who wrote about play and the developing self, is looked at next, followed by Erik Erikson (1902–1994), who theorized about the contribution of play to stages of psychosocial development. Next we turn to research by Parten regarding social participation in preschool play, and to the research of Paley (1984, 1992, 1999), who illuminates the role of play in the socialization of young children.

In the sections that follow, we guide your understanding of the theory and research in education that support the importance of play in the learning of young children and throughout the human life span. We address the theoretical grounding for understanding how play relates to learning and development throughout all dimensions of experience in early childhood, and help teachers formulate articulate responses to the questions of parents and colleagues regarding the role of play in classrooms for young children. We also share our insights as both teachers and researchers on how the joyful, spontaneous, and unpredictable nature of play enlivens and enriches classrooms where teachers are truly able to use play as a window for understanding the development of the children in their care.

A CONSTRUCTIVIST VIEW OF PLAY AND LEARNING

In this book we take the position clearly articulated by twentieth century theorists that development and learning occur through the construction of knowledge in the mind of the learner. In this constructivist view, knowledge is not simply acquired by accumulating information from the environment, or even copying the behavior of others, but is based on what the individual child brings to each situation. The *schemes* or mental patterns that children have already constructed are modified and built upon as children try to make sense of new experiences in light of what they already know. Four-year-old Kim explains the word "invisible" to his friend Tony when the word comes up in a story read by a parent to the two boys. "It's like you go inside visible, and then no one can see you when you're in visible!" Kim asserts, and Tony nods his head in understanding. Kim

The child's development is tied to social life.

bases his explanation on what he has experienced about not being seen in the game of hide and seek; if you hide inside something, then you can't be seen.

From the constructivist view of development, what the child already knows, and his or her patterns for interpreting experience, are modified through the child's own effort and initiative. Piaget placed particular importance on the self-regulating and autonomous activity of children's play in the construction of knowledge. Although Piaget's work focused on the active construction of knowledge through cognition, other constructivist theorists such as Vygotsky (1962) and Mead (1934) and such researchers as Corsaro (2003), Dyson (1997), Forman (2005), and Paley (1992, 1999) have emphasized cultural and social processes central to constructing knowledge and the essentially interactive nature of learning and development. Theorists such as Erikson (1950/85) have emphasized psychosocial development in understanding the role of play in the emotional lives of children. All the theorists we consider note the importance of the close connections between cognition and affect in the learning and development of young children. We first turn to Piaget's work as the foundation for constructivist theory.

PIAGET'S DEVELOPMENTAL THEORY AND PLAY

Piaget viewed the growth of thinking or cognition as one area of development in which the role of play in constructing knowledge is most clearly articulated.

Imagine a world in which every experience you have is new, without mental pictures of previous events in your life to help you organize your perceptions and expectations. Life would be very confusing.

Fortunately, human beings do have the means for organizing experiences so that we can make sense of the events in our lives. According to Piaget, this means of organization is intelligent *adaptation*. In adaptation, humans modify their environments to fit their personal needs. They also modify their own thinking in response to the environment (DeVries, Zan, Hildebrandt, Edmiaston, & Sales, 2002; Fosnot & Perry, 2005; Piaget, 1962b, 1963a, 1969b).

Piaget describes an interactive process between these two aspects of adaptation, which he calls assimilation and accommodation. This interaction is the source of development and learning.

In assimilation, new elements of experience are incorporated into existing structures of thought. Most importantly, these elements are not simply added to the thoughts already there, like items tacked onto a grocery list. Instead, new elements are transformed by the individual's thinking process to fit into the structure or "template" of that individual's thinking.

An example is the assimilative pattern many children develop in playing with playdough or clay. Clay-like substances can be pinched, patted, molded, and rolled using patterns from previous experiences. Schemes or potential patterns of action on clay or playdough are part of the repertoire of mental patterns of many young children. What happens when a child encounters "oublek," a substance made of cornstarch and water that has some of the properties of clay, but also some different ones? Perhaps she is surprised that the new material oozes through her fingers rather than molding into a form. The child's efforts to accommodate to the differences that the new material offers cause a change in the assimilative structure that will be applied to clay-like substances in the future.

In Piaget's theory, accommodation is a complement to the assimilative, meaning-making process. Accommodation allows the structure of our thinking to change when it serves us in adapting to new experiences. Accommodation is the process through which new schemes or mental patterns for potential behavior are created, or existing patterns are stretched and changed in form in order to incorporate new information. Accommodation allows us to meet challenges presented by the environment, such as resolving the cognitive surprise generated by playing with oublek when playdough was expected.

The assimilation process allows us to consolidate, generalize, and apply our current structures of thinking to new situations and materials. It allows us to make sense of our experience in light of what we already know. The accommodation process challenges us to change and adapt our mental structures in the face of new information.

According to Piaget, there is constant interaction between these processes, alternating states of tension and balance concerning what "fits" into our schemes or mental models about experience, and what doesn't fit. Awareness that a new idea or perception does not fit into our structure of thinking calls for a change in our mental models, and results in the continuing development of thought. Through the interaction of assimilation and accommodation, children balance their internal states and meet their personal needs for intelligent adaptation.

In the early childhood years assimilative and accommodative processes are constantly fluctuating. First, the mental patterns fit the new situation. Then new elements are introduced that contradict that fit. Mental structures then change to accommodate these new elements. This process of construction and expansion marks the development of children's early thinking from idiosyncratic concepts about the way the world works to more stable and predictable relationships between internal mental models and the external world.

Because of the changing nature of the child's emerging concepts, young children's behavior is largely governed by play, or a predominance of assimilation. What is essential is that play and assimilation emphasize the child's interests and current structures of thinking as the source of development. In the next section we turn to the contexts in which different types of knowledge are constructed.

Three Types of Knowledge

Piaget delineated three major types of knowledge that serve as the contexts for children's development: physical, logical-mathematical, and social. In their play, children develop all three. *Physical knowledge* is derived from activities with objects that allow children to make generalizations about the physical properties of objects. For example, through physical manipulation in play children may discover that rocks sink and corks float, blocks stacked too high may fall, and sand and water may be used to mold forms (De Vries et al., 2002; Forman, 1998, 2005; Kamii & DeVries, 1993).

Logical-mathematical knowledge, or knowledge about the relationships among objects, people, and ideas, is constructed as children reflect on the relationships between actions or objects, for instance by comparing the sizes of two balls, or the relative lengths of blocks. In logical-mathematical knowledge the concepts employed by the child come not from the objects themselves but from the relationship invented by the child. These two types of knowledge, physical and logical-mathematical, are constructed through the child's own experiences. Play is an opportunity to increase those experiences.

In contrast, *social knowledge* is knowledge imparted by other people and includes labels and vocabulary as well as social conventions such as proper behavior at snack or group time. This type of knowledge falls closer to the accommodative end of the continuum, relying on processes of imitation and memorization for its acquisition. However, social knowledge also depends on the mental structures created through logical-mathematical knowledge for its application. As Kamii (1982) points out, categories such as "good words" and "bad words" are derived from social experiences but it is the logical-mathematical capacity for classification that enables children to decide when a word might meet with the disapproval of adults.

In practice, physical, logical-mathematical and social knowledge are closely connected in any situation involving the education of young children, as we see in this example:

> Four-year-old Enid helps Madeline, the Assistant Teacher, bring food to the snack table. "We need one cracker for each place," Madeline coaches. Enid takes the crackers from the box and places one on each plate, and looks expectantly at her teacher. "There," Madeline says. "Let's count these together—1, 2, 3, 4, 5, 6, 7." Enid counts with her teacher. "Now let's count the crackers—1, 2, 3, 4, 5, 6, 7." They count together again. Madeline asks, "How many cups will we need if we have one for every person?"
>
> Enid carefully takes one cup at a time from the stack and places each next to a plate with a cracker on it. Two of the cups tip over as she sets them down, and as she replaces them upright, Enid looks intently at the uneven places in the table top that have pushed the empty cups off balance. She runs her hand over the table next to the remaining plates to find a smooth spot before she sets down the next cup.
>
> Enid looks expectantly at Madeline, pointing her finger at the first cup. "1, 2, 3," Enid begins, then hesitates. Madeline joins her by counting "4, 5, 6, 7," and they finish the sequence of numbers. "Seven plates, seven crackers, and seven cups," summarizes her teacher, and Enid beams at her accomplishment. "Would you like to ring the bell for snack?" Madeline asks. Enid nods and goes off to accomplish this last task. ✆

In this example we see Enid constructing physical knowledge about strategies for placing crackers and cups on the snack table. She learns something about balance on even and uneven surfaces. Enid also constructs logical-mathematical knowledge about the relationship of cups to surfaces and about one-to-one correspondence. Madeline helps her count using one-to-one correspondence and presents the idea of equivalent sets for the seven plates, seven crackers, seven cups. Madeline also helps her to learn social conventional knowledge about the names and sequence of numbers in English, as well as the position of cups in relation to plates. Enid uses her knowledge of the purpose of the snack bell to call her classmates to enjoy her handiwork.

Teachers' abilities to understand and support children's learning depends on their skill in identifying the types of knowledge being constructed by the child and finding appropriate strategies to enhance that new knowledge. It is too easy for teachers of all-age students to rely heavily on showing and telling as vehicles to imitation and the acquisition of social knowledge. Teachers are challenged to provide opportunities for children to construct their own learning and apply what they have learned from others through playful activity (Forman, 1998, 2005). Both kinds of learning are important—knowledge derived from inner sources and knowledge derived from outer sources—and a balance between the two is necessary for development.

Piaget: The Development of Play

Piaget's theory is intimately tied to the study of play. Many of his important works are filled with observations of his own three children at play during their first 2 years of life and of other children he observed in preschool settings in Geneva, Switzerland.

His important work *Play, Dreams and Imitation in Childhood* (1962b) made play a central part of his theory. Here he showed how children develop the ability to represent their world through a series of stages in which assimilation and accommodation are increasingly better coordinated with each other. Children's ability to represent their inner concerns and understandings is revealed in their play which can be seen to progress through a series of stages. As each new stage is developed, it incorporates the possibilities for play of all the previous states (Figure 2.1). In the following sections, we present a brief description of these stages. (See also chapter 13.)

Practice or Functional Play. The first stage is termed practice or functional play by Piaget and is a major characteristic of the stage of sensorimotor

Figure 2.1
Piaget's Stages of the
Development of Play

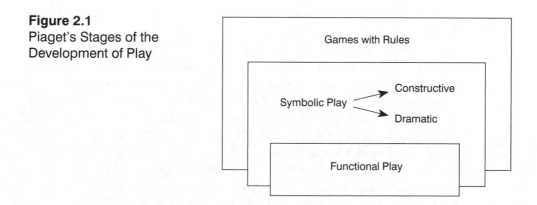

intelligence. Practice or functional play is what Piaget (1962b) called "a happy display of known actions" in which children repeatedly practice their schemes for actions with objects or their own bodies. It is exemplified by the play of the infant, the grasping and pulling, kicking and propelling of arms that infants engage in for the pleasure of mastering the movement. It continues as children take part in activities such as splashing water or sifting sand, honking a horn, or riding a bike. Practice or functional play remains a major form of activity throughout childhood and adulthood. How many adults doodle while talking on the phone, or enjoy the exhilaration of jogging or the body moving to music with aerobics? Opportunities for practice play remain an important source of development and pleasure throughout life and provide an essential feature of school curriculum, as we illustrate in subsequent chapters.

Symbolic Play.   The second stage, symbolic play, begins about 18 months of age and is a major characteristic of the stage of pre-operational intelligence. Symbolic play involves the use of mental representation to pretend that one object stands for another in play, or to take on a make-believe role in play. It forms a foundation of future abstract thinking and the ability to organize both work and play experiences as human beings develop. Three major forms of symbolic play are described by Piaget: constructive, dramatic, and games with rules, which demonstrate the beginnings of conceptual thought (Bergen, 2002; Fein, 1981; Fromberg, 1999; McCune, 1985; Rubin, Fein, & Vandenberg, 1983).

The first, constructive play, provides a natural link between practice or functional play and more sophisticated forms of symbolic play. In constructive play the child uses concrete objects to create a representation of an object: blocks or playdough manipulated to represent a house are typical examples. The intent in constructive play is to approach one's mental representation of the symbolized object as closely as possible. For example, 3-year-old Sandy searches for just the right size and number of sticks to make five candles on her birthday cake.

Following closely on the heels of constructive play, and often overlapping it, comes dramatic play. This play involves the creation of imaginary roles and situations, and frequently accompanies the construction of pretend objects. But the representation is more abstract. Instead of simple object symbols, children use gesture and language to create imaginary roles and situations with complex themes, characters, and scripts (Vandenberg, 2004). Sometimes this play is sociodramatic in nature, involving the negotiation of roles and pretend themes with others (Fromberg, 2002; Goncu, 1993; Howes & Wishard, 2004; Nicolopoulou, Scales, & Weintraub, 1994; Nourot, 2006; Smilansky, 1990). At other times the play may be solitary, with characters, themes, and situations enacted by a single player. So, as Josh finishes his garage of blocks, he may park a toy car in it and pretend that an imaginary family piles into the car for a trip to the beach. Sally may invite several children to play the part of guests at the birthday party as she enacts the role of the birthday girl. She "blows out" the stick candles and the group shares her sand birthday cake.

Both stages of symbolic play, constructive and dramatic, are intellectually and socially complicated. Their mastery sets the stage for playing games with rules, which appear about the age of 5 or 6, and continue as the predominant form of overt play throughout middle childhood, adolescence, and adulthood. Overt play is an important concept here because older children and adults continue to engage in constructive and dramatic play long after early childhood, but in a more covert manner. Dramatic and constructive play take the form of private fantasy and hypothetical thinking, and accompany the daily internal lives of adults in many of the same ways that overt dramatic play enriches the lives of young children.

The games with rules stage involves adherence to an external set of social rules that govern play. A predominance of this type of play marks the transition from pre-operational to concrete operational thought in Piaget's theory. In this play, rules are negotiated and agreed upon by the players before the game begins. Some of these rules, such as those in games of marbles or checkers, are seen by children as handed down from God or other authorities. Others are negotiated on the spot as children spontaneously invent a game, such as one with collections of baseball cards or pebbles. The ability to negotiate and adhere to mutually agreed-upon rules has its roots in the ad hoc negotiation of rules common to sociodramatic play at earlier stages of development (DeVries et al., 2002; Kamii & DeVries, 1980; Piaget, 1965d).

Piaget (1962b) also theorized about the emotional nature of symbolic play, discussing the cathartic or "liquidating combinations" in play that allow children to discharge in play emotions associated with disturbing experiences. He also discussed the compensatory function of symbolic play that provides opportunities to "correct" reality that is confusing or unpleasant. So for example, a child spanking a baby doll might discharge anger about the child's own punishment. Replaying a situation in which the child was not allowed to stay out after dark might prompt a dramatic play sequence of hunting monsters all night in the forest.

VYGOTSKY: DEVELOPMENT AND PLAY

Even though Piaget's research supports the belief that social experience is essential for the development of cognition, his work largely focused on individuals rather than social interactions. Vygotsky, on the other hand, was primarily concerned with social interactions, and the historical and cultural contexts in which development and learning take place. Like Piaget, Vygotsky was a constructivist and believed that conflict and problem solving are essential features of child development. He was particularly interested in the social dynamics that support development. Three important social-cognitive processes are encompassed in his theory: The Zone of Proximal Development, the movement from interpersonal to intrapersonal knowledge, and the transition from implicit rules to explicit rules.

The Zone of Proximal Development

Vygotsky coined the term zone of proximal development (ZPD) to refer to the context in which the child's understanding is furthered as a result of social interactions. Children perform beyond their usual level of functioning when engaged in the social and cognitive collaborations that create this zone. Like Piaget, Vygotsky thought that play was essential to development, and in fact the source of it. "Play is the source of development and creates the zone of proximal development" (1967, p. 16).

By observing children's symbolic play, teachers discover how new concepts, skills, and competencies emerge in the play of each child in relationship to others.

> Steven and Anthony are playing near the tunnel in the outdoor play yard. Steven, lying on his stomach with a face full of mock agony, moans "pretend you gave me medicine." Anthony pretends to feed him medicine, and Steven leaps up, announcing "All better." Then Anthony becomes the patient and Steven feeds him pretend medicine. They each take two turns. Then Anthony says, "I'm hungry," and they rush inside to get their lunch boxes, returning to the outdoor play area with a snack of pretzels. Steven holds up a pretzel and asks, "What letter?" "No letter," responds Anthony, and Steven takes a bite. "Now it's a B," shouts Anthony, and he bites his pretzel. "What letter?" "An O," shouts Steven. The final bite is eaten. "Now what letter?" asks Steven, holding out his empty hand. "No letter!" shouts Anthony delightedly, and they both fall on the ground laughing. ∅

In this observation of Steven and Anthony, we see how in their play they have created a zone of proximal development where their understanding of letters is further developed. In viewing play as the source of the zone of proximal development, we focus on the collaborative construction of a pretend reality that is invented by the players and sustained by the rules they negotiate. Because relationships are of primary importance to young children, their desires to participate in imaginary worlds shared with others lead them to accept and invent new symbolic meanings, regulate their own impulses, and to collaboratively construct pretend realities. This can be observed across a wide range of early childhood settings. For example, early childhood educators and researchers working in integrated classrooms have noted that the play of children with developmental delays is more complex when they play with nondisabled peers (Smith, 1994).

This view of the zone of proximal development differs from the expert-novice model frequently studied in educational research on problem solving. What is left out in the expert-novice model is the acknowledgment of play as a source of development within a zone of proximal development (Nicolopoulou, 1997, 2001).

Interpersonal to Intrapersonal Processes in Learning

Another of Vygotsky's important contributions to understanding play and development is his assertion that every function in development occurs first at the social level (interpersonal) and then at the individual level (intrapersonal) (Vygotsky, 1978). In this view, the social character of situations that promote development is of primary importance. For example, young children frequently learn a new concept or skill with others, such as Amy learning to use a funnel to try to fill a water balloon with her playmates at the water table. She then tries her new concepts and skill in the bathtub at home.

Understanding of Rules

Vygotsky clarified how children develop their understanding of rules. He asserted that all play has rules, and with new levels of development, the rules become more explicit. In this way dramatic play, where rules are implicit, forms the foundation for games, where rules are explicit. Rules in dramatic play govern the organization of roles and behavior in play and events. For example, "Daddies shake hands like this" and "Firefighters have to hook up their hoses first." Yet the following of these rules is largely taken for granted during the dramatic play of children, until conflict among players occurs. Then children assert their versions of the rules governing characters' behavior and hypothetical events.

As children begin to articulate their ideas about rules that govern social behavior from their experiences and their family and cultural backgrounds, they also confront the ideas of others. Through these processes they develop the capacity to negotiate rules of play that are set forth before play begins. This can be particularly challenging for children with developmental delays, children with emotional challenges, or children from families in which the expectations from home and those from school are a mismatch. Yet basic to a play-centered curriculum are mutual understandings that throwing blocks or sand might hurt other children. In this way, children begin to understand why agreed-upon rules are essential to the functioning of society (Curran, 1999; Koplow, 1996; Okagaki & Diamond, 2000).

Vygotsky's Levels of Symbolic Play

Vygotsky also contributed to our understanding of how play relates to levels in the development of symbolic thinking. He observed that very young children merged the meaning of objects with the objects themselves and thus could not think abstractly. In symbolic play, children use objects to represent ideas, situations, and other objects. Objects that represent other objects are called "pivots." Children use pivots to anchor their mental representations of the meanings of words. For example, when Sam selects a book to represent a taco in his kitchen play, he anchors his concept of "taco-ness" with an object that opens and closes, and thus resembles a real taco in important ways. When children's representational competence grows, pivots become less necessary and meaning may be carried completely in the mind, for instance, through the use of an imaginary object. For Vygotsky the use of objects in play as support for the development of meaning-in-the-mind marks a key stage in the development of thought (Vygotsky, 1967, 1978).

MEAD: PLAY AND THE DEVELOPING SENSE OF SELF

Dramatic role play in childhood contains another dimension related to, but separate from, abstract thinking in fantasy and rules. This is the construction of a sense of self.

Mead (1934) studied the relationship of play to the development of a stable sense of self. For Mead, play is the major vehicle for young children to learn to differentiate their own perspectives from those of others in their social worlds. As children take on pretend roles of others and coordinate those roles with the roles taken by their playmates, they come to view their own behavior from the perspectives of other people.

For example, Robert, playing at being a waiter in a restaurant, incorporates the perspectives of his "customers" when he asks them if they are ready to order. He then communicates with his "cook" in the kitchen and tells his customers, "It will take a long time to get a burger here. Better go to McDonald's." This negotiation between the self and others also takes place outside of play scripts, as we see when Robert, his cook, and his customers have to figure out how they will put away the props and furniture for their restaurant when the teacher announces that it's clean-up time.

The Play Stage

According to Mead (1934), the preschool and primary-grade years provide the impetus and context for children to see themselves as unique human beings

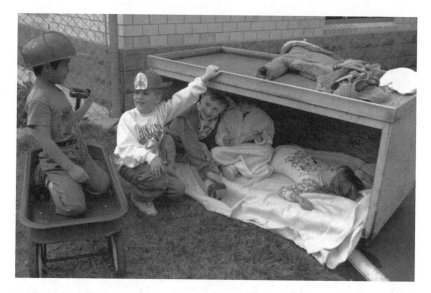

Through interactions with playmates, children learn to respect the perspective of others.

within the community of others. In Mead's theory, the young preschool child operates in the play stage of the development of the self, accomplishing simple role transformations from self to others. This is what Smilansky (1968) describes as the beginning stages of role play. The child simply becomes a tiger, or an astronaut, or a veterinarian, and then returns to being the self, with limited expansion of the components or complementary roles involved in the transformations. For example, 3-year-old Jed announces "I'm a fireman! RRRRRRR!" and races around waving an imaginary hose. Five minutes later he becomes a puppy, barking and crawling on all fours.

In Mead's terms the child is just beginning to differentiate the "I" or spontaneous aspect of the self from the "me" or the sense of the self as a social object. In transforming himself into a puppy, for example, Jed is beginning to figure out how others might view him from their perspectives. This is the stage in which children often create imaginary companions, representing the companion's viewpoint as well as that of the self. Children at this stage form the rudiments of a sense of self that include their own perspectives as well as representations of how others view them. Emphases may differ according to culture, for example, cultural values and interpretations of children's behavior within an individualistic cultural orientation may be different from those with a collective or mutual interdependence cultural orientation (Greenfield, 1994, 1999; Johnson, Christie, & Wardle, 2005; Joshi, 2005; Okagaki & Diamond, 2000).

The Game Stage

As role play becomes more complex, children enter into what Mead called the game stage of the development of the self. In this stage the "I" aspect of self is coordinated with complex representations of the viewpoints of others about the "I." For example, 5-year-old Cindy simultaneously plays the role of mother to her child who is eating breakfast, wife to her husband who is on his way to work, and ballerina to her coach who has just called her on the phone in a typical "morning in the playhouse" enactment. Not only does Cindy need to adjust her voice tone, gesture, and language to what she believes is appropriate for each role, she must imagine the complementary roles of others to each of her roles and coordinate them. All the while she uses cardboard chips to represent scrambled eggs and pours milk from a wooden block. The degree of distancing in such an enactment is impressive.

At this point, the child in the game stage of development of the self is learning to coordinate her representation of herself with the multiple perspectives that others might take with her. She can think about the various aspects of her "pretend selves" in relation to the other players. She shifts fluidly from the "I" to the "me" and considers herself a social object as well as an actor in her play.

The Generalized Other Stage

The third stage of the self defined by Mead is that of the generalized other. In this stage the child not only coordinates the "I" of the self with multiple "me's" but adopts a metacognitive stance regarding the framework within which action takes place. For example, Cindy might begin to comment on the rules of her culture that define authentic roles of mother or ballerina or spouse. Children in this stage often discuss the components of their roles with comments such as "Doctors talk like this" or "Babies walk this way." This is the stage where games with rules become of interest as children coordinate the perspectives of players with their understanding of the framework that governs the rule structure of the game. This behavior reflects the understandings children have about the social rules of our culture, as expressed in both their role behavior within the play and in their negotiations about roles outside the play.

CONCEPTS OF SELF AND OTHER IN "THEORY OF MIND"

Theory of mind research addresses how children come to represent the feelings, intentions, and beliefs of others and to act in socially and culturally appropriate ways. This behavior is based on their understandings of psychological processes of themselves and others, and builds on Piaget's notion of perspectivism and the work of Mead on the child's developing concepts of self and other (Lalonde & Chandler, 1995; Lillard & Curenton, 1999; Lillard, 1998a).

Play is a natural vehicle for the development of theory of mind and is arguably the first context in which children "try on" the feelings, beliefs, and intentions of those separate from themselves in role play. For example, when 3-year-old Anthony pretends to be the doctor examining a patient in the clinic, he takes on the features of a character that may seem threatening or confusing to him in his real life.

In addition, successful negotiation of play roles, themes, and stories depends on children's skill at collaborating and negotiating with their playmates, and their skill in interpreting the responses of others (Astington, 1993; DeVries & Zan, 2005; Fromberg, 2002; Nourot, in press; Youngblade & Dunn, 1995).

Researchers also report cultural and gender differences in children's apparent understanding of others in their play and in social interactions. In Sheldon's research, for example, young girls are found to be more proficient at promoting their own views while considering those of others than young boys (Sheldon, 1992).

Differences in representation of the beliefs, intentions, and feelings of others have powerful implications for classroom cultures and children's styles of negotiation with peers and adults (Bornstein et al., 1998; Greenfield, 1994, 1999). For example, in the area of cultural socialization some families typically tend to emphasize mental states and their relationships to behaviors (e.g. "I think that . . ."), whereas other families emphasize emotional states of self in others in guiding behavior (e.g. "I feel that . . .") (Blake, 1994; Lillard, 1998a). Families from some cultures may be more likely to emphasize mutual interdependence rather than individualistic behaviors (Azuma, 1994; Joshi, 2005; Okagaki & Diamond, 2000).

Another sociocultural contrast emerges in the area of parental views on responsibility and authority. For example, Greenfield (1994, 1999) and Delgado-Gaitan (1994) found that the Mexican families they studied reported that they expected their children to view the teachers' opinion in school as the consistently correct one and expected their children to obey the teachers' authority. Children's cooperative and collaborative behavior was also highly valued by the families they studied. This contrasts with the value of individual achievement and the skill of persuading others of the child's own point of view, values frequently reflected in many elementary schools.

ERIKSON: PLAY AND MASTERY IN THE INNER WORLD OF CHILDHOOD

Erikson stressed the importance of the early years and, in particular, wrote extensively about the importance of play for young children's emotional development

(Erikson 1950/1985, 1977). Psychosocial theory has influenced early childhood education practice for several reasons. Erikson described the development of the healthy personality and also how children's emotional development relates to their families, school, and the cultural contexts in which they live. Psychosocial theory, which extends Freud's psychoanalytic theory, considers both the inner, psychological dimensions and the outer, social dimensions of children's developing identity.

Erikson described eight major stages of psychosocial development that build upon previous stages and are revisited throughout life (Erikson, 1950/1985). The first four stages develop from infancy through early childhood. Rather than being stages that individuals "pass through," Erikson stressed that, although the healthy personality showed the strength of a stage (e.g., trust), healthy individuals continue to rework the balance of the strength of the stage and its antithesis (e.g., mistrust) throughout life. For example, it is adaptable for healthy individuals of all ages to exhibit mistrust in situations where it is dangerous to be too trusting.

Infancy: Trust and Mistrust

During the first year of life, infants are totally dependent on their caregivers. In fact, the word "caregiver" means one who "gives care" as well as "cares for." The caregiver's sensitivity and consistency in care lead not only to the infant's attachment to that caregiver, but to the infant's developing a sense of trust in self and the outer world. The emotionally healthy infant's basic sense of trust is central to the toddler's development of autonomy.

Toddlerhood: Autonomy, Shame, and Doubt

During their second and third years of life, children's growing motor and cognitive competencies contribute to their psychosocial development. This is a time when children develop a sense of their own power, a sense of "I can do it." Children's developing sense of autonomy is shaped by their schools, families, and society. Erikson emphasizes that we examine what young children are allowed or expected to do, and how adults set limits or boundaries on children's behavior, so that autonomy is the outcome rather than shame and doubt regarding their own power in the world.

Early Childhood: Initiative and Guilt

Erikson called the next age, from about 4 to 6, "the play stage." This is the stage of initiative and guilt. Children's greater motor, cognitive, and social capabilities mean that they are able to initiate complex play with others and sustain play for a longer time.

For Erikson, this was the stage where imagination holds sway as children create their own "micro-reality" (Erikson, 1977). He describes how, at this stage, children express their initiative in play by developing complex plots with conflicting turns and twists, and create a wide range of characters.

Children at this stage initiate play to work through past failures and present contradictions. Conflicts between archetypes of good and evil expressed in power roles such as superheroes and space aliens are common themes. Conflicts between child initiative and adult prohibitions are also expressed through fantasy play, such as the "naughty baby." In dramatic play, children enter into fantasies that allow them to explore their concepts of initiative and independence. Play themes that portray children as orphaned or separated from their parents, having to fend for themselves in the woods or at sea, are common in preschool and kindergarten.

Play-centered curriculum supports children's exploration of the psychosocial issues of taking initiative and feeling guilt over violating adult prohibitions. In contrast, curriculum that emphasizes learning by imitating models may undermine the development of initiative. In every teacher-initiated curriculum judgements of right or wrong are consistently made by adults with regard to children's processes and products, and children learn to rely on adult judgment and approval rather than their own internal resources. For example:

> In completing a teacher-modeled project, Rebecca places the pre-cut green strip of "grass" above her name on the page and then places the "trunk" of the tree at a right angle above it. She begins to tear pieces of tissue paper for her "fall leaves." As the teacher circulates about the classroom, she pauses and says, "You've done a good job on your tree trunk, Rebecca, but your grass needs to go along the bottom edge of the paper." The teacher removes the green paper strip of grass as well as the brown trunk, placing them to match her own model. Rebecca puts her hands in her lap and stares desultorily around the room, as the teacher moves on to guide another child's activity. ✇

Too much activity forced upon the child by others, claim Katz and Chard (2000), leads to "damaged dispositions" of intrinsic motivation, concentration, initiative, confidence, and humor that are essential to the learning process throughout children's lives.

Adults can support children's play by providing a safe environment in which developmentally appropriate limits are set to support children's developing sense of initiative. The child who is supported in taking initiative during this stage of development forms a firm foundation for the sense of competence and purpose that develops during middle childhood during the stage of industry and inferiority.

Industry and Inferiority: Play and Work in Middle Childhood

The flexible goals of the initiative stage, where process takes precedence over product, evolve gradually into goal-oriented projects where children's "I can do it" attitude is expanded to include perseverance and self-evaluation. Erikson (1977) writes that play continues to remain important during middle childhood, and children also have the cognitive and motor competencies to participate in the work that the culture values. Children construct their sense of industry or inferiority based on these cultural expectations. He notes that at this stage each culture provides some forms of formal education or training for adult roles (Erikson, 1950/1985). For example, children may apprentice to a local artisan, participate in chores in the home, or begin formal instruction in literacy and math.

RESEARCH PERSPECTIVES ON THE DEVELOPMENT OF PLAY

Every day in preschools, child-care centers, kindergartens, and primary-grade classrooms, differences in the nature of social interaction and the complexity of fantasy, constructive play, and games with rules are observed. These differences reflect aspects of children's cultural, familial, and individual styles, as well as development. Understanding the course of the development of play from preschool to middle childhood is essential for teachers seeking to implement a play-centered curriculum.

When teachers understand the developmental sequences and range of behaviors observed in the play of children of various ages, they are better equipped to support the play they observe. For the basis of this understanding, we expand upon traditional theories of play by looking at research conducted on the development of play in preschool and primary settings.

Parten's Research on Play and Social Participation

Another useful model for looking at the development of children's play was developed by Parten in 1932. She studied the social behavior of children in a parent-cooperative preschool. Based on her observations, she hypothesized a continuum of social participation in play, ranging from onlooker behavior to solitary, parallel, and two forms of group play.

Onlooker Behavior.   Onlooker behavior is defined as when a child watches as others play, either because of reluctance to join, or as a way of scanning for an opening. Less sophisticated players may hang around the edge of a play scene in order to learn by observing and imitating others—at times they may be unsure how to enter a play episode. More sophisticated players use onlooker behavior to help them make choices, to decide which activity to select, or to ascertain the most effective strategy for gaining entrance into an already-established play episode. Sometimes onlookers are simply interested in the play or behavior of others. Sensitive teachers are aware of these possible functions of onlooking and use observation and intervention skillfully to determine what role, if any, he or she might take to help children make choices about their play activities. Onlooker behavior is not simply immature behavior, but, in fact, represents time for children to contemplate their actions.

Solitary Play.   Solitary play is defined as play alone, without overt interaction with peers. For example:

> Four-year-old Amani carefully paints a heart shape at the easel, and fills it in with bright pink. She stops to contemplate her painting briefly, then adds arms and legs. "There!" she says softly. "It's a heart person!" ✆

Parten found solitary play to be typical of the youngest children in her group, but more recent research has shown solitary play performs several functions, depending on the age of the child and the context of play. For example, solitary play may provide the context for complex dramatic play such as enacting a family drama with toy dinosaurs, or it may provide an occasion for needed respite from the demands of negotiating with others, such as solitary play with pegboards. The sensitive teacher is aware that children need opportunities for privacy and solitary play as well as opportunities for sharing and group play in the classroom. For some children who have been traumatized by violence and loss, the need to play alone is paramount (Scarlett, Naudeau, Salonius-Pasternak, & Ponte, 2005).

Because play is inseparable from all facets of development, play itself must develop.

Parallel Play.   Parallel play is defined as play with shared materials or physical proximity without attempts to coordinate play. Nonverbal negotiation of materials may occur but joint play themes and/or constructions are not elaborated. For example, Joyce and Renita are playing parallel to one another with small wooden blocks and a large dollhouse. They each carry on quiet dialogues animating their characters. As one child puts down a block or a piece of dollhouse furniture, the other may pick it up, but they do not overtly acknowledge each other's play. This type of play is thought to represent the earliest, undifferentiated form of group play and teachers may often see it as a prelude to full-blown group play as children test the waters with their peers and gradually begin cooperative efforts. Okagaki, Diamond, Kontos, and Hestenes (1998) found just such processes operating as they studied how children with disabilities used parallel play to participate in play with peers at their own pace.

Group Play.   Parten differentiated two forms of group play. The first, associative play, is seen when children share and coordinate materials and space in proximity to one another, but lack true cooperation. It is similar to parallel play in its form but includes some of the elements of group cooperative play as well. For example, Frank and Mario are playing with Lego blocks at a small table. They negotiate with one another over the number of wheels they may each use out of the basket of parts, but they each continue to work on their own projects, rather than focus on a joint project.

The second form of group play, cooperative play, involves sophisticated efforts to negotiate joint play themes and constructions with peers, and is characterized by children stepping in and out of their play to establish roles or events. For example, three children playing restaurant may alternate their roles in the play as customer, cook, and waiter/waitress with comments about the plot made from outside the play, such as "Pretend the hamburger got burned."

SUMMARY AND CONCLUSION

Teachers of young children gain validation and insight from understanding levels and kinds of play based on the theories of Piaget, Vygotsky, Mead, Erikson, and Parten. Each child in his or her classroom peer culture, shaped by family and community values and histories, plays out his or her understanding of the world in classroom play. By learning as much as one can about the sociocultural factors children bring with them to school, and by observing and listening with care and understanding, teachers enhance the learning and development of children in their care.

Although not all play may be seen as furthering children's development, in our view, play is the necessary core to curriculum for young children. Play provides the teacher with cues and vehicles for assessing children and implementing curriculum goals. Most importantly, it allows children to develop to their fullest potential intellectually, socially, morally, physically, and emotionally as they learn to negotiate their developing sense of self with the demands of the group. Awareness of the possibilities inherent in play for understanding each child in the classroom opens many new doors for teachers. This awareness enhances both the professional knowledge and artistry that make teaching preschool and primary grade children a fulfilling and important profession.

T. H. White (1958), in *The Once and Future King*, tells how King Arthur is transformed into a series of creatures so that he may learn the lessons of each of their perspectives on life. In this way he might become a more sensitive and aware King. During Arthur's stint as a badger he listens to the wise, old badger's story of the Creation:

> God first created embryos for all the creatures of the earth. God called them all before Them [God is plural in this story] and gave each embryo the option of choosing specializations for parts of their bodies as they developed. Some chose to use their arms as flying machines, oars, or shovels; some chose to use their mouths as weapons, or their skins as armor or shelter. When it came Human's turn this embryo chose to remain unspecialized, relying on wisdom alone to guide it to adapt and invent as it encountered experience. God was delighted and remarked that the human alone had solved the riddle of survival in maintaining maximum flexibility for change.
>
> Eternally undeveloped, you will always remain potential in Our image, able to see some of Our sorrows and to feel some of Our joys. We are partly sorry for you, Man, but partly hopeful. Run along then, and do your best. (White, 1958, p. 193)

And so it is in play that we make an investment to protect both the short-term and long-term futures of our children and our society. Play supports the development of specific concepts such as those needed to understand physics or our language system. It also supports more general qualities related to socialization, mastery, imagination, and flexibility of mind that help to ensure a legacy of adaptation to change and freedom to make choices. In the following chapters we begin to provide the detail of the functioning of classrooms that reflect a deep and thorough respect for children's play.

SUGGESTED RESOURCES

Duckworth, E. (1996). *"The having of wonderful ideas" and other essays on teaching and learning* (2nd ed.). New York: Teachers College Press.

These inspiring essays examine the learning processes of adults as well as children from a constructivist perspective. Duckworth's work captures the relationships among playfulness, curiosity, and problem solving for adults as well as children. Readers might be particularly interested in several chapters that describe teachers as learners and their "having of wonderful ideas."

Fromberg, D. P., & Bergen, D. (Eds.). (2006). *Play from birth to twelve and beyond; Contexts, perspectives, and meanings* (2nd ed.). New York: Routledge.

This impressive collection of essays, research reports, and reviews covers every aspect of play in childhood and adulthood, with contributions by many teachers, researchers, and theorists.

Johnson, J., Christie, J., & Wardle, F. (2005). *Play, development, and early education.* Boston: Allyn and Bacon.

This book provides chapters on research and theory related to play and development, addressing many facets of play and education. The suggestions for helping children with special needs are particularly good.

Paley, V. G. (1999). *The kindness of children.* Cambridge MA: Harvard University Press.

Paley describes her life in classrooms with young children and the powerful impact of their play on their development.

Piaget, J. (1962). *Play, dreams, and imitation in childhood.* New York: Norton.

This translation of Piaget's original work on play provides advanced students with an appreciation of the scope and clarity of his observations, as well as a thorough discussion of his theory of the development of play. Piaget shows how representational activity is derived from the psychological invariants of assimilation and accommodation, and relates the development of representation to the transition from preconceptual to conceptual activity.

Scarlett, W. G., Naudeau, S., Salonius-Pasternak, D., & Ponte, I. (2005). *Children's play.* Thousand Oaks, CA: Sage Publications.

This book provides chapters on research and theory related to play and development, addressing many facets of both play and education, including unique perspectives on theories of play and the role of play in therapy.

Vygotsky, L. S. (1976). Play and its role in the mental development of the child. In J. S. Bruner, A. Jolly, & K. Sylva (Eds.), *Play: Its role in development and evolution* (pp. 537–544). New York: Basic Books. Originally published in *Soviet Psychology* (1976), 12, 62–76.

Advanced students will find that this translation of an original work by Vygotsky provides an excellent introduction to his theory. In this brief work, Vygotsky discusses the centrality of play to development. See also, Vygotsky, L. S. (1978) *Mind in society: The development of higher psychological processes,* Cambridge, MA: Harvard University Press, for an elucidation of Vygotsky's views on play, development, and learning.

Play as the Cornerstone
of Development

In chapter 2 we looked at the development of children's play as it relates to cognitive, social, moral, and emotional dimensions of childhood. We emphasized the interweaving of these aspects of development within the fabric of play, and began to elucidate the competencies that children construct through play in the years from preschool through the primary grades.

In this chapter we address in greater detail the question of how play enhances children's development, enabling them to become competent older children, adolescents, and adults. We explore in greater depth the ways in which play leads development in early childhood and supports competence within the peer culture as well as academic achievements at each level. We also describe how play-centered curriculum forms the foundation for effective teaching related to state and national standards for early education, such as those in language and literacy, mathematics, science, social competence, and dispositions for learning.

Early in the history of early childhood education, teachers' views of play in school settings were dominated by philosophical approaches to play. Following the theories of Comenius, Pestalozzi, Rousseau, and Froebel, play was regarded as the natural province of childhood, and teachers believed that play in childhood was valuable in and of itself as part of respecting the vulnerable and malleable nature of children (Nourot, 2005; Wolfe, 2002).

As early childhood educators became more focused on specific outcomes of educational practice, the philosophical views of play were largely replaced by more instrumental rationales for play in the curriculum for young children. Instrumental rationales focused on the future value that play accrues to children and society. This trend has recently been expressed as an increased emphasis on curriculum standards. The integrated nature of teaching the "whole child" was overshadowed by a movement to delineate specific concepts, skills, and competencies at each level of the preschool and primary curriculum. Many advocates of children's play asked a pragmatic question: "What aspects of desirable academic and social knowledge are constructed through play in early childhood?" (Bergen, 2002; Fromberg, 1999, 2002; Gowen, 1995; Jones, 2003; Scarlett et al., 2005).

Much of the recent research in the area of children's play has followed this instrumental focus. Such research argues for the central role of play in constructing and consolidating particular knowledge, skills, and competencies in preschool and the primary grades, or "educational play."

In this chapter we take the position that play has a legitimate postive role in learning and development. We examine how play influences various aspects of child development beginning with intellectual development, followed by a look at its effects on creativity and imagination, and, lastly, its influences on emotional, social, and moral development.

PLAY AS THE CORNERSTONE OF INTELLECTUAL DEVELOPMENT

For both Piaget and Vygotsky, play is intimately tied to representation, that is, how the child expresses ideas about the world, feelings, and needs through symbolic thought, symbolic play, and symbolic role playing. Additional elements of intellectual development include how children come to understand the perspectives of others, how children invent strategies for play with others (as in games with rules), and how children solve problems. We round out our focus on intellectual development with a look at language and literacy and logical-mathematical thought.

Play and the Development of Symbolic Thought

Symbolic activities rest on children's abilities to create meaning in their minds and to express that meaning through gesture (driving a pretend car), language, intonation ("OK, honey, it's bedtime."), and objects (using sand and rocks to make a birthday cake).

The development of symbolic or abstract thought is one of the key aspects of intellectual development centered in the early childhood years. It is also a characteristic of early childhood play frequently studied by child development researchers over the years and, therefore, gives us a major lens for interpreting our observations of children at play (Bergen, 2002; Fromberg, 1999; Frost, Shing & Jacobs, 2005; Gowen, 1995; McCune, 1985; McCune-Nicholich, 1981; Rubin et al., 1983).

> Sally picks up a wooden block and holds it to her ear. She makes pushing button motions with her fingers and says, "Hello, is Mickey Mouse there?" ✄

Beginning at about the age of 18 months, the human mind develops to the point where symbolic thought is possible, evidenced by the use of language and pretend play. From this point on, the ability to transform objects or situations, through the use of imagination, into meanings that are different from the original object or situation forms the foundation for intellectual development and communication (Piaget, 1962b; Vygotsky, 1976).

Symbolic Play with Objects. Building on Vygotsky's notion that concrete objects serve as pivots to "anchor" children's early efforts with imagination and pretense, researchers have studied young children at play with objects. They have discovered that, as children's play develops, they seem able to use objects that are increasingly different in form and function from the object represented in play, building the foundation for abstract thinking (Gowen, 1995).

In playing with representational objects, children explore their culture.

This ability to abstract the essential features of an object and to mentally represent those features is called representational competence, and rests on the notion of symbolic distancing. Sigel (1993) coined the term *symbolic distancing* to denote the degree to which a transformed object represents what it is intended to symbolize. For example, if we want to find something to represent a car, a particular block might be closer in symbolic distance than another because of its shape and size. A toy truck would be closer than a toy cow.

When children engage in symbolic transformations in their play, the use of objects which do not resemble what they symbolize calls for mental effort. This is true of the use of imaginary objects and pretend roles and situations as well. The greater the distance in the transformations, the more intellectually demanding play becomes.

Representational competence increases with development and is largely constructed through play. Some research indicates that older children may actually prefer unstructured objects such as blocks, packing material, or pebbles to real-looking replicas of objects as children's capacity for symbolic representation advances. Presumably, when representational competence is well developed, children do not have to interrupt their ongoing scripts of pretend play to search for an object that closely resembles the one they wish to symbolize (Fein, 1981; Pulaski, 1970; Scarlett et al., 2005).

Symbolic Role Play. Children also make symbolic transformations in their role play. Research indicates that as children's capacities for representing ideas develop, they increasingly create pretend roles and situations without the use of costumes or props, using more subtle behaviors such as gesture and intonation to mark their transformation into make-believe roles in play. Teachers may provide materials for costumes, such as hats or capes for children to use in their role play, and may want to take note of the subtle markers, such as a tone of voice, a walk, or a gesture that children use to enter a make-believe (Bennett, Wood, & Rogers, 1997; Farver, 1992; Fromberg, 2002; Henderson & Jones, 2002; Smilansky, 1968, 1990; Wolfberg, 1999).

The use of symbols is not characteristic of all play. But symbolic behavior underlies the characteristic of pretense that we associate with the play of preschool and primary-aged children. It forms the foundation upon which children construct their abilities to engage in abstract thinking in literacy, mathematical reasoning, and problem solving.

Supporting Symbolic Play for Children with Special Needs. The concept of symbolic distancing is particularly useful when working with young children and children with developmental delays. Some children with special needs have difficulty in separating reality from fantasy (Bergen, 2003; Mindes, 1998; Newcomer, 1993; Odom, 2002). When symbolic distancing is a challenge, most would select an object that is a replica or closely resembles the actual object in form and function. Teachers can support the success of children with special needs in integrated classrooms by including a range of play materials (Hughes, 2003; Neeley, Neeley, Justen, & Tipton-Sumner, 2001). Wolfberg (1999) reports her research on the scaffolding of imagination and pretense in the play of children with autism. She contends that both teachers and peers support children's use of increasingly abstract symbolic representations through modeling and play orchestration

Four-year-old Edna and 5-year-old Jonah, both children with autism in a full inclusion preschool class, are playing parallel in the dramatic play area. Edna drives the grocery cart around the classroom, returning in a ritual fashion to tap the toy cash register on each round. Jonah is also in the pretend store, packing and unpacking toy plastic food in shopping bags repeatedly. Their teacher takes the role of cashier and orchestrates some cooperative play between Edna and Jonah by modeling and coaching how Jonah might load the groceries into Edna's cart and help her to her "car" in the block area. The teacher gradually reduces her coaching role from direct modeling to verbal prompts to observation as the two children master the sequence of pretend, as they laugh and touch one another. ⌀

Taking the Perspectives of Others.   The symbolic distancing of fantasy is not the only demand on the child's mental energy. Playing with peers requires perspectivism, or the ability to mentally represent the viewpoint of others in order to negotiate group play situations.

> Both Samantha and Estelle want to play the part of the princess for the castle they have built of blocks. Play cannot continue until a compromise is reached. Their teacher suggests that one princess has a cousin who visits from another kingdom, and the girls promptly begin discussing how the two princesses' clothing and crowns might look different, and the carriage that they could build to make the journey between the two castles. ⌀

The continuity and stability of the players' joint creation depends on their abilities to marshal enough mental energy to mentally represent and consider the perspectives of others in negotiating their roles and the plot of their play (Ariel, 2002; Curran, 1999; Goncu, 1993; Sheldon, 1992; Sluss & Stremmel, 2004; Trawick-Smith, 1994).

Although young children with cognitive and emotional developmental delays can be observed playing with their peers in integrated classrooms, they may have particular difficulties taking the perspectives of their peers. For example, many have difficulty evaluating how their behavior affects others. Most children with social and emotional special needs are egocentric much of the time. For example, such children might fail to greet peers, but might become upset if peers failed to greet them. Play-centered curricula provide all children numerous opportunities to engage in behaviors, such as compromising and negotiating, that foster the development of friendships (Bergen, 2003; Koplow, 1996; McCay & Keyes, 2001; Mindes, 1998; Newcomer, 1993; Odom, 2002; Wolfberg, 1999).

Weighing the Mental Demands of Play.   Two demands on mental effort, fantasy distancing and taking the perspectives of others, need to be carefully considered by teachers when assessing, planning for, and intervening in play.

Play with familiar peers or siblings provides an interpersonal context that is familiar and has known patterns of social interaction. In these situations of interpersonal comfort, children's mental energy is freed to engage in complicated distancing of symbolic objects and fantasy themes (Ariel, 2002; King, 1992; Meyers, Klein, & Genishi, 1994; Orellana, 1994).

Conversely, children who are new to the group or who may be having difficulties in social negotiations with peers, need the comfort and security of a fantasy script that is not too distanced from what they know well. Almost everyone knows the script for playing house or blocks and trucks, or riding trikes. The less demanding the symbolic distancing requirements of the play scenarios, the more attention children can devote to social negotiation with peers. This may be a particularly important issue for children with developmental delays who may have difficulties with the distancing demands of the play as well as challenges entering the play setting. It is also a consideration for teachers of children with difficulty in self-regulation, or children who are fearful and anxious and may respond aggressively to such frustrations (Ariel, 2002; Bretherton, 1984; Farver, 1992; Goncu, 1993; Scarlett et al., 2005).

This concept of weighing the relative demands of fantasy and social negotiation has implications for the timing of the play curriculum. Familiar scripts and many realistic props are appropriate at the beginning of the year. More distanced themes with prop boxes that stimulate and extend thematic fantasy play are called for later in the school year as play peers become familiar and patterns of communication become more comfortable.

Cultural and Linguistic Contexts for Symbolic Play. Weighing the social and cognitive demands of play situations also has implications for assessing and supporting the development of children from all cultural and linguistic backgrounds. Some children may need the support of familiar play accessories more than others. Children who are English language learners and those from all cultural backgrounds benefit from scripts and play accessories that are familiar and offer opportunities for both repetition and expansion (Reynolds, 2002). Depending on temperament or family expectations, some children will naturally engage in more solitary play or parallel play as a way of meeting their own needs. Others may come from family or cultural contexts in which play in school is not valued or encouraged (Bowman, 2005; Cooney, 2004; Hughes, 2003; Joshi, 2005; Roopnarine, Shin, Donova, & Suppal, 2000).

Inventing Strategies. The most complex level of play, games with rules, is challenging to young children because it represents the most sophisticated levels of both social and symbolic play. Games with rules demand both distancing in terms of object transformations, role transformation situations, and the consideration of the perspectives of all players. Added to this is the dimension of the "generalized other" hypothesized by G. H. Mead (1934). In games with rules, the player is required to reflect on the relationship of all the players within the framework of the rules. For example, a Monopoly player might want to figure out who is playing fairly according to the rules and who is not, or even whom she might make an alliance with to borrow from the bank. These and similar meta-cognitive demands on the skilled games player require even further levels of distancing in order to view both social and symbolic behavior from an objective stance—and then use that information to formulate a strategy (Curran, 1999; DeVries et al., 2002; Zan, 1996).

This kind of strategy-taking does not often appear until children are 5 or 6 years old. As an example, when 3-year-olds play Duck, Duck, Goose, after the goose is tapped and named, all the children get up and run. They understand the basic rule of the game, but cannot coordinate the perspectives of different players with their own. Four-year-olds understand that only the "goose" and "it" run and that the goose must chase and catch "it." But the players chase around the circle and the "goose" inevitably fails to tag "it." At 5 years of age, children begin to employ a strategy with "goose" often circling in the opposite direction in order to tag "it" before "it" can manage to run back to the empty spot.

When children begin to spontaneously invent strategies and discuss and negotiate rules before games begin, games with rules become an appropriate addition to the school curriculum. Game materials and boards may be available but children should be encouraged to invent and negotiate their own rules. In the primary grades, the playing and inventing of games with rules becomes a major component of a play-centered curriculum. Children use this newly emerging stage of

Play can be solitary, parallel, or group.

play development to consolidate their understanding of rules and strategies, and as an opportunity to display and elaborate their new cognitive accomplishments.

Play and the Development of Language and Literacy

Much of the research on children's use of symbols has linked play to language and literacy development. Some researchers have focused on parallels between early language development and the use of symbols in play (Bergen & Mauer, 2000; McCune-Nicholich, 1981; Pellegrini & Galda, 1993; Uttal et al., 1998). Others have studied the ways in which children play with the elements of language such as with sounds or meanings. Children's exploration of sounds, arrangements of words, and meanings of words form the context for children to invent unique forms of language and to master new forms as they are acquired. This play with language and sound also forms the basis for phonemic and phonological awareness. Language play is ubiquitous in classrooms with young children and often occurs in the most mundane of circumstances.

> It's juice time in a preschool setting and James and Eva begin to giggle as they wait for their turns to pour juice. "You're juicy-goosey," contributes James. "You're juicely-goosely-foosley," chortles Eva, and they both dissolve in laughter. ∅

Yopp (1995) and Wasik (2001) report ways in which play with the sounds of language contributes to the development of phonemic awareness. Phonemic awareness includes the ability to recognize and to manipulate individual sounds of words. It involves insights about the sounds of oral language and the segmentation of sounds used in speech communication.

The spontaneous play in the juicey-goosey example above might be supplemented by teachers of young children with songs that play with sounds of language such as "Apples and Bananas," or rhyming in "Down by the Bay"; nursery rhymes such as "One two, buckle my shoe"; and children's books like *The Cat in the Hat*, *Chicka Chicka Boom Boom* or *Barnyard Dance*. The key to playing with sounds is to truly focus on listening and speaking the sounds rather than to focus on print. State and national standards for planning curriculum for early literacy include such concepts as narrative and story comprehension as well as the phonemic and phonological awareness needed to decode sounds and symbols, as illustrated in Table 3.1.

Literacy in Play: Decoding the Symbols.   Research in the field of emergent literacy has looked at how children incorporate literacy play into their make-believe activities. Such play incorporates the social functions of literacy into pretend play scripts, and addresses the early literacy standards related to concepts of

Table 3.1
Examples of Standards for Phonemic and Phonological Awareness

Play Example	Curriculum Standard
Singh makes road sign for block play (Stop; Slow).	Makes letter-sound correspondences
Francisco sings "Down by the Bay," "Willowby Wallowby."	Recognizes and generates rhymes through songs and stories
Tom copies names from cubbies to send a letter in the play post office.	Demonstrates growing awareness of beginning, ending, medial sounds of words

Note: Curriculum standards for this table were drawn from benchmark and standards documents from the following states and countries: California, Connecticut, Great Britain, Idaho, Kansas, Massachusetts, Michigan, New Jersey, Pennsylvania, Rhode Island, Texas, and Vermont.

print and early writing (Davidson, 1998; Einarsdottir, 2000; Neves & Riefel, 2002; Roskos, 2000; Roskos & Christie, 2000a; 2004; Singer & Lythcott, 2004).

In Sandra's kindergarten classroom, children set up a bank, a store and a restaurant, all built with blocks. In order to obtain money from the bank to spend elsewhere, "tellers" in the bank asked their "customers" to pick one of the blank books from the library corner and write their names on it. After counting out paper to represent money, the teller wrote CRTO ("credit to") in the book, and stamped it with a rubber stamp. ✂

In addition to understanding the social functions of print, children's schooling in the written symbols of language and mathematics requires the ability to perform symbolic transformations. For example, the ability to understand that *H* and *K, bat* and *14* are combinations of lines that represent sounds, words, and numbers is similar to the capacity to use a block to represent a truck or a telephone.

Children who become skilled at symbolic transformations in their play are also preparing conceptually to understand some of the subtleties of culturally shared symbolic systems used in written language, aspects that adults take for granted, but that children find confusing. For example, in one first-grade classroom, children were frequently bewildered by the arbitrary meaning assigned to symbols that look the same. The letter *C* is sometimes pronounced as a *K* such as in the word *cake*, sometimes as an *S* as in *city* and sometimes as a new sound *CH* as in *chicken*. This inconsistency among assigned meanings for symbols that do not change in appearance can be very confusing to a child who has not developed the concept of "multiple transformations" in his or her pretend play. For example, the idea that a rectangular block can be a car, a person, or a sandwich, depending on the context of the child's imagination, prepares children to understand these differences when they begin to operate with our system of written signs and symbols. In both symbolic play and phonetic decoding the concept that one object (that continues to look the same) may be transformed by the mind into several different meanings is essential.

A related concept is the idea that several objects that look different may be symbolically transformed to carry the same meaning. In play, for example, you might see Sara appropriate a block, a Lego, or a toy car to represent a walkie-talkie on a spaceship. These choices depend in part on what is available and also on the child's ability to abstract salient features of objects in order to use them as symbols for alternative meanings. This concept is called upon when children learn to identify symbols of written language, for example, in understanding that *A* and *a* both represent the same sound in our alphabet. These competencies are closely related to the concepts of print and early writing as seen in Table 3.2.

Table 3.2

Examples of Curriculum Standards Related to Concepts of Print and Writing

Play Example	Curriculum Standard
"That P starts my name," says Pamela as she surveys the photos labeled at the sign-in table.	Understands that letters make up words and distinguishes between print and pictures
"And one day the littlest bear . . ." Maddy pretends to read to the teddy bear in the book area, turning pages and orienting the book with pictures on top and text below.	Handles books appropriately and respectfully (front-back; top-bottom; left-right)
Alesha uses a note pad and pencil to take Jonathan's order in the classroom restaurant. "Do you want fries with that?" she asks.	Uses symbols and forms of early writing to create more complex play
Hannah makes a sign to lean against her completed block tower. It says, "Du not dstrub!"	Uses letters and/or phonetically spelled words and basic punctuation

Note: Curriculum standards for this table were drawn from benchmark and standards documents from the following states and countries: Alaska, California, Connecticut, Great Britain, Kansas, Michigan, Minnesota, New Jersey, New York, Pennsylvania, Rhode Island, Texas, and Vermont.

Table 3.3
Examples of Standards Related to the Development of Narrative

Play Example	Curriculum Standard
Jeremy and Kayla head out to the grassy area under the trees, each carrying two books. "Let's look at the frog one first. It's my favorite," comments Kayla.	Chooses to read books for enjoyment
At sharing circle Manuel dramatizes the Scarecrow's walk from the *Wizard of Oz* play seen the week before.	Retells, re-enacts, or dramatizes stories
"I think Charlotte will go to the fair with Wilbur," predicts Flavia as she forms a pig out of clay. The class has been listening to *Charlotte's Web* read aloud at storytime.	Reads or listens to a story and predicts what will happen next

Note: Curriculum standards for this table were drawn from benchmark and standards documents from the following states and countries: Alaska, California, Connecticut, Great Britain, Idaho, Massachusetts, Michigan, Minnesota, New Jersey, New York, Pennsylvania, and Texas.

The Development of Narrative.   The capacity to enter the "as if" or hypothetical frame of reference in which animals talk, such as that created by E. B. White in *Charlotte's Web,* or the ability to create such a frame oneself in telling or writing a story, rests on concepts constructed in dramatic play. The ability to negotiate multiple roles and hypothetical situations in housekeeping play or to dictate and enact an episode of superheroes' adventures calls on the same capacities in young children's symbolic thought as those needed to write a poem or a narrative of one's own.

Taking on the roles of different characters and sequencing events to tell a story form the foundation for the important aspect of literacy learning called narrative. Reading comprehension, particularly with characters, motives, and plots, also rests on alternative perspectives and sequencing events in order to create and interpret meaning (Bruner, 1986; Fein, Ardeila-Ray, & Groth, 2000; Fromberg, 2002; Gallas, 2003; Kim, 1999; Nel, 2000; Roskos & Christie, 2000a; Williamson & Silvern, 1990). This ability to demonstrate a concept of story also appears in early education standards for literacy development. These and other aspects of play and literacy are considered in detail in chapter 8. See Table 3.3 for some of the academic standards related to the development of narrative.

Play and Logical-Mathematical Thinking

Another relationship between play and development is the construction of logical-mathematical knowledge. One expression of this is seen in children's construction of cause-effect relationships through physical activities. Block building, bike riding, and sand and water play all foster the construction of spatial relationships, gravity, and other concepts of physics. These cause-effect relationship experiences are essential to children's future understanding and abilities to solve problems, and form the foundation for learning science concepts as children develop (Bodrova & Leong, 2003; Chalufour & Worth, 2004; De Vries et al., 2002; Forman, 1998, 2005; Jarrell, 1998; Kamii & Devries, 1993; Kamii, Miyakawa, & Kato, 2004; Wolfe, Cummins, & Meyers, 1998). Table 3.4 shows some of these early education standards in science.

In the development of logical-mathematical thinking, original experiences are more valuable than imitating adult models. When children develop their own schemes or mental patterns for organizing and interpreting meaning in the environment, they form the basis for classification abilities. Play brings children a wide array of opportunities to develop concepts based on classification, and also allows them to construct categories at their own pace (Dominick & Clark, 1996; Kamii with Housman, 2000).

For the past two weeks Marie has been playing almost daily with a set of thick crayons, eight colors. Today there is something new. She chooses a large box of thin crayons, a total of 40 colors. She picks out all the crayons that have a red color and arranges them separately from crayons of orange and pink shades. As she colors a piece of scrap wood with multiple shades of red, she comments, "This is for my mom." Lily sits down next to her. Marie turns, offering a crayon. "There's more reds over here." ✆

Table 3.4
Examples of Curriculum Standards Related to Science

Play Example	Curriculum Standard
Fran solves the problem of finding equivalent blocks for a racing track.	Children engage in play as a means to develop questioning and problem solving.
Amy weighs her baby doll on the scale at the pretend hospital.	Children begin to use scientific tools and methods to learn about the world.
Brad and Raj mix playdough to make their farm animals just the right colors.	Children learn that properties of substances can change when mixed, cooled, or heated.
Sid uses wood chips and clay to make a mask.	Earth is made of materials that have distinct properties and provide resources for human activities.

Note: Curriculum standards for this table were drawn from benchmark and standards documents from the following states: California, Connecticut, Massachusetts, Michigan, Minnesota, New York, Pennsylvania, Rhode Island, Texas, and Vermont.

In this example, Marie is coordinating relationships of "more than" and "less than" and "similar" and "different." The coordination of these relationships is the beginning of classification abilities in early childhood. In fact, more mature play in preschoolers has been found by some researchers to be positively related to sophisticated classification skills (Johnson, Ershler, & Lawton, 1982).

Dramatic play can also contribute to the development of classification concepts in another way. In the following example, for each symbolic transformation, Sam identifies similar characteristics of familiar objects to form the basis of his decision of what to use as a prop. Before choosing the cookbook, presumably because of its qualities of opening and enclosing that are compatible with his idea of a taco, he scans the area, rejecting the pencil and a tennis ball in favor of the book. He later uses the pencil to represent the hot sauce bottle. This selective attention to similar characteristics of objects is another concept essential to the development of classification abilities.

> Six-year-old Sam is fixing dinner for his "son" John. John says, "But I want a hot dog for dinner!" "OK. I can make good hot dogs," notes Sam as he scans the playhouse area for a prop that exemplifies "hot dog-ness" for him. He selects a paperback cookbook from the shelf, opens it, and "stuffs" it with a plastic marker. "Do you want mustard?" he asks. John nods emphatically and Sam shakes a pencil over the "hot dog," pretending that it is a bottle of mustard. ✆

Another relationship between play and logical-mathematical thinking rests on the symbolic transformations inherent in role play. The child who transforms himself or herself into a veterinarian, a puppy, or an astronaut, and each time returns to the mental concept of self, is beginning to show evidence of reversibility, a feature of thinking that accompanies the development of concrete operations in middle childhood in such competencies as basic addition and subtraction. Some researchers have hypothesized that such successive mental transformations in pretend play form the foundation for the Piagetian notion of conservation (Golomb, Gowing, & Friedman, 1982). Conservation involves the understanding that matter does not decrease or increase with a change in its position or form just as role play involves understanding that the identity of a person remains the same when a role is taken (Forman & Kaden, 1987).

> Four-year-old Cassie asks as the family leaves a performance of *Seussical*, "Those people don't really look like that, do they? I mean they had to be real people in costumes?" Her parents went over the program with her and noted the names of the actors who had played particular roles. The next week, Cassie dressed her stuffed animals and dolls in feathers and bits of cloth and yarn, creating "weird animal" costumes, and confirming her concepts of how identities change. ✆

Table 3.5
Examples of Curriculum Standards Related to Mathematics

Play Example	Curriculum Standards
Sandy counts aloud to time the baking of pretend cookies in oven.	*Concepts of Number* Counts to 10 by rote memorization
Frank asks for more red paint at the easel.	Uses comparative words, such as many-few, big-little; more-less; fast-slow appropriately
Marcus counts out six coins to pay for ice cream at pretend restaurant.	Understands numbers and simple operations and uses math manipulatives, games, toys, coins in daily activities (e.g., adding, subtracting)
Laura measures sand or water to pour.	*Measurement* Uses measuring implements
Jake says, "I need about two more blocks."	Estimates
Matt orders toy dinosaurs by size on edge of sandbox.	*Ordering/Seriation* Orders objects from smallest to largest
Mary comments, "That doll needs a straw hat like the big one."	*Sorts and Classifies* Describes how items are the same or different

Note: Curriculum standards for this table were drawn from benchmark and standards documents from the following states and countries: Alaska, California, Connecticut, Great Britain, Idaho, Kansas, Massachusetts, Michigan, Minnesota, New York, Rhode Island, Texas, and Vermont.

All of these competencies seen in children's play—classification, reversibility, quantity, comparisons, ordering and measuring, for example—appear in academic standards for early mathematics, as illustrated in Table 3.5.

Play and Problem Solving

As we see in the example above, young children persist in their efforts to make sense of new information through their play, developing the ability to entertain alternative possibilities in a given situation. For example, the flexibility in thinking that allows one to solve a problem from a fresh perspective or use a tool in a unique way is part of critical thinking. Play contributes to this ability by allowing children to "play through" their ideas, in the same way that adults "talk through" alternatives to problems they face and imagine consequences from varying perspectives. This process also leads to the discovery of new problems or new questions to be asked as children play and think more deeply about their experience (Fantuzzo et al., 1995; Holmes & Geiger, 2002; Tegano, Sawyers, & Moran, 1989; Wyver & Spence, 1999).

This playing through of alternatives may be nonverbal, as in the first example below, or it may include verbal communication as in the second example of negotiating with peers.

> Second graders Darren and Peter are making a sand mountain with a road around it designed for a ball to roll down. The moist sand is beginning to dry in the hot sun and pieces of the road are crumbling. They first try a "patching" job with more sand, but it is too dry to stick. When that doesn't work, they dig under the dry sand to find more of the damp sand they originally used. ✆

Research on children who are popular with peers indicates that children who are flexible in their thinking frequently come up with unique alternatives for resolving disputes and suggesting compromise (Howes, Unger, & Matheson, 1992).

> Four-year-old Mara and 3-year-old Juan are playing with a hospital bed, medical props, and two dolls. They agree to have their "patients" share the toy bed, but there is only one pillow. Mara takes a blanket and folds it several times, placing it under the head of her doll. "Now we both have pillows," she concludes, and the play continues, uninterrupted by disputes. ✆

Researchers who have studied children's play speculate that the conflicts and subsequent negotiations that occur as children shift from actors "in play" to directors "out of" play, force children to consider the perspectives of their playmates. In play, children enact roles and move the storyline forward with action and dialogue. Out of play, children step out of make-believe roles to negotiate new roles, behavior appropriate to roles, and ideas for the plot of their play. If one wants play to continue, then compromises must be made (Fromberg, 2002; Giffin, 1984; Goncu, 1993; Reifel, Hoke, Pape, & Wisneski, 2004; Reifel & Yeatman, 1993; Sawyer, 1997; Sheldon, 1992; Snow, Burns, & Griffin, 1998). All of the state standards for early education that we reviewed include this ability to negotiate and resolve social problems as an essential goal for early education. Table 3.6 presents some of these competencies related to social development.

Play-Centered Curriculum Supports Children with Special Needs

Play-centered curricula can be beneficial for those children who are unable to resolve problems when they arise. This includes many children with social and emotional disabilities and children with developmental delays (Bergen, 2003; Koplow, 1996; Odom, 2002; Wolfberg, 1999). Flexibility is an important dimension of problem solving (Holmes & Geiger, 2002). Because of the links

Table 3.6
Examples of Curriculum Standards Related to Dispositions for Learning

Play Example	Curriculum Standard
Sam and Marcus play spaceship for 15 minutes outdoors. Sam negotiates role of pilot and co-pilot so both can use the controls.	Negotiates with peers to resolve social conflicts and cooperate in play
Fran falls and hurts her knee. While the teacher is coming from across the yard Sam hugs her and says, "We'll get you fixed up!"	Expresses empathy or caring for others
Sam and Elaine set up paint cups for Nancy and tilt her easel so she can reach it from her wheelchair.	Demonstrates respect for differences in interaction with others from diverse backgrounds and with different abilities
Three days in a row, Sam returns to the road project, adding new signs and persisting at building a bridge with buttresses.	Demonstrates persistence in play and projects

Note: Curriculum standards for this table were drawn from benchmark and standards documents from the following states: California, Connecticut, Michigan, Minnesota, New York, and Rhode Island.

between flexibility, language, and cognition, certain children with special needs lack this flexibility and react to the environment in a rigid manner. Extended opportunities to interact with peers in play can support the development of problem solving skills. For example:

In a second-grade integrated classroom, Danny and Michael are playing with small race cars. Danny has a learning disability which includes challenges with visual processing and visual discrimination. As Danny pushes his car on the carpet, he says, "I want my car to go faster." Michael looks around the classroom, spots a table and says, "We can use a table 'cause it's smooth." Danny then looks around the room and exclaims, "Let's go over there," and points to an area of the classroom that is covered in shiny tile. The children take their cars to the slick surface of the tile floor and begin racing them. ✆

Although some of the research and writing in the field of special education, such as that cited above, suggests that children with special needs are unable to solve problems, this example of Danny's success in problem solving in collaboration with Michael demonstrates that it is important to observe each child's abilities in different contexts.

A related issue is the role of the teacher. Genishi and DiPaolo (1982) and Pellegrini (1984) suggest that the teacher's presence during peer play negotiations may inhibit children from solving their interpersonal problems on their own. On the other hand, researchers such as Smilansky (1968, 1990) discuss the ways that the teacher's presence may support children's ability to work out solutions to disagreements during play. Teachers may find the issues of roles and timing especially challenging when working with children who have cognitive, social, or emotional delays or who are overly aggressive when others do not play according to their wishes.

In these and all interventions in play, the teacher's sensitivity and support for children's capabilities and patience for their intended meanings is paramount (Bergen, 2003; Brown & Marchant, 2002; Fromberg, 2002; Jones, 2002; King, 1992; Ramsey, 1998; Wolfberg, 1999).

As we discussed in chapter 2, the idea that play leads children's development is a major feature of Vygotsky's notion of the zone of proximal development (Vygotsky, 1967, 1978). He set forth the idea that children function above their normal level of ability when challenged by peers in their play. Children's desire to maintain social interaction and to encounter and coordinate perspectives other than their own contributes to the developmental stretch evident in play. Researchers studying children's play in mixed-age groups or classrooms with mainstreamed children report that younger or less sophisticated players play at higher levels of complexity when playing with older or more expert peers (Katz, Evangelou, & Hartman, 1990; Stone & Christie, 1996). Children who are imaginative in their symbolic play transformations and flexible in their negotiations with peers are building concepts essential to critical thinking expertise and social problem solving.

PLAY AS THE CORNERSTONE OF IMAGINATION AND CREATIVITY

Qualities that are sometimes taken for granted when reviewing the value of play for future development are imagination and creativity. Much has been written concerning the curriculum appropriate for the 21st century. Bruner (1976) perhaps stated this dilemma best by asking: How can a system that prepares the immature for entry into the society deal with a future that is increasingly difficult to predict within a single lifetime?

One possibility is to foster adaptive, flexible, and creative thinking. These qualities, which represent key elements in determining the survival of our ancestors and in the future, will remain equally essential because "whenever the environment is changing it selects for playful individuals" (Ellis, 1988, p. 24). Concerns about the effects of didactic teaching and skills-based curricula have

Computers in classrooms may engage children in a number of ways.

led to research and writing urging educators to consider more carefully the need to foster imaginative and flexible minds, and to provide rich and varied opportunities in the visual and performing arts. (Elkind, 1990, 2003; Gallas, 2003; Holmes & Geiger, 2002; Isenberg & Jalongo, 2001; Lieberman, 1977; Singer & Lythcott, 2004; Singer & Singer, 1990). See Table 3.7 for samples of academic standards in the arts.

Singer and Singer (1990, 2005) have written extensively about the contribution of play to the imaginative thinking of children. In the Singers' view, make-believe play is essential to the development of the capacity for internal imagery. It contributes to the development of creativity by opening children to experiences involving curiosity and the exploration of alternative situations and combinations. In addition, their research emphasizes the psychosocial benefits of imaginative play: Children who engage in much make-believe play are likely to be happier and more flexible when they encounter new situations.

Three Aspects of Imagination and Fantasy

Egan (1988) developed Vygotsky's claim that play "leads" development in early childhood. He claimed that fantasy and imagination are the appropriate content of early childhood curriculum because they highlight for teachers

Table 3.7
Examples of Curriculum Standards Related to Visual and Performing Arts

Play Example	Curriculum Standard
Melanie appropriates scarves from the dress up box and creates a dance on the stage built in the block area. She requests some "ballet" music.	Children develop self-expression through visual arts, dance, music, and drama
Chase has steadily produced a series of pumpkin people at the easel, making a whole family with different shades of orange, faces, and stem and leaf shapes.	Children create artwork from memory or imagination
In her storyplay Cassie becomes the wicked Queen, snarling and lowering her voice to threaten the "sad princess."	Children assume the role of something or someone else and talk in the language/tone appropriate for that person or thing
"I think I'll use collage like Eric Carle does," says Isabel as she cuts parts for a tree and a sheep, I'll use that fluffy stuff for the sheep fur."	Children develop appreciation, interest, and knowledge of the arts

Note: Curriculum standards for this table were drawn from benchmark and standards documents from the following states and countries: California, Connecticut, Great Britain, Massachusetts, Michigan, Rhode Island, and Vermont.

the passionate concerns of young children. Egan's work emphasized three major aspects of imagination and fantasy in early childhood: (1) the oral nature of the peer culture in the early years, (2) the importance of binary opposites in creating dramatic tension in play themes, and (3) the sense of wonder, magic, and joy inherent in pretend play.

The Oral Culture of Early Childhood.   Egan (1988) found the seeds of the ability to create story in the orally expressed fantasy of early childhood. As each aspect of the story told in fantasy play unfolds, its meaning is clarified and extended in relation to other aspects of the play. In solitary dramatic play these stories are told to the self, and in sociodramatic play the play's meanings are communicated and negotiated within the peer culture of the classroom (Ariel, 2002; Dyson, 1997, 2003; Fromberg, 2002; Katch, 2001; McEwan & Egan, 1995; Nicolopoulou, Scales, & Weintraub, 1994; Paley, 1981, 1994, 1995; Perry, 2001; Sawyer, 1997).

The accompanying ability to extend knowledge of characters, situations, and events from the everyday into the realm of the improbable or impossible is a primary form of logic that encompasses ambiguity and paradox and merges thought and feelings. This ability to make meaning through narrative forms is one of the first examples of the ordering and classification of human experience (Bruner, 1986, 1990). This early use of contradictory forms of logic in play is what Egan calls "mythic thinking," and is seen in both the fantastic series of events that children may imagine in play and in role play. For example, when 4-year-old Erin pretends that she is an undersea monster, she knows that she simultaneously is and is not the role that she plays. This early embrace of paradox lays the foundation for noncontradictory forms of logic that emerge in middle childhood. Egan believes that one must create and entertain a variety of possibilities before narrowing them through logical thought, and that young children's grasp of reality begins by stretching the borders of the known world into new dimensions and possibilities in play (Nourot, in press).

Bipolar Opposites in Play.   Researchers of children's play frequently note binary oppositions in children's play themes such as love/hate, danger/rescue, the permissible/the forbidden, big/little, good guy/bad guy, death/rebirth, and lost/found (Bettelheim, 1989; Corsaro, 1985; Egan, 1988; Garvey, 1977/1990; Katch, 2001; Paley, 1988). These oppositional tensions help children discriminate features of their physical and social worlds, and to define themselves within those worlds. The unity of thought and emotion animates their abilities to make sense of life through the stories told in dramatic play. The following example shows how children move flexibly between sense and nonsense, the physically possible and impossible, the mundane and the exotic, the safe and the threatening, and, for some, the permissible and the forbidden. Here they define the borders of their physical, cultural, social, and emotional realities.

Cathy and Marla are pretending to be witches, and pretend that they are taking blood from their playmates by touching their arms with a spoon, and then running back to the pot on the stove in the housekeeping area to add the imaginary blood of each victim, cackling as they stir the brew. Brian is a witch too, wearing a sparkling cape and carrying a cup with a plastic lemon in it. "This drink has poison and fingernails in it," he announces.

Cathy sends Marla to find a new victim. Marla comes back, spoon held aloft over the pot. "Yes, yes, good," encourages Cathy. Marla pretends to take some blood from one of the teachers who observes on the outskirts of the play. Marla comments to the teacher, "I have your blood and now you will be dead forever," using a high-pitched cackling voice and waving her arms majestically.

Brian holds up his cup. "But if you drink this magic potion, you can come alive again," and he offers some to Kelly, who has just joined the play. "Can I play?" Kelly asks. "Yes," agrees Cathy, "but you have to be a witch, like us." Kelly pretends to take blood from Marla, imitating the high cackling laugh she has heard Cathy use. Then Brian offers his cup to Marla, "This will turn you from a witch into a princess." She pretends to drink the princess-making potion and then the other witches try to turn her back into a witch. "No, no, drink this one." The tension between the bad witches and the good witch Brian with his magic potion continues a few more minutes until clean-up time is called. ✇

The framing of ideas for character, plot, and setting through bipolar oppositions, such as the good witch/bad witch/princess, and the death and rebirth in the above anecdote also define these emerging aspects of story, even as it clarifies children's sense of themselves. Children want passionately for play to continue despite the potential pitfalls of differing ideas about characters or events in the play. The shared understanding that comes from framing play themes and characters in binary themes such as good guy/bad guy or danger/rescue supports the shared understanding and the subsequent negotiation that allows play to flourish (Nourot, 1997, in press).

Wonder, Magic, and Joy.   Although the development of logical thinking and skill in negotiating meanings with others are laudable aspects of imaginative play in early childhood, the essence of play is captured in the magical and ecstatic experiences that define creative processes throughout life (Ariel, 2002; Weber, 1978; Csikszentmihayli, 1993; Egan, 1988; Nachmanovitch, 1990). The joy and wonder encompassed in imaginative play are powerful links to others and an incentive to self-regulation and perspective-taking (Bronson, 2000; Lewis, 1995). The desire for this sense of wonder and joy to continue creates a powerful incentive for children to move beyond their own viewpoints to encompass the perspectives of others, a quality described in children they deem "Master Players," as children experience the power of both friendship and fantasy in their play (Jones & Cooper, 2006; Jones & Reynolds, 1992; Reynolds & Jones, 1997).

PLAY AS THE CORNERSTONE OF EMOTIONAL DEVELOPMENT

The joy and sense of connection that children experience in play is closely connected to emotional development. Children's emotional development refers to their capacity to feel or experience a wide range of emotions such as happiness, sadness, anger, jealousy, excitement, wonder, and fear. Emotional development also involves children's capacity to manage or regulate their emotions and the manner in which they express them. Teachers, theorists, therapists, and researchers emphasize the importance of play in children's emotional development.

For example, Sofia, Elijah, and Jenna are playing in the sand area. They have constructed a volcano and invented a danger and rescue plot for their characters. Sofia and Elijah laugh with delight as the water cascades over their wet sand volcano. They "use their voices" to protest when Jenna begins to stomp on the sand. Later in the play, the three children express conflicts between archetypes of good and evil in their superhero rescue roles. ✆

Dramatic play themes that portray children as orphaned or separated from their parents, having to fend for themselves in the woods or at sea are common in preschool and kindergarten. Other common themes involve life and death, as the example of magic potions involving Cathy, Marla, and Brian illustrates. At times, conflicts between child initiative and adult prohibitions are expressed in the classroom through fantasy play, such as the "naughty baby."

Theorists such as Erikson, Vygotsky, and Piaget have written about play as a cornerstone of emotional development. Erikson wrote, "The play age, as we said, offers the child a micro-reality in which he can use toys (put at his disposal by those who sanction his play) in order to relive, correct, and re-create past experiences . . ." (Erikson, 1977, p. 99).

Erikson's (1950/1985, 1977) work also shows that, through their sociodramatic and pretend block constructions, children respond emotionally to the major life themes that their new cognitive capabilities present. Themes such as death and life, love and hate, care and jealousy occur frequently in the play of young children.

In their play, children reassure or frighten themselves, often at the same time. Erikson also reminds us that, in play, children further develop their sense of purpose. In dramatic play, children enter into fantasies that allow them to explore their concepts of initiative and independence.

Piaget (1962b) also writes about play as a cornerstone of emotional development. Like Erikson, he describes the "liquidating" function of play that allows children to neutralize powerful emotions and release them by reliving them through make-believe. He also describes the "compensatory" nature of fantasy play that helps children rewrite events in which their feelings of helplessness or fear are overwhelming.

Similarly, Vygotsky (1976, 1978) discusses play as the primary matrix for children to develop self-regulation of their behavior and emotions in early childhood.

Contemporary theorists and writers emphasize the importance of emotional development. Entry into school presents additional challenges to emotional development centered on the home and family. With school comes the advent of social comparisons and the need to come to terms with challenges such as insecurity, envy, humiliation, pride, and confidence. Learning to interact with others in a responsible manner, to wait for one's turn and to regulate one's own emotions present major milestones in the development of emotional competence. Gardner (1992) writes that "interpersonal and intrapersonal intelligence" is characterized by the ability to accurately read and respond to the feelings, motivations, and desires of others and access one's own feelings and use them to guide behavior. Similarly, Goleman (1995) explains that "emotional intelligence" is characterized by empathy and self-regulation.

Play and the Harsh Realities of Some Children's Lives

The degree to which contemporary play invites realities that are both incomprehensible and frightening to children remains a thorny issue for both teachers of young children and researchers of play (Ariel, 2002; Katch, 2001; Lancy, 2002; Levin, 2003b; Milne, 1995; Osofsky, 1999; Wallach, 1993; Waniganayake, 2001). Much of play that teachers see as risky or full of violence and aggression may stem from children's need to repeat and revise frightening or confusing experiences through imagination in much the same way that adults talk through emotional distresses (Katch, 2001).

> Six-year-old Josh organizes his classmates to pick dandelions from the school lawn at recess time. They create bouquets and stash them in their cubbies when they return to their first-grade classroom. At their play and project time later in the day, the children construct a pretend casket from blocks complete with handles for pallbearers and enact a pretend funeral with Josh coaching them on the prayers and songs. Other children join and the bouquets of dandelions are shared and thrown on the "casket" as it is lowered into the gravesite marked by tape on the classroom rug. Josh's 19-year-old aunt was killed in a drive-by shooting the previous Saturday.

Josh's teacher understands that "righting" the imbalance in a world in which community violence is frequent and the evening news shows vivid and repetitive images of catastrophe and violence is an important aspect of play in schools. The children are all playing through a disturbing event in their community, and their active collaboration with Josh contributes to his healing. She wonders what to do.

Children also try to make sense of frightening images and scripts from the national media. For example, in the aftermath of September 11, 2001, teachers across the nation reported children repeatedly crashing toy planes into buildings in their play, and confusion about the continual replay of the images on television.

Children often play out the frightening themes and challenge school-based rules regarding weapon play, violence, or use of language in efforts to create meaning for themselves. These emotional roots of play and the possibilities for healing they present must be carefully interpreted by teachers (Katch, 2001; Koplow, 1996).

But sometimes stress levels are too high for children to use play to cope with their emotions. It is important that teachers seek professional resources when children's play takes forms that are disruptive or upsetting to the other children or to the teachers themselves. School counselors and psychologists have long explored the ways in which children struggle to make sense of frightening and/or confusing events (Axline, 1969; Erikson, 1950/1985, 1977, Koplow, 1996; Winnicott, 1971). For example, Erikson (1963) wrote about "play disruption" in children as they reached levels of stress and anxiety in which play was absent or severely curtailed. Children who have been severely trauma- tized may not be able to use play to represent and work through stress and conflict in more typical ways. These children require sensitive and careful or- chestration from specialists as well as teachers in school and in theraputic set- tings. (Goleman, 1995; Koplow, 1996; Scarlett et al., 2005).

PLAY AS THE CORNERSTONE OF SOCIAL-MORAL DEVELOPMENT

Just as play forms the cornerstone of intellectual, creative, and emotional de- velopment, it is also the major cornerstone for social and moral development. For example:

> In one kindergarten classroom, Jon and Rio were happily engaged in building a "ranch" out of blocks. Their intimacy was evident as they giggled and whispered to one another their plans for the fantasy occurring within the block structure. "And then pretend the bad guys can get in here," one boy said to the other. Paul watched from the sidelines and finally began to build his own structure next to Rio and Jon. "But what about me?" Paul said plaintively, as the ranch builders began to expand their construction site. "I'll tell you what," said Rio, "we'll make a line right here and you can build, too. We won't cross the line." ✇

In this example, we see Paul learning to assert his rights, and Jon and Rio learning to understand and accommodate the perspective of a third player, without giving up their investment in keeping their ranch to themselves.

Kamii (1982, 1990) draws upon Piaget's theories of moral development (Pi- aget, 1965d) when she discusses autonomy and heteronomy in classrooms for young children. Moral autonomy is characterized by being governed by oneself. Moral heteronomy means being governed by others. Children who develop moral autonomy come to see moral values as internal guides, independent of whether they may be "caught" doing something inappropriate by a parent or a teacher. In a classroom that promotes moral autonomy, children construct be- liefs about what is fair and unfair based upon their experiences with their peers. Through social-moral dilemmas that involve reciprocal interactions with their playmates, children learn to make informed choices about their behavior and practice factoring in the perspectives of others (DeVries & Zan, 1994, 2005). In the above example, Jon and Rio were able to factor in Paul's desire to play with them and still preserve their own interactive play space. They compromised, treating one another with respect and consideration.

Play and Peers

Cognitive representation, self-concept, emotional intelligence, and social competence are not the only aspects of children's play with objects and other people that contribute to learning and development. Corsaro and colleagues draw upon the theories of Piaget, Vygotsky, and Mead to paint a picture of play as it contributes not only to the child's individual sense of self, but the creation of peer cultures among children at each level of development.

Corsaro (2003) contends that play is the primary context for socialization in childhood. Children's experiences as individuals are nested within a series of peer cultures that evolve at particular ages or levels of cognitive, social, emotional, and physical development. The characteristics of each peer culture are intimately connected to the integration of all levels of developing competencies and knowledge for children. From this view, the peer culture of toddlers differs from that of preschoolers, and that differs in turn from the peer culture of third graders, and so on through adolescence into adulthood. In their peer cultures at each level of development, children represent their interpretations of the larger culture, including the behavior of adults and older children as a compelling theme. For example, playing the role of teenager has a special allure in the peer culture of preschoolers—a view characterized by seeing teenagers as having the privileges of adulthood without the responsibilities of adult life. Young children's interpretations of the culture that surrounds them are shaped by cognitive developmental characteristics, such as young children's abilities to represent the perspectives of others, to reason about categories and sub-categories, and to use objects, gestures, and language to represent objects and ideas (Corsaro, 1985, 2003; Corsaro & Elder, 1990; Gaskins, Miller, & Corsaro, 1992; Perry, 2001).

Children's play also reflects the social norms of their classrooms, and the contexts and values of the adult culture (Hughes, 2003; King, 1992; Meyers, Klein, & Genishi, 1994; Schwartzman, 1978). While the socially constructed meanings of objects, roles, and rules change with the developing series of peer cultures a child joins, Corsaro (1985) also notes that there are common qualities of each successive "layer" of peer culture in which children participate as they grow and develop. He delineates control and communal sharing as key elements of any peer culture, whether manifested by 3-year-olds or 11-year-olds.

Paley (1981, 1986, 1990, 1992) in research from her own classroom illuminates these themes of control and communal sharing by describing the appropriate curriculum for young children as one that includes "fantasy, friendship, and fairness" (1986). Paley's reflections on her own classroom illuminate the powerful connection between children's play and narrative. Play is the first context for considering the "landscapes" of narrative (Bruner, 1986) and serves as the vehicle for constructing the joint history of a group of children and their teachers in a classroom. Who plays with whom, and what roles are coveted and negotiated, are of key importance in a play-centered curriculum, themes we illuminate in chapter 8, Language, Literacy, and Play, and chapter 11, Play and Socialization. All the competencies of development—intellectual, social, emotional, moral, and physical—are drawn into serving this agenda: Who am I in my group of friends, and what stories can we create together?

SUMMARY AND CONCLUSION

In chapter 2 we explored the development of play as viewed by a number of theorists. In this chapter examining how play supports development, we explored some of the many ways in which play influences development and learning. Some of the material we presented is a further examination of these theories. In addition, we discussed the considerable range of research that has been conducted in this area.

We have seen that play has a critical role in all facets of human development. These include, but are not limited to, the large domains of social, emotional, and intellectual growth. With regard to some of the issues considered here, we have examined some of the specific ways that play influences symbolic thought, expressive language, literacy, perspective taking, a sense of self, social cooperation, logical-mathematical thinking, imagination, creativity, and moral reasoning. (See chapter 13 for a more general discussion of the role of play in development.) Understanding how play develops, as well as how play supports children's development, leads to the curricula strategies that will be discussed in chapters 4 and 5.

SUGGESTED RESOURCES

Frost, J., Wortham, S., & Reifel, S. (2005). *Play and child development* (3rd ed.). Upper Saddle River, NJ: Merrill/Prentice Hall.

This volume reviews many aspects of children's play, including cross-cultural influences, classroom practices, and research on play and playgrounds.

Gallas, K. (1994). *The languages of learning: How children talk, write, dance, draw, and sing their understanding of the world.* New York: Teachers College Press.

Gallas, a primary-grade teacher, describes the multiple ways in which children learn as they represent their world through play and other media. Her discussion of the arts in her curriculum and her insights into children's learning is inspirational, as well as practical.

Jones, E., & Cooper, R. (2006). *Playing to get smart.* New York: Teachers College Press.

The authors discuss the ways in which play contributes to the development of critical life skills, such as creativity and problem solving amid the current climate of high pressure for academic standards. It is written with a playful approach for teachers, and underscores the reasons why high quality play is essential for children of all backgrounds.

Klugman, E. (Ed.). (1995). *Play, policy, and practice.* St. Paul, MN: Red Leaf Press.

This volume presents work from a conference on play held at Wheelock College in Boston in the summer of 1992. The conference was attended by teachers and play researchers from the United States and Israel and explored a range of issues related to play in schools and across cultural contexts.

Paley, V. G. (1990). *The boy who would be a helicopter.* Cambridge, MA: Harvard University Press.

This book recounts the case study of one child whose development is profoundly affected by his symbolic play. Paley's sensitivity to the processes inherent in play and her insights gained from careful observations of play are inspirational to teachers.

Roskos, K., & Christie, J. (Eds.). (2000). *Play and literacy in early childhood: Research from multiple perspectives.* Mahwah, NJ: Erlbaum.

This book presents current research on the relationships of play to many aspects of early literacy with many examples of classroom practice.

Orchestrating Children's Play: Setting the Stage

In Ann's K–1 combination classroom, the environment invites play. The house-keeping area includes kitchen furniture and accessories, and a small couch and rocking chair. A girl doll with Asian features and two boy dolls, one with African American and one with Caucasian features, rest in two small beds near the rocker. The children have made a VCR and a television screen from different-sized card-board boxes. Hats and costumes are stored on shelves and hooks, doll clothes in drawers. An accessory box with props for hospital play sits open in the block area adjacent to the house, along with the ever-useful blank clipboards with paper and pencils attached. Ann considers these staples of her play environment. She explains that a local pediatrician had visited the class the day before, and introduced children to terms and medical tools that she hoped would be recast in today's play.

Outdoors, the climbing structure has several levels with platforms, and invites children to create their own level of challenge, with soft rubber matting as a cushion below. Ramps lead to the slide and there is ample space for Angie, who uses a wheelchair, to get out of her chair and maneuver onto the slide. The pathways around the structure are soft mats so that the wheelchair can easily be moved for entering and exiting the play structure. There is a small garden area, with benches and a table for potting plants. Drawing and painting supplies are stored in a small cart, as many children like to draw and paint representations of the plants and rabbits housed in the outdoor yard. The pathway into the garden is wheelchair-accessible, as are the shelves and garden table. ✑

Using the knowledge of theories and research that guide teachers' understanding of the development of play presented in chapters 2 and 3 is the first step in the complex and rewarding process we call "play orchestration." Awareness that 3-year-olds are more dependent on replica objects to sustain their play because of their emerging ability to symbolize, or that 5- and 6-year-olds frequently play games with rules that shift with each round, gives teachers a frame of expectations for behavior and learning in a play-centered curriculum.

The next step in the orchestration process is to bridge expectations based on knowledge and understanding of development and learning to practical strategies for supporting play in settings for young children. These strategies are illuminated by an interpretive approach to teaching. In this approach, teachers always view children's behavior within the sociocultural context in which it occurs, noticing factors such as the social history and social hierarchy of a group of players, or the dynamics of a newcomer, a child with special needs, or an English language learner within the play. In addition, teachers draw on their knowledge of a variety of theories of learning and development to find the lens that fits what they observe (Corsaro & Elder, 1990; Henderson & Jones, 2002; Hughes, 2003; Paley, 1999; Reynolds, 2002).

This book addresses curriculum in settings for young children as well as the phenomenon of childhood play. As such, we value teachers' keen observation, planning of explicit strategies for orchestrating play, and the assessment of learning and development evident in play.

A play-centered curriculum is not made of fixed components but is emergent, finding its direction in the themes and concepts children generate in their play. For a play curriculum to be effective, the teacher must orchestrate the dynamic flow of its elements by matching play to the child's levels of functioning and by providing opportunities for developmental stretches to occur for each child and for the group as a whole. Skilled teachers employ a myriad of strategies for "upping the ante" to encourage these developmental stretches, and foster feelings of trust and safety for all children in the group within play contexts (Barnes & Lehr, 2005; Bowman, 2005; Clawson, 2002; Derman-Sparks & Ramsey, 2005; Joshi, 2005; Swick, 2002).

PRINCIPLES GUIDING PLAY ORCHESTRATION

Four general principles guide our thinking about the ways that teachers may support play in the curriculum. We believe that each of these principles applies across contexts that involve spontaneous play and those that involve guided and directed play. We describe in examples that follow how these principles may apply for different ages of young children and in classrooms that include children with special needs and those from a variety of cultural, socioeconomic, and linguistic backgrounds.

Taking the Child's View

The first principle involves the teacher taking the child's view of experiences and materials in the classroom. Developmentally Appropriate Practice (DAP), a term coined by the National Association for the Education of Young Children

Teachers help children sustain their play by sensitively entering into their activities.

(NAEYC), involves understanding age-appropriate development in young children (Bredekamp, 2004; Bredekamp & Copple, 1997). Knowing that younger children are likely to need replicas of real objects in their play, while older children often prefer blocks, marbles, or other unstructured materials for their play, is an example of using child development theory and research to inform practice.

Developmentally appropriate practice also involves understanding the individual development of each child, and the cultural context in which development occurs. What does Raul bring to school from his home that is unique and different from the concepts and attitudes brought by Miko or Frances? How does the impending divorce of Jo Ann's parents affect her development and behavior? What special accommodations does Brian, who has spina bifida, need to have access to the slide or have an opportunity to swing? In taking the child's view of experience and materials, teachers work with both of these aspects of developmentally appropriate practice: understanding the normal development of a particular age group, and understanding the life experiences in and out of school that shape meaning for each individual child. For example, what does Emil's preoccupation with gunplay and soldiers mean in light of his family's recent immigration from a war-torn country to the United States? Will the addition of a private small space outdoors encourage Fran and Celine to interact, rather than just watch others play?

Teacher as Keen Observer

The second principle of orchestrating play in the curriculum involves the teacher functioning as a keen observer of children's behavior. His or her observation skills are supported by planning specific times to circulate through the classroom, to jot anecdotal notes on peel-off labels, or to sit and observe in a given area of the room. The teacher also uses observational strategies when working with a small group of children on a focused activity and takes time to write down children's observations, questions, experiments, and hypotheses as they work and play.

Seeing Meaning as It Is Constructed

Under the auspices of this third principle, the sensitive teacher recognizes that children construct meaning through many aspects of their experience. Sometimes meaning emerges as playmates suggest a new block to support a building or offer a costume for a role. Sometimes meaning emerges as teacher and child sit together to figure out the spelling of a new word. Children's interactions with adults and other children in classroom settings create contexts where knowledge is relevant. Observing and interpreting children's play enables teachers to skillfully intervene in ways that fall along a continuum of subtle to active participation in play, or even to decide to step back and allow children to resolve their own challenges or conflicts.

Teacher as Stage Manager

The fourth principle involves the teacher's skill in organizing the environment. The teacher plans experiences for children, anticipating the spatial arrangements, basic materials, accessories, and time frames needed for children to construct knowledge through their play. In this role, the teacher supports play by indirectly orchestrating the physical environment and time for children's play (Curtis & Carter, 2003; Greenman, 2005; Hand & Nourot, 1999).

In this chapter we first present some general definitions of strategies and concepts for setting the stage for play in the classroom. Chapter 5 lists more detailed descriptions of teachers' interactive orchestration strategies and examples of their uses in classrooms for preschool and primary-grade children. Chapter 6 focuses on how assessment and play-centered curriculum go hand in hand.

Greater numbers of children with special needs are now included for part or all of the day in preschool and primary-grade settings. Adaptations to the environment, careful selection of play materials, and curriculum are described extensively in the early intervention literature, and we include many of these strategies in our examples and suggested resources. We believe that play "leads" development for all children, those who develop in atypical as well as more typical ways.

A CONTINUUM OF PLAY ORCHESTRATION STRATEGIES

The model we present in Figure 4.1 represents play orchestration strategies ranging from very indirect to very direct roles on the part of the adult. The most indirect of these strategies involve arranging and accessorizing the physical environment for play, and then planning curriculum based on observation and recording of children's play. Increasingly directive techniques for guided play orchestration are described in depth in chapter 5. Although we present these as separate play orchestration strategies, skilled and observant teachers frequently employ several strategies in supporting children's play, often beginning with more indirect strategies, perhaps moving to more directive ones, and then, as they phase out adult involvement, returning to a less directive role on the part of the teacher.

SETTING THE STAGE FOR PLAY

As adults, we look at an office, a restaurant, an outdoor barbecue, and know what kinds of activities and behaviors are expected. As children play in different areas of the classroom, they learn the implicit and explicit rules about what is expected, and, in effect, come to read the social and physical cues of that particular area. The environment, then, is not only "responsive," but children

Figure 4.1
Continuum of Play
Orchestration Strategies

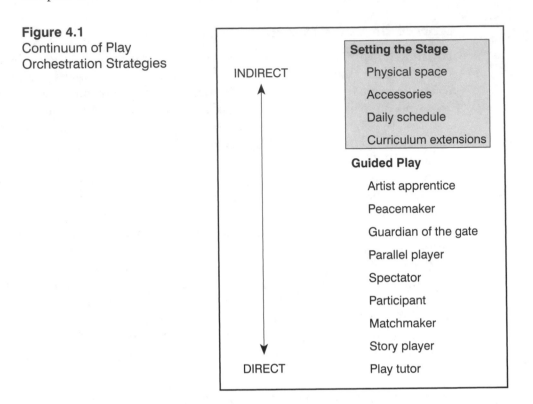

also respond to it by bringing their own knowledge of their cultures, situations, events, people, and things to bear on their understanding of what others may expect of them.

At the indirect end of the continuum, teachers orchestrate play by setting the stage for it to occur. They first provide the physical space conducive to children's play needs, a process that illuminates the respect of teachers for children's special abilities, needs, families, and communities. They also use their professional skills to elaborate and extend curriculum based on the children's play that they observe. Accessories for play are changed frequently as the teacher responds to the children's needs, or are readily available for children to appropriate on their own (Chalufour & Worth, 2004; Curtis & Carter, 2003; Reynolds, 2002).

Preparing the Physical Space for Play

In structuring the physical environment for play, questions to consider are: How is the space arranged, both indoors and outdoors? Is there a place for rough-and-tumble play, an area to run and jump and chase? Are there clearly marked spots with "soft" spaces such as soft chairs or a small grassy area outdoors in which children may find privacy? Are there other areas that have clear boundaries for children, such as the housekeeping, reading, and block areas? All of these features contribute to children's developing play complexity by fostering choice-making and the protection of ongoing play episodes.

Research on children's play environments indicates that between 30 and 50 square feet of usable space per child represents an ideal size for indoor environments. Spaces with less than 25 square feet per child may lead to increases in aggression and unfocused behavior for children (Smith & Connolly, 1980). For teachers, crowded physical spaces promote more directive teaching and limit opportunities for social interaction among children. Outdoors, a variety of choices and natural environments that include trees and grassy areas have been found to increase participation in play and reduce aggressive play (Moore & Wong, 1997).

In thinking about environments, teachers need to consider both units (the spaces arranged for children's play) and the surrounding space (the area around a unit needed for people to move about). Space invites children to pause and attend, to play alone or with others, to move randomly or purposefully, and to combine materials or separate them. Space generally shapes the flow of play and communication in the classroom or outdoors (Clayton & Forton, 2001; Curtis & Carter, 2003; Frost, Wortham, & Reifel, 2005; Hand & Nourot, 1999; Kostelnik, Onaga, Rohde, & Whiren, 2002; Kritchevsky, Prescott, & Walling, 1977; Trawick-Smith, 1992). Figures 4.2, 4.3, and 4.4 show indoor and outdoor plans that support play-centered curriculum.

Adapting Spaces for Special Needs. Considerations of the physical space are extremely important when integrating children with special needs into the classroom. According to McEvoy, Shores, Wehby, Johnson, and Fox (1990), educators cannot assume that children with special needs will be socially integrated merely by placing them in classrooms with nondisabled children. It is imperative for teachers to be aware of the particular alternative learning strategies of each child (Barnes & Lehr, 2005; Erwin, 1993). In some cases, adaptive equipment for children who cannot stand for long periods of time, such as a tabletop easel or exercise ball placed at a regular easel, may be needed to promote active engagement (Hanline & Fox, 1993; Sandall, 2003; Thomas, 2005). Based on this awareness, teachers can then plan environments that support the child's development of self-initiated solitary play as well as play with peers. For children in wheelchairs, or in the case of Jake, whose wide rigid leg braces made movement around the classroom a challenge, less may be more. Teachers and children may need to think about what furniture or materials could be left out of the room or stored in order to provide more access or movement.

Outdoor environments that provide linkages among play areas such as platforms, slides, or tire nets are most conducive to sustained play. Multiple levels of

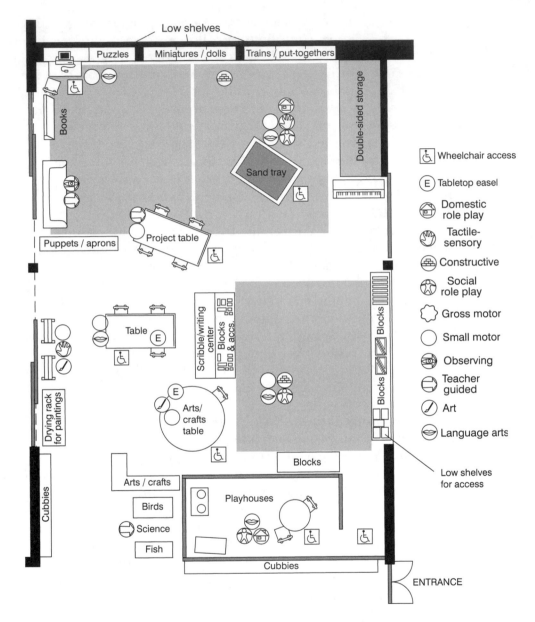

Figure 4.2
Preschool and Kindergarten Setting

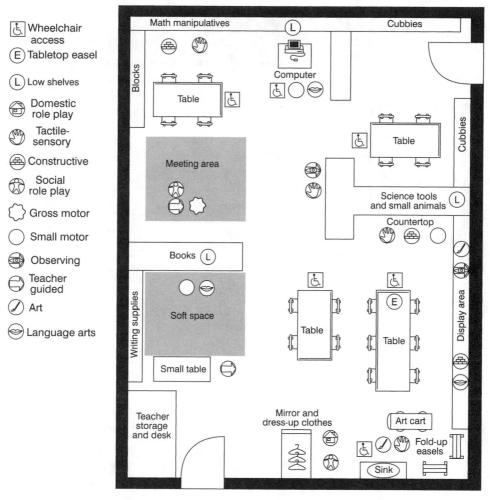

Figure 4.3
Primary Grade Setting

challenge and diverse materials help children to make choices, and pathways need to accommodate wheelchairs and other mobility aids. Ramps, decks, and stationary bridges are useful for parking wheelchairs so that children may access climbing areas (Burkhour, 2005; Frost et al., 2005; Rivkin, 1995).

Paths and Boundaries. Research on children's environments indicates that clear boundaries between interest areas, and clear paths of movement between them, help children to focus on their play and support their protection of interactive space (Perry, 2001; Ramsey & Reid, 1988). Boundaries must be low enough, however, for children to view available possibilities in the environment,

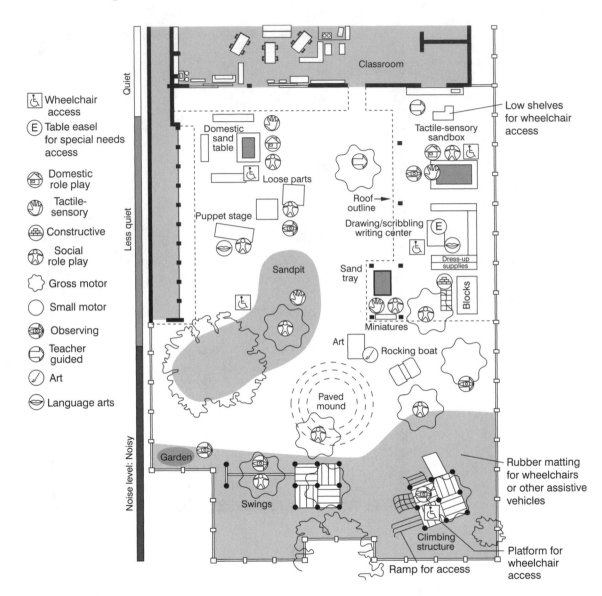

Figure 4.4
Outdoor Setting—Preschool and Primary Grade

and for adults to observe children. Low adult-child ratios also contribute to the maintenance of play themes, perhaps by having the mere presence of an adult nearby to act as a buffer against interlopers or distractions.

John and Sara are playing airport in the block corner. They have just painstakingly completed a control tower and runway when Andrew and

Playful interactions with adults are just as essential as those with peers.

Colin chase through the block area on their way outdoors to try out the magic capes they have made from yarn and paper. The block structures fall, and there are angry tears and accusations. If the pathway from the art area to the outdoors were re-routed around the block area, such events would be less likely. ⚥

Quiet and Noisy Areas.   Another set-up strategy involves separating quiet and noisy, or private and group, activities in different parts of the setting. Activities likely to foster social interaction and busy noise are blocks, dramatic play, reading and writing corners, number activities, and climbing structures. Sandboxes, water tables, art activities, and computers are variable—in some situations with some children, they may be conducive to social interaction; in others they may promote more parallel and solitary play than cooperative play (Curtis & Carter, 2003; Ramsey & Reid, 1988). In general, activities that encourage gross motor play, such as tricycles and outdoor climbing structures, foster more social interaction than those that encourage small motor skills, such as puzzles, table toys, miniatures, or Montessori materials, and in fact may support more sociodramatic play. Teachers may find that small motor toys promote more solitary and parallel play (Hendrickson, Strain, Trembley, & Shores, 1981; Sim, Harvey, & Shelly, 2001).

Activity units that offer children privacy for playing alone or with one or two friends are created by furniture that defines the space. These "hidey-holes" for children to find respite from the group seem particularly important for children who may spend 8–10 hours a day in settings with other children.

Including Children with Special Needs.   Areas that support social activities are critical in classrooms practicing inclusion. Many children with special needs are challenged by the social skills necessary for appropriate development, and it is important that teachers do not make assumptions about these social skills, and carefully observe and support children's efforts, even if they appear to be characteristic of much younger children (Creasey, Jarvis & Burke, 1998; Kostelnik, Onaga, Rohde, & Whiren, 2002; Odom, 2002; Okagaki, Diamond, Kontos & Hestenes, 1998; Sheridan, Foley, & Radlinski, 1995). Beckman and Kohl found that providing interactive toys leads to increased social interactions among disabled and nondisabled children (Beckman & Kohl, 1984, as cited in McEvoy et al., 1990). Similarly, Horner found that disabled children's adaptive behaviors were increased by adding large numbers of toys to a free-choice setting (Horner, 1980, as cited in McEvoy et al., 1990).

Children with health impairments may benefit from play spaces that foster less physically demanding play while allowing children to be part of the group, and to make choices about when to observe and when to join play (Burkhour, 2004; Frost et al., 2005). Quiet places are particularly important for some children who are easily distracted or frustrated (Bronson, 2000; Kostelnik et al., 2002; Kranor & Kuschner, 1996; Odom, 2002).

Hannah is a student with special needs, diagnosed as having ADHD and language delays. With the supportive teamwork of her parents, the school psychologist, and the special education teacher, Hannah has been fully integrated into Pam's first-grade class. Pam finds that Hannah frequently has difficulty sustaining interactions with the other children. As part of Hannah's Individualized Education Plan, Pam and the school psychologist are attempting to assess and support her progress in social activities with peers.

In addition to interacting with peers in Pam's class, Hannah's participation in after-school day care means that she is with large groups of children for 10 hours each day, from 7:30 a.m. to 5:30 p.m. Pam observes that Hannah spends quiet time each day by herself in the classroom's reading loft, looking at picture books or talking quietly to the stuffed animals. When Hannah becomes frustrated, Pam finds that she can help Hannah self-monitor her behavior by suggesting that she go to the loft or another quiet place. ✑

Soft Spaces. Children also benefit from soft areas in the classroom that provide privacy and refuge. The cozy nature of a corner with pillows and rocker, carpeting, and materials that invite sensory exploration such as sand or clay evoke comfort, collaboration, and friendship in the environment. When children become angry or frustrated, teachers can give them a chance to retreat to a quiet, soft space by themselves, a place with no hard objects to throw or hurt themselves. Adults may need to accompany children who are, at that moment, very aggressive or have behavioral disabilities (Rivkin, 1995).

> The book corner is in a central area of the room. It is carpeted in a mellow beige tweed, which was selected both for its sturdiness and softness. The rug is bounded on one side by a piano that faces a low rose-colored couch. Several thin rectangular pillows, covered in a washable, leaf-colored velour, are available for sitting on or leaning against the piano legs during circle time. At the wall end of the rug, two birch book display stands each put five rows of picture books within easy reach of rug sitters. (Beardsley, 1991, p. 52)

Some of the outdoor spaces may be soft as well. A tree for shade, a grassy carpet to just sit on and watch or read or play alone or with a friend provide havens from the frequently active pace of outdoor play. For example:

> In the outdoor garden area Josh and Taylor sit with their backs against a row of hay bales quietly looking at picture books. They're propped on the edge of the planter box that holds the newly blooming daffodils and crocuses planted by the children the previous fall. ✆

Forms of Life and Forms of Beauty. Freidrich Froebel (1782–1852) wrote about the importance of nature and forms of life and forms of beauty as elements in a kindergarten or "garden of childhood." Providing materials that invite real life experiences with plants and small animals, such as gardens, and terrariums for fish or lizards, and opportunities to care for these living things is essential. Activities such as gardening or woodworking, or washing dishes or furniture give children a sense of competence with using real tools. Forms of life also include culturally diverse objects and representations of experiences from children's lives such as photographs and music.

Patterns, color, light, and visual and auditory harmony are all aspects of forms of beauty in the environment. The use of texture, paintings, color on walls or floors, music and plants all convey a feeling of respect and care for the environment and for children themselves in aesthetically pleasing forms. Access to water and to natural environments outdoors are all important aspects of forms of beauty (Hand & Nourot, 1999; Wolfe, 2002).

Outdoor Play Spaces.   Although much of what we have discussed as important in play environments applies across indoor and outdoor spaces, outdoor play environments offer unique opportunities for learning and development. Outdoor play offers choices to children in the use of natural materials such as sand, water, and plant life that are constrained indoors. Outdoor play offers opportunities for children to develop the "naturalistic intelligence" that Gardner (1999) describes, and to reap the benefits of fresh air, live plants, and perhaps the care of small animals to which many children have little access. Opportunities for fine and gross motor play abound. Natural materials such as pebbles, leaves, sticks, flowers, and feathers find their way into children's dramatic play. Natural materials such as leaves, stalks, seeds, and flowers become treasures to sort, to touch, and to use in creating art pieces (Topal, 2005; Torquati & Barber, 2005). In Berkeley, California, an asphalt playground was replaced with soft spaces, a grassy field, and small garden areas and trees. The outcomes were reduced rates of accidents and aggressive behavior (Moore & Wong, 1997). Barbour (1999) looked at the effects of outdoor playgrounds on peer relationships among physically disabled children and typically developing peers. She found that outdoor playgrounds that offered more options than the typical open "exercise" play space fostered more integration of children with physical limitations in play with typically developing peers. Fisman (2001) studied third graders' responses to actual and ideal playgrounds, and discovered that children expressed a desire for many more choices, flexible use areas, and soft private spaces for their outdoor play.

In another urban school setting, a working farm is at the school site. Nourot takes her class there in the fall, winter, and spring to observe the changes in the seasons. Gardens, ducks, chickens, rabbits, goats, two horses, and a pig offer opportunities for children to observe and care for plants and animals, and teachers at the school use the farm as part of their planned curriculum.

Unfortunately, many short sighted educators have limited the access to outdoor play for children, especially in elementary school settings (Jarrett, 2003; National Association of Early Childhood Specialists in State Departments of Education, 2002). There is a growing movement among educators to ensure that children in school settings have access to healthy and appropriate outdoor play environments, and the time during the school day to play there. See Resources at the end of this chapter for position statements and research related to the importance of recess and outdoor play.

When Space Is Limited.   In classrooms where space is at a premium, often in public school primary-grade settings, teachers may be creative in the use of portable accessories or "Murphy space." For example, in one first-grade classroom, where desks grouped as tables occupy a large part of the classroom, the teacher constructed easels that fold into the wall, much like a Murphy bed, that can be pulled out and set up during free play time. He complements this with a rolling cart that includes art and carpentry materials that may be transported outdoors or to a table area.

Other teachers have decided that table space for all children to sit down at one time is not necessary in a room where the play goes on in specific areas of the classroom. For one teacher, freeing the room of large tables has enabled him to rotate the use of center areas according to the play experiences he has planned, and has left open space in the room for block play and a large dramatic play area.

Adjacent Areas.   When setting up, teachers might also think about the effects of placing activity areas adjacent to one another. For example, in one teacher's classroom, the dramatic play and block areas were moved next to one another. Groups of children who normally played in only one of those areas began joint fantasy play using props from the housekeeping corner to equip a "space station" under construction in the block area. Another teacher found that the placement of block and housekeeping areas adjacent to one another generated crowded conditions. Each environment is unique and each teacher needs to experiment and evaluate changes.

Adjacent areas also invite opportunities for the cross-fertilization of the ideas of children engaged in play even when the play areas remain distinct. For example, in one first-grade classroom, ongoing play at the carpentry table adjacent to the block area prompted the construction of airplanes and helicopters to be housed at the block area airport. In a second-grade classroom, a post office created to encourage letter writing soon expanded to a bank and an office on either side where children integrated literacy and mathematics concepts.

To encourage the cross-fertilization of ideas in activity areas, Griffin (1998) recommends that teachers keep a box of game parts, puzzle pieces, rocks, and miscellaneous small objects that children may use in their dramatic play. In this way, the puzzle pieces and objects associated with more structured activities are more likely to remain in their respective areas, while allowing children to appropriate flexible materials for their own uses. Cultural and family factors may affect children's understanding of the school culture's conventions for returning objects to their original storage places. For example, a child who lives in a trailer or a crowded home may have learned to store toys out of view rather than displayed on a shelf. Conversely, children who come from families where the adults do the clean-up may have no rationale for the expectation that they put classroom materials away.

Accessories for Play.   The provision of accessories in the environment relates to our discussion of symbolic distancing in chapter 3. For sociodramatic play, younger or less sophisticated players need more realistic props to support or scaffold their play themes and roles. Their symbolic distancing skills are not well enough developed to appropriate a block or an imaginary gesture when a real-looking prop such as a toy telephone is not available. Generally, younger children (ages 2–3) prefer to have several sets of realistic props to use in their dramatic play. Multiple sets of brooms and phones, toy food and dishes, fire trucks and toy animals are necessary elements for the scaffold supporting their dramatic play. If not available, play fantasies may give way to object disputes and the symbolic distancing of roles and situations has little chance to get underway.

On the other hand, sophisticated dramatic players like to have lots of un-structured props—that is, props with limited specific use of their own—available for their dramatic play. Cardboard packing, rocks, sticks, and blocks are examples of unstructured props. Such non-realistic props offer much leeway to the child to make successive transformations—for instance by using pebbles as money, food, buried treasure, and circus tickets—all in the course of a single play episode.

School-aged children (ages 7–10) enjoy having hats and scarves available for the more formal plays they enact, and will generally use both unstructured props and imaginary ones in their play. They also use miniatures, models, and games with rules as accessories to their fantasy play. Many children in this age group also enjoy collections, and are supported by soft spaces and trays for or-ganizing their collections.

> Randall and Amber have been making a volcano scene in a cardboard box for several days. After constructing the volcano from playdough, they use red and orange tissue paper to represent flames from the volcano and toothpicks and paper to make trees and homes on the sides of the volcano. They spend time coloring branches of their trees to represent ash and burned wood and discuss the escape and rescue operations of the people and animals who lived in the houses. ✍

Timing in the introduction of props is important. Replicas of real objects and props that relate to familiar scripts are appropriate at the beginning of the year, as children get to know one another. Accessory boxes that augment the familiar scripts of housekeeping or cars and trucks in the preschool and kindergarten may be introduced later in the year. Many teachers have a large selection of accessory boxes built around themes such as restaurant, office, beach trip, and camping that they introduce to correlate with curriculum themes or have available upon request by children. Accessory or prop boxes may be made from cardboard boxes, ice cream containers, or plastic bins (Desjean-Perrotta & Barbour, 2001; Myhre, 1993). Figure 4.5 provides sugges-tions for themes and contents for prop boxes. Some teachers offer a rotating variety of theme boxes in a designated area of the room, others periodically re-place or augment equipment in the housekeeping area or outdoor climbing

Office
stapler
tape
old adding machine or fax
    machine
copier made from cardboard
box
telephones
computer keyboard
computer monitor made from box

Paint Store
painter's hat
bucket
brushes, scrapers
paper color chips in
    graded colors
cash register and "money"
order pads and pencils
home improvement catalogs
telephone

Flower and/or Fruit Stand
plastic flowers, fruits,
    vegetables
boxes or crates, tables
    for display
cash register and "money"
chalkboard for prices

Bakery
playdough, paper confetti
cookie sheets, tubes for
    decorating
oven
telephone
labels or chalkboard for prices
cash register and "money"
blocks for display cases
cookbooks

Gas Station
trikes, wagons
large boxes for pumps
    plastic hoses

cash register and "money" or
    "credit cards"
window-washing supplies
    (spray bottles, squeegies)
large box for car wash

Restaurant
aprons
chef's hat
menus
tablecloths
silverware
dishes
play food
chalkboard and chalk for
    "specials"
order pads and pencils
cash register and "money"
telephone

Bank
tellers' windows
cash boxes
bank books
office supplies
play money

Shoe Store
shoes and boxes
foot measure, tape, ruler
socks
telephone
receipt book
price labels
cash register and "money"

Camping Out
sleeping bags
tent
camp cookware
flashlight
backpacks

Travel and Passport Office
computer keyboard, box for
    monitor

toy camera
drawing and writing supplies
blank books
travel brochures

Hospital or Doctor's Office
bandages
toy medical tools (e.g., blood
    pressure cuff, syringe)
cots or mats
waiting room with magazines
white coats
medical hats
rubber gloves
files, clipboards, and paper for
    patient information
telephone
computer keyboard, box for
    monitor

Pet Shop
toy animals
boxes for cages,aquariums
cash register, receipts, "money"
materials to make collars, pet
    toys, and animal food

Laundromat
washers and dryers made from
    cardboard cartons
plastic or straw baskets
clothing to "wash," sort, and
    fold
toy iron and ironing board
clothes rack and hangers
cash register or change
    machine
bulletin board and notices
magazines

Figure 4.5
Some Suggested Accessory Box Themes and Contents

structure. In the primary grades, these accessory boxes are valuable as prompts for enacted plays and story writing.

Play Materials for Children with Special Needs. Older children with special needs characterized by autism, some speech disabilities, or developmental language delays may benefit from having multiple realistic or replica play accessories to support their fantasy play, much as toddlers do. Such costumes and props for pretend play enable children who are challenged to communicate their ideas with language to more fully participate in pretend play role and situations. (Marvin & Hunt-Berg, 1996; Wolfberg, 1999).

Adaptive toys with technological features such as a battery-operated bubble blower or electric dice roller enable some children with physical disabilties to more easily participate in play (Locke & Levin, 1998; Stone & Stagstetter, 1998).

Familiarity Balanced with Novelty. Children need a balance of the familiar and the novel. In addition to the traditional housekeeping props, the teacher must consider the cultural backgrounds of his students. Does the family eat with chopsticks and cook in a wok? Does the family use a barbeque? Might cherry-picking baskets, beads and yarn, western hats or coal miners' hats be familiar objects in some children's homes? If we want all children to find a familiar script in the classroom, we must scaffold their symbolic behavior on what is comfortable and home-like to them (Derman-Sparks & Ramsey, 2005; Hughes, 2003; Reynolds, 2002).

Areas where materials for art and music are available open opportunities for new accessories or modifications of old ones (Bronson, 1995). In one classroom, film cans filled with rice, beans, or pebbles, and then taped closed were placed next to the xylophone and rhythm instruments, with materials for creating individual shakers set out nearby. In another setting, a discussion of a Pisarro painting prompted the teacher to mix muted pastel colors and thicken the paints so that children might try the "painting in pokes" that they had noticed in the print borrowed from the public library (Beardsley, 1991).

Play Materials Offer Alternatives. Teachers may set up environments that encourage a particular kind of play by combining or rearranging materials. For example, setting out toothpicks with clay may encourage more social interaction than clay alone, as children link structures they build or construct birthday cakes or bridges in play that involves others.

Quiet and private materials offer children opportunities for exploration before they begin to play. In initial exploration, the focus is on "What can this object (or material) do?" After time to explore the material at hand, children begin to truly play, when the implicit question becomes, "What can I do with this object or material?" (Hutt, 1971; Wohlwill, 1984).

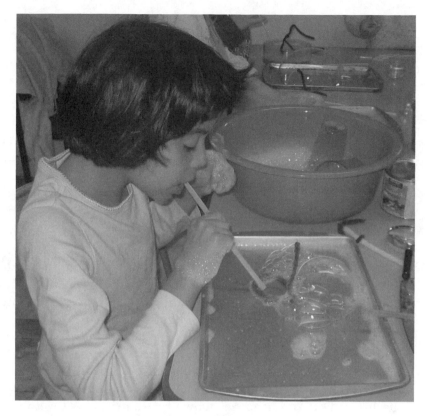

Materials offer children opportunities for playful exploration.

Sandy approaches the used adding machine that another child has just left. She pushes keys and watches the numbers print for about 10 minutes. The next day she returns and continues her exploration, systematically trying each key to note the number it produces on the tape. On the third day she invites Mark to play. "Come to my store. You can buy cookies," and she rings up a pretend purchase. ✆

Materials that offer opportunities for exploratory and self-correcting activity include pegboards, form boards, miniatures, and picture lotto. These activities give children a relaxed time away from the mental effort of negotiating with their peers and help them restore a sense of order and control to their lives. Materials that support solitary play may also provide important relief from the pressures of social interaction for children learning English as a second language or those with language disabilities (Clawson, 2002). This function seems to be age-related. McLloyd (1983) found that 3-year-olds used these materials in more solitary ways, whereas 5-year-olds engaged in more cooperative play regardless of the structure of the materials. This relates to the finding that solitary play represents an option for older children, who may be better able to verbalize their needs for privacy.

Play Safety

One of the most compelling issues related to play environments for young children is the question of the safety of toys and play environments. Each year, hundreds of children are injured while playing with commercial toys. Many of these injuries occur in school settings. Therefore teachers need to be knowledgeable and observant.

Government regulation of toy safety standards increased with the Hazardous Substance Act of 1973 and the Consumer Product Safety Act of 1978. These standards include the important requirement that toy manufacturers clearly label products with age appropriateness. For example, toys containing tiny pieces or sharp edges must be clearly labeled to warn adults that they are not designed for children under the age of 3. Toys that are electrical in nature, and thus present a potential hazard of burning children, must be labeled as hazardous for children 8 and younger.

Consumer publications inform teachers and parents about toy safety issues. The U.S. Consumer Product Safety Commission offers resources such as *For Kids' Sake: Think Toy Safety* (2005) and *Toy Safety Shopping Tips* (2005), available online at no cost, that are designed to help prevent toy and playground injuries. The American Academy of Pediatrics lists toy safety tips for the holidays. The Toy Industry Association offers a Toy Safety Hotline, and Safechild.net offers tips for toy safety as well as updated information on toy recalls. See resources at the end of this chapter for relevant Web sites.

The Toy Manufacturers of America, in conjunction with the U.S. Consumer Product Safety Commission (1994), developed and published guidelines for guarding against potential accidents involving toys. These guidelines include:

1. Select toys that are appropriate for children's interests and stages of development. This includes avoiding toys with long strings or small parts for infants and toddlers. "Choke tubes" are available to measure the size of pieces in toys that are suspected of being dangerous.

2. Read labels on packaging carefully and dispose of packing material (such as plastic wrappers) that might be dangerous to children. Choose toys with nontoxic paints and flame-retardant fabrics.

3. Keep toys clean and in good repair. Store toys designed for older children out of sight and reach from those at earlier developmental stages.

4. Supervise the play of children, particularly very young children, to see that they do not use toys in ways that are dangerous to their health or safety.

Not all products are screened under consumer safety guidelines. Parents, teachers, and other professionals who work with children and families still must be vigilant. Many products available by mail from overseas do not meet these standards. Toys that children acquire from someone's attic could be in poor repair or have pieces missing that make them potentially hazardous.

Playground Safety.   Another issue is playground safety. Although space limitations do not allow us to treat this topic in depth, we have read several resources useful for planning safe, outdoor play areas that have high play-ability. The National Association for the Education of Young Children (NAEYC) requires 75 square feet of play space outdoors per child as part of their accreditation criteria, and recommends the following six elements of playground safety:

1. Careful supervision of children
2. Arrangement of space that protects against access to streets, standing water, and other hazards
3. Sturdy and safe equipment designed for the physical and developmental level of children
4. Resilient surfaces for landings
5. Regularly scheduled maintenance and clean-up
6. A variety of choices for play (National Association for the Education of Young Children, 1996)

One of the most user-friendly resources is the manual on playground safety written by Jambor and Palmer (1991). These authors offer general guidelines and specific criteria for playground safety in a checklist. They discuss three general principles for school playground safety. First, enclosures that shelter play environments should have no visual barriers so children are supervised adequately and protected from hazards outside the play area. Second, adequate space is needed to accommodate children safely using equipment on their own. Jambor and Palmer include guidelines for space surrounding slides, swings, and climbing structures. Third, play surfaces must minimize the impact of children's falls. In general, Jambor and Palmer recommend that softer surfaces (such as grass or packed dirt in comparison with cement or asphalt) are less likely to contribute to injury when children fall. (See Frost et al. [2005] for a detailed review of playground safety issues.)

Planning the Daily Schedule

Another element of the infrastructure of curriculum is the daily schedule in the setting. Powerful messages are sent to children about the value of their own choices and the activities they construct for themselves by the way that teachers structure the days. This scheduling includes not only the content of the classroom, but also how much time is allotted for playful purposes (Hand & Nourot, 1999; Trawick-Smith, 1998; Wassermann, 2000).

In the most free-flowing environments, the room is arranged with activities available for children to choose. Furniture and materials are flexible, and the teacher floats, interacting with small groups of children more often than the entire class. Traditional nursery schools and open classrooms based on the British Infant School model are examples of this design. Teachers who use this design in their classrooms have noted that lengthening the total time for free choice activities and play increases the focus and engagement of children in their chosen activities and also encourages children to try new experiences after they have touched base with their old favorites (Paley, 1984).

In other environments, more teacher direction and less child choice is evident. Small- and large-group direct instruction alternates with free-choice time. Teachers spend more time with designated groups and less time attending to the flow in the total classroom. The pitfall of this model is that what teachers perceive as play (e.g., building an airport with blocks) may be seen by the children as labor because their choice of activities really rests with the teacher. Teachers may also miss out on important learning events when they attend to only one group.

The most structured environment leaves little time for free play. Play is regarded as recreational rather than as a vehicle for learning. Small- and large-group direct instruction characterize this design, and the teacher's attention to children's play rests primarily on concerns about safety rather than on aspects of social or intellectual development. Skills-based academic programs exemplify this model.

Another source of reflection for teachers is the "match" between teachers' beliefs about play and their practice in their classrooms. For example, one teacher who voices a belief that play is a valuable aspect of developmentally based practice only allows play that serves as time to discharge children's energy pent up after long periods of passive instruction. Another may espouse a belief in play but play in his classroom is really "work disguised as play." There are activities in which children have little or no choice about the materials, challenges or direction of their experiences, and there is little room for self-generated challenges or negotiation. Yet another teacher who values play offers a selection of genuine choices and uses a variety of questioning strategies and elaborated materials that fully support children's initiation and construction of knowledge.

A play-centered curriculum that serves children's intellectual development and construction of new and meaningful knowledge achieves a delicate and important balance between teacher-initiated and guided play and child-initiated and directed play. Teachers who are sensitive to the distinction between labor required by others and playful work selected by children in their settings will note the importance of choices for children, as well as ample time for children to elaborate and complete activities they have begun. In any activity, teachers need to ask themselves: How much of it is truly chosen by the child? Does the child have choices about where, when, how, and with whom she or he plays? How engaged are children in their play?

EXTENSIONS FOR PLAY

Setting the stage for play and curriculum planning go hand in hand. It represents the backstage versus the on-stage aspect of teaching when we focus on play as the center of the curriculum.

Play-Generated Curriculum

One facet of curriculum planning is play-generated curriculum, or curriculum that emerges directly from the interests of the children. In this aspect of setting the stage for play, teachers draw upon their observations of children's interests and themes in their play to provide opportunities to extend and elaborate their learning. For example:

> In one first-grade classroom, several of the children had participated over the weekend in a community art fair called "Art in the Park." They had all contributed their efforts to a huge wall mural on which both adults and children had painted images and experimented with color. On Monday, three of the children asked if they could have some large paper to show the other children "how you make a really big picture." The teacher set up large sheets of butcher paper and multiple containers of paint housed in small tote boxes during the week. Children experimented with recipes for making paint and mixing colors. Later in the week the teacher brought in books from the library depicting murals in other communities around the world. The following week, the teacher introduced new media such as collage and group wood sculptures for the children to try. ✆

Curriculum-Generated Play

This facet of curriculum planning involves a more direct role for the teacher. In planning curriculum-generated play, a teacher's observation of children's play leads her to include materials or techniques that she suspects will create a match with children's spontaneous interests (Bennett, Wood, & Rogers, 1997; Hand & Nourot, 1999; Stegelin, 2005). In this way, the teacher's knowledge of the content area such as science, mathematics, art, or literacy intersects with her sense of children's previous experiences and their current interests.

Judy, the teacher of a second-grade science program, noticed children's interests in the concept of water pressure as they experimented with dish soap bottles outdoors. She related these interests to requirements for physical science activities and the introduction of scientific terms in the state department of education's science framework and state curriculum standards. Judy placed holes in containers at different levels and set up plastic piping material with a water source, challenging the children to find out which arrangements would make the water squirt farther. She introduced terms like "pressure" in the context of their observations, and introduced the term "hypothesis" in conjunction with the "guesses" that the children made about their experiments. ✐

In a kindergarten classroom, Jennifer spent her choice time over several days creating a book she called "The Very Hungry Clowns" which consisted of clowns with butterflies in their tummies, a new one drawn for each day. Jennifer's merging of a phrase she had heard at home with the format and structure of Eric Carle's book *The Very Hungry Caterpillar* read earlier in the week were evident in her play creation. ✐

The technique of curriculum-generated play has elements in common with the thematic curriculum design seen in many programs for preschool and primary children. We believe curriculum-generated play enhances the best of thematic curriculum. Some thematic curriculum is based on the teacher's interests, children's families, past experiences, and resources. Truly play-centered curriculum integrates teachers' interests and concerns with those observed in children as they play.

This continuity among families, community, and school curriculum is reflected strongly in the Reggio Emilia approach to early schooling (Edwards, Gandini, & Forman, 1993; Forman, 2005; Hendrick, 1997; New, 2005). Within this approach, the contributions of families and community and the relationships and interaction among children as they construct knowledge in small groups are all highly valued aspects of curriculum planning. Time for themes, concepts, hypotheses, and multiple representations to emerge and evolve to completion is valued. The spiral curriculum approach that revisits and revises representations of experience is shared by both children and teachers.

The way in which learning is documented is particularly important in the Reggio Emilia approach. Physical space supports many displays of children's representations of their experiences and thought processes. Programs for young children include an "atelier" (studio) and "atelierista" (artist in residence) whose training in the visual arts supports both teachers and children in documenting their thinking (Edwards, Gandini, & Forman, 1993; Gandini, Hill, Cadwell, & Schwall, 2005; Houck, 1997; New, 2005; Trepanier-Street, Bock Hong, & Donegan, 2001; Wurm, 2005).

As noted in the theoretical foundations for play as the center of the curriculum presented in chapters 2 and 13, children's capacities to represent and to engage in reflective abstraction support the ongoing construction of knowledge. In the process of reflective abstraction, children symbolize their thoughts and feelings through a variety of media such as language, gesture, drawing, music, drama, and sculpture. The implicit relationships and understanding that children perceive as part of their developing view of the world around them become publicly as well as privately represented as they share their expressions of knowledge.

Representation that serves the process of reflective abstraction includes both multiple representation, in which an experience is symbolically represented with several media, and re-representation in which the representations of experience and thinking are themselves represented by subsequent symbolic constructions in new media.

In Jackie's multi-age class of 5-, 6-, and 7-year-olds, ongoing curriculum centers on the concept of living things. A day trip to the beach was represented by small groups of children playing and working collaboratively. One group painted a mural; another made a set of flannel board pieces to tell a story; another group arranged snapshots of the trip into a book with both dictated and child-written narrative; a fourth group enacted the trip outdoors in the sandbox, creating an imaginary bus and making props for the picnic and sea creature discoveries they remembered.

Jackie and her co-teacher Peggy solicited children's drawings of their ideas about the beach before the trip, after the trip and then again as the unit was drawing to a close. They showed these "before" and "after" drawings to the children so that they could reflect on their own learning. The drawings were also placed in children's portfolios as assessment data.

"I didn't even know about the rocks and those teeny little animals before," exclaimed Jared as he compared his own before and after drawings. Jackie and Peggie also tape recorded children's comments about their representations of the beach. The tape recordings served as transformative representations as the children reflected on both the content and processes symbolized in their developing knowledge about the beach. ∅

Bruner (1963) coined the term *spiral curriculum* to represent the idea that, at many stages of their development, children may grasp basic concepts, each time returning to the same ideas at a more sophisticated level of understanding. So, rather than focusing on the themes of curriculum, such as whales or dinosaurs, the teacher focuses on the concepts that might be revisited as children encounter those themes several times during their school experience. For example, the study of both whales and dinosaurs involves concepts related to comparisons—of size, of environments, of ways of living that are different from humans. Concepts of time and historical contexts are also embedded. These are some of the essential concepts that emerge gradually as children study creatures great and small, and compare them to their own perspectives and experiences. Such lessons may be revisited many times from varying perspectives and with deeper understanding as development spirals upward.

Play-Centered Curriculum Addresses Experiences from a Variety of Cultures.   One drawback of thematic curriculum that is not directly based in children's experiences is the unsatisfactory treatment of multicultural issues. Topics such as ethnicity and race, culture, and language may be overlooked or misrepresented. For example, teachers with good intentions may address cultural diversity in a manner that has come to be known as the "tourist curriculum" (Derman-Sparks & A.B.C. Task Force, 1989; Derman-Sparks & Ramsey, 2005). In this approach, foods, festivals, and music from different cultures are introduced once a year, often in conjunction with a holiday. In addition, some teachers have fallen into the routine of presenting out-of-context knowledge of culture, such as depicting stereotypes of American Indians at Thanksgiving or Chinese culture at Chinese New Year, without addressing the real issues of cultural diversity in our daily lives. Instead, the "anti-bias" approach advocated by Derman-Sparks and A.B.C. Task Force includes diversity as a regular aspect of the curriculum where teachers foster children's positive attitudes toward the acceptance and celebration of differences among cultures. It is important that the environment reflects children's cultures and languages, and that the physical space and materials for play become vehicles for learning about our country's rich diversity.

Consistent with this view, in a play-centered curriculum, aspects of the physical environment and accessories for play reflect diversity of culture, through such items as the tortilla press, yogurt maker, seaweed toaster, rice bowls and chopsticks, as well as day-time planners and briefcases that are available in Janice's kindergarten room.

In a play-centered curriculum, art, music, literature, science, and mathematics experiences reflect cultural diversity in a manner that makes it part of everyday life in the classroom, not just an infrequent glimpse of fragmented information or a song or two. For example:

In Consuelo's first-grade classroom, she observed the Southeast Asian children pretending to make rice and shrimp dishes in their sand and water play. She contacted one of the parents of the children and included frequent cooking projects. The projects introduced some of these foods and the techniques used to cook them to everyone in the class and offered the Southeast Asian children foods that seemed familiar and delicious to them as part of the regular snack menu. ∅

In a second-grade classroom, the teacher incorporated literature describing the creation myths of several cultures into his curriculum on astronomy. He invited families of children to tell bedtime stories and family stories to the class and was pleasantly surprised when over half of the families participated. Family members, including parents and grandparents, aunts and uncles even took time off from work to come to school and share stories from their childhoods or family traditions and rituals. ∅

The cultural values of some families may provide an additional challenge in advocating for play-centered curriculum. For example, Joshi (2005) describes a common response of Asian Indian families to play at school, reflecting the belief that education should be focused on learning correct behaviors and habits rather than playfulness and creativity. He recommends that teachers take the time to explain and describe how concepts, skills, and academic standards are embedded in play-centered curriculum at school, and to respect the families' beliefs by offering suggestions for activities at home to enhance these academic goals. Documenting children's play and projects through photographs, visual arts, and writing can make the links between play and academic learning more evident to families.

Integrating Academic Standards.   Wassermann (2000) designed an interesting approach to curriculum-generated play specifically targeted at primary-grade teachers. Her technique, which she calls play, debrief, replay, involves careful planning of the environment and materials as well as keen observation of children's activities. Her approach also calls for skilled debriefing questions that elicit children's reflections and support construction of knowledge in the particular curriculum areas embedded in children's play. This planning is directly related to academic standards and benchmarks. For example:

Kitty introduced a unit integrating history and science to her third-grade class in a rural area school. Studying present day tools and comparing them to tools used in the past, using artifacts, photos, maps, and written sources are all components of the third-grade history and social studies curriculum for her state. The guided play focused on machines for agriculture, and built on the concepts from a unit on small machines completed earlier in the year. During that unit, the class visited the county historical agricultural museum, where a docent actively engaged the children. Kitty brought the class pictures from the museum as well as real objects gathered from her own grandparents and their friends and the families of the children in the class. These objects included apple corers, flour sifters, models and pictures of tractors, huskers, and combines. One of the families brought in several looms and the parents discussed the growing and transformation of fibrous plants.

In the play phase of the activity, children were prompted to play with their ideas about the characteristics of the machines; spontaneous sorting and hypothesizing about their uses occurred, as well as interesting speculation about the division of labor between men and women, and the children's chores.

In the debriefing phase, Kitty asked each group of children to describe what they did and to draw some representation of their discussion. Each group reported on the questions she set for them: What do these machines do? How do they work? Who used them? How are they alike and different?

Hypotheses about all these topics emerged during the class discussion. Kitty invited each group to return for the replay phase in which they added to their drawings and wrote about their objects based on the new information they had learned. They created their own museum of tools and became "docents" for other children and adults in the school who came to view their project. ✍

Recasting the Curriculum Through Play. Another curriculum strategy represents subtle orchestration on the part of the teacher and calls for finely tuned observation skills. In this strategy, the teacher provides opportunities and asks questions that encourage children to use newly constructed knowledge derived from the curriculum in their play. We return to the notion presented in chapter 2, that play is a predominance of assimilation, and represents opportunities for children to consolidate and generalize their emerging mental concepts. We see this aspect of play as extremely important. The true test of whether experiences orchestrated by the teacher help children learn a specific concept or skill, such as counting money or using a calculator, is to see it "replayed" spontaneously by children in their play.

In one first-grade classroom, the teacher complemented a mathematics unit on measurement with the creation of a shoe store in the dramatic play area. She was delighted to hear children use terms like "same size" and "half an inch shorter," as they used rulers, yardsticks, and shoe measurers in their play. As part of the language and literacy curriculum, she facilitated the making of a shoe sale sign and sales receipt books, while children wrote about shoes they love to wear. The unit was expanded to include other stores that children knew about in their local shopping mall, and integrated literacy, mathematics, art, and social studies concepts in the play. Table 4.1 illustrates the curriculum standards addressed by the shoe store project and the environmental supports provided for the children's play.

Table 4.1

Examples of Standards Addressed by the Shoe Store Project

Curriculum Standards	Play Example	Environmental Support
Phonemic and Phonological Awareness		
Makes letter-sound correspondences	Children make signs for shoe sale and labels for shelves	Supply blank signs and pens in block area
Demonstrates growing awareness of beginning, ending, medial sounds of words	Sandra writes receipts for shoe sales	Provide signs with words for sneakers, sandals, running shoes, dress-up shoes
Numeracy		
Uses comparative words, such as many–few, big–little; more–less; fast-slow appropriately	Discusses small, big, long, short in trying on shoes	Different size shoes are available in play props
Understands numbers and simple operations and uses math manipulatives, games, toys, coins in daily activities (adding, subtracting)	Counts out 6 coins to pay for shoes at pretend store	Pretend money and cash register
Measurement		
Uses measuring implements	Measures using foot measure	Yardstick and shoe measure from local shoe store
Estimates	"I need a smaller sandal"	
Ordering and Seriating		
Orders objects from smallest to largest	Lines up shoes on shelf in order	Shoe rack and shelves with space for ordering pairs of shoes
Sorting and Classifying		
Describes how items are the same or different	"Those shoes have Velcro and these have buckles"	Shoes of similar kind (e.g., running shoes) but with different features

WHEN TEACHERS TALK

Helping Parents and Educators Value Play

Educators who implement play-centered curricula can consider strategies that go beyond their own classrooms to foster a school and community culture that values play. Since many teachers often feel they must defend the importance of play, a significant part of implementing a play-centered curriculum is for teachers to have a network of colleagues, including parents, who support play. This network can form the basis of a purposeful community with participants who share experiences, books and articles, and arrange programs—creating a community of players.

Teachers from several schools shared attempts to involve parents and other educators in discussions about the value of play. Several tried the idea of a slide show that Anna described in the first chapter. This was a lively way to begin discussions about their programs. Seeing slides of the children engaged in different types of play made it easier for everyone to understand, particularly parents who spoke little English. It was also successful at producing a good turnout for "open house," reaching and engaging some parents who rarely came to school.

One teacher said that she explained how the children's activities shown in the slides related to children's understanding in academic areas. A student teacher who had worked on a slide show said that she made sure that each child was included. When parents spoke with her, they spoke about what their own child did in the slide. That gave her the opportunity to discuss how that specific example of play supported development in several ways.

Shelley, a teacher-director of a parent cooperative nursery school, wrote short letters to parents. This is part of one:

> This week, with your assistance, the children and I are turning the dramatic play area into a clothing store. We have chosen a clothing store because all the children are familiar with it and will feel comfortable playing out familiar roles like salesperson and customer. We think that this theme will promote cooperation and creative dramatic play.
>
> "The clothing store" play promotes practice with basic vocabulary words like shirts and dresses as well as extended vocabulary such as "accessories," "pleated," "paisley," and so forth. This theme promotes other literate activities as children write and read signs ("boys' clothes"), receipts, and newspaper ads. ✍

Scott, a third-grade teacher, commented on his discussions with other teachers, including special education teachers, the school counselors and psychologists who worked with several children mainstreamed into his class, and administrators. He was interested to learn more about their perspectives and experiences. For example, several of them had read articles that gave them the impression that particular children with special needs were not capable of the self-direction and mastery he observed in children's play. Scott explained: "When I feel that I'm leading people to a better understanding, I feel different than when I feel that I'm defending my position. When I use theoretical perspectives along with examples from my own classroom to show how play is related to developmentally appropriate practice, people begin to understand."

SUMMARY AND CONCLUSION

Teachers use knowledge of developmental theories and research when setting the stage for a play-centered curriculum. Rather than following a fixed curriculum, the teacher guides orchestration by providing opportunities for development. Guiding principles include (a) taking the child's view, (b) being a keen observer of children's behavior, (c) seeing meaning as it is constructed, (d) serving as stage manager to organize the environment, and (e) planning new curriculum.

The continuum of strategies discussed in this chapter are subtle and complex. Therefore, it is helpful if teachers work with others and think of themselves as working within their own zones of proximal development. For many of us working in classrooms, new challenges are related to addressing the needs of all children, including those with identified special education programs, and children whose cultural and socioeconomic backgrounds are varied. Children who are learning English in addition to their home languages offer further stretches to the imaginations and resourcefulness of teachers. All teachers continue to develop and refine their abilities to set the stage, prepare the physical space, plan the daily schedule, and develop curriculum-related extensions for play. In these extensions, teachers think about children's play to inspire and generate more formalized curriculum, as state and national curriculum standards and benchmarks affect even the youngest children in our schools. The chapters on the arts, science, mathematics, and language and literacy that follow will provide further consideration of these extensions.

SUGGESTED RESOURCES

Basche, K. (Writer/Producer) (1995). *Respecting how children learn through play* [Videotape]. (Available from Child Development Media, Inc., 5632 Van Nuys Blvd., Suite 286, Van Nuys, CA 91401.)

This videotape gives lively examples of children in kindergarten as they learn through their play and the play-centered curriculum orchestrated by their teachers. It features discussion among teachers about planning for play, as well as narrative discussing the skills and concepts evident in the sequences of children's play.

Cadwell, L. B. (1997). *Bringing Reggio home: An innovative approach to early childhood education.* New York: Teachers College Press.

A powerful collection of stories by a teacher of young children about implementing ideas drawn from the Reggio Emilia program in Italy in her own classroom in the United States.

Curtis, D., & Carter, M. (2003). *Designs for living and learning: Transforming early childhood environments.* St. Paul, MN: Redleaf Press.

This book is a rich resource for teachers. The authors provide the rationale for a rich collection of ideas to create more complex learning and development in play spaces. The photographs help readers to visualize possibilities, and to think through the potentials of their own play environments.

Infinite potential through assistive technology.

Much information and many links to other sources on accommodations for special needs. Online at www.infinitec.org/play/outdoor/playgrounds.

Jambor, T., & Palmer, S. D. (1991). *Playground safety manual.* Birmingham, AL: American Academy of Pediatrics.

A concise and practical guide to promoting safety on children's playgrounds. The authors offer checklists and resources for planning for outdoor play spaces that reduce the risk of injury to children. Other resources for playground safety include:

National Association of Early Childhood Specialists in State Departments of Education (2002). *Recess and the importance of play: A position statement on young children and recess.* Washington, D.C.: Author. Available online at http://naecs.crc.uiuc.edu/position/recessplay.html.

This position statement online also includes statements for the National Association for the Education of Young Children and the Council on Physical Education for Children on the importance of outdoor play.

Natural Learning Initiative, College of Design, School of Architecture, North Carolina State University. Retrieved October 9, 2005, from http://naturalearning.org.

Perry, J. (2001). *Outdoor play:* Teaching Strategies with young children. New York: Teachers College Press.

This book provides an engaging account of Perry's research in her own classroom and the dynamics of the peer culture as play develops. It also presents in practical detail the challenges of orchestrating an outdoor play space.

Ramsey, P. (2004). *Teaching and learning in a diverse world: Multicultural education for young children* (3rd ed.). New York: Teachers College Press.

This book uses rich examples of teachers' reflective practice to illustrate children's understanding of race, socioeconomic class, culture, and gender, and how teachers may promote equity and respect into their curricula for young children.

United States Consumer Product Safety Commission. (2005). *For kids' sake: Think toy safety.* Document #4281. Online at www.liveandlearn.com/toysafe.html.

This resource is a comprehensive guide to selecting and maintaining children's toys that meet national standards for safety. Other resources for toy safety include:

The toy manufacturers of America guide to toys and play. (2005). Online at www. openseason.com/annex/library/cic/X0085-toysply.txt.html.

Safechild.net's top 5 toy safety tips. (2005). Available online at www.drtoy.com/tips-on-toys/safechild-nets-toysafety-tips.html.

United States Consumer Product Safety Commission. (2005). *Handbook for public playground safety.* Accessed online September 23, 2005, at www.cpsc.gov/CPSCPUB/ PUBS/ 325.pdf.

Wassermann, S. (2000). *Serious players in the primary classroom; Empowering children through active learning experiences* (2nd ed.). New York: Teachers College Press.

This book presents arguments for developing a sense of "can do" in primary-grade children and gives teachers specific suggestions for designing and implementing a guided play curriculum in several academic subject areas.

5

Orchestrating Play:
Interactions with Children

Pam, a first-grade teacher, watches as three children begin to play a board game, counting out marbles as they move to designated spaces on the game board. Peter counts whatever numbers come to mind, although he uses one-to-one correspondence as he pulls them from the barrel (1, 2, 3, 4, 7, 10). Marcia counts hers quite precisely, using the conventional number sequence, and one-to-one correspondence. Emily grabs a handful without counting, and Peter shouts, "You're cheating!" Pam asks if she may join the game and models counting in sequence and with correspondence when it is her turn. Soon Emily is imitating her strategy and Peter is attempting to master the sequence for counting from one to 10. ✆

The 3- and 4-year-olds in Grace and Dorothy's classroom had just returned from a field trip to the outdoor farm at their local regional park as part of their project curriculum on the theme of mothers and babies. The mother pig at the farm, "Sophie," has four piglets and the children were excited about their opportunity to observe the piglets nursing, and watch them as they learned to move on their own. In the midst of their mural making and block play, the local news reported that the baby pigs from the regional park had been stolen from the farm. Of course the children were distressed and worried. They contributed their theories about what happened. "One day the baby pig woke up and Tilden farm was gone," "Maybe they just rolled down the hill" were two suggestions. After a phone call to the park ranger they had met, the news was not promising for the pig's safe return. Grace and Dorothy supported the children's discussion and play speculating about the pigs' fate for a few days. Then they turned the discussion from the fear and violence that dominated to the ranger's plan that the park would build a pig-napping-proof pen, and to feelings of empathy for Sophie and her babies. "She is missing her babies," went one dictated story. "The baby pigs are scared and sad without their mama," went another. The children set to work eagerly, using clay, blocks, sticks, and drawings to work on their designs for the "safe pig pen." They use the toy farm animals to test their designs and to play through their fears. "Where did all my piggies go? Cow, will you help me find them?"

"Here we are—in the barn!"

"You scared me silly, babies! I couldn't see you. Remember, stay close to me!" (Stewart, 2001b) ✆

In each of these anecdotes we see how the teacher's ability to set up, observe, enter, and exit play with sensitivity and grace is crucial to the successful sustaining of children's play. Each teacher does this by considering factors of age-appropriate and individual development. For example, Pam knows that 5- and 6-year-olds are just beginning to understand games with rules, and that children's emerging abilities to use both conventional sequences and one-to-one correspondence in counting vary at this level of development.

Grace and Dorothy understand the fears raised by the pig-napping at the local park, especially since the children have already begun to construct their representations of the mother pig-baby pig relationship they had observed first hand. After supporting a discussion of their fears, Grace and Dorothy introduced ideas that shifted their thinking from fear and violence to empathy for the pigs and more positive alternatives, such as imagining ways to keep baby pigs safe.

A key role for the teacher lies in the ways he or she interacts with children as they play and think. The most important aspect of this role is the attitude that teachers maintain towards children's play. Teachers' respect for both individual and cultural variations in play themes and activities is essential, along with the cultivation of their own disposition of playfulness and humor (Bergen, 2002; Cooney, 2004; Lancy, 2002).

PLAY AND SCAFFOLDING

The notion of "scaffolding" was developed by researchers who studied the ways in which adults support and elaborate children's early language. Just as scaffolds on a building support the new construction, adults' interventions in play assist children's attempts at effective communication (Cazden, 1983; Ninio & Bruner, 1976).

Scaffolding includes the ways that teachers support and facilitate meaning-making in children's play. As we noted in chapter 4, the environment acts as a context for play at school. Various environmental elements scaffold for certain kinds of play. For example, the housekeeping corner supports both constructive and dramatic play as well as the use of cooperative language; bubbles and blowers in the water table suggest extensions for water play, small tables and chairs scaffold solitary or parallel play, and rugs and cushions scaffold opportunities for cozy sharing or privacy (Beardsley, 1991; Henderson & Jones, 2002).

The impact that teacher presence has on children's play is an important aspect of scaffolding. In one classroom, interaction among children at tables with toys and puzzles was considerably muted because much of the interaction was dominated by the teacher, who took over such tasks in conversation as initiating topics, and controlling turn-taking. In a contrasting setting, teachers lingered close to children's play areas doing productive work of their own such as weeding the garden or untangling a ball of yarn, remaining available but unobtrusive as children sought to negotiate turns on a rope swing (Lederman, 1992).

Acquiring skills to negotiate their own interactions is basic to children's social and communicative competence, and does not rest solely on adult modeling. Play provides the occasion for children to corroborate, question, experiment, and stretch their understandings of the world and their places in it.

Other examples of scaffolding include the use of music to encourage persistence at clean-up time or while on a hike. Along with scaffolding the group's efforts, songs with open-ended phrases also support children's developing abilities to hear and reproduce rhymes.

Ted sings, "Exploring we will go, exploring we will go. We'll catch an ant and put him in our. . . ." He pauses as Sarah and Luis complete the phrase with "pants." Nessa calls out "bants" and Anthony offers "shoe." More children join in as the singing continues, "And then we'll let him go!" (Beardsley, 1991, p. 115)

Scaffolding also supports children whose play reveals and expresses frightening or confusing experiences, such as some of the children in Dorothy's class. Scaffolding is also important for children for whom the construction and negotiation of a pretend reality is a challenge, such as children with autism or Pervasive Developmental Delay (Griffin, 1984; Koplow, 1996; Kostelnick et al., 2002; Phillips, 2002; Wolfberg, 1999). In the following example, two children with autism are supported in their efforts to engage in cooperative play.

Jeremy enters the rug area where Todd is building with blocks. Jeremy watches, and jumps up and down in place. The teacher suggests, "Jeremy, ask if you can play." Jeremy says tentatively, "Can I play?" as he looks at Todd. Todd nods his head and Jeremy sits down. They begin to build a tower cooperatively. With a sudden kick, Todd knocks the tower down. They begin rebuilding the tower, and this time Jeremy kicks it down with his foot. Todd admonishes Jeremy, "No kicking!" as Jeremy jumps up and down in place. They rebuild the tower twice, taking turns knocking it down with their hands until it is time to clean up (Lovsey, 2002). ⌀

Questions that arise for most teachers are: How much scaffolding is helpful, what form should it take, and when should it be modified or removed?

Teachers need to consider both the physical environment and the ways in which they intervene (or refrain from intervening) as integral elements of scaffolding. In the sand or water area, for example, the teacher might move a new basket of sand toys into the area, or redirect attention from a dispute over materials by using a play voice to signal a "flood" or an "avalanche." Keen observational skills and a willingness to wait and watch as children construct their own meanings are key elements of successful scaffolding in play (Henderson & Jones, 2002; Jones & Cooper, 2006; Perry, 2001, 2003).

SPONTANEOUS, GUIDED, AND DIRECTED PLAY

Play orchestration is possible in three contexts of play among young children. In spontaneous play, the teacher's role is nearly invisible, just as setting the stage represents a prelude or backdrop to a drama. In guided play, the teacher's role is more directive, although these strategies, too, range along a continuum of less to more teacher direction. Guided play strategies differ slightly depending on the nature of the materials and the content area of the

Figure 5.1
Continuum of Play Orchestration Strategies

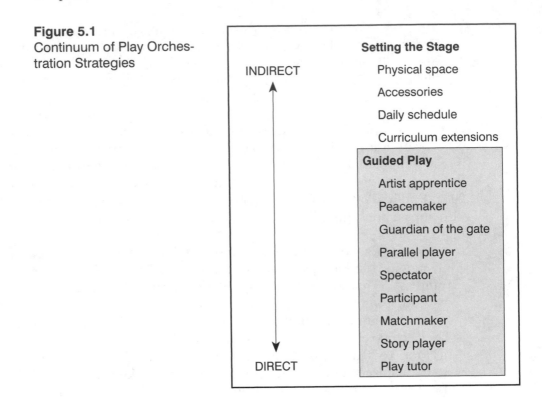

Setting the Stage

INDIRECT

Physical space

Accessories

Daily schedule

Curriculum extensions

Guided Play

Artist apprentice

Peacemaker

Guardian of the gate

Parallel player

Spectator

Participant

Matchmaker

Story player

DIRECT   Play tutor

curriculum. For example, art play and music play may call for more guidance when new materials and techniques are introduced. The strategies listed in Figure 5.1 are appropriate for orchestrating children's exploration, sociodramatic, and constructive play in the classroom. Subsequent chapters delineate guided play strategies appropriate to specific content areas such as language and literacy, science and art. In each case, the teacher orchestrates play in all its facets—intellectual, social, physical, and emotional—by being first and foremost a keen observer.

In addition to possessing keen observational skills, the teacher who orchestrates children's play needs to learn to "dance" with the children as she facilitates their play. The first element of this dance is determining if and when she should join the children (Roskos & Christie, 2001). First she needs to ask herself: Will the children benefit by my intervention or shall I simply watch?

Many teachers are uncomfortable with this notion of simple observation, since it seems at odds with cultural stereotypes of teaching as adult-directed activity (Henderson & Jones, 2002; Joshi, 2005; Yang & McMullen, 2003). One useful strategy to help teachers extend their observation skills and at the same time model representation, reflection, and recording is by taking the role of "scribe." In this role, the teacher draws or writes about children's play, and then shares her recordings of her observations with the children (Jones & Reynolds, 1992). For example:

> In Gail's kindergarten classroom, Tom and Alexis have built "a machine for seeing inside your suitcase" as part of the extended thematic play unit on airports. Gail draws their construction of blocks, playdough, cardboard, and paper, and then invites the children to label parts and discuss their functions with their classmates at group time. Alexis points out that Gail has forgotten to draw an essential piece—a small ball of aluminum foil. "You forgot that important shiny part that makes the light go inside the suitcase," she says, and Gail adds it to the drawing, writing a label next to it. ∅

Vivian Paley (1984, 1986, 1992, 1995, 1997, 1999) is masterful at recording children's play and then using it as a frame for group discussion or as raw material for drama. Paley reports frequently asking children "I noticed that you were playing. Can you tell me more about it?" and recounts an aspect of their play that she found interesting. This form of authentic questioning in which the teacher asks questions he or she does not already know how to answer, both acknowledges play for the children and adds to the teacher's information about them as individuals and as a group.

> Sally, a first-grade teacher who teaches in an ethnically diverse community with many English language learners, frequently uses this technique in her classroom. For example, Sally took handwritten anecdotal records during the candy store sociodramatic play in her classroom. She noted that Javier modeled the invention and use of pretend money for Lee, who seemed at first confused, then enthusiastically began to count his change: "1, 2, 3, 4, 5—that is five dollars!" Sally noted this in Lee's portfolio, and then used the event to launch a discussion at group time about objects that could be used as pretend money.
>
> "We could use those plastic buttons, because they're round," suggested Frank, representing in language his thinking about a perceptual feature of both money and buttons.
>
> "Or shells," contributed Fran.
>
> "Or make our own dollar bills with paper," shouted Emilia enthusiastically. A plan was made to extend their play by adding a bank the following day. ∅

What are some ways teachers can be more directly involved in children's play? Table 5.1 shows some orchestration roles that involve direct teacher intervention

Table 5.1
Spontaneous, Guided, and Directed Play

Curriculum Standard	Spontaneous Play	Guided Play	Directed Play
Demonstrates equivalency with blocks	Eric uses four triangular blocks to finish his yellow brick road of squares.	Teacher sets out tangram blocks and patterns; Sara and Ari negotiate use of smaller rectangles to complete a house pattern.	Teacher sits with Matt and Brita and asks them to help her stack the blocks so they are all in squares.
Uses scientific tools and methods to learn about the world	Sandra uses a toy thermometer to take her doll's temperature. "Oh, it's 100. She needs to go to the doctor!"	Teacher sets out ice cubes and containers of warm and cold water and thermometers, asking the children, "What do you think will happen? How can you tell?"	Teacher directs small group to measure temperatures of pans of water placed in the sun with varying numbers of ice cubes, and to measure and mark time for melting the ice.
Uses pictures and letters to express thoughts and ideas	Jeff answers the phone in the playhouse. "She's not here. Can I take a message? She will be glad you can come!" and scribbles on a notepad, using M for mom and drawing a smiley face.	Teacher sets up card-making center with templates for Valentine hearts and paper letters to glue or copy.	Teacher directs children to make labels for their block structures, asking them to label parts of their constructions so they can photograph them.

in children's play and range from the most subtle and indirect to the more active and direct.

The Artist Apprentice

The most subtle of these guided play strategies is what Griffin (1982) calls the Artist Apprentice role. In this role the teacher helps to remove clutter in the physical spa ce around an ongoing play episode, or offers accessories for play, much like a set assistant in a theater.

As Mark, Donelle, and Beth launch their spacecraft, land on a planet, and discover aliens, Ms. Toms, their teacher, helps to tidy the blocks when the spaceship "crashes," and the players move their play to the housekeeping corner. She provides a red scarf for their flag and a cardboard box for their control panel. ✆

In doing this, Ms. Toms helps the children to maintain their thematic focus in play. If the blocks were to become scattered, the space travel might degenerate into block throwing. Alternately, the extended theme might become sidetracked in the search for appropriate accessories to represent the flags and the control panel. In the Artist Apprentice role, the teacher does not intervene with accessories or action unless she perceives that her action is helpful to sustaining children's play. Another example is described by Phillips (2002). Teddy, a 6-year-old, is a child with autism who repeatedly takes books from shelves and stacks them on the floor. The adult intervenes first by clearing space for his purposeful play with books and then uses her words to give voice to his actions.

Another technique used by the Artist Apprentice is to physically protect an ongoing project and help others set up their own projects in adjacent spaces. In one preschool, a plastic hoop was used to designate "in-progress" constructions in the block area, so that new players would know that someone was saving the materials to play with later (Beardsley, 1991).

The Peacemaker

The next intervention role along the direct-indirect continuum is the Peacemaker who may help children resolve conflicts that appear in their play in several ways. First, the teacher may offer accessories that help to resolve disputes. For example, as 3-year-olds Mary and Jesse argue over a toy typewriter for their office play, the teacher might find another toy typewriter or help the children to imagine how they could use blocks to make another typewriter.

In terms of roles, teachers can help children resolve conflicts by suggesting related alternatives for disputed roles. In chapter 3 we described a situation in a kindergarten classroom in which several children wanted to play the princess role in an ongoing dramatic play episode. The teacher asked if the princess might have a sister or some cousins who weren't in the movie the children had seen and the children agreed on new but related roles. These kinds of suggestions model for children the flexible thinking and problem solving that ideally occur in play and help them to generate solutions to role disputes on their own as teachers encourage them to invent their own alternatives.

Teachers also act in the role of the Peacemaker when they help children to invent roles that stretch their thinking beyond the need to possess disputed materials.

An observer to Mrs. Paley's classroom in Chicago noticed a child standing, arms outstretched, in front of the unit blocks. No one else was able to use the blocks, as a consequence. When the children complained to Mrs. Paley, who was seated at the story dictation table, she asked, "Ben, how can they get the blocks they need?" Ben replied (after a long pause), "They have to order them!" The other children immediately picked up blocks and "telephoned" their orders to Ben. ✆

Mrs. Paley remarked later that she could see that Ben "was a character in search of a part." Her one-line query to Ben provided the scaffold for successful negotiation and maintenance of the play episode by inviting the player to stretch himself and invent a part.

The teacher may serve as an interpreter of children's motives to their peers when conflicts occur, or when children disrupt the play of others. Some children slip easily in and out of play and learn to give their fellow players "meta-messages" about their intentions. Bateson (1976) coined the term *meta-communication* to describe the behaviors that people use to signal play. Such behaviors include winks or smiles, laughter, play voices, or exaggerated movements. Verbal markers may be as obvious as "Let's pretend that I'm the babysitter and you're the bad baby" or as subtle as the change in voice pitch to mark the role of the "Papa Bear."

Children whose play is characterized by imitation of content from television or video or whose speech and language are delayed are frequently misunderstood by peers in their attempts to initiate and maintain play (Katch, 2001; Levin, 2003b; Ogakaki et al., 1998; Wolfberg, 1999). These misunderstandings also occur in settings in which children speak different languages or dialects.

Teachers can help children interpret meanings of others signaled by such meta-communicative cues and invent explicit strategies for finding out meanings when they feel confused. Such techniques may be particularly important in helping children interpret the cues of play fighting or rough and tumble play so that the play remains a healthy and safe exercise in physical challenge rather than an escalation into violent confrontation (Ariel, 2002; Blurton-Jones, 1972; Pellegrini 1998, 2002).

Guardian of the Gate

How can the sensitive teacher help children gain entry to play without violating the rights of the players in an already-established episode or, alternatively, to judge when it may not be appropriate to interrupt?

Corsaro (1985, 2003) reported that 75 percent of the time preschool children's initial bids to enter ongoing play episodes are rejected. Young children seem to intuitively protect their shared fantasies from interruption by interlopers. After two or three attempts at entry, 50 percent of children seeking to enter others' play are successful.

How can teachers help children develop effective strategies for entry and the confidence to try again if rejected at first? Intervention strategies on the part of the teacher to monitor the gates of play parallel those for the Peace-maker role.

One way teachers can encourage children is by introducing an accessory. Griffin (1982) tells of a child who rode a trike every day around the periphery of other children's play, watching but never joining. She gave him an old cam-era, simply saying, "Take this with you on your travels." Other children soon noticed the camera and asked to be "photographed." Gradually, the child be-came included in play groups, and developed the confidence to play with oth-ers through the accessory that was uniquely his.

Sometimes teachers may suggest a new role. One teacher, seeking to help a child she had observed as an onlooker on the edge of play, asked her to help deliver a large package to the ongoing houseboat play. The "delivery people" were then invited to stay for lemonade and the onlooker child became includ-ed in the play, with her teacher there as security. In another classroom, the teacher asked a group of children who were playing camping, "What could Carl be, a Forest Ranger?" In this way, the teacher opens up possibilities for the children to negotiate new roles within their play without interfering with the integrity of the ongoing episode.

Teachers also can interpret the social context of play. Schwartzman (1976) wrote that play offers teachers "sideways glances" at make-believe. First, it reflects the social status of children in the group. Children with high status often play the most powerful roles and also assign roles to their peers. Children with lower status in the group may hold that status due to un-skilled attempts to enter the play of others. Play also reflects children's un-derstanding of the peer culture in the classroom. Teachers can explain children's motives to others in terms such as, "I see Sandy really wants to join your group. She is looking for a friend to play with. Would you like to be her friend?"

Orchestrating Play Entry for Children with Special Needs. Teachers may find that some children with special needs have less experience, confi-dence, or ability when engaging in play activities. Some consistently look to adults to help them enter the play of others. This is often true of children who are unable to communicate their needs clearly (McCay & Keyes, 2001–2002). Some children with special needs may have lower status than their nondis-abled peers due to the difficulties they have in entering play. In the role of Guardian of the Gate, teachers can provide the additional involvement that might be needed without increasing children's dependence on adults (Neeley, Neeley, Justen, & Tipton-Sumner, 2001). For example, a teacher might make a child's motives known in order to increase social interaction between disabled and nondisabled students (Allen & Brown, 2002; Bartolini & Lunn, 2002; Han-line & Fox, 1993).

Emma, a kindergartner with delayed expressive language, loves to play catch, and frequently approaches other children holding the ball and saying "Emma, Emma" pointing to her chest. Her teacher has helped other children understand that Emma is asking them to play ball, and prompts Emma to say "to me" as the ball play begins. ✆

Parallel Player

An even more active role for the teacher involves playing parallel to children. In this scenario the teacher plays next to but not with the child, using similar materials, but not interacting. The teacher might first imitate the child's behavior, such as pouring sand into a container, establishing a basis for reciprocity. Next, the teacher might introduce a variation in the play, such as using a funnel and watching to see if the child imitates the variation. In this way, reciprocity builds at a nonverbal level. In dramatic play, the teacher might use a prop in a new way, subtly extending the child's symbolic distancing, for example, by using a pretend gesture or an unstructured prop to make a telephone call within the child's view (Forman & Kuschner, 1977).

Parallel play is a strategy children frequently use for entry into ongoing play and works for teachers as well.

In Jackie's multi-age primary-grade class, Ted, Martha, Elisa, and Kim were calling themselves "ocean scientists" as they played on the carpet. They were sorting, ordering, and counting seashells, discussing their criteria for classification, and speculating about which was bigger, a large, flat, thin shell or a smaller, round, dense one. Periodically, one child would say "We're scientists doing our work," and the others would nod in agreement. Jackie sat down on the carpet with the children, first manipulating shells and informally observing and joining their discussion. She then brought out a small plastic balance scale from the shelf and began to place large shells one at a time in one bin of the balance scale and count smaller shells into the other bin, watching until it balanced. The children began observing and commenting on Jackie's actions. Jackie then began to verbally describe her own hypotheses and behavior as she manipulated the shells and the balance scale. Soon another scale was produced and the children began to play in pairs, returning to their original questions about which shells were bigger, now reframed as which ones weighed more. Jackie gradually withdrew from the play context, continuing to take anecdotal records for later inclusion in their portfolios and to support the class debriefing about choice time that would occur later in the day. ✆

Spectator

The teacher comments from outside the play about the themes and content of play when she orchestrates play from the perspective of Spectator. In this way she indirectly coaches play from the sidelines, by taking the role of an interested spectator or a peripheral participant. For example, as Maggie and Keisha approach their teacher carrying their suitcases, the teacher might ask about their imagined travel plans, "Have you bought your tickets yet? Do you have enough suitcases?" By referencing a present context and extending it to a future event, the teacher invites the children to elaborate their play to incorporate the teacher's comment. In this way, teachers validate children's dramatic play and may subtly suggest extensions.

As with all intervention strategies, particularly those that involve a more active role for the adult, teachers must be careful to gauge the situation and determine if comments, even from outside the play frame, might disrupt the flow of children's play or introduce elements incongruent with their intentions (Ghafouri & Wien, 2005). Williams (2002) suggests that this form of orchestration may be typical of some parents who, while valuing play, see it as a means of teaching cultural skills by directing play through their comments to children.

Giffin (1984) developed a scheme for analyzing strategies that children use to coordinate shared meaning in their make-believe play from both outside the play frame and as players inside the frame. For example, teachers, as spectators outside the pretend frame, can support children by implicit pretend elaboration, such as in the travel and suitcase example above. In this role the teacher is an implicit and undefined onlooker to play and may suggest extensions or clarifications that help move play forward.

Participant

In the next role, the Participant, the teacher moves from outside the pretend frame into an active role in the play, perhaps as a neighbor knocking on the door to borrow eggs, or as an ambulance driver bringing an injured person to the hospital. Once the teacher is part of the enactment of a shared script, she can indirectly communicate actions, themes and verbalizations in her role as Participant.

After the make-believe theme of an airplane trip had been established in Matt's kindergarten class, he noticed that children were boarding the pretend airplane, and just sitting in the seats. He boarded as a passenger, and asked Carlos, the flight attendant, what was on the menu for dinner. Carlos responded with "You could have pizza or fried chicken," and then began to enact the rolling of a food cart down the aisle of the pretend plane. ✍

Another participant strategy that allows adults to enter the play space is the use of a direct or indirect comment in order to shift or extend the play in a particular way by interjecting high drama into the script. The teacher might report a warning or foretelling of an imaginary event as if it were real. "Quick, we need a nurse! Call 911," prompts Matt, as he enters his kindergartners' superhero play and encourages them to extend the make-believe play beyond the fight, die, and resurrect sequence he has observed in this play all week.

Through both dramatic underscoring and storytelling, teachers can interject verbal comments into the stream of play without disturbing the shared illusion of the pretend frame. In underscoring, the teacher might sing or use a sound effect to model the communication of pretend actions, roles, or objects.

Matt speaks urgently to children playing firefighter as they have arrived at the burning house with sirens blaring and limited action. "I'll turn on the hose-sh-sh-sh-sh" (making water sounds as he mimes turning on a faucet) to douse a pretend fire. ✆

Storytelling is a verbal strategy that allows the player (adult or child) to communicate pretend transformations using narrative forms. For example:

First-grade teacher Sally shops at the pretend candy store in her classroom, elaborating the plot to extend children's problem solving as she tells her story. "It's my sister's birthday and she really likes gummy bears, do you have those? We are having a big party for 10 people and we need two bears for everyone. Can you sell me enough? Also, I need a birthday card. Do you have those?" ✆

As in the Spectator intervention, the teacher must be sensitive to cues from children and not enter into play unless it is called for (Bennett, Wood, & Rogers, 1997). If the teacher does enter the play as a Participant, then he or she needs to play a supporting rather than starring role. Many teachers of young children enjoy engaging in play as a Participant and may have a tendency to control the flow of play without realizing they have usurped the power of the children. For example, in one preschool classroom, an over-enthusiastic parent volunteer offered to play the injured party in hospital play. She ended up directing the entire play episode, assigning roles to children and suggesting what the doctor and nurse players should say and do.

Matchmaker

In this role the teacher may deliberately set up pairs or groups of children to play with one another. He may, for example, pair a more sophisticated player with a less sophisticated player. Providing there is not too great a difference in their play styles and personalities, both children may benefit from this arrangement. Complementary emotional needs may also serve as a basis for matchmaking.

> In one classroom, Sandy, whose parents were divorcing, sought out situations she felt she could control and in which she could feel power. Paul, on the other hand, distressed over the birth of a baby sister, created a baby role for himself whenever possible. These two children were a perfect match in terms of their complementary emotional needs and spent long hours in house play with Sandy as a powerful and nurturing mother to the helpless baby Paul. ⌀

Wolfberg (1999) recounts her research in which she paired children with varying severity of autism with typically developing playmates in playgroups. Situations in which the child with more skilled play was able to bring his or her peer into a zone of proximal development in play abound in this interesting and valuable research.

Matchmaking may also be an effective strategy for orchestrating play with English language learners. Children who are more proficient in English may be able to smooth communication among players with less fluency in English.

Storyplayer

Vivian Paley (1981, 1986, 1990, 1999) introduced the technique of story play for supporting children's play that structures its form, but not its content. In her approach, children dictate stories to a teacher who writes them out, to be enacted later in the school day with the class group. The text is written down exactly as it is dictated and reread in the child's language. Each author chooses the part he or she would like to play and selects who will take the parts to be enacted. The author serves as director as the teacher reads the story aloud. Elaborations of the plot are often enacted as the story unfolds in drama. Comments such as, "I forgot, the little bear does come home to his mom at the end," are sometimes added to the story's text. Props are not usually used to ensure that the children's imagination is exercised, although teachers may want to consider the developmental level of the child in making decisions about props. In chapter 8, Language and Literacy, story playing is described in greater detail.

Play Tutor

The teacher as Play Tutor takes on the most direct role of all by re-creating the emotional security of the caregiver-infant dyad that is the source of human beings learning to play. In this context the child feels safe and is able to take risks involved in using symbols and language to represent the meaning of the concrete. The teacher models and directs children's play in this role, providing reinforcement to their efforts to symbolize and interact.

A computer station offers many opportunities for guided play.

Researchers who study childhood play have been guided by the work of Smilansky (Smilansky, 1968; Smilansky & Shefatya, 1990) for many years. Smilansky focused on intervention with preschool children whose dramatic play lacked complexity. Direct tutoring may benefit those children whose play consists of repetitive one-liners imitated from television, or whose attempts to enter the play of others are awkward and intrusive (Bartolini & Lunn, 2002). Smilansky's strategies guide teachers in their attempts to help children elaborate their play through such elements as extended role play, social interaction, verbalization, persistence, and object transformations in a process she calls sociodramatic play training. Smilansky's scheme for assessing play complexity is presented in detail in chapter 6.

Other researchers have employed a technique they call "thematic fantasy role play" (Saltz & Johnson, 1974) in which the teacher assigns roles and directs the enactment of stories read aloud to the children. This technique assigns more control to the teacher than sociodramatic training, where children form their own story lines with teacher support. It also differs from Paley's story-playing approach in its emphasis on stories authored by adults, and roles selected and directed by the teacher.

Another strategy involves both matchmaking and play tutoring. Teachers may ask children to serve as "play coaches" and help other children invent roles, pretend with objects, or join in a play episode. In many classrooms, children are given this role with regard to computer use, writing, or other activities in which the status of "expert" encourages children in particular roles to reflect on their own thinking and communicate it to others. It adds the dimension of expert-novice to the already powerful zone of proximal development created in pretend play. Smilansky (1990) found that the play coaches as well as their players benefit from this process.

Because play tutoring represents a very direct role for the adult, it must be used carefully (Trawick-Smith, 1998). Children who have difficulty with symbolic play distancing and/or social play negotiations might be better served by less direct teacher strategies. For example, a multi-age setting often encourages more advanced play on the part of younger children and prosocial behavior on the part of older children, and may be a more desirable alternative than play tutoring.

CHOOSING A STRATEGY

Considerable skill and thought is required to determine which context, in combination with which child, calls for a given strategy. For example, the child who plays parallel functional play with blocks or sand is a likely candidate for the Parallel Player strategy. The child who hangs around the edges of play groups might benefit from an accessory or entry strategy. As a general guideline, wise teachers intervene with the most indirect strategy possible. Many teachers begin by changing the setting for play, perhaps by adding new accessories. If that doesn't work, then the teacher proceeds to increasingly more direct strategies along the continuum.

Another combination involves both matchmaking and play tutoring. Teachers may ask children to serve as "play coaches" and help other children invent roles, pretend with objects, or join in a play episode. In many classrooms, children are given this role with regard to computer use, writing, or other activities in which the status of expert encourages children in particular roles to reflect on their own thinking and communicate it to others. It adds the dimension of expert-novice to the already powerful zone of proximal development created in pretend play. Smilansky (1990) found that both the play coaches and their players benefited from this process.

Challenges in Play for Children with Special Needs

In intervening with all children in their play, there are several factors to consider. We believe it is essential for teachers to keep in touch with the power of the zone of proximal development created through play. All children, regardless of their current developmental capacities, stretch their competencies in play with others. For some children, playful interactions with adults are just as essential as those with peers. Smilansky's play tutoring approach and the overt modeling of pretense may be called for. For most children, however, the teacher in his role as Matchmaker and stage manager serves to support play opportunities that are productive and engaging for all. The matchmaking and tutoring roles present promising avenues for orchestrating pretend play with children with special needs (Bartolini & Lunn, 2002; Henderson & Jones, 2002; Kostelnik et al., 2002; Odom, 2002; Phillips, 2002). Wolfberg (1999) describes an ongoing play-group consisting of normally developing peers who are coached by the teacher to interpret, elaborate, and scaffold the play of autistic playmates.

One drawback of play in inclusive environments is that, while young children frequently empathize with their peers who have special needs, most young children are unable to take the perspective of another child and act altruistically on that understanding. For example, in one kindergarten classroom, Pauline, a child with Down syndrome, was consistently manipulated by two of her peers into giving up her play materials in exchange for less desirable objects.

Another consideration is that children who are typically developing sometimes feel pressured to include peers who have special needs. They may subsequently comply with adult expectations by allowing the child with special needs in the play area, and then ignore him or her (Trawick-Smith, 1994). Conversely, peers may overdo their helpfulness by treating special needs children in a patronizing manner or by doing too much for them. For example, in a preschool classroom, 4-year-olds Alkicia and Emily consistently spoke for Theresa, a child with communicative delays. In doing so they often squelched Theresa's efforts to communicate with others and her developing sense of initiative.

Challenges in Play for Children Who Are English Language Learners

Play with peers provides a safe context for negotiating turns, roles, and problems that arise in play. Linguistic skills are evident in these negotiations and in the enactment of play themes and entry in play. Given the importance of language for social competence and success in play interactions, English language learners present some unique challenges to orchestration (Saracho, 2001).

One challenge is the observation made by many teachers that children prefer to play with peers who speak the same language (Clawson, 2002). Whether the groupings occur as a result of English speakers or from English learners, the results call for sensitivity on the part of the teacher. Matchmaking children who are interested in similar things may be one approach. In this way children who do not speak the same language begin to form a social history with one another as they share play (Orellana, 1994).

Other challenges call for different orchestration strategies. For example, in observing children a teacher may notice that the onlooker behavior of a child masks a desire to join the play.

Selena hovers at the edge of the restaurant area watching as Mark and Cecilie cook a pretend dinner. Ann, their teacher, is a customer in their play restaurant. She comments from the Participant role, "I'd like some cake after my dinner. Is it on the menu?" "Oh I don't know if we have any," responds Mark. Ann asks Selena in Spanish if she knows how to make cake. Selena nods, and slowly begins to approach the pretend restaurant. "Selena knows how to make cake," Ann suggests to the two other players, and they hand her a bowl and spoon, as she joins them in the kitchen. Selena begins to mix pretend cake ingredients, and asks Ann in Spanish, "Do you like chocolate?" ∅

Timing Is Everything: Entering and Exiting Children's Play

When teachers enter and exit children's play or shift from one strategy to another, timing is crucial. Manning and Sharp (1977) and Reynolds and Jones (1997) suggest guidelines for entering play. First and foremost, teachers need to observe play long enough to see if any intervention is called for or if the children are best served by the teacher in a less direct role. As part of this observation phase, the teacher has an opportunity to ascertain the themes, characters, plot, and vocabulary negotiated by the children.

If the teacher chooses to enter the dance of interaction played out by the children, she must do it seamlessly, joining the flow of the play without disrupting its progress or integrity. Respect for children's ongoing shared make-believe is critical. Adult entry is more suitable at transition points during which children are "stepping out" of the play frame to negotiate rules about the play or ongoing themes or roles, rather than at the times when children are deeply engaged in pretend play (Bennett, Wood, & Rogers, 1997).

Leaving the play and returning control completely to the child players is just as important as a sensitive and flowing entry. Since the teacher's purpose is always to support children in their efforts to sustain and elaborate play on their own, the timing of exits is critical. Phasing out of play is one exit strategy that gradually returns the control of the play to children. As a participant within the play frame, a teacher might use storytelling to explain her departure or take a less active role. For example:

Karen entered the train play of a group of five preschool children with the intention of facilitating Heidi's entrance into the play. Karen sees that Heidi is now engaged with others eating "lunch" in the dining car. Karen announces, "Oh good. The next stop is mine, so I'll see you next Friday on the train." She says to the engineer, "I'll be getting off at the next station." ∅

Sometimes teachers may unobtrusively leave the area when children are very involved in play, as Jackie did when the children appropriated the seashell balancing activity. At other times, the teacher may speak from a different stance: "I promised some children in the block area I'd come visit their airport. I'll come back to watch you when I finish." This effectively places the teacher on the outskirts of play as a Spectator and reminds the children of her real-life responsibilities as the teacher (Trawick-Smith, 1994, 2001).

PLAY AND THE CULTURE OF SCHOOL

Play always occurs within a social context and in relation to the various cultures that co-exist within the classroom and the school. The "school culture" (Heath, 1983) represents the norms of school behavior commonly accepted in our society and shaped through teacher behavior. The peer culture represents an alternative and, to some degree, a complement to the school culture in the classroom.

King (1992) studied the three types of play that commonly occur in school settings: instrumental play, recreational play, and illicit play. Each is defined by the way in which the teacher responds to children's play and the context in which it occurs.

Instrumental play is sanctioned and employed by the teacher to meet goals consistent with school curriculum. Examples are blocks or games with rules that teach vocabulary or concepts, and dramatic play. In dramatic role play,

Children engage in complex spatial reasoning and imaginative play with blocks.

teachers find that the negotiation of the features or implicit "rules" of adult roles provides fertile ground for children to test their mental concepts about gender and adult occupations with other children whose backgrounds may have created a different set of rules and expectations. In one preschool classroom, Nat and Katherine argue over who will fix the dinner, the mom or the dad. In Nat's home, his father is the primary caregiver and usually prepares the evening meal. In Katherine's home, her father commutes to work in a large city and her mother generally prepares the meals.

Recreational play is sanctioned by the teacher as a means to let off steam, but it generally occurs outside the teacher's view. Playground play at recess and free play outdoors in some preschool and kindergarten settings are examples of this type of play.

Illicit play is not sanctioned by the teacher and, in fact, may be expressly forbidden. Children engage in illicit play either behind the teacher's back or as a direct challenge to the teacher's authority. Such play is thought to provide children with a sense of mastery and autonomy within the school setting that limits the range of acceptable behavior. Examples commonly seen in early childhood settings include transforming Tinker Toys into guns when such play is prohibited, "group glee" activities, such as coughing or snapping Velcro shoes, and passing secret notes or pictures (Corsaro, 2003; King, 1992).

One aspect of illicit play that proves to be increasingly difficult for teachers are the consequences of outlawing weapon and violent play in the classroom (Katch, 2001, 2003a; Levin & Carlsson-Paige, 2006). Strategies for coping with the behind the scenes strategies that children use to circumvent teacher-made prohibitions about the content of play are addressed later in this chapter.

Other kinds of illicit play are described by Scarlett et al. (2005) as "risky play" in which children endanger themselves and others, for example by throwing sand or rocks. In this "mean-spirited play," characterized by teasing and bullying, and "mischievous play," children deliberately flaunt school rules, such as rolling around on the carpet at circle time. Scarlett et al. (2005) also describe "ambiguous play" in which children seem to be using play as a means of mastering strong emotions, such as putting the baby doll in the oven (Ardley & Ericson, 2002), or tearing apart the housekeeping area as "naughty" kittens.

Although instrumental play in educational settings or, as Sutton-Smith (1995, 1997) calls it, "play in the rhetoric of progress" is sanctioned by educators, we wish to remind ourselves and other teachers of the importance of play that is not sanctioned by adults. This mischievous or silly play represents another arena in which we find the social skills and concepts of young children developing.

Just as play serves an "equilibrating" or balancing force in our lives, by its paradoxical nature, play also allows us to invert reality, to throw off balance what we know to be normal or sensible. This represents the power of both nonsense and festive play (Fromberg, 2002; Sutton-Smith, 1995). One of the outcomes of this kind of play that is mischievous, rebellious, and nonsensical is the powerful social bonding that occurs among players as they jointly oppose traditional social norms and a sensible view of the world in a playful manner.

> David and Brad are playing with a squirrel doll in the playhouse. David squeaks the squirrel and taps it on Brad's shoe. Brad shouts "Stop, squirrel!" "I'm not a squirrel. I'm a squirmmy!" responds David in a high-pitched voice, hopping the squirrel doll up and down. He grabs a baby doll out of Brad's hand and makes a pouring motion over his head with it. "Sh-h-h." Brad questions, "Hot coffee?" "No, hot caw-caw," David responds, laughing loudly. "Hot caw-caw!" He and Brad fall together onto the floor, laughing hysterically. ✆

In their evolving peer culture, children confront the differing perspectives of one another and also that of the school culture represented by the teacher. As Corsaro (1985, 2003) advises, teachers must walk a fine line between respecting children's needs to ally themselves against the constraints of adult authority (to look the other way on occasion) and their own need to provide firm and consistent limits about what is acceptable in the school setting. "Adult ideas, materials, rules, and restrictions can be seen as frames or boundaries within which features of peer culture emerge and are played out" (Corsaro, 1985, p. 289). A good example of this dilemma is the ongoing debate in early childhood education centered on the use of toy and imaginary weapons and fantasies involving violence in preschool and primary grade settings.

RESPONDING TO VIOLENT PLAY

Although pretend weapons and war play issues have plagued the curriculum and classroom culture decisions of teachers for decades, the increase of numbers of children in schools whose lives are filled with violence and the increased access for all children to violent imagery via television, videos, and video games have sharpened the debate. Children who are unduly repetitive in their imitation of characters' dialogue and scripts gleaned from television, movies and video need intervention from teachers to expand their limited repertoires to more complex representations of characters, settings, and plots (Katch, 2001; Levin, 2003a; Levin & Carlsson-Paige, 2006).

Teachers struggle with alternatives to outright censorship to help children make sense of frightening and confusing images seen in the media, such as themes of bullying and violence that occur in the following example of Leo and Jeremy playing out an episode from the television series *Survivor.*

Seven-year-old Jeremy and 6-year-old Leo are playing in the outdoor lawn area of their elementary school playground. "I'll make you eat these worms!" snarls Jeremy, attempting to stuff a handful of leaves and wood shavings into Leo's mouth. When Leo protests, Jeremy counters, "But that's how your team can win! You want us to win, don't you?" ⏀

What can teachers do to mitigate the themes of violence in their classrooms? In what situations might children be playing out confusing and disturbing images from their own lives, rather than imitating scripts from television, movies, video, or even videogames? These and other questions regarding violence and play have surfaced in our work with teachers, children, and families.

One compelling question that intersects with some of the thinking regarding violence in high schools is the relationship of violence to exclusion, both for the child who is excluded and for those who are sought as play partners. Katch (2001) addresses these issues with her powerful insights to the hearts and minds of children whose violent imagery in play both attracts and repels others. Both the rejected children who retaliate with violence and the popular children who strike out in frustration at being continually solicited to play have feelings with similar roots.

Paley (1992) writes eloquently of the problem with the tradition of early childhood educators to accept children's often painful rejection of one another in play as a natural part of growing up. In implementing a "You can't say you can't play" rule in her own classroom she brings the issues of inclusion and exclusion and their accompanying social and emotional consequences to the forefront of the debate.

Ascertain Children's Purposes in Play

Another question that calls on teachers to examine their beliefs about the media and contemporary popular culture is the relationship of development to violent play. Young children are just learning to reliably negotiate the lines between reality and fantasy. Crossing those boundaries frequently in pretend play helps children to clarify the meaning of violence in our contemporary culture. But how much of this play is too much? What are the fine lines between "playing through" confusing or frightening images or experiences and becoming obsessed with them (Katch, 2001; Koplow 1996; Levin, 2003b)?

In considering the motives for children's aggressive play, teachers need to ask: To what degree does the play reflect the desire to be powerful in the world, and to what degree does it reflect children trying to make sense of what they have seen on the evening news or even in their own neighborhoods? Schwartzman (1976) pointed out that an important aspect of play is its "inward perspective" or the process by which children repeat experiences that are puzzling, confusing, or disturbing to them. For example:

> Tracy's home had been fire-bombed and her older brother injured. For several weeks, her kindergarten peers, in their roles as paramedics and firefighters, carried the "injured" Tracy to hospitals they constructed in the block corner, under tables, and in the sandbox. ✆

Schwartzman also described the "upwards view" of playing, asserting that in play, children rehearse roles and experiences they hope to have when they are older. This function of play is certainly part of the appeal behind Barbie dolls and Power Rangers. Still, many teachers wonder if play with toy weapons and play fighting encourages these activities as desirable goals for the future.

A related issue is identifying the sources of violent imagery. Many teachers report impatience, anger, and frustration with media-based violent play. "How can their parents allow 5-year-olds to watch those teenage horror videos?" one teacher laments. On the other hand, teachers express more empathy for children whose play includes violent images and themes that are derived from their home lives, such as Josh's enactment of his aunt's funeral or the repeated firefighter and rescue play flowing from the firebombing of Tracy's home, or the death of a relative in the World Trade Center attack.

Still another source is the personal histories and stories of children whose families were tortured or killed before fleeing to the United States. Wanigarayake (2001) describes the ways in which Australian early childhood teachers in community programs serving immigrants observed preschoolers quietly and seriously pretending to slit each others throats in their play. She describes how teachers were forced to abandon their "comfort zones of accepted policies and practices that prohibit violent play" (p. 291) in their efforts to support children's need to play through the violent experiences they had witnessed before they came to Australia. They used the information gleaned from the play to talk with families, and to bring mental health professionals into the dialogue.

How Willing Are Teachers to Confront Their Own Beliefs and Experiences?

Many teachers of young children cope with frustration about violent play by outlawing toy weapons and violent themes, hence driving the play "underground" into the peer culture. Is it more effective to illuminate children's fears by openly discussing the violent content of play or by creating more empathetic and rich contexts for play than to ignore children's fears (Ardley & Ericson, 2002; Katch, 2001; Levin, 2003a; Levin & Carlsson-Paige, 2006).

When pretend play is largely an attempt to order what is confusing, chaotic, or frightening to children, then is it important to consider the sources before invoking classroom rules about weapon play or violence? For example, in the days and weeks following the September 11, 2001, attack in New York, many teachers believed that the block play, dramatic play, dictated stories, and story play enacting the violence were appropriate avenues for healing and making sense of fear. Similarly, Dorothy and Grace's children needed to play out their fears regarding the lost baby pigs in order to move to a more empathetic stance. Does replay of violent imagery desensitize children or offer them an avenue of control?

Diffusing Violence in Play

When does the discharge of frightening feelings become obsessive? How can teachers and families work together to diffuse violence in children's play?

Educators and families can collaborate in early childhood programs to reduce aggression and violence. Some war play or aggressive "good guy/bad guy" play is often typical for many young children in our culture. The loud noises, fast pace, and especially the thrill of the chase that have been elements of diverse forms of sociodramatic play for decades often appeal to children. The themes of good versus evil, life and death, lost and found, and danger and rescue that occur in war play and other aggressive play give children opportunities to deal with these archetypal concerns. However, as we shall discuss further in chapter 12, Play, Toys, and Technology, the explicit violent details of television, movies, and computer games, as well as the many toy weapons on the market today, seem to spur children on to greater heights of aggression. In "firing" a toy gun, for example, children may lose sight of the story line of the pretend play and end up hurting one another through their aggression (Carlsson-Paige & Levin, 1990; Levin, 2003a; Levin & Carlsson-Paige, 2006).

In contrast, in the "best" play derived from media, children use characters, settings, and events typical of a television program, film, or video as raw material for the creations of their own imaginations, with complexity characterizing their play structure. In a classic example of media-based superhero play:

Ran and Marty are playing Teenage Mutant Ninja Turtle characters Leonardo and Michelangelo. They swagger around the playhouse with cardboard and tin foil swords and discuss how they will track and capture "the bad guys" by rigging traps for them in the forest (represented in the adjacent block area). "I know how to make a tent in a tree," offers Michelangelo, "so we can have a secret hideout." Leonardo elaborates, "We'll leave a map to our secret hideout so they will come there." "And then, when they smell our hamburgers cooking, they'll be hungry," proposes Michelangelo. "Yeah, and then when they get close, we'll grab 'em," continues Leonardo. They transform their swords into horses and gallop into the "woods" to pitch their tent and lay their traps. ✆

In this example we see homemade weapons transformed into horses and a typical good guy/bad guy theme elaborated from the children's own experiences of camping out. Although the heroes are drawn from a media source, the plot and objects are of the children's own invention.

Many teachers report that they can follow the plot of the latest violent movies or the morning's TV cartoon shows by observing children's play. However, teachers can help children to use characters, play themes, and props derived from popular media in constructive ways. Levin and Carlsson-Paige (1998, 2006) suggest several strategies for parents and teachers to cope with war play. These are easily integrated with the strategies already discussed in this chapter.

Observe Play Carefully.   By keeping informed about popular cartoons, videos, films, and television series, as well as toys that may be popular in the peer culture of the classroom, teachers are better able to understand the play they observe. Through close scrutiny of children's play, teachers may determine if some children are "stuck" in repetitive imitations of what they have viewed. Teachers may then orchestrate play to help children expand character roles, elaborate story lines, and use props beyond the level of simple imitation following strategies suggested in these chapters.

Look Beneath the Surface of Play.   When teachers are sensitive to the underlying themes of play, they may suggest nonviolent alternatives that appeal to children. Good guy/bad guy play encompasses themes such as danger and rescue that are central to children's socioemotional development (Corsaro, 2003; Katch, 2001; Paley, 1990; Perry, 2001). Once the theme is identified, teachers may introduce literature with new characters and plots that elaborate these themes in new ways.

In a preschool directed by one of the authors, teachers and parents embarked upon an experiment to diminish the frequency of television-limited play that imitated cartoon violence. Noting that themes of good and evil, life and death, and lost and found dominated much of this play, the teachers and parents read various versions of *Peter Pan* and helped children make costumes and props, and act out their interpretations of the characters and events in their play. Later in the year, *The Wizard of Oz* and *Peter and the Wolf* were explored in similar ways. Children still used pretend weapons and fought and chased adversaries, but their repertoire of characters and actions

Play often reflects daily activities.

for these themes was expanded. For example, after the *Peter Pan* theme was explored, one child noted that "turning bad guys into toads or rocks was better because if you shot them, they just came alive again." ✇

Set Limits.   Teachers may also keep children "safe" by setting limits. For some children, the appeal of war play or media-derived play is especially irresistible when it is violent in nature. Since the script for war play or media play is usually simple and well-known, children with limited social skills or language abilities are often drawn into the vortex. As the cast of the play grows, the level of aggression can become out of the children's control. By setting limits and carefully monitoring this play, teachers can help assure that at-risk children are protected. It is also important for teachers to understand the circumstances in children's personal lives that might be leading to an overabundance of this type of play.

Several teachers we know set these limits by banning real-looking weapons from their schools, while acknowledging children's need to do battle with imaginary ones. In this way they avoid the phenomenon of children imitating action from television with single-use weapon toys. Other teachers make a point of talking to children about alternatives for their play plots when aggressive play careens out of control, perhaps suggesting strategies for tricking bad guys instead of shooting them.

WHEN TEACHERS TALK

Building a Peaceful Classroom

In the preceding sections we focused on the multiple ways that teachers can respond to children's violent play, both directly and indirectly. We conclude this chapter by going beyond strategies for violence prevention to integrated strategies for peace promotion. Peace promotion is central to our ideas of a play-centered curriculum.

> Kindergartners were drawing their ideas of "our wishes for peace" as part of a teacher-initiated activity in the aftermath of September 11. As they talked about each child's wish (e.g., getting along with everybody, cooperating, and helping others), children pointed out with some surprise that "that's what we do, too."
>
> In Dorothy and Grace's preschool classroom, the children began to consider remedies to the sadness of Sophie the mother pig on losing her children. They decided to paint a mural and to learn "Old MacDonald Had a Farm" on the bells. After weeks of mural construction and practice, the children went back to the farm to present Sophie with the mural and play their bell concert for her.

In the classroom, just as at the international level, peace is more than the absence of violence. Violence is not only direct, clearly visible violence, but also insidious structural violence. Structural violence refers to inequalities in schools, communities, and societies that disadvantage some and privilege others, such as racism, sexism, religion, nationality, and inequalities based on economic class (Christie, Wagner, & Winter, 2001).

Peace educators and psychologists make the useful distinction between a negative peace and a positive peace. A positive peace is marked by the absence of violence, as well as equity and opportunities to enhance growth for all, and by nonviolent conflict resolution (Derman-Sparks & Ramsey, 2005; Alvarado, Derman-Sparks, & Ramsey, 1999).

Early childhood educators and researchers have long emphasized the priority of programs that promote a positive peace. Peace education is truly an "umbrella concept" (Gustafson, 2000). Reviews of early childhood education for peace and nonviolence theory, research, and practice shows that conceptions of peace have always been multifaceted (Harris, 1999; Hinitz & Stomfay-Stitz, 1998; Van Hoorn & McHargue, 1999).

With the growing concern about youth violence during the past decade, teachers have seen many K–12 curriculum that are promoted as violence prevention programs—focusing on negative peace. Early childhood educators find that a growing number of books and curricular materials describe approaches to promoting peaceful classrooms. We have also found that the more developmentally appropriate programs and materials are those that promote a positive peace, have a multifaceted approach, and promote play (Adams & Wittmer, 2001; Kreidler & Whittal, 1999).

For example, in *That's Not Fair: A Teacher's Guide to Activism with Young Children* (Pelo & Davidson, 2000), the authors underscore the importance of looking carefully at children's play. One vignette relates to equity and inclusion. When boys exclude Julia from their Winnie the Pooh play ("there are no girls in Winnie the Pooh for real . . ."), Julia asserts her rights and negotiates, "I could pretend to be a different character, a new one that's a girl." A discussion ensues, and everyone agrees that Julia will be Tigger's sister.

SUMMARY AND CONCLUSION

We think of *Play at the Center of the Curriculum* as "play at the center of a curriculum for peace and nonviolence," for these are the values that are embedded in each chapter. Many of the classroom examples of play described in this book show children cooperating, considering the feelings of others, developing friendships, and playing with peers who speak different languages and come from diverse family configurations and ethnic backgrounds. These are all aspects of building a culture of peace.

The considerations for setting the stage discussed in chapter 4 lead to more peaceful classrooms. There are subtle strategies as well as more visible ones. For example, teachers consciously set the stage so that children have sufficient space as well as materials that foster cooperation. Teachers plan a time schedule that balances activities so that children do not become overly tired, and consider children's needs for private play. Environments welcome all children and their families, and help all to learn about living in a diverse society.

Strategies discussed in this chapter for intervening in children's play promote children's development of dispositions and behaviors inherent in a peaceful classroom: empathy, prosocial behavior, and cooperation. How can newcomers to the United States like Ben and Carl find a place in the social group? What about Sandy and her physical limitations? When play is at the center of the curriculum, children are more autonomous and have multiple opportunities to develop social problem-solving abilities and to take the perspective of others.

Early childhood programs that promote peace are characterized by a pervasive culture marked by inclusiveness, empowerment of all, nonviolent conflict resolution, cooperation, and empathy. We firmly believe that the play-centered curriculum leads to a peaceful classroom and nurtures peaceful children.

SUGGESTED RESOURCES

Brown, C. R., & Marchant, C. M. (Eds.) (2002). *Play in practice: Case studies in young children's play.* St Paul, MN: Redleaf Press.

This rich book is a collection of teachers' stories from their classrooms. Each example highlights issues that teachers face in orchestrating play, and their thinking as they struggle with choices that enhance children's play and learning.

Derman-Sparks, L., & A.B.C. Task Force. (1989). *The antibias curriculum: Tools for empowering young children.* Washington, DC: National Association for the Education of Young Children.

For many years, numerous teachers have turned to this resource, which provides practical and theoretical guidance to teachers of young children.

Katch, J. (2001). *Under deadman's skin: Discovering the meaning of children's violent play.* Boston: Beacon Press.

Katch writes about her own kindergarten–first-grade classroom and the effects of media-derived violent play on her classroom peer culture, individual children, and her own practices as a teacher.

Levin, D. (2003). *Teaching children in violent times—building a peaceable classroom* (2nd ed.). Cambridge, MA: Educators for Social Responsibility & Washington, DC: National Association for the Education of Young Children.

This book offers practical suggestions for teachers to cope with children's fears and behavior related to images seen in the media and in their lives.

Levin, D. E., & Carlsson-Paige, N. (2006). *The war play dilemma: What every parent and teacher needs to know* (2nd ed.). New York: Teachers College Press.

This is an updated edition of a classic tool for parents and teachers to navigate the complexity of guiding children in the understanding of the media and the escalating violence in the world.

Reynolds, G., & Jones, E. (1997). *Master players: Learning from children at play.* New York: Teachers College Press.

The authors discuss how educators can use the concept of master play and players to observe children and support their development. They guide the reader to become more skilled in observing and analyzing children and their play through their superb, lengthy case studies.

Teachers Resisting Unhealthy Children's Entertainment (TRUCE). (2004–05). *Toys and toy trends to avoid.* Somerville MA: Author.

Each year this organization publishes a list of objectionable toys, books, and other products for children that include themes such as making violence the focus of play, encouraging age compression, encouraging gender stereotypes, and linking non-nutritious food to play. They have also written a Toy Action Guide and the Media Violence Guide for families and teachers. Available online at www.truceteachers.org.

Wolfberg, P. (1999). *Play and imagination in children with autism.* New York: Teachers College Press.

Wolfberg, a therapist, describes her research in developing techniques for children with typical development to support children with autism in developing play skills.

Play as a Tool
for Assessment

In Kathy's kindergarten classroom, four children have set up a "bank." They have stacked two rows of large hollow wooden blocks to form a counter and built chairs for themselves out of smaller blocks. Additional small blocks on the countertop form windows and have the "teller's" names taped to them. Pat, an adult visitor to the classroom, walks up to the teller's window. Shawna, one of the tellers, asks Pat if she brought her bank book. When Pat responds "No, I don't have one," Shawna directs Pat to the basket of small blank paper books that Kathy makes available in the classroom. "Write your name on it," Shawna tells Pat, and Pat prints her name on the front. "P-a-t," Shawna says as she touches each letter, and then remarks that her grandmother's name is Pat too. "Does she spell it like this?" Pat asks. "I don't know," replies Shawna, "I'll ask her."

Returning to her place behind the bank counter, Shawna takes the bank book and opens it to the first page. She carefully writes "CRTO," and then asks Pat how much money she wants. Pat says, "Fifty dollars." "I can't count that much, you know," says Shawna, "How about ten?" Pat agrees and Shawna takes out a piece of 8 × 11 white paper, folds it in half and makes a series of horizontal cuts. She then cuts the paper down the middle and counts out 10 pieces of paper. She writes a "1" on each "bill" and counts them out carefully on the counter in front of Pat. "Here you go," Shawna says as she uses a rubber date stamp and a stamp pad available for children's play to stamp the bank book. "Just come back when you run outta dollars." ✆

ASSESSING DEVELOPMENT THROUGH PLAY AT THE BANK

Later that day Kathy, the teacher, discusses the dramatic and constructive play at the bank with Pat, who teaches kindergarten in a neighboring school. She talks about the ways in which Shawna's play yields information about her developing concepts and skills in literacy, mathematics, and social studies as well as her social and emotional development.

Kathy has taken digital photographs of the bank in its various stages of construction over two days of free play periods. Both Pat and Kathy are impressed with the complexity of the block representation of the bank environment. Kathy's anecdotal records indicate that the children who built the structure discussed and negotiated their experiences of how banks look. They used spatial reasoning, including part-whole relationships, to select blocks for the counter, the chairs, small blocks for the name plaques, and long rectangular blocks for the teller's windows. Her notes indicate that Shawna was one of the children who persisted with the project over several days' time, while two other children lost interest after the first day. Shawna and her "new" best friend Emily continued the project and directed the creation of the tellers' roles, which they were eager to play. The tellers have each written their names and fastened them to the "name plaques," using a social form of literacy they have observed in banks and, at the same time, practicing their own renditions of their names.

Kathy and Pat discuss the conversation about Pat's name, and how Shawna spontaneously identified each letter. "Shawna is still working on the idea that some names are spelled the same way every time—probably because not all the adults who work in this classroom know how to spell her version of 'Shawna,' " Kathy informs Pat.

Another example of how Shawna is working on the consistency of letters to spell words is shown in her careful writing of "CRTO" in the bank book. Apparently there was quite a bit of negotiation when the bank "opened" before the children agreed on "the thing you hafta write in the book." Emily's mother works in a bank and had apparently used the term "credit to" in talking about accounts. Emily was quite emphatic that this was the proper term and used her invented spelling concepts to create the notation "CRTO." The date stamp is another form of social literacy that children have observed in the real world.

"Shawna's awareness of the limitations of her counting amazed me," said Pat. "I thought of offering to help her count to 50 and then realized she had already come up with her own, better alternative. I also wondered how she learned to cut paper that way." ✐

Kathy explained that weeks earlier they had experimented with paper folding and cutting in order to make shapes for valentines. Shawna was apparently replaying this skill and applying it in a new situation. Kathy and Pat agreed that Shawna's writing of a "1" on each bill and then counting them out carefully for the customer not only showed Shawna's counting skills, but also informally contributed to the concept of place value she will construct in the future.

Kathy is interested in Shawna's progress as an individual and as part of her kindergarten group. Kathy uses information from her assessments of children to plan curricula for her classroom and to monitor the learning that has taken place. Recently adopted state standards in the curriculum areas of language and literacy, mathematics, science, social studies, and visual and performing arts provide a framework for Kathy's assessment of learning and development in her kindergarten classroom. She uses developmental charts, checklists, and portfolios to organize her assessments.

Play is a natural "piece" of the assessment "pie" because it offers perspectives on children's progress in all areas of development as they are spontaneously integrated into daily experience. Ongoing observation of spontaneous play such as the "bank" is an ideal complement to assessments made during guided play with specific goals and to more direct measures of children's achievement in subject-centered activities.

In play, many facets of children's development are revealed. Educators increasingly call for a refocusing of our goals for young children's programs based on what we know from child development theory and research. Standardized tests target attention to surface skills such as memorizing the alphabet or numbers, and away from deeper concepts such as classification or the nature of narrative. We need to use assessment that recognizes the value of easily observable skills as well as the more subtle concepts children construct during their early years of education. Play assessment allows us to observe both.

ASSESSING AGE-APPROPRIATE DEVELOPMENT

These examples from Kathy's classroom illustrate age-appropriate development for 5- and 6-year-olds in the areas of emergent literacy and mathematical concepts. In addition, the assessments themselves are "authentic" with both content and methods of collecting data on children's progress aligned with widely held expectations about the development of kindergarten children. Such assessments include the teacher's knowledge of the typical stages of development for children in a given age range on a variety of skills and concepts, and the assessment process itself promotes learning and development (Shepard, Kagan, & Wurtz, 1998). The criteria of authenticity in both content and assessment strategies is a key element in ascertaining the developmental appropriateness of assessment for children in preschool and primary grades (Bredekamp & Copple, 1997; National Association for the Education of Young

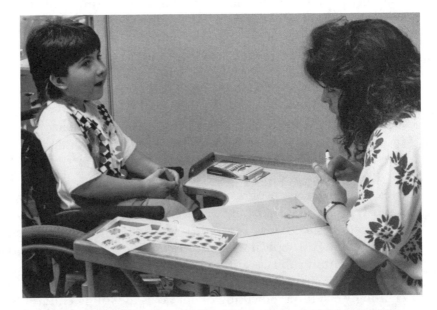

One-on-one interactions provide opportunities to assess children's skills.

Children & National Association of Early Childhood Specialists in State Departments of Education, 1991; National Early Childhood Goals Panel, 1998).

Assessing Skills and Concepts

For example, Kathy and Pat examined Shawna's assessment portfolio, which contained handwritten observations, called "anecdotal records," of Shawna's spontaneous and guided play since the first week of school. They compared Shawna's rendition of her name with well-formed letters and adequate spacing in March to the shakily written backwards "s" followed by a series of curved lines that Kathy had placed in Shawna's portfolio in early October.

Pat and Kathy looked at Shawna's early attempts at spelling words other than her name, beginning with the pictures and letters on a shopping list made in the playhouse in November, and then random letters in December and January. Her most recent writing, like the "CRTO" (Credit to) at the bank showed attempts to use some beginning and ending consonant sounds. "I lk wtrmln" (I like watermelon) is Shawna's recent contribution to a class book about favorite letters of the alphabet.

In the area of geometric and spatial reasoning, Kathy collected snapshots of Shawna's block structures, some built along with peers and others individually. Kathy also showed Pat an observation form on which she records anecdotal records of children's spontaneous and guided play (Table 6.1), and links them to the state academic standards for kindergarten.

Kathy also records notes from guided and directed play, as in this example from earlier months of the school year when she informally questioned Shawna regarding her understanding of number concepts.

> In the playhouse, Shawna was setting the table for "breakfast" for four stuffed animals. She had each animal sitting at a chair at the table and was passing out napkins. She took the napkins one at a time from the playhouse cupboard and placed each at an animal's place, walking across the playhouse each time. She went through the same process with spoons and cups until each diner had a place setting. After discussing Shawna's breakfast guests and the menu with her, Kathy asked Shawna how many of each—napkins, spoons, and cups—there were. Shawna counted each set aloud, "1-2-3-4." "Four and four and four," she said, smiling, "for my four friends." Kathy noted Shawna's competence with number concepts, including one-to-one correspondence in counting to four on the record of mathematics skills. ✍

> Later, in January, Kathy's anecdotal records showed that Shawna had set the table for her snack group of six children. She had carefully counted the number of places aloud, then gathered sets of six napkins and six cups and placed one of each at each setting.

Table 6.1
Record of Mathematics Skills and Concepts for Kathy's Kindergarten

Curriculum Standard	Play	Dates	Contexts
Number Concepts			
Counts to 10 by rote memorization	S. and E. press leaf patterns into sand, counting to 10 and laughing as they check results.	9/27	Outdoors—sand area
Counts with one-to-one correspondence	Sets table for stuffed animals, counts 1 to 4 to place cups and napkins.	11/6	Housekeeping area—play alone
Uses comparative words, such as many–few, big–little, more–less, fast–slow appropriately	"I need more blocks; you have too many."	12/4	Block area—negotiates with boys "Girls need blocks too!"
Understands numbers and simple operations and uses math manipulatives, games, toys, coins in daily activities (e.g., adding, subtracting)	"I need 2 more to make 10 dollars."	3/27	Pretend bank—customer role
Sorts and Classifies			
Describes how items are the same or different	"Put all the red food in this basket and the yellow food in here."	9/14	Pretend store—packing groceries

"Sometime in those three months Shawna learned to count and mentally match equivalent sets instead of doing it one at a time," remarked Kathy. "In October, when I discovered that many of the children were just beginning to construct the idea of one-to-one correspondence, I planned a series of guided play activities where I set up materials like straws and cups and brushes and paintboxes. I asked children to help me set the places for children to work, and found out how they were thinking about counting and correspondence. My observations of play helped me plan a curriculum that was a good match for children's needs and also see how successful my ideas were." ∅

Fine Motor Skills with Scissors.   Kindergarten is a critical time for the development of children's motor skills. Kathy's assessments include both fine and gross motor skill competencies. She collected samples of Shawna's cutting projects over the course of the school year. Shawna's early attempts at using scissors were characterized by cutting straight short lines, and then tearing the paper with the scissors the rest of the way. Kathy recalled guiding Shawna's hand to show her how to close the blades of the scissors on each cut and how Shawna and a group of friends spent most of their time for nearly two weeks in November making collages for people from magazines and paper scraps.

After that, Shawna's cutting showed smooth edges and control over different shapes. By February, her creations at the valentine table and her subsequent use of folding to make multiple sets of a cut shape were a great advance from her cutting skills earlier in the year.

Documenting Social Development. Up to this point Kathy and Pat had discussed the aspects of Shawna's development seen in her portfolio and through anecdotal records that reflected Shawna's progress in "age-appropriate development" in academic subject areas. Shawna's development of such concepts as the use of letters to represent spoken language, one-to-one correspondence, and spatial representation with blocks are aspects of development Kathy focused on in her observations. Skills such as counting in conventional order, using scissors, and writing her name also fell within the range of accomplishments Kathy expects of kindergarten children. More importantly, Shawna's records indicated growth in all areas from September to April.

Kathy's anecdotal records and samples of Shawna's writing also document the development of Shawna's friendship with Emily. Although Shawna still chooses to spend part of each day in solitary play, Kathy was pleased to see the development of a close friendship with Emily, since she believes most kindergarten children should have at least one friend. Her district has taken the lead among others in the state by incorporating standards of social and emotional development in their systematic assessment instruments. An example of standards is shown in Table 6.2.

Kathy felt that Shawna's ability to negotiate with other children seemed to have been bolstered by the bond she formed with Emily. For example, Kathy believed that part of the reason Shawna was able to confront a group of boys over taking more than their share of blocks was because she felt she was speaking for her friend as well as herself. Kathy also showed Pat samples of notes with pictures and Emily's name on them that Shawna had written. She recalled that Shawna had proudly spelled out Emily's house number when she drew a picture of Emily's house after visiting one day after school.

Table 6.2

Curriculum Standards for Approaches to Learning and Social and Emotional Development for Kathy's Kindergarten

Date	Curriculum Standard	Play Observation	Notes
9/14	Children become more comfortable with taking risks and with generating their own ideas.	Sam finally joins the block play. "I can make good garages!"	B
	Children approach tasks and activities with increased flexibility, imagination, inventiveness, and confidence.		
	Children demonstrate the ability to follow a sequence of steps to create a finished project.		
	Children are increasingly able to persist in and complete a variety of tasks, activities, projects, and experiences.		
11/7	Children show growing capacity to maintain concentration in spite of distractions and interruptions.	Maddy and Joan continue to build their sand restaurant despite the noise and disruption from the nearby chase and rescue game.	C for M O for J
	Children use more and more complex scenarios in play.		
	Children develop greater self-awareness, and have positive feelings about their own gender, family, race, culture, and language.		
	Children identify a variety of feelings and moods (in themselves and others).		
2/27	Children increase their capacity to take another's perspective.	"I think she's sad because her dad went on a trip," comments Doug in response to Carrie's tears.	C
	Children show progress in developing and keeping friendships.		
	Children manage transitions and follow routines most of the time.		
	Children use materials purposefully, safely, and respectfully, and take care of their own needs with the support of adults.		

B = Beginning; O = Occasionally; C = Consistently

ASSESSING INDIVIDUAL DEVELOPMENT

The second aspect of assessment that is equally important as widely held expectations for a given age is that of individually appropriate development (Bredekamp & Copple, 1997). This aspect of development takes into account each child's cultural, linguistic, and family background as well as personality qualities such as temperament and interests. Teachers often intuitively assess children's development with regard to individual personality and temperament, and consider factors related to language, culture, and family background. Because these factors do not appear on report cards or find their way into "developmental norms" charts, individual aspects of development may go by the wayside in favor of more skills-oriented goals. In her assessment, Kathy makes a point of including children's "dispositions" or "approaches to learning," such as taking initiative, curiosity, and cooperation. These approaches to learning are now more frequently included in state and national standards regarding appropriate assessment for children ages 3 to 8. Kathy also looks for ways in which children's play reflects their experiences at home, their styles of interaction, and ways of representing their ideas (Hughes, 2003; Katz & Chard, 2000; Murphey & Burns, 2002; National Educational Goals Panel, 1992). For example:

> Shawna comes from a family where she has two teenage brothers. Kathy and Shawna's mother have speculated that some of her interests in block building and her ability to assert herself with the boys in the classroom may come from this experience with her brothers. Kathy continues, "As a much younger sibling, her situation is somewhat similar to that of an only child in the family—Shawna seems to need a lot of time to play by herself. Although she has Emily and one other blossoming friendship in the room, she often will go to the library corner or the table toys and play alone. I also think her home situation has fostered her ability to assert herself with adults and talk easily with them. She often includes parents who visit the classroom in her play, just as she did with you today." ℊ

Intelligence Is Multifaceted

The issue of addressing multiple facets of children's learning and development is the subject of ongoing local and national debate. Current assessment efforts at local, state, and national levels have been criticized for overreliance on language and mathematics (Chen, Krechevsky, Viens, & Isberg, 1998; Kamii, 1990; Krechevsky, 1998). Early childhood educators are concerned that schools recognize the need to support a variety of modes of expression and understanding in order for us to acknowledge the potential of each individual (Epstein, Schweinhart, DeBruin-Parecki, & Robin, 2004; Kohn, 2001; Meisels, 2000; Seefeldt, 2005; Shepard, Kagan & Wurtz, 1998; Wien, 2005; Wesson, 2002).

Given these concerns, another aspect of individual development that is essential for teachers to include in assessment is the interests and aptitudes observed in children's play in the classroom. Gardner (1993, 1999) extended the notion of "intelligence" beyond the paper and pencil language and math evaluations traditionally seen in school settings. He discusses how abilities in music, spatial reasoning, and other aspects of personal expression are more often seen as special "gifts," but not integral to adapting to the world in an intelligent manner. Gardner reminds us that all these intelligences are present to some degree in everyone. Most of us have strengths in two or three intelligences that shape the way in which we see the world and express ourselves. Gardner believes that educators need to pay serious attention to alternative avenues of expression as well as the traditional *linguistic* and *logical-mathematical* intelligences emphasized in schools and assessed on standardized tests.

Gardner proposed five other intelligences that operate in people's daily lives. One of these is *musical intelligence.* Musical intelligence is expressed as children hum and sing to themselves. They often find patterns of sounds in literature, such as alliteration, and are interested in musical instruments, dance, and singing in the classroom.

Another intelligence is *bodily kinesthetic intelligence.* Children who readily express this intelligence are very active, expressing their thoughts and feelings through bodily movement. They may dance or leap across the room, exhibit coordination beyond their years in large motor activities and be particularly interested in and skilled at the mechanics of objects. Children who commonly express themselves through bodily kinesthetic intelligence may be interested in careers as dancers and choreographers, mechanics, athletes, or physicians.

Visual-spatial intelligence may be seen in children who are very interested and skilled in constructive play. Their block structures are very sophisticated in terms of design elements such as symmetry, color, and form, and their dramatic play is often characterized by elaborate use of objects to represent settings for their play. They may be very interested in art, using several different media to convey their ideas, or may focus on the similarities and differences in the shapes of letters and numbers as they begin to use written symbols. In the example above, Shawna exhibits many of the qualities associated with spatial intelligence.

Gardner (1993) also describes the personal intelligences that teachers see in young children. Children who express themselves through *interpersonal intelligence* are very interested in and savvy about other people's thoughts, feelings, and perspectives. They are often very social and well liked by other children and adults. Others may exhibit more *intrapersonal intelligence.* These children are very introspective, reflecting on their own thoughts and feelings and are often able to discuss just how they solved a particular problem or how they felt in a certain situation. As noted in chapter 3, interpersonal and intrapersonal intelligences are linked to the concept of "emotional literacy" described by Goleman (1995).

More recently Gardner (1999) posits a *naturalistic intelligence* that is characterized by particular sensitivity to the natural world. We see this in the child who loves to watch spiders spin a web, sowbugs move in the garden, and care for plants and animals.

Careful observation of children's play, in terms of both the process and content of their activities, offers teachers important clues as to the individual development of each child within this framework of multiple ways of making meaning. For example, Kathy emphasizes standards, such as those shown in Table 6.3, related to the visual and performing arts. Her district includes these as well as mathematics, science, literacy, history, and social studies.

Case studies, such as the information Kathy has collected on Shawna, are excellent examples of holistic assessment processes that include multiple aspects of children's representational abilites. For example, Carini (2000) gives examples of the Prospect Center's "descriptive review" process. In this approach to assessment, teachers discuss their observations focused on individual children, addressing particular areas of interpretation and reflection. They structure these observations and interpretations around children's body language and gestures, dispositions and temperaments, connections with others,

Table 6.3

Standards for Visual Arts for Kathy's Kindergarten

Date	Curriculum Standards	Play Observation	Evaluation
10/15	Children use a variety of art materials (e.g., paint, clay, wood, markers) to express their ideas.	Mandy uses wood glue to make a plane and draws windows with a red marker.	C
	Children share their ideas about their art work, and show interest in the artwork of others.	Mandy and Sarah at the easel. "Let's make butterflies, ok?"	O
	Children plan and carry out projects with increasing persistence.		
11/6	Children show growing awareness and use of elements such as line, shape, color, and texture.		
12/18	Children discuss and demonstrate appropriate use and care of tools such as scissors, paintbrushes, markers, and paper.	Mandy paints spirals and then creates a border of circles around her easel painting.	O
	Children experiment with mixing and shading color.	Mandy shows Cathy how to use scissors. "You have to hold both sides."	C

B = Beginning; O = Occasionally; C = Consistently

interests, and modes of thinking and learning. See Clyde (1994), Gallas (1997), Katch (2001), and Paley (1986, 1990) for other case studies.

Children Need to Reflect on Their Own Learning.   A major element of assessment approaches that provide multiple forms of representation is the provision of opportunities for children to reflect on their own learning and development. For example,

> As Shawna and Emily sorted through photos of the bank in its various stages of construction, Shawna remarked, "We got the name tags for the tellers, but next time we have to make a sign that shows people where to get in the line." ✆

The many projects described in this book, such as Kathy's "bank project" described at the beginning of this chapter, the post office project described in chapter 1, and Sophie and the lost pigs project and others described in chapter 5, are examples of how play and representations of play claim a central role in how children reflect on their own experiences and learning.

HOW PLAY INFORMS ASSESSMENT

Play is the ultimate "integrated curriculum." It offers teachers windows to view all aspects of children's development, including concepts, skills, dispositions, and feelings. These aspects of development, such as classification concepts or cooperative behavior, inform teachers about how to orchestrate more complex play.

Play occupies a privileged role in constructivist theories of learning and development. Therefore, it is the natural vehicle for assessing children's understanding of their experiences. In their play, children naturally emphasize concepts or broad patterns of thinking and problem solving rather than isolated skills. Play also offers a multidimensional look at skills, concepts, and dispositions that are valued by teachers and appear in state and national curriculum standards. It helps teachers to see a myriad of different avenues for developing and expressing understanding of these concepts among individual children. Although there is much discussion in the early childhood community regarding the developmental appropriateness of many curriculum standards and benchmarks imposed by schools, much of this discussion comes down to the means by which these competencies are assessed, rather than the benchmark itself. Play-centered assessment enhances the developmental appropriateness of many curriculum standards.

For example, one competency within the state curriculum standard for understanding of numbers in kindergarten, "counts with one-to-one correspondence," is reflected in Kathy's goals. But each child approaches this concept in a slightly different way. Jonathan develops his understanding by counting the number of blocks he needs to make the fence around his "lion cage" exactly

A teacher may assess such dispositions to learn as taking initiative, curiosity, and cooperation.

the same on each side. Shawna sets the table in the housekeeping corner, and Emily arranges the paintbrushes and the cups in correspondence to one another as she mixes colors for the day's easel painting.

A play-centered curriculum provides an atmosphere for assessment that is both comfortable and challenging. Children have many opportunities to make choices regarding their modes of expression and their playmates. In a classroom well equipped for play, children will find familiar objects and means of expression that scaffold their performances and allow them to create and problem solve in ways most comfortable to them.

Play enhances reliability of assessment by assuring that the results of an assessment are based on many opportunities for observing children at play with familiar materials and playmates. In this way, play-centered assessment differs from assessment that occurs only once or twice during a school year in which children are confronted with unfamiliar materials and intimidating contexts and are expected to perform to a standard of achievement.

Play also enhances the validity of assessment. Children are best assessed by their performances in real contexts. For example, it makes sense to evaluate children's spatial reasoning while they are constructing with blocks or collage materials instead of administering a paper and pencil task.

In Roseanna's K–2 multi-age primary class, a pretend restaurant begins as the "Don't Forget the Olives Pizza Parlor" and evolves to include Chinese food. The first week, children labor over a large wall menu that depicts the food choices and combinations in both print and pictures. After making pretend pizzas with playdough made from a posted recipe, Matt and Sam introduce sushi, rice, and noodles made from playdough as well and Celia and John write menus that show the pizza choices on one side, the Chinese food on the other and drinks and desserts on the back. Their teacher helps them xerox copies to color and mount on colored paper for their customers as they enter the restaurant. "Then everyone can see what we have on the wall, and at their table!" exults Angie, as she dons her chef's hat. ✆

Embedded in these experiences, Roseanna plans several of the curriculum standards from her state:

- The standards, "Understanding the concept of exchange and use of money to purchase foods and services" and "The specialized work that people do to manufacture, transport, and market goods," are part of learning basic economic concepts for grade 1. They are exemplified in the group's study of ingredients for foods for the restaurant and the pricing and pretend sale of foods and drinks.
- The standard, "Writing with a command of standard English, including sentence structure, grammar, punctuation, capitalization, and spelling" as part of understanding the conventions of written language for grade 2, is illustrated in the signs and menus children make for their restaurant.
- The standard, "Identifying, sorting and classifying objects by attributes," as part of the concept of sorting and classification for kindergarten, is embedded in the arrangement of food on the serving trays and in grouping items for the menu.
- The standard, "Learning that properties of substances can change when mixed, cooled, or heated" as part of the physical science concept that "matter comes in different forms" for grade 1, is evident in the playdough recipes that the children follow.
- The kindergarten-level visual arts standard, "Using a variety of art materials such as paint, clay, wood, and markers to express their ideas," is addressed by the making of playdough food, costumes for restaurant employees, placemats, tablecloths, menus, and advertisements.

ASCERTAINING THE CHILD'S VIEWPOINT

A major challenge for the teacher in implementing play-centered assessment is the development of observation strategies and questioning strategies that illuminate children's progress, while at the same time respecting children's right to control their own play. When Pat discovered Shawna could not yet count to

50, she might have asked Shawna how high she could count. Pat decided, however, that interrupting the flow of Shawna's play in order to do direct teaching or to ask her to perform a task was not appropriate in that context. Kathy's anecdotal record in which she questioned Shawna about the numbers of spoons, cups, and napkins demonstrated a situation in which questioning was not disruptive to the play. Shawna seemed pleased to show off the setting, "Four and four and four—for my four friends" to her teacher.

This judgment call on the part of teachers is one that requires sensitivity, thoughtfulness, and a repertoire of strategies for determining when to assess by careful observation and when to guide or directly question a child. As teachers use their careful observations of children's play, they grow in their understanding of how children think and feel and develop a deeper insight into children's purposes and conceptions concerning the world, as well as an appreciation of how the peer culture in the classroom influences learning.

As teachers gain an understanding of children's worlds, they become better able to plan curriculum that is relevant and appropriate to children's development. In guided play experiences, teachers have specific goals in mind. They may use these guided play contexts to assess children's progress in ways that pinpoint the questions they have about the development and learning of individual children and the group.

In the following sections we turn to the work of Selma Wassermann (2000), who developed principles for assessing and guiding children's play through questioning strategies and the introduction of new materials. Her model involves setting up materials for children to investigate concepts through their play, and asking questions that encourage children to communicate their thoughts and to elaborate their thinking.

Principles for Framing Play Questions

According to Wassermann, the first rule of thumb in formulating questions for children regarding their play is to *carefully attend to the child's behavior and/or verbalization*. This may involve making eye contact with the child and certainly listening to children with full attention and interest. It may mean getting down to the child's level or moving close enough so the soft-spoken child may be heard. Attention also means looking for nuances of feeling in the child's behavior, voice pitch, or tone. For example, many young children sing as they play with objects, sometimes creating a running monologue about what they are doing.

A second principle emphasized by Wassermann *is respect for the child's intentions and autonomy*. This means, in the most basic way, not passing judgment on the child's play behavior or on the product of that play. Respect may take the form of the teacher's decision not to ask a question, but instead to subtly and quietly put forth a new object or material the child might choose to use, and see what he or she does with it. This is part of the Artist Apprentice strategy for orchestrating play that we discussed in chapter 5.

If the teacher does decide to ask a question after determining that it will not be too intrusive, then a third consideration arises: *Does the adult's question empower the child or does it foster dependence on adult judgment?* For example, if Pat had offered to teach Shawna to count to 50, rather than accept the alternative of 10 dollars offered by Shawna, she might have conveyed that her adult knowledge was the only alternative in this situation. On the other hand, Pat might have felt that Shawna was eager to perform her counting skills and asked, "How high can you count?" In this way she would have invited Shawna to show off her rote counting skills. Instead, Pat chose to accept Shawna's suggestion of 10 dollars, believing that to do otherwise would have interrupted the flow of the play.

Ask Authentic Questions.   Paley (1981) notes that she tries never to ask a question to which she already knows the answer. Along with others such as Duckworth (1996), Paley suggests that teachers' questions need to represent an authentic curiosity about how children are thinking about their experiences. This is qualitatively quite different from finding out if the child knows what the teacher knows. The challenge is not to impart the teacher's knowledge to the child, but to objectively and without judgment observe the process the child uses to interpret his or her environment. In addition, many educators have noted that children who do not come from middle-class homes are frequently bewildered by teachers asking questions to which there are obvious answers, such as "What color is the grass?" Genuine interest in children's own thoughts and perspectives is a more respectful and more meaningful approach to questioning (Delpit, 1995; Tizard & Hughes, 1984).

Successful assessment of children's development in their play depends largely on keeping these principles in mind. Our viewpoints as teachers are transformed as we listen to children, and open ourselves to children's purposes and meanings.

Challenge Children's Thinking in Play.   Other questioning strategies challenge children to analyze or to generate hypotheses about their play. Asking children to predict, verbalize, or draw their plans for play, or to explain how their ideas might be tested are all examples of questions that challenge children to stretch their thinking. Ask, for example: I wonder if there's another way to do that? What do you suppose the lion would do if you allowed him out of his cage? Do you think you could make that same color again with paints?

Context is another dimension to assessing children's viewpoints as expressed in play. In an extension of the Matchmaking strategy for orchestrating play described in chapter 5, teachers wisely might consider structuring individual, small-group, and whole-group contexts for play. Wolfberg (1999) and Elgas and Peltier (1998) describe how teachers can use small-group projects and stable play groups to assess the development of children with special needs, as well as their typically developing peers.

STRATEGIES FOR COLLECTING AND ORGANIZING INFORMATION

In Kathy's classroom, several strategies for systematically collecting information about children's progress are evident.

Anecdotal Records

The first and most essential strategy is observation and anecdotal recording of spontaneous and guided play. Kathy says that she targets one or two children each day to observe during play and project time. She records her thoughts on Post-it Notes or on sticky mailing labels and then completes her notes after school. She says she finds that keeping observations to a maximum of three children a day makes the task easier to accomplish and that she can put together her notes on each child rather quickly. The dated observation then goes on the form. (See Table 6.1 on page 144 and Table 6.4 on page 156 for example.)

Other teachers simply place their notes taken on Post-it Notes or mailing labels on a paper in the child's folder, but Kathy says she prefers to "log" the observations as she takes them. "Then I can see where a child is spending most of her time. I can also see if I am really getting a good picture of the child's activities or if all my observations arc too narrowly focused. For example, I looked at Mario's chart a few days ago and realized that nearly all my observations of him were taken on the outdoor climbing structure playing with the same group of boys. I have to make an effort to find him on his own and record his play."

Another strategy for collecting information about children's development is through anecdotal observations of guided play experiences that teachers set up. For example, in her first-grade classroom, Anita frequently sets up a store as one of the centers. She is often a participant as well as an observer, focusing on children's counting and understanding of money. A center where leaves and rocks are available for classifying, or one with a variety of objects and a tub of water, are setups that afford teachers opportunities to observe children's play and converse with them about their thinking.

Checklists

Yet another useful strategy in assessing development through play is a checklist. Checklists might include stages of early writing (Table 6.4) or stages of sociodramatic play drawn from Smilansky's work (Table 6.5). Other checklists might

Table 6.4

Checklist of Beginning Writing for Kathy's Kindergarten

Dates	Observed Behavior	Evaluation	Comments and Play Context
9/14	Uses scribble writing or approximations of letters	Beginning___ Consistently_X_	Kayla holds a pen and makes a row of circles. "This is my letter!"
	Tells about writing	Beginning___ Consistently___	
	Uses strings of letters	Beginning___ Consistently___	
12/5	Writes left to right	Beginning___ Consistently_X_	K. begins "Happy Birthday" at left side of card.
	Knows difference between writing and drawing	Beginning___ Consistently___	
	"Reads" pictures	Beginning___ Consistently___	
	"Reads" writing	Beginning___ Consistently___	
12/3	Dictates "art notes" to pictures	Beginning_X_ Consistently___	"And write sun here and then the moon, 'cause it's night" as K. points to images she has painted.
	Dictates stories	Beginning___ Consistently___	
	Copies name	Beginning___ Consistently___	
10/7	Writes first name, last name—Copies words other than name	Beginning___ Consistently_X_	K. writes first name with reversals.
		Beginning_X_ Consistently___	
12/5	Writes independently	Beginning___ Consistently_X_	K. begins "Happy Birthday" pretend writing of card.
2/18	Uses upper and lowercase letters	Beginning_X_ Consistently___	"Does 'Mom' have a big M or little?" K. asks.
	Spaces writing	Beginning_X_ Consistently___	
	Uses begin/end consonants in writing	Beginning___ Consistently___	
	Invents spellings	Beginning___ Consistently___	
		Beginning___ Consistently___	

include strategies observed in children's problem solving, block building, or cooperative group play. A comprehensive checklist for assessment of young children on many dimensions of development is the 1993 Work Sampling System developed by Meisels (Marsden, Meisels, Jablon, & Dichtelmiller, 2001; Meisels, 1993).

Checklists have the advantage of giving the teacher "quick glance" feedback regarding the stages of development of both individuals and the group. For example, if in looking at a class checklist for stages of block play, a kindergarten teacher notes that many of the children are not yet constructing elaborated structures, she may want to consider some of the intervention strategies suggested in chapter 4. She may want to introduce some accessory boxes for new play themes that might stretch children's block representations to more complex levels. Checklists may also work to help summarize information from audiotaped or videotaped sequences of children's play, guiding the teacher to organize a large quantity of information into a succinct form.

Checklists have the disadvantage of giving the teacher little information about the context or detail of children's play when the observations are made. Just marking the stage and date of the observation is useful as a broad measure of development but may lack the richness of detail provided by anecdotal observations, videotapes, audiotapes, and portfolios.

Some teachers combine checklists with portfolios and observations. In his first-grade classroom, Mark takes observations and materials from portfolios every three months and summarizes the stages of development they represent on a checklist of early writing. This way he gives himself a picture of individual children's progress as well as the progress of the whole group, and ensures that he has collected a representative sampling of each child's experiences in his classroom.

Portfolios

Portfolio assessment at all levels of education is currently widely discussed. Historically, teachers have gathered samples of children's "work" and collected them in files. But too often this work represents only a child's efforts to copy a set of sentences from the board, a teacher-modeled art project, or a set of math workbook computations. Contemporary children's portfolios reflect much more of children's processes (Gronlund, 1998; Smith, 2000; Strickland & Strickland, 2000; Tierney, Carter, & Desai, 1991; Wortham, 2005). For example, Tierney and his colleagues (1991) recommend that children select their own samples for a language and literacy portfolio and include drafts as well as their final writing and drawing projects.

A preschool teacher holds a monthly art show in which children display their work. She asks children each month to pick out a piece of their artwork that they would like to be included in their portfolios.

Tommy's family is part Chinese and he has recently become interested in the written forms of both the Chinese and Japanese languages. The family hosted a Japanese exchange student in their home for the summer. Tommy was impressed by the Japanese writing on the boxes of Japanese toys he was given as gifts, and by the student's translation of the symbols for him. Tommy's pretend writing "in Japanese" is clearly marked from the pretend writing he has also done "in English." His teacher has a short audiotape of him "reading" his writing to her. For the Japanese symbols, he makes sounds that he thinks are like the language he has heard. Then he translates it into English for his teacher. ✆

Documentation Assessment

Teachers can also take photographs of projects in process, and write captions and ongoing questions and insights. For example, in Greta's second-grade classroom, open-choice playtime, called "project time," was the context for group projects that extended over several days or weeks.

As part of a project in social studies focused on tools and inventions in the past, present, and future, one group designed a whole series of robots, starting with the "X-100 model" that could serve soft drinks, extending to the "X-500 model" that could clean the whole house. The children created a collection of promotional brochures for their robot series and Greta helped them videotape their pretend television commercial showcasing their products. She kept records of their constructions as they developed and the drafts of their brochures and scripts for the television commercial. She marked the development of their thinking as a group as well as their individual contributions to the project. Over time, it became clear that Sonia was the budding engineer of the group, suggesting additional functions and parts for the robots each day. Mauricio carefully wrote their scripts and illustrated the brochures. Lila, a child who recently moved to the area from Mexico, and who had been reluctant to speak English, starred in their commercial, which was presented in both English and Spanish. This project addressed Grade 2 social studies, technology, and literacy standards for Greta's district. ✆

A key feature of documentation assessment is the opportunity for children to revisit their experiences and to elaborate their play in new ways. Documentation assessment also provides a powerful avenue for communicating with families about the play-centered curriculum and its outcomes for children.

Documentation assessment has been widely promoted by educators using the Project Approach based on the work in Reggio Emilia, Italy, and is thoroughly described by teachers and researchers such as Alkon (2004), Berry &

Allen (2002), Ganzel and Stuglik (2003), Helm and Benecke (2001), Kogan (2003), Nacif (2005), and Wurm (2005).

Videotape

Richard teaches a kindergarten–first-grade combination class in a rural area. Many of the children in his classroom speak English as a second language and their parents work in the nearby electronics industry. The parent group at Richard's school purchased a video camera a year ago. Richard videotapes children's open-choice playtime and occasionally large group-time discussions. Sometimes Richard sets the camera on a tripod in a given area of the classroom and lets it run. In this way he sees what goes on over time with a play project. He recalls two boys who came into his kindergarten without preschool experiences or much contact with other children. Both boys were limited in their social negotiation strategies, and both chose to play in the block corner nearly every day. Richard videotaped their play periodically over two months, documenting on videotape their progress from grabbing blocks and shouting "Mine!" to cooperative constructive play projects.

He often tapes play in the housekeeping area as well. Because Richard does not speak Korean, he is frequently at a loss to discover the content of some of the children's dramatic play sequences. With videotape as a tool, he is able to record sequences of play and then show them to a colleague who speaks Korean. She helps him to determine both the content and developmental level of the play he has taped.

"Letting the tape run" is also a strategy that Richard uses to assess what happens "on the periphery" of his classroom, and to plan curriculum accordingly. He observes and reflects on what the camera picks up. He often invites the children to watch some of the tapes and solve the problems they reveal. For example, Richard noted that some of the block and manipulative accessories were not being used much by the children. Through the videotape, it was revealed that the children seemed to have difficulty taking out the materials and putting them away. The class watched the tape together and some of the children explained their frustrations as they watched. They brainstormed a new way of storing the materials in the future.

Interview Children About Their Play.
Another technique that Richard developed is interviewing children about their play during playtime. He circulates through the room with the camera, and children explain their constructive play projects, science experiments, or dramatic play. For example:

During one play period, Juan described the three-story house he built of Cuisenaire rods while he and Richard conversed in Spanish. In the housekeeping area, a group of children had opened a restaurant and took Richard's order for spaghetti, writing his order on a clipboard and using invented spelling.

Richard checked in with children at various stages of their play. Richard's tape showed that Amanda and Jerry persisted for 45 minutes in making "magic potions," proudly reciting their newest ingredients each time they were interviewed.

He recorded Juan and Marty arguing over their block play early in the hour, then returned much later to two smiling boys peeping out of a structure. "You wanted to build a firehouse and you wanted to build an office. What did you finally decide?" asked Richard. "A police," announced Marty and they proudly showed off their telephone for "when people call 911" on the desk they built.

ASSESSING PLAY AS PLAY

One of the major points of this book is that there is a reciprocal relationship between the development of play and the development of other aspects of cognitive and social-emotional functioning in childhood. Therefore, although play serves as a context for assessing the development of such qualities as representational thinking, emerging literacy, problem-solving strategies, and mathematical concepts, the development of play as play in a variety of contexts also concerns teachers of young children.

Smilansky (1968) developed a system for viewing children's sociodramatic play that is widely used for assessing young children. Sociodramatic play might appear in several contexts, such as the housekeeping area, around the climbing structure, in the sandbox, or with the blocks. In all contexts the features of sociodramatic play that mark social, linguistic, and cognitive complexity are the focus of assessment. The six components of Smilansky's system for evaluating play complexity appear in Table 6.5. Sophisticated sociodramatic play of preschool and primary-grade children includes all of these elements in good measure. Children's developing complexity in their play may be traced through anecdotal observations or videotaping of dramatic play episodes.

For example, in Kathy's kindergarten class, two children, Amanda and Curt, spent much of their time in the housekeeping area arguing over who would use objects such as the toy telephone or the teapot. Both children's capacities to perform make-believe transformations were unsophisticated according to Smilansky's scale. In story play activities that Kathy offered three times a week, Amanda and Curt watched as others used gestures to represent imaginary objects, and tried it themselves as actors in story play productions. Kathy modeled for them the use of blocks for a variety of pretend objects, as she guided the resolution of their play disputes. After six weeks, Kathy repeated her play observations using the Smilansky scale and determined that both children had made progress in their use of make-believe props for play.

Although the Smilansky scale is the most concise assessment of symbolic play that we have found, teachers who care to look in more detail at the kind

Table 6.5
Complexity of Children's Play

Benchmarks	Evaluation/Date	Play Examples
Using Make-Believe Roles		
Children declare their roles ("I'm the the firefighter.") and engage in behavior consistent with that role (hosing down a pretend fire).	**Not yet**___ **Occasionally** _10–18_ **Consistently**___	Sandy announces "I'll be baby—you're the sister." "Help me, sister! I'm stuck!"
Using Make-Believe Props		
Children use objects to represent as he other objects (a block for a walkie-talkie); gestures or words to represent pretend action ("Whoosh! Whoosh!" while pretending to hose a fire), and/or verbalize a pretend situation ("Pretend the baby was trapped in the house").	**Not yet**___ **Occasionally** _2–13_ **Consistently**___	"9-1-1 please," says Zack as he picks up a block and hold it to his ear. "We have a fire!"
Using Make-Believe Episodes		
Make-believe play is coordinated into an elaborated episode ("Call the ambulance. This baby is really hurt bad.")	**Not yet**___ **Occasionally**___ **Consistently**___	
Persistence		
Children sustain their dramatic princesses play over time (5 minutes of more sustained play for preschoolers and kindergartners. 20 minutes for first and second graders and even continue story lines over several days' time)	**Not yet**___ **Occasionally**___ **Consistently** _1–25_	Selena and Chris play for a week, each day making more rooms for their castle out of blocks and playdough.
Social Interaction		
Two or more children are engaged in enacting a play episode.	**Not yet**___ **Occasionally**___ **Consistently**___	
Verbal Communication		
Children use words to communicate make-believe transformations in play and to "direct" the play, by assigning roles or planning story sequences ("I'll be the ambulance driver, and you give me the baby").	**Not yet**___ **Occasionally**___ **Consistently**___	

Sources: Based on *The Effects of Sociodramatic Play on Disadvantaged Preschool Children* by S. Smilansky, 1968, New York: Wiley. *Facilitating Play: A Medium for Promoting Cognitive, Socioemotional, and Academic Development in Young Children* by S. Smilansky and L. Sheftaya, 1990, Gaithersburg, MD: Psychosocial and Educational Publications.

of play children engage in and its relationship to language might also wish to use the play complexity instrument described by Sylva, Roy, and Painter in their 1980 study *Child Watching at Play-groups and Nursery School.*

Reynolds and Jones (1997), in their work on "master players," also present a scheme for assessing the sophistication of play. They found that children who were skilled at pretend play with others coped effectively with social constraints, showed mutuality in their interactions, added new elements to play, and were able to see patterns or to structure play for themselves and others.

The Penn Interactive Play Scale (PIPPS) is an instrument developed for teachers to assess children's interactive skill and social competence in play. In contrast to other measures to assess play as play, the PIPPS was specifically designed to be responsive to the strengths in the play of young children who live in urban environments characterized by poverty. Head Start teachers, parents, and children were involved in the development of this assessment. The PIPPS guides teachers in identifying techniques that children use to sustain play with one another. It includes descriptors for positive play interaction such as sharing ideas, leadership, helping, and inclusive behaviors. Descriptors for negative play or disruption include starting fights or arguments, refusal to share or take turns, and physical and verbal aggression. A third factor labeled "disconnection" in play is characterized by behaviors that indicate nonparticipation in play, such as aimless wandering, refusal of invitations to play, and unhappy demeanor (Fantuzzo et al., 1995).

Rubin and his colleagues developed a system for combining Piaget's and Parten's levels of play (Rubin, 1980; Rubin, Maioni, & Hornung, 1976). They nested Piaget's categories of functional, constructive, dramatic, and games with rules within Parten's social categories of solitary, parallel, and group play (Figure 6.1). In their research, Rubin and his colleagues point out that play sophistication ranges from the simplest combination, solitary functional, to the most complex, group games with rules.

Figure 6.1
Stages of Cognitive Complexity of Play Nested Within Categories of Social Play

Solitary Play	Parallel Play	Group Play
functional	functional	functional
constructive	constructive	constructive
dramatic	dramatic	dramatic
games with rules	games with rules	games with rules

Source: Adapted from "Free Play Behaviors in Middle- and Lower-Class Preschoolers: Parten & Piaget Revisited" by K. Rubin, T. L. Maioni, and M. Hornung, 1976, *Child Development, 47,* pp. 414–419.

In chapter 11, we describe the detailed analysis of social play discourse that helps teachers to assess children's intentions and goals for play. In chapter 8, we discuss how longitudinal analysis of story play provides teachers information about the development of children's play and their concepts of literacy over time.

DEFINING THE PURPOSES OF ASSESSMENT

Assessment of children's progress is a complicated and multifaceted issue in early childhood education. While most teachers agree that the primary purpose of assessment is to inform their professional judgment about curriculum, other purposes of assessment frequently cloud this goal. Adding to and sometimes supplanting the primary purpose of assessment to determine individual strengths and approaches to learning are recent initiatives at local, state, and national levels to assess the progress of young children on expectations for learning from preschool through the primary grades (Meier, 2000; Seefeldt, 2005; Wien, 2004; Wortham, 2005).

Following the Federal No Child Left Behind Act of 2001, early childhood educators across the United States began discussing the implications of this legislation for the assessment of young children. Policy groups formalized the discussion. The National Early Childhood Assessment Panel (Shepard, Kagan, & Wurtz, 1998) outlined four major purposes of assessment for young children:

1. To inform the teaching-learning process for children and their teachers
2. To identify children in need of special education services
3. To inform program evaluation and staff development
4. To focus on accountability for students, teachers, and schools

The first two of these purposes are focused on the teaching-learning process. These provide a natural context for play-centered assessment. The third purpose, serving program evaluation and staff development needs, also links to play through evaluation of the learning environment for play and the observed and self-identified needs of teachers to improve their skills at orchestrating play. Communication with parents regarding the processes and outcomes of play-centered curriculum also relates to this purpose.

However, the fourth purpose, "high stakes" accountability, is not a good fit for play-centered curriculum and assessment, nor is it a fit for children aged 3 to 8. The National Early Childhood Assessment Panel recommends that the standardized tests that characterize such high stakes assessment be postponed until the end of third grade and preferably until fourth grade. As we discuss in chapter 1, when the results of group measures for accountability are used to make decisions regarding individual children, teachers, or schools, the ethical issues are serious. The NAEYC/NAECS/SDE position statement on Early Learning Standards (2003) notes, "assessment and accountability systems should be used to improve practices and services, and should not be used to rank, sort, or penalize young children" (p. 7).

Because teachers, administrators, and policymakers use standardized assessment to evaluate programs and to come to decisions about groups of children, these assessments are by their nature designed to be cost- and time-efficient. The assessment instruments selected frequently reduce complex capabilities to a single score that may be interpreted readily by those who are not educators (Pellegrini, 1998; Shepard, 2000; Shepard, Kagan, & Wurtz, 1998; Wesson, 2001).

Features of Play-Centered Assessment

In contrast to standardized tests, are classroom-based or "performance-based" assessments that are centered on children's play. This kind of assessment involves complex and ongoing measures that focus on individual styles and paces of learning. In addition, play-centered assessment serves as a means of learning and reflection for the student as well as the teacher. If children are to develop the ability to reflect on their own developing concepts and take responsibility for their own learning, their participation in their own assessment process is critical.

We also need to observe and measure the long-term dispositions about learning and thinking developed during children's early years: How does the way that a skill such as identifying short and long vowel sounds is learned relate to children's enjoyment of reading and their interest in literacy? Play allows us to see the cognitive as well as the emotional aspects of children's development and the ways in which they are connected.

Play-centered assessment also naturally includes social-moral development in addition to the more traditional questions of cognition and attitudes toward learning. In a society that is increasingly diverse in its values and perspectives, the development of children's abilities to negotiate, to understand the perspectives of others, and to communicate effectively becomes essential. Play-centered assessment helps teachers shift their thinking to see social-moral development as a priority on a par with cognition and motivation, and offers a window to document progress and plan curriculum in these areas (DeVries & Zan, 1996; Kamii, 1990; Leavitt & Eheart, 1991).

Play is the window to view both age-appropriate development and individual development. In play, teachers may discern whether children's understandings of concepts such as correspondence or classification fall within a range expected of a given age group. They may determine how many children in their group exhibit complex sociodramatic play according to Smilansky's guidelines, or how many need particular orchestration strategies to enhance their development of symbolic thought.

Play also illuminates the development of individual children. It allows teachers to notice and appreciate the interests and values a child brings from home, and the special kind of intelligence he or she may use to express thoughts and feelings (Clyde, 1994; Graue, 1998; Himley & Carini, 2000; Zimmerman & Zimmerman, 2000).

For example, in one second-grade classroom, Juan Pablo, a recent arrival from Costa Rica, spends his playtime drawing detailed soccer games on paper, talking to himself in Spanish, and animating the imaginary soccer games with sounds and comments made by the players. His teacher can see that Juan Pablo's understanding of the game of soccer is a special window through which she can communicate with him.

Play and Assessments of Children with Special Needs

Another purpose of assessment in programs for young children is identification and intervention for young children with disabilities. Transdisciplinary, play-centered assessments are being incorporated in some early childhood special education programs (Bergen, 1994, 2003; Eisert & Lamorey, 1996; Sheridan, Foley, & Radlinski, 1995). There is growing awareness among researchers, teachers, and parents of children with special needs that play-centered assessments provide valuable information regarding all children's development, and that traditional standardized assessment tools present a limited picture of children's abilities. For example, many standardized tests do not allow the examiner to change items or the order of item presentation which may prove difficult for all young children, both those with typical development and those with atypical developmental patterns.

A number of researchers have developed play-centered scales that are appropriate for determining eligibility for special education services and making program decisions. For example, Eisert and Lamorey (1996) report on research using their Play Assessment Scale (PAS). The scale includes 45 items that measure both spontaneous and elicited play development in infants and preschool children. They emphasize that play-centered assessments allow us to observe children with special needs using their skills functionally in natural environments.

Van der Kooij (1989a) developed two scales appropriate for use with school-age children. The scale consists of three concepts related to play: intrinsic motivation, internal locus of control, and suspension of reality. Van der Kooij's Mental Activity Scale provides information about a child's cognitive functioning during play.

Myers, McBride, and Peterson (1996) point out that practitioners have been adopting transdisciplinary, play-centered assessments because parents and educational professionals rate them highly, even though it is a relatively new area for research. Myers et al. (1996) report that their assessments yielded a high rate of agreement with developmental ratings, and were highly time-efficient, taking fewer days to complete. In addition, they indicate that professionals found that play-centered assessments provided more information than standardized assessments on communication, social skills, and motor skills. Other early childhood special educators present guidelines for creating Individualized Educational Plans (IEPs) for young children that focus on developmental frameworks including play (Edmiaston, Dolezal, Doolittle, Erickson, & Merritt, 2000).

Sheridan et al. (1995) offer a comprehensive scheme for assessing play and strategies for supporting the development of play in children with disabilities. Detailed checklists of play behaviors, patterns that limit play, and case studies describing the application of their "supportive play" model make this an excellent resource for teachers of all young children who are concerned about supporting a range of individual play styles and levels of sophistication. Koplow's (1996) excellent case studies, play therapy techniques and discussion of play that supports emotional development in the classroom is another resource for teachers who seek to assess the play of young children and its developmental motifs.

Using Videotape for Assessing Special Needs.   Richard has found that video records of children's behavior have been very helpful in documenting his assessments of children who have special educational needs. In one instance, the parents of Maureen, a child whom Richard believed needed special help, refused to believe that their daughter needed to be referred for special education. Richard documented Maureen's behavior at group time where her need to be touching Richard at all times was evident. He documented Maureen's play with other children in which she would frequently lash out and hit others. Because Maureen was an only child and their home was at the outskirts of this rural community, she had had few playmates. Consequently, her parents had little opportunity to compare their daughter's behavior with that of other children her age. The videotape helped Richard and Maureen's parents agree on special needs assessment for Maureen and helped them to plan some strategies together that would smooth Maureen's relationships with others.

COMMUNICATING WITH PARENTS ABOUT PLAY AND ASSESSMENT

As noted in the above example, play is a valuable tool teachers can use in communicating with parents about their children's progress. It illustrates for parents the individual flavor of their child's expression. Play anecdotes also offer an opportunity for the teacher to explain what is being learned in the play-based curriculum as examples of the child's progress are cited. Brandon, the child in the opening anecdote in chapter 1, spends part of his 26th day in kindergarten building a maze for Fluffy, the pet rat, and then represents his play with a map. He gets carried away with firefighting fantasies, and some of the aggressive behavior his preschool teacher saw comes out in his play with others. Brandon's parents will appreciate hearing of his progress in map making, and of the complexity of his maze. They will enjoy hearing about his nurturing concern for Fluffy. They may be able to help the teacher understand his aggressive outbursts of behavior at school by comparing his behavior at home and at school.

The study by Myers et al. (1996) found that play-centered assessment may increase parent involvement. Parents are an integral part of some assessments, and may physically support a child or help elicit responses. This study also demonstrated that parents felt more comfortable in seeking information from professionals during play-centered assessments and perceived the identified goals as important.

In Richard's K–1 combination class, videotape became useful in giving parents an opportunity to observe their children in particular and the whole curriculum in general. Twice a year, he prepares a videotape with edited segments of children's activities and progress. At "Back to School Night" in the fall, he shows parents scenes from a typical day in his classroom and examples of play

Play-centered assessment may increase parent involvement.

projects children have done in previous years. At "Open House" in the spring, Richard shows video clips of children's block constructions, dramatic play sequences, story plays, science experiments, and other events and projects that he has captured on tape. He creates a video "yearbook" for children and their families from clips of classroom life throughout the year so that children may keep a permanent record of their kindergarten experience.

WHEN TEACHERS TALK

School Readiness and Academic Standards

The notion of *readiness* to enter kindergarten, preschool, or the next grade and the accompanying debate regarding subject area curriculum standards and retention is complicated. These ideas emerge frequently in communication with teachers of young children, parents, administrators, and policy makers. Debates about what expectations for concepts, skills, dispositions, and behaviors are age- and individual-appropriate, as well as tuned to family and community norms and expectations, are exacerbated by recent trends in early education.

One of these is the current trend to push didactic, narrowly focused curriculum into lower grades, including kindergarten. Many early childhood educators believe this is closely linked to the "high stakes" testing prevalent in public schools which make scores on standardized tests the primary if not the sole measure of individual and school success (Andersen, 1998; Graue, 1998; Kohn, 2001; Meisels, 2000; Wesson, 2001; Wien, 2004).

Linked to this trend for didactic, narrow curriculum is the practice of "redshirting"—a term borrowed from school athletics, in which families keep children out of kindergarten for social reasons (Graue & Diperna, 2000). Some families then expect programs designed for 5-year-olds to more closely resemble those for 6-year-olds when their children enter school a year "late." We believe this kind of curriculum inflation distorts the purpose of kindergarten as a beginning formal schooling experience.

Another issue is equitable access to schooling. The majority of states have no laws for kindergarten attendance, and kindergarten and first-grade curriculum standards frequently do not account for children who have not had access to preschool or whose families choose to keep their children within the family rather than send them to school at age 3, 4, or even 5 (Graue & Diperna, 2000). For example, one kindergarten teacher, whose year-round school program began in July, had mostly 4-year-olds enrolled, and only 4 of 20 children had attended preschool. Yet the curriculum standards for assessment more closely resembled those appropriate for the end of first grade, or 6- and 7-year-olds.

Curriculum standards, as well as widely varying criteria for readiness, reflect a range of assumptions about child development and family and cultural values and expectations (Ballenger, 1999; Graue & Diperna, 2000; Greenfield, 1994, 1999; Joshi, 2005; Yang & McMullen, 2003). Varying interpretations of the term readiness begin early in the schooling experience to position some children disadvantageously. In contrast, a developmental approach to school entry views children as coming to school with their own strengths and styles of learning, and turns the question of readiness to one that asks, "Are the schools ready for all learners?" (Graue & Diperna, 2000; Hand & Nourot, 1999). In a thoughtful review, Murphey and Burns (2002) identified community notions related to school readiness that include separation from caregivers, play with other children and appropriate interactions with adults, social problem-solving skills, appropriate expression of emotions, flexibility in adapting to transitions, persistence, enthusiasm, and curiosity. In our own conversations with teachers and families, we have found that these social and dispositional competencies are at the top of the list for readiness criteria for children as they enter kindergarten.

Also critical to all of these assessment issues is the notion of time. Time for children to inhabit their classrooms, develop relationships, competencies, and dispositions, as well as time for them to develop their concepts of themselves as learners and meaning makers is the missing element in the ubiquitous press to have children perform more and sooner (Elkind, 1990, 2003; Graue, 1998, 2001). As Almy (2000) wisely advised, the adults in children's lives are the ones responsible for ensuring that children do indeed have time to play and to enjoy childhood in the twenty-first century.

TENSIONS REGARDING PLAY-CENTERED CURRICULUM AND EARLY LEARNING STANDARDS

In addition to questions regarding school readiness, the adoption of curriculum standards for programs serving young children presents multiple challenges. In our review of state and national standards we find that many are consistent with play-centered curriculum. However, tensions are created between basic principles of developmentally appropriate practice and the simplistic skills and concepts listed in some standards documents. Honoring children's interests and choices about learning and offering time for exploration, play, and reflection in order to construct meaningful knowledge are frequently threatened by pressures for teachers to isolate skills and concepts and teach in a didactic fashion. Another serious concern is the damage to children's self-esteem and dispositions to learn as side effects of these measures (Meisels, 2000; Wien, 2004).

Celeste, a kindergarten–first-grade teacher in an urban district comments,

"When my principal visits my classroom, she wants to see evidence that all the children have learned the concepts and skills and demonstrated their knowledge in the same way. This goes against everything I know about how young children approach learning. At the beginning of the year, she insisted that they all complete the same workbook pages, but after meeting with the primary grade team she is coming around to understanding development of 5- to 7-year-olds more deeply. She's open to our collecting data in a systematic way for portfolios and documentation panels from our projects. I'm relieved because I felt like I couldn't teach simply using workbooks to structure and evaluate the success of my curriculum."

A related issue is the narrowing of curriculum, a trend increasingly reported by teachers in light of high-stakes assessment pressures.

Pamela and Ben are kindergarten teachers in a rural school district that serves many English language learners. They have taken a strong stand with their administrators regarding the "sacredness" of their project and play time each day.

"We do more small group directed play early in the day," explains Ben. "We focus on specific skills such as phonemic awareness using rhymes and songs, and letter and numeral formation using mazes and patterns, but we have sixty minutes of play time as well. Then the children are free to make choices about their learning and we have many opportunities for block building, cooking, painting, clay, puppetry, and dramatic play that have always been the "bread and butter" of good kindergarten programs. We also offer projects such as our Bubble Unit that integrate social studies, science, math, literacy, and the arts."

Pam continues, "Teachers we know in south county have given up nearly all their art, science, and social studies experiences to focus on preparing children to take tests in math and literacy. It seems like such a disservice to everyone." She notes, "The combination of free-flowing play and small-group teaching and assessment gives us both very focused and spontaneous information about each child. It's a critical time of the day for our English language learners to develop both receptive and expressive language. I also think kids will take more risks when they are creating and solving their own problems in play. For example, Gary loved our Bubbles Project. His enthusiasm inspired him to measure his bubbles everyday for a week and to record their widths. A month ago he out and out refused to try to write any numerals—context is everything!" ✒

SUMMARY AND CONCLUSION

In this chapter we have looked at some of the ways that play episodes inform teachers in their efforts to assess children's progress. Teachers' anecdotal observations of children's play and portfolios of the products of play offer an ongoing record of children's development in cognitive, linguistic, and social-emotional domains.

Play-centered assessment paints a portrait of the "whole child," as individuals express their unique views of the world through play. Play-centered assessment is a means for teachers to evaluate the success of their curriculum planning, to see if children replay the concepts and skills embedded in the curriculum and use them in their own play. Play-centered assessment is appropriate for use with all children, and may have special advantages for assessing the development of children with special needs. Play provides information that informs teachers' future designs for curriculum and serves as a means of evaluating the progress of groups of children as well as the progress of individuals.

We have discussed multiple means of collecting information on children's play, including forms for organizing anecdotal observations, checklists of age-appropriate development, and audiotaping and videotaping techniques. We have looked at ways to assess how play contributes to development in traditional academic areas such as literacy and problem solving. We have also looked at ways to assess play as play, to highlight the reciprocal relationship of play to other aspects of early childhood development.

In this chapter we have addressed some of the major issues surrounding the use of standardized tests for young children and contrasted these methods with the more spontaneous, contextualized assessment that play provides in classrooms for young children.

Finally, we have discussed some of the ways that teachers use play-centered assessment to communicate with parents. Using observational records, photographs, and audiotaped or videotaped samples of children's experiences in the classroom helps parents understand what their children are learning through their play as well as appreciate their children's unique styles of development and expression.

Our view is that play-centered curriculum is the avenue that offers the opportunity for children to develop and learn in ways led by children's own strengths and interests as they enter school. Careful observation, orchestration, and documentation of children's play across a variety of contexts build the foundation for more formal instruction in traditional school subject areas such as mathematics, literacy, science, social studies, and the arts, as children develop and construct new knowledge in more formal school contexts.

SUGGESTED RESOURCES

Chen, J. (Ed.). (1998). *Project spectrum vol. 2: Early learning activities*. New York: Teachers College Press.

Chen, J., Krechevsky, M., & Viens, J. (with Isberg, E.) (1998). *Building on children's strengths: The experience of Project Spectrum* (Vol. 1). New York: Teachers College Press.

Genishi, C. (Ed.). (1992). *Ways of assessing children and curriculum: stories of early childhood practice* New York: Teachers College Press.

This book presents numerous classroom examples that illustrate how teachers can use alternative assessments to document children's development. Many illustrations demonstrate assessment techniques for a play-centered curriculum. The authors also consider multiple, often novel, methods of assessing children from diverse backgrounds and with varied special needs.

Helm, J., Beneke, S., & Steinheimer, K. (1998). *Windows on learning: Documenting young children's work.* New York: Teachers College Press.

This book provides a detailed, step-by-step description of documentation assessment, as well as an engaging case study of a post office project in a primary-grade classroom. The accompanying forms for assessment, including checklists and templates for documentation, are practical and easy to understand.

Himley, M., & Carini, P. (Eds.) (2000). *From another angle: Children's strengths and school standards.* New York: Teachers College Press.

The "descriptive review" process and the many examples that the authors provide inspire teachers to think beyond traditional means for assessing children in the elementary grades and to document interests and dispositions as well as competencies revealed in children's behaviors, including play.

Kamii, C. (Ed.). (1990). *No achievement testing in the early grades: The games grown-ups play.* Washington, DC: National Association for the Education of Young Children.

This book offers numerous perspectives on the assessment of young children. It considers the viewpoints of educators, from teachers to state departments of education, offering arguments against standardized testing and suggesting strategies for authentic assessments in language and mathematics.

Krechevsky, M. (Ed.). (1998). *Project Spectrum vol. 3: Preschool assessment handbook.* New York: Teachers College Press.

This set of books based on Project Spectrum is a comprehensive resource for teachers who wish to understand the multifaceted nature of play, as well as other forms of representation in designing and assessing curriculum.

Sheridan, M., Foley, G., & Radlinski, S. (1995). *Using the supportive play model: Individualized intervention in early childhood practice.* New York: Teachers College Press.

This resource describes the supportive play model for assessing and orchestrating the play of children with disabilities. Detailed developmental checklists and case studies provide a valuable resource for teachers who are challenged to interpret and support a range of play behavior in their classrooms.

Wortham, S. (2005). *Assessment in early childhood education* (4th ed.). Upper Saddle River, NJ: Merrill/Prentice Hall.

This book explores a range of assessments for young children, including standardized tests, and more naturalistic forms such as observational scales, checklists, and portfolios. Many examples and discussion of the strengths and weaknesses of each approach make this a practical tool.

7

Mathematics in the Play-Centered Curriculum

The blocks have arrived! After weeks of anticipation, the students in Virginia's first-grade class get their first opportunity to create with blocks. Some of the 27 children have never played with unit blocks before. Until this year, the school's three first grade classes had no blocks. Virginia is the first of the first-grade teachers in the school to use them.

Chhoun runs to the blocks purposefully. He builds a two-tiered structure and divides it into symmetrical sections. Several towers add an interesting touch of asymmetry. In front of the structure he builds four small, separate constructions that look like animals. He groups three to his right and a single one to his left. Leah and Becky work together to build a castle. It has a triangular base, so that one looks into the structure as if looking onto a stage. They also emphasize asymmetry by adding a second tier on one side. ✆

Virginia was surprised at the children's skillfulness in block building and their sense of design. She wondered about their previous experiences with block building. When discussing their constructions, Virginia emphasized their use of balance and symmetry, and how they "decorated" the more regular, symmetrical structures with small shapes to make them a bit asymmetrical. She pointed out that the limited number of blocks available sometimes led to exchanges in which children discussed issues of fairness concerning the number of blocks each child could take. Children traded one longer block for two shorter blocks. They counted the total number of blocks different children had. They searched for particular triangular or cylindrical blocks to complete their structure or provide greater stability.

As Virginia's comments indicate, block play provides opportunities for children to consolidate and extend their mathematical thinking. In constructing with blocks, children deal with relationships involving concepts that are basic to mathematics during the early childhood years, such as space (geometry), quantity (number), measurement, and patterns. Blocks have always been a favorite play material of young children. They have long been recognized by early childhood educators and researchers for their appropriateness in supporting the development of mathematical abilities within a playful context, fostering the development of the whole child (e.g., Chalufour & Worth, 2004; Geist, 2001; Hirsch, 1996; Reifel & Yeatman, 1991). In this chapter, we consider how the play-centered curriculum supports the development of children's mathematical interests and understandings.

THE PLAYFUL NATURE OF MATHEMATICS

Mathematicians have often written about the playful, creative aspects of mathematics. Holton and his colleagues (2001) write that, "Mathematical play involves pushing the limits of the situation and following thoughts and ideas wherever they may lead . . . it is designed to allow complete freedom on the part of the solver to wander over the mathematical landscape" (Holton, Ahmed, Williams, & Hill, 2001, p. 403). In this playful spirit, mathematicians creatively generate new ideas and experiment to solve problems.

This description of mathematical play in the work of adult mathematicians is also characteristic of the play of young children as they explore the mathematical dimensions of their environments. The vignettes in the following sections illustrate how spontaneous and guided play foster dispositions central to doing mathematics, such as curiosity and the desire to explore and experiment. The vignettes show that mathematical processes such as problem solving and inquiry involve "wandering over the mathematical landscape" as well as trying a particular path to reach a solution.

MATHEMATICAL CONCEPTS IN THE PLAY-CENTERED CURRICULUM

Through play, children begin to construct understandings of many basic mathematical concepts. In the following sections, we discuss some mathematical concepts related to spatial relationships and quantity that begin to develop during early childhood and provide illustrations of how typical spontaneous play activities help children develop, consolidate, and extend their understanding of these concepts.

Subsequent sections in this chapter focus on how teacher-guided interventions in play as well as teacher-initiated or directed mathematics activities can complement spontaneous play activities in order to provide a well-balanced mathematics curriculum.

Spatial Relationships

We begin with concepts that involve spatial relationships. These form a foundation from which more sophisticated geometric concepts can develop as children grow. Spatial relationships and basic geometric concepts are just as fundamental to children's understanding of the physical world as numerical concepts are. As we observe children's interactions with their surroundings, we find that much of young children's experiences involve spatial relationships; yet, most adults—and mathematics texts—emphasize children's understandings of numerical concepts.

Young children often explore and play with their spatial environment. As infants, they crawl around and over furniture. Later, they construct mazes with pillows or obstacle courses with chairs. They roll down hills, slick slides, and beanbag chairs. They play with their bodies' shapes as they dance, their round, fluid movements becoming linear and staccato. Perhaps this is the first awareness of spatial relationships—awareness of one's body and its environment. As adults, we see that this fundamental exploration and play involve basic concepts of spatial relationships. These include proximity, enclosed versus open space, vertical versus horizontal movements, and numerous shapes. From this example, we see that such conceptual development takes time, literally from infancy to adulthood.

Proximity.   Proximity refers to the closeness or separation between objects. When one object is near another, we can say that it is in close proximity.

> Janet paints a tree right next to the house she has just finished painting. She paints grass around it so that the green fills in the space between the tree and the house. In one spot, the tree almost touches the house. After mistakenly painting a small section of the house green, Janet selects a narrower brush that her teacher has made available and carefully traces around the area between the house and the tree. Through this activity, she is learning about the proximity of the tree to the house. ✆

Vertical and Horizontal.   When something is vertical, it is perpendicular (upright) to the ground or another reference point. When something is horizontal, it is parallel to the ground or another reference point.

> Tomás uses red and blue pegs to make four horizontal rows of alternating colors across the pegboard. He then makes a brilliant strip of yellow pegs that runs vertically to the bottom of the pegboard. ✆

Shapes.   The concept of shape refers to the form of an object. Children frequently have experiences that involve regular shapes such as triangles, circles, and squares. These shapes are called Euclidean shapes. In this vignette, the children jointly develop a complex design, and their teacher responds to the children's curiosity.

> Together, Nick and Emma stretch rubber bands across the nails of a geoboard, making hexagons and octagons. Noticing the students' interest, their teacher first informally introduces the terms *hexagon* and *octagon*. When the children show interest in these unusual words, he explains the derivation of *hex* (meaning six) and *oct* (meaning eight). He then introduces more advanced pattern cards for the geoboard and suggests that they try making their own cards, as well. ✆

Children also have numerous experiences with irregular or non-Euclidean shapes. For example, 2-year-old Peggie delights in squeezing the light green playdough through her fingers. She then opens her hand and looks at the play dough form in her palm. It certainly is an irregular, though very interesting shape!

Relationships Involving Quantity

"Five little monkeys jumping on the bed. . . ." When people think about math, they generally think about relationships involving quantity. How many monkeys were jumping? What is the value of *x* if 6 times *x* equals 30?

In early childhood, children begin to develop an understanding of the many ways in which we take measure of our world. When we describe aspects of the physical world, we often use concepts that indicate how much there is (e.g., "That's too much milk.") or how many there are (e.g., "Six glasses of milk!").

Continuous Quantities. Continuous quantities refer to those objects whose amounts we don't count, like "a lot of milk" and "a little rice." Although preschool and kindergarten programs traditionally have included materials that foster the exploration of continuous quantities, such as sand, clay, water, and even mud, primary-grade teachers as well are recognizing the value of providing these special materials that playful people of all ages enjoy.

> Steve takes big handfuls of playdough to make giant hamburgers. He rolls out two large, circular forms, and exclaims, "These buns are still too small," and places the hamburger inside. ✇

Discrete Quantities. These are the objects whose amounts we count, like "seven cookies" or "three grains of rice." Discrete quantities are also called non-continuous quantities.

> In sustained, spontaneous play, Laurie, Sandra, and Marie are jointly exploring a collection of shells. They divide the collection into three sets of 26 shells each. They then begin to classify their sets (e.g., large, multicolored spiral and small, multicolored spiral). Linda, their second-grade teacher, notes that Marie, who knows little English, is participating enthusiastically and showing her understanding of the relationships between the supraordinate class, all multicolored spiral shells, and the subordinate classes, large and small multicolored spiral shells. ✇

Estimation. When children estimate, they form a judgment of the approximate quantity. They will use estimation processes throughout life to make preliminary judgments and to assess how reasonable an answer might be. For example, a fifth grader estimates that 31 times 33 is about 900. Therefore, if she gets the answer 10,230, she knows that there is an error in her calculation. In play-centered curricula, children have many opportunities to develop estimation abilities.

> Sandra says they need two big blocks. However, Melinda finds only small ones and returns to Sandra with an armful of five small blocks. ✇

Quantifiers.   When children are learning to deal with quantities, initial concepts include "some," "fewer," "all," and "none."

> Bradley selects all the red pegs. When none are left in the tray, he asks Cheryl if she has any red ones. "No," she answers, "none of these are red." ✇

Equalities and Inequalities.   At a young age, children develop the ability to make judgments as to whether two objects or groups are equal or unequal. Indeed, some children seem to spend much of their time focused on whether they have the same quantity of whatever it is that their classmates have.

> *Steve:*   "You took more red [playdough] than me."
>
> *Karen:*   "Well, I'm the grandma so I get more."

Seriation.   After children are able to sort objects by one property, for example, the color blue, they learn to order the objects according to "how much" of that property the objects have, for example, light blue to dark blue.

> A second-grade teacher has worked with the children to create flannel board cutouts of dolls of four different sizes, each having backpacks and objects of corresponding sizes that fit in the backpacks. Some children are intrigued by these multiple seriation problems and create others of their own, such as making cars of different sizes for the dolls to ride. ✇

Young children's construction of number concepts involving quantity develops over several years. Before children can truly understand number concepts, they begin to understand the concepts of one-to-one correspondence. They learn number names and to count by rote. They also learn the numerals that represent number concepts and begin to understand the difference between ordinal and cardinal numbers.

One-to-One Correspondence.   We begin with two sets of objects, such as paper dolls and paper umbrellas. If we place one umbrella next to each doll we have established one-to-one correspondence between the objects in the set of dolls and the objects in the set of umbrellas.

> Craig and Karen establish one-to-one correspondence between the four dolls in their chairs and the quantity of plates and utensils. ✇

> Tomás has placed the red and blue pegs in one-to-one correspondence in two horizontal rows. ✇

Number Names.   Number names are the names we use (in our language) to represent the number concepts.

> Maria tells Jason, "I got three, three buttons." Later, in playing in the housekeeping area, she talks to Rosa in Spanish, "Tengo tres, tres botones." ∅

Rote Counting.   Children first develop the skill to say the names of numbers in correct order without understanding the meaning of the number concepts or, consequently, the importance of the order. In rote counting, the order of numbers has no special significance, like the order of letter names when chanting "a, b, c, d. . . ."

> While filling a jar with cupfuls of water, Jeremy counts "five, six and seven, eight." (But the words do not correspond to the actions of either filling or pouring the cup.) ∅

Numerals.   Numerals refer to the notation or symbols we use to represent the number concept. The same number concept is represented by *15* and *XV.*

> Jeffrey sits outside next to the compact pile of weeds pulled from the garden. He bends a stem into different configurations, exclaiming, "It's a 7. . . . Look, now I put a foot on it and it's a 2!" ∅

> One of the girls in Kristin's first-grade class is seated at a desk, working by herself. She draws a picture of a woman with a bubble caption above her head. In the bubble she has printed the numerals in order from 1 to 21. When she notices Kristin looking at the picture, she explains that "she's counting in the picture." Then she begins to draw another picture of a counting lady. ∅

Ordinal Numbers.   Ordinal numbers indicate the place order of the object such as "the third child in line." They answer the question "Which one?"

> Alvin looks at the line forming behind him for turns on the new scooter. "I'm first!" he announces. ∅

Cardinal Numbers.   Cardinal numbers indicate the quantity of the set. They answer the question "How many?"

> Mary turns over a Candy Land game card: "I've got two yellows." ∅

> Two girls in Shelley's kindergarten class are playing with a flannel board. There are a dozen flannel pieces for the story. The girls divide

them evenly before beginning to make up their own story. They put out one piece for each girl until they both have six. ✆

Number Concepts.   When children truly develop concepts of number, they understand the relationships among numbers, for example, eight is "bigger" than seven. They also understand that a set of objects can be rearranged without changing the number of objects in the set.

> *Tomás:*   "I need three red ones to fill this line."
>
> *Karen:*   "We don't have three. We just have two."

Mathematics and Problem Solving

Most of the examples just described also involve problem solving. In building a symmetrical design with attribute blocks, Ricky adds a green triangle and a yellow hexagon to the right side and then must decide what to add to the left side. Tuan tries to glue a big piece of wood on top of several smaller ones. After the pile falls over several times, Tuan tries putting a larger piece on the bottom and finds that it works. Problem solving is frequently a social activity, as illustrated in the following example. In chapter 1 we described the activities of Lisa and Peter, busy wrapping packages at the post office, who were involved in estimating how much paper they needed to cover the package and figuring out how to solve the problem that arose when the sheets of paper were too small.

Problem Solving Is Basic to Mathematics.   The problems children face in their spontaneous play and everyday life situations are their own problems. Perhaps it is their ownership of these problems and the social nature of their play that contributes to the extraordinary competencies that Vygotsky saw in children's play which led him to hypothesize that play leads development (see chapter 2.)

MATHEMATICS IN THE EARLY CHILDHOOD INTEGRATED CURRICULUM

Our approach to math education parallels our approach to education in all the content areas. Developmentally appropriate programs are based on the understanding of mathematics as well as the understanding of children's development and interests. As we have noted, though adults sometimes think about students' learning as occurring in separate subject areas, young children's own subjective experiences are not limited to the activities of one subject area. Children participating in an engaging, inclusive activity experience no such

Playing "post office" reflects children's lives in a number-literate environment.

boundary; they don't think of themselves as being in "math land." Instead, they experience social interactions with lively communication and an involvement in thought processes related to a variety of areas, such as the arts, science, and literacy. This is one important rationale for considering the full continuum of play, from spontaneous play to play in which the more didactic curriculum is recast in children's play.

The Goal of Early Childhood Mathematics Education

In their joint position statement, *Early Childhood Mathematics: Promoting Good Beginnings,* the National Association for the Education of Young Children (NAEYC) and the National Council of Teachers of Mathematics (NCTM) (2002) explain that,

> Throughout the early years of life, children notice and explore mathematical dimensions of their world. They compare quantities, find patterns, navigate in space, and grapple with real problems such as balancing a tall block building or sharing a bowl of crackers fairly with a playmate. Mathematics helps children make sense of their world outside of school and helps them construct a solid foundation for success in school. (p. 1)

These national organizations emphasize that if we are to have mathematics programs that help children make sense of their world and construct a solid foundation for success in school, we must commit our efforts to supporting children's competencies in mathematics learning, just as we have in literacy. In setting goals for mathematics education in early childhood programs, *Early*

Childhood Mathematics: Promoting Good Beginnings includes important recommendations, some of which are included below:

1. Enhance children's natural interest in mathematics and their disposition to use it to make sense of their physical and social worlds . . .

2. Provide ample time, materials, and teacher support for children to engage in play, a context in which they explore and manipulate mathematical ideas with keen interest . . .

3. Build on children's experience and knowledge, including their family, linguistic, cultural, and community backgrounds; their individual approaches to learning; and their informal knowledge . . .

4. Base mathematics curriculum and teaching practices on knowledge of young children's cognitive, linguistic, physical, and social-emotional development . . .

5. Introduce mathematical concepts, methods, and language through a range of appropriate experiences and strategies. (pp. 4–7)

The Nature of Mathematics

Before delving deeper into our consideration of mathematics education and young children, we begin with a brief discussion of the nature of mathematics. Mathematical thinking involves dispositions such as curiosity, playful risk-taking, and experimentation.

Mathematics involves all three types of knowledge that Piaget described: physical knowledge, social knowledge, and logical-mathematical knowledge. Mathematical thinking involves physical knowledge because we use mathematics to describe relationships in the real world; for example, these tomatoes weigh 3 pounds and cost $1.29 per pound.

Mathematical thinking also involves social knowledge, information we learn directly from others. English-speaking children learn the number name *seven*, just as French-speaking children learn the number name *sept*. Not only do children in different places call numbers, shapes, and mathematical procedures by different names, this socially constructed knowledge also includes a particular way of seeing the world. For example, most people in the world use the metric system for measurement. Young children learn that their weight is measured in kilograms, the distance to school is measured in kilometers, and the amount of milk in a container is measured in liters. Procedures for arithmetic operations also differ from culture to culture, sometimes based on differences in systems for counting (Ma, 1999; Saxe, 1991).

The basis of mathematics is logical-mathematical thinking because solutions to mathematical problems involve the logical relationships that our mind constructs rather than the information our senses observe (physical knowledge) or that we obtain from others (social knowledge). Over time, each of us constructs our own mathematical concepts with help or interactions with others, and based upon our culture and time in history. In this way, children reinvent for themselves what adults and older peers in their social environment already know (Kamii with DeClark, 2000; Kamii with Housman, 2000). When we think mathematically, we use our logical abilities to solve problems.

What do we mean by logical-mathematical thought? We know that Sally is taller than Marie. We know that Marie is taller than Melody. Even if we have never seen Sally and Melody together, we know that Sally is taller than Melody. We understand the relationship of Sally's height and Melody's height as a logical relationship that "must be." As adult thinkers, we are certain of our answer without seeing the physical evidence. We do not have to see Sally, Marie, and Melody standing next to each other. Young children have not yet constructed this logical way of thinking about problems involving height, volume, or area, or even ideas that seem as simple to us as the idea of number (see chapter 13).

Logical-mathematical thought is the foundation of our understanding of many aspects of the physical world: How many floor tiles will we need to cover the kitchen? How many miles per gallon does our car get? Throughout childhood, children's grasp of relationships involving mathematical concepts develops. Children, too, grapple with problems requiring applications of logical-mathematical thought. How many sheets of paper do we need so each student in the class can have four? How many forks do we need to set a table with four places? Logical relationships are at the heart of all mathematical thinking—all everyday problem solving.

The early childhood years are marked by major developments in several areas of logical mathematical thought. For example, in a study that focused on very young children (ages 1 to 4), Kamii, Miyakawa, and Kato (2004) examined the development of young children's logical mathematical thought in the context of typical activities such as block building and painting. Based on their analysis of these playful interactions, Kamii and her colleagues identified five types of logical mathematical thought that Piaget described (see Table 7.1).

Logical-operational thought does not emerge at once, like a butterfly emerging from a cocoon, but occurs from infancy into adulthood. Like studying the metamorphosis of a butterfly within the cocoon, we can assess evidence of the many small changes in a child's development. (See, for example, the review of the research by Baroody, 2000). Three- to 5-year-olds might delight in showing that they can arrange four "candles" in multiple ways on the "cake" they have made out of sand and know they still have four. Older children attain a more mature understanding when they realize, in this example, that no matter how large the number is, merely rearranging the "candles" does not alter the number.

Table 7.1
Five Logical Mathematical Relationships

Type	Example
1. Classification relationships	"Smocks" vs. "ordinary clothes"
2. Seriation relationships	The "big" vs. the "small" paintbrushes
3. Number relationships	"Three paints at the easel"
4. Spatial relationships	The paint drips down the paper
5. Temporal relationships	Wet paint takes time to dry

Source: Based on "The Development of Logico-mathematical Knowledge in a
Block-building Activity at Ages 1–4," by C. Kamii, Y. Miyakawa, and Y. Kato, 2004,
Journal of Research in Childhood Education, 19(1), p. 46.

Geist (2001) suggests that it is useful to consider mathematical understandings as "emergent," just as the development of literacy. When early childhood educators and other adults attempt to rush the processes of development, young children's lack of a firm foundation can lead to frustration and damaged dispositions not only in preschool and the primary grades but later on, as well (Helm & Katz, 2001). The development of basic concepts such as number sense and abilities such as problem solving is a complex process that takes time and experience. The Joint Position Statement of the National Association for the Education of Young Children and the National Council of Teachers of Mathematics (2002) emphasizes that teachers of young children must take time to provide a variety of strategies, activities, and materials. If we are to address the needs of all students, we need to provide adequate time for rich experiences that draw upon children's interests and strengths.

Children often show that they have informal knowledge that they have developed from their everyday experiences rather than from direct mathematics instruction. Young children also show that they can use informal strategies to solve problems (Baroody & Wilkens, 1999; Geist, 2001; Ginsberg, Inoue, & Seo, 1999; Kamii, Miyakawa, & Kato, 2004; Macmillan, 1998). Informal knowledge forms the basis of more complete conceptual mastery.

Assessing Children's Development of Mathematical Thinking

It is often difficult for teachers to assess the children's understanding of mathematical reasoning, both what they know and what they can do with the support of others. In the series *Young Mathematicians at Work*, Fosnot and Dolk (2001) emphasize the importance of assessments that take place as children engage in mathematical thinking. Teachers use assessments to make children's thinking processes visible in order to inform curriculum decisions. When we

Logical mathematical knowledge is constructed by acting on objects.

make children's thinking visible, we are more likely to make valid assessments. This is particularly true when assessing the understandings of English language learners who face challenges in assessments that require understanding English and providing oral or written responses.

For example, Amy is a student in Leni's first-grade class. How does Amy understand the concept of number? On dittos, she can draw the numeral *9* under the circle with nine ducks. When Leni asks her to show with her fingers "how many" nine is, Amy counts on her fingers from one to nine and holds up nine fingers. At first glance, it seems that "nineness" is a concept that Amy understands. Leni now follows one of Piaget's assessment procedures (Piaget, 1965a) to see whether Amy has developed the mental ability to understand conservation of number. When a child understands that a given number of objects can be rearranged and that a change in the arrangement does not result in a change in number, the child is able to conserve number. The ability to conserve is fundamental to a true understanding of number.

Leni places a pile of pennies on the table in front of Amy. Leni selects nine pennies and places them in a row. She asks Amy to take pennies from the pile and to make a row for herself that will have the same number as Leni's row. Amy does this easily (see Figure 7.1).

Next, Leni moves the pennies in her row so that they are close together. Her row is now shorter than Amy's row, as Figure 7.2 shows. She asks Amy if they both have the same number of pennies or whether she has more or Amy has more.

Figure 7.1

Figure 7.2

Amy replies without hesitation: "I have more pennies because my row is longer." ✄

Although she can count and recognize the numerals used in mathematical recording, Amy does not completely understand the concept of the number. Young children like Amy rely on their perceptions of how things look. Amy might be able to tell us that when four pennies are rearranged, four pennies are still present (Baroody, 2000). However, when the number is too large to grasp perceptually, she becomes confused. When nine pennies are rearranged, she looks at the two groups to determine which group looks bigger. Answers to problems involving logic are not "out there" in the physical world through better observation. Amy must use logic to construct the answer that rearranging the pennies does not change the total number of pennies.

Some children are in a transitional phase between what Piaget referred to as preoperational and concrete operational reasoning. They realize that counting the objects is a strategy for solving the conservation of number problem. These children respond that the same number of pennies is in each line because "both have nine." However, a complete understanding of number comes only when children no longer need to count or check the appearance of the rows, but rather when they understand the logical relationship that "must be so." In time, Amy will master the concept that "the number nine" refers to a relationship among objects that remains stable even when the arrangement of the nine objects changes.

Children's abilities to understand these logical relationships between objects develop during the primary grades. A few children will understand concepts such as conservation of number and length in preschool, many more will get it in kindergarten and first grade, and most children will understand by second grade.

Assessments of children's abilities need not be as formal as the example just given. As we discussed in the assessment chapter, ongoing, formative, informal assessment, particularly observations of young children's play, provides teachers with the information they need to respond to the needs of each child.

Mathematics Education Based on the Nature of Mathematics, Children's Development, and Children's Interests

If mathematics education is based on an understanding of mathematics and of children's development and interests, which programs are appropriate for early childhood settings? As we have noted, *Early Childhood Mathematics: Promoting Good Beginnings,* the Joint Position Statement of the National Association for the Education of Young Children (NAEYC) and the National Council of Teachers of Mathematics (2002) recommends that high-quality education programs for young children include building upon children's individual and cultural experiences; fostering their interests in making sense of their world; basing the curriculum on knowledge of children's development; and, we emphasize, providing "ample time, materials, and teacher support for children to engage in play, a context in which they explore and manipulate mathematical ideas with keen interest" (p. 4).

Daily Life Situations and Play Are Cornerstones of Early Childhood Education Programs.   We think that daily life situations and play are the cornerstones of mathematics education in early childhood. A mathematics program centered on daily life situations and play can be a vital dimension of partnerships with parents, particularly because most parents recognize the importance of children's developing competencies in mathematics. Teachers and parents can share examples of how daily life situations and play can foster play and mathematical thinking at school and at home.

Daily Life Situations.   Daily life situations are one cornerstone of an early childhood mathematics education program in that they provide opportunities for children to make sense of their world and to develop mathematical understandings informally within the context of their own lives and the lives of people in their community. This now-classical principle of John Dewey is

emphasized by many math educators. As children encounter and try to solve problems in daily life that involve logical-mathematical thinking, they realize that as their understanding grows, they will become better at solving problems that matter to them, not simply problems on a worksheet.

> As children enter the kindergarten classroom each day, Theresa places a survey at the front door, allowing children to "vote" on different classroom decisions for the day, like whether to have snack inside or out. A few weeks after this classroom routine had begun, Ila and Erin began taking "surveys" of their classmates' preferences, using classroom clipboards, scratch papers, and tally marks to query friends about their favorite color or their favorite place to play at school. ✐

In their book *Young Investigators: The Project Approach in the Early Years,* Helm and Katz (2001) include a wonderful example of a fire truck project that drew upon the spontaneous interests of many children. As the project developed, the children were involved in such activities as making a map of the fire station and counting the fire truck's doors and ladders. They mirrored their understandings in their own construction, using materials such as blocks and Legos. Through experiences such as these, children come to regard math as something that "happens in your head," rather than as the mindless repetition of drills and worksheets.

Play, a Second Cornerstone of Mathematics Education.   Like daily life, play situations provide numerous activities in which children can use their emerging logical-mathematical abilities. Some play situations are children's own reconstructions of events in daily life: setting the table in the housekeeping area so that everyone will have one of each utensil, or making playdough hamburgers that are "just as big" so no one will complain. The children in Pat's kindergarten class have begun to play "gas station," discussing quantities of gas and payment of cash as an extension of play with trikes and wagons.

Play has two characteristics not always found in daily life situations that offer further advantages. First, play is flexible. Situations from everyday life sometimes have a single solution, but problems encountered in play more often have many possible solutions and provide the opportunity to "wander over the mathematical landscape."

Second, play involves children in problems of their own choosing. In play, as the joint National Association for the Education of Young Children and National Council of Teachers of Mathematics statement (2002) points out, children explore mathematical ideas with "keen interest" because, we believe, children select both the content and the level of difficulty. This makes it more likely that children are working within their own zone of proximal development.

Four-year-old Miriam discovered yesterday that she could make smaller triangles within the larger triangles she constructed on a geoboard. Today she is using colored rubber bands and four geoboards combined to make a square and is "going to town on triangles," Mrs. Ward, a participating parent, reports. Miriam's play with the geoboards illustrates how she integrates and extends her mathematical understanding through play. ⌀

In Susan's kindergarten class, some children carefully count out stamps, "take money, and make change." They write numerals in the receipt book complete with carbon paper. Susan notes that other children simply take the letters, stamp them, and put them in the box. ⌀

Games with rules are one form of play that DeVries, Kamii, and others strongly recommend as experiences that encourage the use of logical-mathematical thinking. *Young Children Reinvent Arithmetic* (Kamii with Housman, 2000) provides an account of how, through collaborative research, Kamii works with teachers to develop math curriculum based on group games and situations from everyday life. It includes a chapter by DeClark that chronicles her change from a teacher who relied on direct instruction and worksheets to one who advocates a game-centered curriculum. Hildebrandt and Zan also describe how group games help children to take the perspective of others, because they must understand and play by rules others have proposed (DeVries et al., 2002).

Supporting Children from All Cultures and Children Who Are English Language Learners

Throughout this book, we have emphasized the importance of an inclusive curriculum that promotes the developing competencies of all children. Today, as in the past, we find that the assurance of an appropriate and free education has not led to equal education. Consistently, national and state statistics show that school success in mathematics is less typical of children who live in poverty and who are members of linguistic and ethnic minority groups (e.g., see the National Association for the Education of Young Children and the National Council of Teachers of Mathematics Joint Position Statement, 2002). The vignettes throughout this chapter show that an inclusive curriculum addresses the needs of children from diverse backgrounds, cultures, and who speak a language other than English.

The Joint Statement of NAEYC and NCTM (2002) provides guidance regarding the developmental appropriateness of standards as well as guidelines for connecting current and future expectations. This is in keeping with practice that is developmentally, culturally, and individually appropriate. For example, the Statement underscores the importance of learning about and building upon the experiences and knowledge that children bring to school from their family and community cultures.

The concept of the play continuum and the principles related to orchestrating children's play are the bases for principles that promote inclusiveness and equity, in mathematics as in all areas. We hope that the following examples from teachers' experiences and our own will encourage further discussions of promoting competence in mathematics for all children.

The Environment.   First, we can make sure that we consciously arrange the environment to promote rich mathematical experiences for all children. In chapter 2, we noted that in early childhood, play is the cornerstone of logical-mathematical thinking. Even though logical-mathematical thinking is central to many disciplines, mathematics is a specific discipline with a specific vocabulary. While most early childhood educators pay careful attention to opportunities for supporting literacy, mathematics education may not be an important program focus. It is critical to assess the curriculum carefully, lest we discover that by assuming that "math is everywhere," we find instead that "math is nowhere."

We can reexamine the environment to assure that multiple possibilities for mathematical thinking as well as the use of mathematical language are everywhere. Are graduated containers provided for measuring and pouring in several areas? Are instruments for measuring, such as calculators, rulers, and scales, accessible? Are materials such as blocks and manipulatives organized so that differences in size and shape are readily apparent?

Culturally Relevant Mathematics.   Ensign (2003) introduces the concept of culturally relevant math, especially in urban schools. How can the classroom mirror aspects of the community? For example, could we make signs in children's home languages for the dramatic play, block, or outdoor areas that are similar to signs in the community? Are there photos of familiar places in the community? In addition to numerous books that illustrate numbers and shapes, can children who are learning English as a second language also turn to books with pictures or simple but interesting texts that follow a sequence of events? As we have mentioned, it is also essential that we use assessments that reveal the abilities and understandings of children who are learning English. As we have noted, informal and formal assessments of mathematics usually have a strong language component so that all English language learners are at a disadvantage, even those gifted in mathematics.

Considerations of Teacher-Initiated Activities.   In this book, the concept of math in a play-centered curriculum includes teacher-initiated activities as part of the continuum. In some programs, we might consider a special area designated for mathematics. Based upon her observations in local classrooms,

Scales (2000) noted that few preschool classrooms had areas designated for mathematics, as they did for literacy and science. In addition to an environment where math happens "everywhere," teachers can consider a designated "math happens here" area. Scales also observed that many preschool programs lacked a mathematics curriculum. This could result in "hidden disparities in informal math learning." In such programs, teachers might not assess children's development of spatial reasoning and numeracy, and might not consistently support children's development in these areas.

Supporting Children with Special Needs

A commitment to equity does not mean, for example, that we always respond by maximizing direct teacher instruction for children who are not learning number concepts or operations as quickly as their peers. How can we address children's strengths as well as their needs?

> Eight-year-old Brendt has a keen eye for symmetry and yet experiences developmental delays in many areas. He has spent several days cutting squares and triangles of various colors and sizes, using large, beginners' scissors. He carefully places them on the large mosaic he is constructing, exploring the relationships between shapes and sizes by superimposing the triangles on the squares. ✆

Inclusive mathematics curricula address a wide range of children's needs. For example, there are children with disabilities related to mathematics, such as disabilities with calculations (developmental dyscalcula); those who understand mathematical concepts but have limited language ability; those with developmental delays; and children with auditory and visual impairments. Lastly, it is important for teachers to be skilled observers so that during the early childhood years children's special needs and individual interests in the area of mathematics can be identified.

Children's Interests

Throughout this book, we have discussed children's interests in the play materials found in traditional early education programs, such as clay, blocks, manipulatives, sand, and water. In this chapter, we see that children are often actively engaged in mathematics when it might have appeared that they were doing something else. In a rich, play-centered curriculum, children develop mathematical understandings in all areas of the environment and all times of the day. Art materials lend themselves to explorations of geometry and arithmetic. If we listen closely, much of the conversation in the dramatic play area involves math in some way, such as when we hear children count out plates for the table or count out money at the store. Though teachers have often thought of mathematics as part of the "indoors" curriculum, teachers of young children can promote the playful development of both informal and formal mathematical concepts outdoors, as well (Basile, 1999; Macmillan, 1998).

> In a community near the ocean, 3-year-old Nicky and 2-year-old Schyler are playing outside on a wooden boat. While Jo, their teacher, rocks their vessel, they sing "Row, row, row your boat." They finish the song by counting, "one, two, three, we all fall out!" Laughing and tumbling out, they quickly board the ship to play again. ᗢ

Another area of interest reflected in children's play is their desire to learn about the adult world and to understand the things adults do. This is shown when they play house, store, or pretend to read or write because they are in a literate environment. Similarly, their interest in numbers is shown when they use calculators when playing store, yardsticks to measure a block structure, or telephones and computers when playing office, thus reflecting their life in a number-literate environment.

ORCHESTRATING PLAY IN MATHEMATICS

The general guidelines for setting up the physical environment and developing schedules of routines presented in chapter 4 apply to our specific concerns about setting up an environment that fosters the development of mathematics, particularly logical-mathematical thinking.

Setting the Stage

How is the physical space arranged? Do the children have room to work on block constructions without constant interruptions from others in a crowded space? Should the small wood table be located near the water table so children can have a place for their assortment of measuring cups and containers?

Are sufficient materials available that will allow children to explore with shapes and number concepts as they play? For example, are blocks of all kinds available? Is an adequate quantity of differently shaped unit blocks set out for creating diverse structures? Are there several kinds of table blocks, such as pattern blocks, attribute blocks, Construx, and Lego blocks? Different types of clay provide opportunities for children to explore non-Euclidean shapes. Pattern boards, tangrams, and pattern blocks give children experiences with Euclidean shapes that they can also use to sort. The multitudes of peg-type manipulatives give children chances to think about quantity, as well as patterns.

The sandbox and the water table are sometimes neglected areas stocked with cast-off materials and odd containers. Although it is useful to have containers of different shapes, it is also important to provide graduated sets. A measuring set with a quart pitcher, a pint pitcher, a cup pitcher, and a half-cup pitcher gives children a chance to explore equivalencies. As Murray (2001) points out, "If we are to make math experiential, we must present children with tactile tools with which they can learn, opportunities to interact with each other and the teacher, and diverse methods of arriving at the correct answer" (p. 29).

Time considerations are important here as in all aspects of play. How long do children have to work uninterrupted? What are the rules about leaving a Lego construction overnight? What should be done about Cindy, a student with special needs who tends to need close supervision after 15 minutes in the block area? And if Jonny has been working intently on his Lego construction for 20 minutes, must he stop because it is his turn to make an apple snack that looks like a turtle?

Accessorizing: Transforming the Environment to Extend and Enrich Play

Virginia observed that block play in her classroom had settled into a routine after 5 weeks. At the beginning, she enjoyed the great variety of construction. Now she wondered whether things had gotten into a rut. Day after day, block play involved building ramps and racing. The same boys tended to play in the same groups with the same repetitive themes. When car racing first came into vogue, several girls were involved, and the ramps had become more complex each day. This was no longer the case.

Rather than intervene directly through out-of-play suggestions or through entering and redirecting the play, Virginia decided to experiment with accessories placed near the blocks. She placed a box of toy people and animals on the block shelves. This brought several children, including several girls, back to the block area. New themes evolved. The castle-like structures that had been built during the first few days re-emerged. The car races even seemed more complex, with drivers and teams. ⌀

Pat decided to use an explicit approach to include measurement with her kindergartners. Three of the children riding trikes had appropriated a hose to play gas station. Pat asked them what other things a gas station had and what they could use. Within a few days, the drivers were busy adding measured oil, checking tire pressure, and pumping gallons of gas. ⌀

Accessorizing is a playful activity for teachers, as well as for children. All parts of the environment can be enriched further to stimulate mathematical

Block play supports mathematical thinking.

thinking. This not only helps children acquire mathematical abilities within a meaningful context but also helps them apply their skills and abilities in numerous situations. What can we add to the housekeeping area? Are measuring spoons, food cans of different sizes, and silverware settings for six or eight available? Dramatic play accessory boxes can be assembled easily. What is needed to play store? Post office? Bank? Office? What can be added to foster social interactions and support the inclusion of all children?

Play-Generated Curricula

Children's play in a rich environment leads to curricular innovations that are more challenging and sophisticated than most traditional curricula. Martine is building a *pyramid* of cubes. Stevie needs another *cylindrical* block. Many preschool and primary standards and benchmarks include problem solving as well as identifying and naming the basic two-dimensional Euclidean shapes: triangle, circle, square, and rectangle. As experienced block builders, sand castle designers, and artists, children have the background to support a much more sophisticated mathematical vocabulary. Furthermore, as these examples illustrate, children have a need to use these terms in their daily activities.

Ideas for numerous activities and extended curriculum units that relate to mathematics and address standards arise through careful observation and reflection on children's play. (See Burns, 2003; Copley, 2004; Seefeldt & Galper, 2004.) For example, after discovering that the "car racers" were fascinated with measuring, Virginia developed a unit on measurement that addressed state curriculum benchmarks such as using non-standard and standard units of measurement; and mathematical processes such as communication and problem solving. She introduced a measured roadway for cars, which she marked with colored paper. She then removed the paper and introduced nonstandard units such as Popsicle sticks, knots on a string, and Unifix cubes, along with standard measuring units such as rulers, yardsticks, and the popular tape measure. Based on her observations of children's play and her knowledge of children's interests, she included activities that reflected children's fascination with the minuscule and the gigantic, from sprouting seeds to measuring the length of the playground. Many children spontaneously wrote about measuring in their journals, reflecting their interest in numeracy, as well as literacy.

Pat decided to extend her kindergartners' gas station play by including the gas station in her social studies curriculum that centered on "our neighbors." This emergent curriculum built upon their interests. Pat was able to explain to parents and administrators how this project addressed standards because of her knowledge of her state's mathematics and social science frameworks and standards.

The children discussed their own experiences at gas stations. Many had significant experiences involving cars that they wanted to share—cars breaking down and being fixed, getting stuck on the highway with flat tires, tales of stolen cars, and accidents. These were important communications, and the storytellers received serious attention and sympathy from their classmates. The children then drew and wrote about these experiences in their journals. A trip to the school's library resulted in a great assortment of books about vehicles and transportation.

Pat then arranged for a tour of the local gas station. The children saw where the big gas truck pumped the gas into the underground tanks. They first estimated, then asked the truck driver how many gallons were in the tank. The garage mechanic showed them different tools. Many, like wrenches, came in graduated sizes. He demonstrated how he measured the oil and how he used a funnel when he added oil. ✆

Play-generated curriculum can forge critical links between math, literacy, and science. For example, in the article "Reading in Math Class: Selecting and Using Picture Books for Math Investigations," Thatcher (2001) emphasizes that teachers select books that have meaningful math connections and topics that are meaningful to children, and that stimulate children's sense of wonder. It is our view that books that relate to the children's interests, as shown in their play, are particularly powerful. Kroll and Halaby (1997) remind us that children not only read to learn mathematics, but write to learn mathematics as well.

Curriculum-Generated Play

Children consolidate and extend the experiences they have in their math education program through their spontaneous play. As we have shown, teachers can consciously create bridges from many mathematics programs that address particular standards to playful activities. This presents a serious challenge, however, when the curriculum involves adopted texts or dittos that rush from topic to topic. This results in an emphasis on memorization rather than the approach taken by the National Council of Teachers of Mathematics. When the mathematics curriculum involves children interacting with each other to address real problems, both children and adults find numerous bridges to play. (See, for example, Copley, 1999; De Vries et al., 2002; Griffin, 2004; Kamii with Housman, 2000; Seefeldt & Galper, 2004.)

The number and scope of early childhood mathematics curriculum projects is growing. Projects include *Making Sense* (Richardson, 2004); the *Berkeley Math Readiness Project* (Klein & Starkey, 2004); *Number Worlds* (Griffin, 2004); *Building Blocks,* a technology-based curriculum (Serama, 2004); and a language-arts-based supplementary program focused on the development of spatial sense (Casey, 2004).

When providing an environment with the basics for rich play, accessories can be chosen that relate to specific aspects of math curriculum goals, including the standards and benchmarks defined by the teacher, the district, or the state department of education. As in all other subject areas, teachers can promote curriculum-generated play by making materials from mathematics activities available during choice time, as well as by assuring that a wide selection of materials is available during this time.

> Souvanna has been working with her second- and third-grade students to put together several boxes with materials for playing store. They decided on a post office, a grocery store, and a computer store kit. Souvanna makes sure that students have multiple opportunities to practice adding, subtracting, and multiplication by including scales, timers, calculators, and student-made pads of sales slips. ✍

> According to her state and district's kindergarten math curriculum, Marilyn is expected to teach rote counting and recognition of numerals from 1 to 20. She also decides to experiment with turning the dramatic play area into a store. In addition to a balance scale, she is lucky enough to obtain an old hanging scale. She includes a Bates stamp with numbers

that the children can rotate and change. She has several hand calculators and an old adding machine borrowed from a third-grade teacher. She also includes tubs of small objects, like Unifix cubes, that can be sold. She is delighted to find that she now has a use for out-of-date coupons and the weekly ads from local supermarkets. The pictures and the numbers make the messages understandable for kindergartners. The store is now open for business! On opening day, workers and customers discover that Marilyn has forgotten an important component: They need money. This leads to a group project of making bills and coins. ☙

ADDRESSING STANDARDS IN THE PLAY-CENTERED CURRICULUM

In 2000, the first national conference was held that addressed the issue of standards for prekindergarten and kindergarten mathematics education. The goal of the conference was to bring leaders in early childhood mathematics together in order "to help those responsible for framing and implementing early childhood mathematics standards (Clements & Sarama, 2004, p. xi).

One outcome of the conference was a series of recommendations for early policy makers and leaders. The first recommendation for the area of Learning and Teaching relates to the central role of play, "Mathematical experiences for very young children should build largely upon their play and the natural relationships between learning and life in their daily activities, interests, and questions" (Clements & Sarama, 2004, p. x).

As Table 7.2 shows, all the vignettes in this chapter can be used to illustrate the ways that play-centered curriculum addresses standards.

The National Council of Teachers of Mathematics and the National Association for the Education of Young Children Joint Position Statement (2002) includes numerous recommendations to promote quality, developmentally and culturally relevant early childhood mathematics education for all children. Importantly, this document also articulates six guiding principles to guide practice that are key considerations in discussions of standards and assessment:

1. Equity: Excellence in mathematics education requires equally high expectations and strong support for all students.

2. Curriculum: A curriculum is more than a collection of activities; it must be coherent, focused on important mathematics, and well articulated across the grades.

3. Teaching: Effective mathematics teaching requires understanding of what students know and need to learn and then challenging and supporting them to learn it well.

4. Learning: Students must learn mathematics with understanding, actively building new knowledge from experience and prior knowledge.

Table 7.2

Addressing Mathematics Standards in the Play-Centered Curriculum

Example of Curriculum Standard	Example
Geometry and Spatial Awareness	
Learners will use visualization, spatial reasoning, and geometric modeling and solve problems.	In their play, Peter and Lisa estimate the amount of paper they need to wrap the package to mail to Lisa's grandmother.
Problem Solving	
Learners will engage in problem solving. Learners will use a variety of mathematical tools.	Pat's kindergarten students measure oil, check tire pressure, and pump gas as they play in the gas station she has helped them create.
Numbers & Operation, and Problem Solving	
The student applies kindergarten mathematics to solve problems connected to everyday experiences and activities in and outside of school.	Marilyn has turned the dramatic play area into a store. The children select food to buy, decide on the quantity, count "money," and make change.
Patterns and Relationships	
Sorting, classifying, seriating objects by shape, size, number, and other properties.	Second-graders have created a camping scene. They seriate dolls of different sizes with the corresponding backpacks of different sizes.
	Using numerous colored pencils, Tomás draws horizontal rows of alternating colors and adds a bright vertical line.
Geometry and Spatial Awareness	
Learner identifies, names, and creates common two-dimensional shapes in the environment and play situations.	Using the colored rubber bands placed near the geoboard, Nick and Emma make multiple hexagonal and octagonal shapes.
Problem Solving	
Students make decisions about how to set up a problem.	Laurie, Sandra, and Marie divide a shell collection into three sets of 26. Each then sorts the collection by various properties.

5. Assessment: Assessment should support the learning of important mathematics and furnish useful information to both teachers and students.

6. Technology: Technology is essential to teaching and learning mathematics; it influences the mathematics that is taught and enhances students' learning (pp. 2–3).

WHEN TEACHERS TALK

Standards and Professional Expertise

In speaking with teachers, we heard many concerns about state and district interpretations of state standards and also about high stakes, standardized assessment tests for young children. For example, in our examination of state standards, we found that problem solving and computational skills as used in daily life were embedded in the written standards. However, many schools and districts encourage teachers to address math standards mainly through drill worksheets that are unrelated to the contexts of daily life. This is one example of how the implementation of standards, rather than the standards themselves, can be developmentally inappropriate.

What can teachers do? *Early Childhood Mathematics: Promoting Good Beginnings* (NAEYC & NCTM, 2002) emphasizes the importance of educators and families being key participants in decisions:

The process of developing and reviewing early learning standards involves multiple stakeholders. Stakeholders may include community members, families, early childhood educators and special educators, and other professional groups. In all cases, those with specific expertise in early development and learning must be involved. (p. 7)

Early childhood educators have great expertise to contribute to the dialogue and decisions about developmentally appropriate practices in mathematics education.

SUMMARY AND CONCLUSION

Marilyn's and Virginia's curriculum development flows from formal math curriculum to guided and spontaneous play and back to the development of math curricula activities related to play. This flow is characteristic of integrated and appropriate early childhood education mathematics curricula. When early childhood environments provide opportunities for play with blocks and materials such as clay, sand, and water, children develop and consolidate mathematical concepts as they play. The centrality of play in quality mathematics programs for young children is recommended by the national associations for teachers of young children and teachers of mathematics. We can observe activities in which children deal with spatial concepts such as proximity, symmetry, Euclidean, and non-Euclidean shapes; with concepts of measurement such as area, volume, and weight; and with relationships involving classification, seriation, and quantity.

Children think mathematically as they use their developing logical abilities to solve the real problems that confront them in play. In solving their own problems, children develop an appreciation for the usefulness of mathematics.

Teachers then can extend play activities into the more formal curriculum. The play-centered curriculum provides the conceptual framework to address standards in an integrated, developmentally appropriate manner. In programs that provide a balanced continuum from child-initiated to teacher-initiated activities, we find children who bring energy, joy, and imagination to their own relationships with mathematics.

SELECTED RESOURCES

Althouse, R. (1994). *Investigating mathematics with young children*. New York: Teachers College Press.

Althouse suggests strategies for helping children connect mathematics to daily life. These activities involve students in exploring themselves and their environments; for example, ourselves, our day, our room, our shapes in the classroom, our houses, our city, and our playground.

Clements, D. H., & Sarama, J. (Eds.). (2004). *Engaging young children in mathematics: Standards for early childhood mathematics education*. Mahwah, NJ: Lawrence Erlbaum Associates, Inc.

The purpose of the Conference on Standards for Prekindergarten and Kindergarten Mathematics (2000) was to bring together experts in the fields of early mathematics education and early childhood education to discuss the movement towards standards and develop recommendations for policy makers. This book includes chapters by participants, all leaders in the field, that report on the issues discussed and the recommendations for developmentally appropriate standards and guidelines proposed. This useful resource includes chapters in which the authors describe their major early childhood mathematics curriculum initiatives; a section on professional development; and a section on implementation and policy.

Copley, J. V. (Ed.). (1999). *Mathematics in the early years*. Reston, VA: National Council of Teachers of Mathematics, Washington, DC: National Association for the Education of Young Children.

This comprehensive book, by numerous well-known authors in the field, includes chapters on teaching mathematics in an integrated curriculum involving play, the arts, literature, reading and writing, social studies, and daily life activities. The chapters that address culture and language and the acquisition of mathematical understandings have important implications for classroom practice.

De Vries, R., Zan, B., Hildebrandt, C., Edmiaston, R., & Sales, C. (2002). *Developing constructivist early childhood curriculum: Practical principles and activities.* New York: Teachers College Press.

This book addresses the broader issues regarding play and constructivist teaching, including the "political problem." Detailed descriptions of classroom practice illustrate how understanding principles of constructivist education is truly "practical" for classroom teachers. Specific chapters relating to teaching mathematics include "Developing geometric reasoning using pattern blocks" and "Using group games to teach mathematics."

Hirsch, E. S. (1996). *The block book* (3rd ed.). Washington, DC: National Association for the Education of Young Children.

Teachers have valued this classic book for several decades. *The Block Book* explains how teachers working with children in preschool through the upper elementary grades can use the many different types of blocks to support development. This updated edition presents the many ways that blocks relate to all areas of the curriculum, including math.

Kamii, C., with Housman, L. B. (2000). *Young children reinvent arithmetic: Implications of Piaget's theory* (2nd ed.). New York: Teachers College Press.

Kamii and Housman provide insights into early mathematics learning and teaching based on classroom practice. This book provides a detailed analysis of the ways in which children construct mathematical knowledge through math games and daily life activities.

Seefeldt, C., & Galper, A. (2004). *Active experiences for active children: Mathematics.* Upper Saddle River, NJ: Merrill/Prentice Hall.

In this comprehensive resource for early childhood educators, the authors describe how a comprehensive mathematics program can be based on children's own interests and experiences. Seefeldt and Galper show in detail how a carefully crafted emergent curriculum can address basic standards in all areas: number, geometry, algebra, measurement, data gathering and analysis, and problem solving.

Language, Literacy, and Play

At Patrick's school, "story playing" is a regular activity. Children have the option daily to dictate a "story play" to a teacher. Later, it will be enacted by their friends during circle time. Three-year-old Patrick has attended his school for only 2 weeks. He has not yet made friends with anyone. He spends most of his time near his teachers, where he has observed the story play dictation frequently but has not yet dictated a story play of his own.

An important breakthrough happens when Patrick quietly tells the teacher he has a story to tell. His first story dictated, he is assured it will be enacted at circle time.

At circle time, Patrick is invited to the "stage" (a taped rectangle on the rug). He shyly steps forward. Patrick's story is "I have lots of friends." Patrick picks himself to be one of his friends. He also picks Margaret and Barbara (two teachers) to be his friends. His teacher begins to read Patrick's story.

Teacher: Now, listen to what Patrick's story said. "I have THOSE friends." Who wants to be THOSE friends? If Patrick points to you, come right on the stage. All right, Patrick pick someone who has a hand raised. All right, Sophia, you were picked. Who else?

With the teacher's active assistance, Patrick chooses Mary, Ian, and Catherine.

Teacher: Good! All right, now, those are THOSE friends. Now the last part of Patrick's story is "I have THESE friends." If you want to be THESE friends, raise your hand and Patrick will pick. Patrick, would you like to pick Kelly? You want Felix to be one of THESE friends? All right, Felix, you're one of THESE friends.

Patrick then picks Nathan, who comes on stage and then follows with Jessica, Sam, and Patrick.

Teacher: Now, Patrick, you've got THOSE friends and THESE friends. Lots of friends. Do you want your friends to do something while they are on the stage?
Patrick: Yes.
Teacher: What would you like them to do?
Patrick: (looking at the piano just outside the circle) Play piano.
Teacher: Play the piano? All right, all of you sit down and pretend you're playing the piano. Because that's what THESE friends and THOSE friends do. All of Patrick's friends are piano players. Good! ✍

What an important day for 3-year-old Patrick! Not only has his story launched him as a member of a community of "storytellers," it has established him as a person who, having started with only two friends, his teachers, now has new friends, his peers. For sure, Patrick will be chosen to have a part in the plays of others.

This example of how play motivates the development of language and literacy and how literate behaviors, in turn, enhance play is one of many that could be taken from early childhood classrooms using play-based curricula. Patrick's story playing is a guided-play situation in which the teacher's presence, comments, and questions serve to scaffold learning. Patrick's teacher has supported his first tentative effort to engage in a responsive dialogue with others. Participation in the story play activity leads children to an early awareness that language contains within it the expectations of a responsive "other." Patrick must tell his listeners what to do. With their response, his own sense of self within a social world will grow (Richner & Nicolopoulou, 2001). This awareness will allow Patrick to begin to build competence in communicating with a responding other (Bahktin, 2000).

In this chapter, we take the position that play provides the motivating context for the "literate behaviors" that precede the development of more specific literacy skills (Heath & Mangiola, 1991). Literate behaviors are numerous forms of expression, verbal and nonverbal, that fulfill the fundamental purpose of communicating the child's needs, interests, and desires. For the young child, these larger purposes of language provide the motivation and framework for later literacy development. Taking a broad sociocultural perspective derived from Vygotsky, we see language and literacy being constructed from the collective resources of the classroom, not just in a dyadic mentoring relationship with the teacher.

With this orientation in mind, we first consider how play and literate behavior support one another and then how a play-based curriculum differs from more traditional approaches that emphasize the direct teaching of isolated literacy skills. Special attention is paid to balancing spontaneous and guided play and classroom "authoring" activities: sociodramatic play, story dictation, story playing, and narrative construction in journals and booklets. We also discuss developmentally appropriate standards for literacy.

PLAY, LANGUAGE, AND LITERATE BEHAVIOR: A NATURAL PARTNERSHIP

In play-centered programs, communication through gesture, action, talk, and written symbols supports play everywhere, from the library corner and the language arts center to the sand table and the dress-up corner. This opportunity to communicate allows children to establish a theme in play and a role for themselves in that play. Signs, even when not legible to everyone, can label things, mark turns and designate a territory. Through play, literate behaviors develop most readily. Here are some of the ways the developmental thrust of play and literate behavior serve each other:

Many children spontaneously read in a print-rich environment.

1. Play provides a motivating context for literate behavior as children communicate through language to themselves in solitary play and to their peers in social play. Noah is talking to himself at the easel—"Now there is blue, blue, and now white"—thus schooling himself in the creation of a new color. Or, as Maria answers Juan, "I know what to do to help make a tunnel! You have to dig another hole."

2. Language and communicative actions allow children to create and share imaginary worlds and participate in the beginnings of narratives. Lizzy, whose mother is ill, wants to play hospital so she can be a doctor who cures someone. She needs to communicate and use language in order to get the play going, attract other actors, and carry out the theme.

3. Language makes collaboration in play with others possible and facilitates the development of "friendship." Patrick had just two friends before he dictated his "I have lots of friends" story, but a whole classroom of buddies thereafter.

4. Language in collaborative activities with others enhances the complexity of play by deepening, lengthening, and diversifying play forms. Lizzy's hospital starts with one ward but expands as the children pursue the theme over many weeks to include a "chief of staff" and everything from an operating room to an eye clinic, a pharmacy, and an ambulance unit.

5. The partnership of play and language supports the development of children who are English language learners. Through her interest in the class's story play activity, Russian-speaking Masha communicates her desire to play with others and rapidly acquires English skills in this motivating context.

6. Language in play enables children to share and exchange their knowledge about literacy skills. For example, in the social context of one first-grade classroom, children are encouraged to exchange ideas spontaneously and share what they know about writing during their regular "Booklet Writing Time." In this way, not only the teacher, but also classmates are resources for language learning.

Thus, literate behavior, as developed and expressed through play, introduces children to language as the medium through which all humans construct a personal identity and participate in the social forms of their culture.

Communication as a Prerequisite for Play with Others

In spontaneous play with peers, children recast their knowledge of the world in terms that are compatible with their interests, competencies, and levels of cognitive, social, and affective development. Play in the home corner is not simply a copy of what "mommies and daddies" do, nor is such play merely the children's attempt to repeat stories that have been read to them or seen on television.

Spontaneously created play narratives are occasions for children to share and develop a sense of "topic" and "sequence"—the basic elements of written texts. In such collaborative literate behaviors, a topic and an ordered sequence are coordinated with play partners, thereby successfully maintaining the narrative thread of a cohesive interaction.

Jelani, playing at a sand tray, initiates the topic of "saving freezing bunnies" by hiding several miniature bunnies in a "safe sand mountain." Cody stays on topic by sprinkling dry sand over the mount, exclaiming, "It's raining, it's raining." He has followed successfully with an appropriate sequence of activity and expanded the initial topic as the two collaboratively construct a theme in their play discourse (Corsaro, 1997; Jaworski & Coupland, 1999). ⌀

In this vignette, Jelani and Cody verbally coordinated their constructive and dramatic play. Nonverbal expression, however, also contributes and often provides the communication needed for shared spontaneous action sequences. Tag, chase, or superhero games immediately come to mind. One child sounds the theme music from a familiar media program, and then others take up the theme. Soon a highly coordinated activity of swooping or "flying" gets underway.

Other nonverbal initiation of topic and sequencing actions occurs in settings such as the home play corner, where the function of the props is familiar to many of the children. For example, when Josh brought the laundry basket to Amanda, who had just picked up the iron and ironing board, he was on topic. When Ethan entered the play and began wielding a plastic carrot like a sword, he was clearly off topic and not in synchrony with the ongoing interaction.

Play as a Form of Communication

Long before acquiring verbal competency, young children are able to convey their needs and desires, likes and dislikes, competence, and knowledge in the language of their culture. They do this through gesture, expression, and choice of objects and activity, in solitary as well as interactive play. In a vignette we discuss in detail in a later chapter, Matthew, a child with speech impairments, indicates his interest in entering into play with two other boys by the nonverbal act of kicking a tire near their play space. In response to Matthew's nonverbal overture for entry into play, the teacher might move in closer to this spontaneous play and assist the potential play partners in finding a role for Matthew. In dialogue, children express their unique personal identity and cultural heritage in play with others (Genishi & Dyson, 2005). They learn to adapt to the communicative needs of others in the sociocultural diversity of the classroom (Dyson, 1997, 2003; Genishi, 2002; Hughes, 2003; Jaworski & Coupland, 1999; Reynolds, 2002). The wise teacher monitors the language of play closely, finding in it much of the source of a developmentally appropriate play-based curriculum.

FOSTERING LITERATE BEHAVIORS

The Value of the Play-Based Curriculum

In contrast to some approaches, which stress only "drill and practice" and the acquisition of isolated skills such as rote practicing of letter formation or memorization of phonics rules, play-centered language arts programs do not foreground the unnecessary honing of skills. We turn the natural processes of language learning upside down when we attempt to teach such skills to children before they have shown interest and motivation through their spontaneous attempts, for example, in dictating a text or attempting to write a text themselves. Although they often play at letter formation, young children do not use or learn a word's component sounds before they articulate the word—they do not practice the "d," "o," and "g" sounds before saying "dog"—and they do not start with more simple sentences before expressing complex emotions or desires. It is through nonverbal communication—gesture, interaction, expression—that children initially communicate desire or pain. Only after using language in these ways do they come to consider adult norms.

Contrary to traditional views, the rate and direction of the learning process is not necessarily linear and progressive. Research tells us that for some children, the direction might be curvilinear or cyclical, and even sometimes regressive, only to spiral out again later (Heath & Mangiola, 1991). For example, in guided-play activities, Nathan dictated many stories, all of which revolved around the Beatles and seemed to be attempts to mimic adult fiction he had heard. As he became more integrated into the peer-group culture of the school, his stories began to have greater personal impact. At this point, teachers noted that his previously long-winded and convoluted narrative style seemed to shift to a more age-appropriate level. The urgency of Nathan's need to express something meaningful to his peers took precedence over literacy skills that were not well established.

Learning for young children is determined largely by what they want to know and when they need to know it. To illustrate this point, we look at the development of an accurate concept of gender in children's storytelling efforts.

Early Story Constructions

Three-year-old children typically begin story constructions with fuzzy, gender-undifferentiated bunnies and cuddly creatures. Often, 4-year-old children, as they achieve greater narrative competence, may begin repetitively to relate gender-stereotypic stories derived from the media and peer culture (Nicolopoulou, 2001; Nicolopoulou & Scales, 1990). This period of seeming stagnation and creative impoverishment marks the children's membership in their peer group. It is followed, generally at about ages 5 and 6, by a spurt of more creative and elaborate narrative, encompassing and interweaving this same stereotypical material with material based on personal interests, and family experiences and expectations (Nourot, Henry, & Scales, 1990).

As Dyson (1993, 1997, 2003), Paley (1995, 1997, 2004), and others (including Tobin, 2000) have noted, children's narratives are often centered around issues of power, fairness, gender, ethnicity, and culture. Dialogue about such issues provides not only a motivating context for the growth of language and literacy, it can also provide the context for the construction of more accurate and more equitable notions of a social self within a social world. Dyson (1993) explains:

> In their plurality, in their diversity, our children offer us the opportunity to widen our own worldview, to see aspects of experience that might otherwise remain invisible to us, to understand better ourselves as situated in a complex world of multiple perspectives.

She goes on to say:

> Thus, in working to create permeable curricula, we further the development of young people with complex visions of themselves, whose varied and varying voices will enrich the cultural conversations of us all. (p. 230)

The impetus for literacy and social development is augmented by honoring children's authoring in all its multiple forms and by providing many opportunities to play at story construction during well-defined periods of the day. When children have opportunities for spontaneous play in early childhood classrooms, they generate a curriculum that integrates all their experience and knowledge and that is, therefore, naturally relevant to their cultural and personal lives (Fein, Ardlila-Ray, & Groth, 2000).

Angela's Story.   This is poignantly revealed by the case of Angela, who illustrated her traumatic story of poverty and homelessness (Figure 8.1), then dictated its text to a teacher she trusted.

Angela's story reveals not only the sadness of her life outside of school, but also her need to communicate her special story. It demonstrates the efficacy of the play-based curriculum to meet that need. Furthermore, the story's wording—"Once there was" and "The End"—reveals that Angela is beginning to grasp the social conventions surrounding the literate activity of storytelling. For homeless Angela, "school" learning was intertwined with other more basic lessons in mere survival.

This kind of storytelling activity is highly motivating and a precursor to more formal, self-directed journal writing in later schooling. In preschool and kindergarten, it is a form of early writing along with script-like scribbling. It reveals much about the child's beginning knowledge of writing conventions and the function of texts. In the Continuum of Children's Development in Early Reading and Writing laid out in a Joint Position Statement of the International Reading Association (IRA) and the National Association for the Education of Young Children (NAEYC) on appropriate standards for reading and writing (1998) as well as the early indicators adopted by a number of states, we find many correspondences to the competencies Angela has learned through play. For example:

- Angela uses illustrations or pictures to represent oral language.
- She describes people, places, and things in her story.
- She identifies the purpose of illustrations in a story.
- She includes a main idea in oral descriptions and drawings.

Once there was a
lady who lived
in a house and
didn't have anything
to eat.

Figure 8.1
Angela's Drawings

- She has dictated sentences.
- She has dictated the beginning, middle, and end of the story.
- (And more advanced) She uses her illustrations and dictation to create a consistent writer's voice and tone.
- She uses descriptive words and dictates a complete thought.
- She recounts experiences or presents the story in a logical sequence.
- When her story was bound together with staples like a book, she demonstrated the ability to use correct book handling skills, e.g., book is right side up and pages turn in correct direction. (Scales, 2004)

How the Play-Based Literacy Curriculum Serves Children of All Cultures and Languages

As we can see, today's classroom is richly peopled with children of diverse backgrounds. These children bring to school markedly different cultures, languages,

and ways of handling the English language. Traditionally, educators have attempted to ignore sociocultural differences in the classroom. However, differences arising from the uniqueness of race, culture, gender, and lifestyle can be used in the service of education. In attempting to attain equity by neutralizing our classrooms, we fail to notice that children of different backgrounds bring rich variety to play patterns and language (Genishi, 2002; Genishi & Dyson, 1984, 2005; Derman-Sparks & Ramsey, 2005).

Books of traditional stories from different cultures, tapes of songs in different languages, and ethnic dress-up clothes and eating utensils help all children learn that people can live and communicate in different ways. In one classroom, parents helped label the centers and materials in English, Russian, and Chinese to reflect the various cultures and languages of the students. Some of the English language learners in this classroom had younger siblings, or other relatives as well as parents who frequently volunteered. Opportunities to use both their first language as well as English were therefore available. This created an atmosphere in which all cultures were recognized, accepted, and celebrated, and all children felt valued (Genishi, 2002).

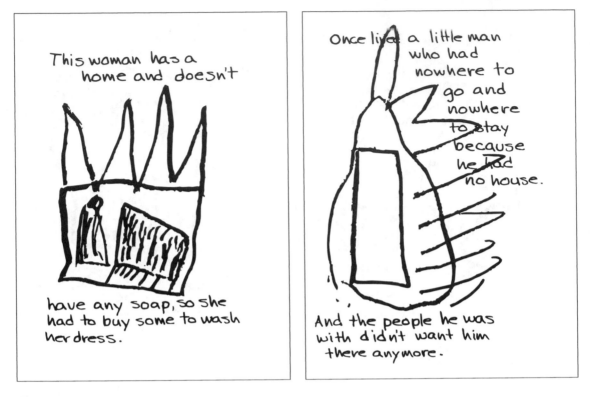

Figure 8.1
Angela's Drawings (*continued*)

It is in play-centered environments that opportunities for second language acquisition are paramount. In contrast to traditional classroom settings where adults often control the language spoken, the play-based program exposes children to the full range of their peers' language abilities. Play encourages young English language learners to develop their language competence for its strategic value in social relations. But it is also important to involve native speakers who can extend children's opportunities to use their primary language, as well as learn English. Bilingual teachers, aides, parents, volunteers, and cross-age tutors can all support a program that is language-varied for all students.

English Language Learners: Masha's Story

In the following, more lengthy anecdote drawn from records of story plays created by an immigrant child, we document Masha's acquisition of a second language, as well as her integration into the play culture of an American preschool classroom (Scales, 1997). The richness she and her family brought

to this classroom demonstrates how English language learners in our classrooms come with a cultural glass that is much more than half full (Genishi, 2002).

Having recently arrived from Russia, Masha spoke little or no English on entering a preschool program. She had attended preschool in Russia and was very accomplished in dance, movement, and gymnastics as well as drawing, painting, and crafts. At the school, Masha contented herself with these pursuits for most of the fall and winter, rarely going outside to the play yard. In these activities she received a great deal of acknowledgment from her teachers, and much time was spent near them at the drawing table. At circle time she was very attentive when children's story plays were enacted. Despite this interest, Masha had laboriously dictated only one story in October, near the beginning of the school year. This is what Masha dictated:

"My head and my eye.

My veil . . . white.

And play veil.

Someone pull my veil and play."

In her beginning English she has tried to recapture the excitement of whirling with colorful scarves in spontaneous dances with the other children.

After this first attempt, Masha did not dictate any stories for many months. But she had begun to make friends at the drawing table, where she was also near a teacher most of the school day. Finally, early in April, Masha rushed to Janet, her favorite teacher in the school, announcing urgently that she had a play to write, her first since October. It was a pivotal story that reflected her social development at the time. In her story, we hear a poised 4-year-old obliquely announcing that she is now ready to enter the world of her peers fully. She symbolically bids her teacher and mentor (and the drawing table as well) a gracious farewell. Tactfully, she honors her teacher by giving the only character in this play the teacher's name. Listen to Masha's story:

> "Once upon a time there was a little girl named Janet. And she so much liked to draw pictures, beautiful pictures. And she stopped drawing beautiful pictures and then she started to climb up the tree. And that's the end."

Masha furiously dictated 19 stories between April and the first of July. They vividly reflected her advancing development through the expression of her changing social motivations and her acquisition of greater and greater fluency in English as well as a grasp of the peer culture. First to appear was the familiar character of Cinderella, which she also knew in Russian. Soon other Disney-inspired figures began to enter. She made sure that there were many roles so that all her new friends could participate; sometimes she multiplied the characters so that no one was left out. Some stories involved two Cinderellas and several others had multiple characters named Pocahontas, distinguished as "a big one" and "a little one." She wrote several stories about "Fly Horses" and, much to the teacher's consternation, many little horses began "flying" about the play yard as Masha's Fly Horse theme daily became more integrated into the peer culture. Masha, despite admonitions to slow down, kept flying. She had made the whole school her own and she was not about to stop flying at this point. ✆

A story dictated in May about Pocahontas demonstrates Masha's mastery of English over a very short period of time. While only a little over a month has passed since the story about "Janet," she has grown not only in her fluency in the use of English, but in her use of literacy conventions as well. In terms of social development, she displays a well-developed sense of herself as a participating member of the peer group as she integrates and reproduces themes of her life in a new school in a new culture. Casting for this story included everyone in the story circle.

By June, a few months before kindergarten, Masha's stories began to express her growing awareness of herself as ultimately becoming independent not only from her teachers, but also from her parents. Listen to Masha reflect on growing up.

> "Once upon time there was a little baby with her mother. And then the mother said to her little child, 'Look, child, there's your father who's coming.' The father, he come and he showed the little child a toy. And the little child grew up into a grown-up girl and that's the end."
>
> But the ending of childhood carries a bit of anguish for Masha, which is expressed in her very next story, also dictated in June. It is a brief tale about two friends whose parents die while the friends "play hide and seek."
>
> ". . . And then they were sad for a long time they didn't see their family and their family was dead."
>
> Possibly the consideration of independence from her family was a bit too frightening for Masha, and she modified the ending of her story by saying:
>
> ". . . and then they come alive again. They said 'hello, we missed you, we didn't be dead, wc was only sleeping.'" ✂

Masha's stories are a vivid record of one child's growth in language acquisition and social integration and reveal, in a minor way, how her personal play theme (Fly Horses) was integrated into the culture of her American classroom (Scales, 1997).

Seefeldt and Galper (2002) suggest that young English language learners generally follow a pattern of second language acquisition that parallels the development of their first language. In this example we find:

- A silent period (throughout this period Masha conversed in Russian with her mother and bilingual cousin Alex).
- A tentative use of new language (Masha's first story) that was marked by use of simple syntax and grammar, and very short sentences.
- Complexity of language structures increased gradually, e.g., use of verb tenses includes past and future as well as present (This was transitional for Masha at school's end.)
- Use of very short sentences.
- Moving from present verb/noun construction to past and future (transitional for Masha at school's end). (Seefeldt & Galper, 2000)

We see this pattern reflected clearly in language Masha used to dictate her stories.

Variations in this pattern may, of course, occur, as was the case for Masha's younger cousin, Sonia.

In the second month of school, after beginning to tentatively use English, Sonia acquired an English-speaking friend who began to "speak" for her. Sonia stopped using English in the preschool and did not speak in Russian while at school. No more of the "ABC" song was heard at naptime. Sonia and her new friend were inseparable, although their interactions did not involve speech. Teachers were alarmed and saw this as a warning flag, a possible indicator of a speech or emotional disorder. They consulted frequently with her parents, who reported that their child was becoming ever more fluent in English at home. Everyone doubted this until evidence of Sonia's bilingual competence finally arrived many months later in a tape recording Sonia's father shared with teachers. Sonia's English was more fluent than her parents! However, Sonia continued to remain mute at school until she separated from her new friend on entering kindergarten. ⊘

This anecdote certainly indicates the complex ways that second language learning may impact socioemotional development. This anecdote illustrates that the idea that the "one size fits all" way of learning language or literacy must be resisted. It also demonstrates how difficult it is to be a young English language learner in a classroom where the primary language spoken is English. It gives us a greater appreciation of the countless, sometimes unruly but always original, ways children learn (Dyson 1997; Genishi, 2002).

HONORING THE IMPORTANCE OF LITERATE BEHAVIORS

A group of fast-paced, 4-year-old superheroes was stimulated to elaborate their play when their teacher suggested they draw pictures showing the features of their characters' costumes. The children excitedly drew their characters, and the teacher then labeled each character's essential items of apparel—one character, for example, wore a belt with an *M*. As superhero experts, the children used their language skills to give the teacher the information she needed to label their characters accurately. Had the children been older, the teacher might have asked for their help in spelling, and some of the children could have rendered their own labels, and language certainly would be used to verify and dispute the details of the pictures and the order of the story's sequences. Because they require consideration of a responsive other, all these types of communication—writing, drawing, oral expression, and the use of different media—serve as stepping stones to more developed literacy concepts (see Figure 8.1).

Writing and Graphics

Writing is critical in helping young children grasp the concept of "story" or "narrative" and the perspective this implies (see, for example, Dyson, 1989, 2003;

Children's ideas are given importance when written down by adults.

Dyson & Genishi, 1994). Writing, in turn, occurs as part of a social context. It often emerges from the shared verbalizations surrounding scribbling, drawing, labeling, letter writing, or dictating that lead to a first understanding of the requirements of written communication. Whether the subject that is shared with friends is superhero lore or other fantasy creatures, children come to grasp the relationships of an author to a text and a text to a reader.

Subsequently, children will come to understand that stories follow specific narrative conventions characteristic of their cultures (such as "once upon a time" or "the end"), and will use such conventions appropriately as they become storytellers for themselves and others. Angela began her story by marking new episodes with "Once there was . . ." and closed with "The End," and has marked sequences within her story with "and then." Later she will link events causally (using "because," "and so") as she encounters the need to explain her sequencing.

Opportunities for writing in the classroom should be abundant. Children can be encouraged to send notes to each other by making a mailbox for intra-class mail out of sturdy, 12-section beverage boxes. Each box is laid on its side, exposing 12 mail slots, each slot labeled with a child's name and a small photo-graph. Bookmaking and publishing are additionally encouraged by setting out a few pages of paper stapled together or with holes punched to receive yarn ties. In one class, an autograph book proved a successful activity for all when one child introduced the idea (Koons, 1991). More high-tech activities for children in the primary grades can involve computer journals, PowerPoint presentations, e-mail, and speech-to-text programs (see chapter 12 for more examples).

Another exciting possibility involves journal writing, wherein the child cre-ates a written and/or drawn record of his or her experiences. The writing itself can be done by the child independently, with the assistance of a speech-to-text program, or it can be dictated directly to the teacher. Journals can be prepared by adding pages to a construction paper cover or using binders with fairly sturdy paper, unlined for the younger children and with lines for older beginning writers.

Awareness of Sounds and Patterns of Language

In chapter 2 we distinguish between knowledge children construct or discover for themselves (ideas and concepts) and social knowledge, which is arbitrary. For example, the name *table* is social knowledge and must be taught. This is also true of letter-sound correspondence. The more meaningful the context for introducing such correspondence, the more effective. An example of a meaningful context would be to start with a child's name. What is the sound of the letter that begins it and what is the sound of the letter that ends it? Patterns in the rhythm and structure of language, such as syllables, can be introduced by clapping on the accents in the child's name. Seefeldt and Galper (2001), in *Active Experiences for Active Children: Literacy Emerges,* have included many activi-ties for children that provide a meaningful context. The authors indicate the following as essential concepts in developing phonemic awareness. Phonemic awareness includes:

- The ability to detect rhythm and alliteration
- Phonological memory
- The ability to break down and manipulate spoken words and isolated sounds in words

Although the terms sound similar, phonemic awareness is not the same thing as phonics (International Reading Association and the National As-sociation for the Education of Young Children, 1998). While phonemic awareness is a precursor to understanding letter sounds in words, it is not the systematic presentation of letter sounds in words. Whatever the method used to teach reading (whole language, systematic phonics, or a combination of the two), children first need a strong basis in phonemic awareness (Wasik, 2001).

Another key to developing phonemic awareness is in knowledge of *rimes* or *word families*. While recognition of rhymes develops relatively early and easily, awareness of rime may require explicit instruction. With knowledge of rimes along with onsets, such as *will* and *still*, children are able to decode words that are new to them. With knowledge of common and familiar rimes, such as *ack, ail, est, ice, ink,* and *ight,* children would be able to read nearly 500 words typical to primary-level reading books (Seefeldt, 2005).

Teachers can introduce letter-sound correspondence with one of the most meaningful things children have—their names—for example, pronounce the initial consonant of a child's name and then ask "whose name am I thinking of?" (Seefeldt & Galper, 2001). Changing the beginning letter of children's names to create a new variation is another game that draws attention to letter sounds and creates a hilarious response.

For example, patterns in the sequence of sound in language can be foregrounded by a game that changes a vowel following a consonant in a little chant such as "Apples and Bananas." Children delight in its silliness and quickly pick up the pattern by changing the vowels to "o" or "i" or "u."

LANGUAGE AND LITERACY LEARNING IN THE PRIMARY GRADES: THE MOTIVATING POWER OF PLAY

Erikson noted that elementary school age children become interested in mastery and the need to prove themselves competent in the activities that their culture values (i.e., industry and conformity) (Erikson, 1985). For example, by first grade, they are more ready to participate in the lives of adults and are coming to terms with social expectations of their teachers and parents in academic areas such as literacy.

Parents of children involved in play-centered programs sometimes question how children progress from the drawing, scribbling, dictation, pretend writing, and invented spelling that we know so well from preschool, to the necessary formal conventions of literacy. To answer these questions about elementary school as a context for play and learning, we examine an important element of an effective curriculum developed by a primary-grade school teacher whose school is located in a large, urban area (Scales, 1997).

While many of the literacy activities we describe may be familiar, Harriet, the teacher in the following anecdote, developed her approach through participation in workshops conducted by the Bay Area Writers Project (University of California, Berkeley). She views herself, her classroom environment, and her students as the major resources in a sociocultural context that enhances language and literacy learning. She does believe in teaching specific skills (spelling tests are given, for example). But, importantly, she is wise enough to provide ample time for children to integrate their emerging knowledge through playful engagement with the social resources of this classroom. The motivation and practice necessary to acquire skills in letter-sound recognition, rules for capitalization, punctuation, and dictionary spelling augmenting children's invented spelling are provided primarily through the children's spontaneous acts of writing about things that interest them rather than through unrelated repetition.

A respect for "authoring" in many forms manifests itself in the centrality of a small group activity called "Booklet Writing Time," during which Harriet and trained parent volunteers support children in guided play surrounding writing and drawing. After Booklet Writing Time, opportunity is provided for children to take the "author's" chair to read or tell the class about what they have written or drawn. Sometimes Harriet points out special features she notices like, "Listen to Michelle's story and when we get to the point where people are talking, put your hand up, and when they stop, put your hand down. That's called 'dialogue.' Doesn't it make this piece of writing more interesting?" This intrinsically engaging activity not only involved children in constructing knowledge of concepts and ideas about language, but provided the occasion for the teaching of necessary social knowledge, such as vocabulary, the structure of language, spelling, letter-sound correspondence, and phonemic awareness. Such social knowledge arose from the context of a self-directed, developmentally appropriate activity.

After lunch, a period of spontaneous play again offers opportunities to write and draw and numerous pieces are produced by the children during this time. These can be as simple as a block builder's sign saying, "Don't shake the table," or a "Kwyot plas" sign. On the other hand, the writing could be as complex as the letter to the principal (Figure 8.2) written by Emilie and Vanessa requesting better "pensiels." Some groups might even create more extended pieces, such as a play or a class newspaper.

During these spontaneous and guided play periods, the generative power of play provides the motivation for children's authoring. Like the ephemeral quality of play itself, the creative flow of writing is fleeting, not to be interrupted by premature corrections of "form." In this classroom, neither the teacher nor parent volunteers spell words for children; they encourage the children to try to figure out for themselves how words should look. Later, children are guided to learn correct form as individual development dictates. Here is an observation from this classroom:

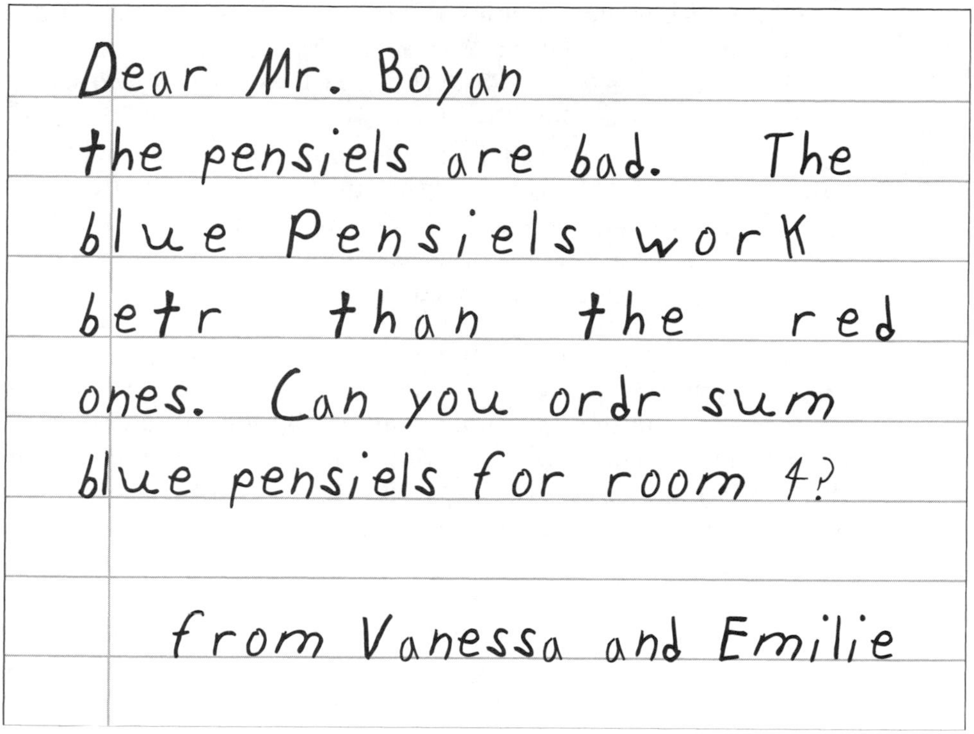

> Dear Mr. Boyan
> the pensiels are bad.   The
> blue Pensiels work
> betr   than   the   red
> ones. Can you ordr sum
> blue pensiels for room 4?
>
> from Vanessa and Emilie

Figure 8.2
Vanessa and Emilie's Pensiels Letter

It is Booklet Writing Time, and Jomar invites his teacher to look at his booklets. He has filled the pages of several. Each entry is dated, and he and his teacher start with the earliest. A vivid illustration accompanies this first story: "THiS Is MY SPASMANHEEIZFLIEEN."

Pointing to the word *THIS*, Jomar's teacher Harriet comments, "I noticed you changed *THIS*. How did you know the dictionary spelling?"

Jomar murmurs, "I learned it and I changed it."

"It was a spelling word and you went back and fixed it," his teacher responds.

Carefully drawing a line with a ruler well below Jomar's writing and illustration, she says to Jomar, "Let's do some dictionary spelling because you already know a lot about dictionary spelling." She carefully copies the first word of Jomar's story and then comments enthusiastically that *Is* is spelled "just right too, except would we put an *I* like that there?" Jomar has used a capital *I*.

"No, we would dot it," Jomar replies. His teacher carefully writes *is* with a lower case *I* after *This*. Harriet and Jomar read through his story, and Jomar is invited to point to the three words in his story that he would like to be able to spell the "dictionary" way.

Jomar points to SPASMANHEEISFLIEEN, and they discuss the "soft" sound of *c* in *spaceman*. Then Jomar is invited to spell along as his teacher writes the word *spaceman*. Later she comments, "You remember, we have just learned about 'ing' endings," and Jomar is guided in his dictionary spelling of the word *flying*. As they proceed through his story, she demonstrates that a "two finger space" is a good rule for separating words from each other (Morrison & Grossman, 1985). ✄

Jomar's teacher talked not about his most recent piece of writing, where he still might be integrating recently acquired knowledge, but about one of his earliest efforts. In this way, Jomar comfortably appropriates formal skills he has already nearly acquired in the context of his own writing. In the process of "proofing" his earliest efforts at "authoring," Jomar becomes what Harriet likes to call a witness to his own growth and development. As Michelle, one of Harriet's other students, reflects on her own growth as an author, she exclaims: "At first you couldn't even read what I wrote!" In this classroom, Michelle knew she was an author before she knew how to write (Morrison, 1985b).

The children's frequent engagement in writing during their spontaneous play periods in this classroom is a testament to play's value as a catalyst in their appropriation and integration of the resources of a rich social-cultural context. The varied pieces of writing children produce in this first-grade classroom as well as the story plays created by preschoolers provide documents through which the children can observe their own personal progress as authors or playwrights.

Multimedia Extends Meanings of Literacy

The wealth of different media today argues against narrowly defining literacy as the acquisition of specific reading skills. Consider the range of possibilities. Oral storytelling stimulates the imagination of the listener and contributes to reading as a habit. Books, of course, contribute to knowledge of literature and, if illustrated, appreciation for art. Recordings and radio contribute strongly to imagination and can influence speech ability and comprehension. Movies, videos, and television, today's principal storytellers, contribute to the child's imagination, speech, and ability to listen and comprehend, as well as to an appreciation of music and art. Interactive computers may make the broadest contribution across all areas, from imagination to potential for control of the medium and creativity in its use (Brown, 1986; Sarama & Clements, 2002; Singer & Lythcott, 2004; Singer & Singer, 2005; von Blanckensee, 1999). (See chapter 12 for more examples of technology-based literacy.)

DYNAMIC APPROACHES TO PROMOTING LITERACY THROUGH PLAY

Young children spontaneously initiate sociodramatic play. Careful observation of the cadence of children's speech and gestures reveals when sociodramatic play is coordinated and cohesive, if the children know who is taking part in it and who is not, and what the play is about (Cook-Gumperz & Scales, 1982, 1996; Scales & Cook-Gumperz, 1993). A well coordinated play scenario is, in a sense, a story the children are telling with an agreed-upon theme and cast of characters.

Sensitive teachers can enhance the development of this literate behavior by responding to or even helping establish sociodramatic play interactions by taking a participant role (see chapter 4). They will want to avoid dominating the dramatic play with their power as grownups, but, on the other hand, abdicating educative responsibility must also be avoided. In other words, a balance must be struck between spontaneous and guided play.

Using Drama Techniques to Enhance Sociodramatic Play

One way to support more complex sociodramatic play is for the teacher to enter into what English drama educator Dorothy Heathcote called "role" within children's sociodramatic play (Heathcote & Bolton, 1995; Wagner, 1999). Heathcote developed an extensive repertoire of drama techniques for the classroom, emphasizing strategies that enable children to create and elaborate roles in spontaneously created dramas that center around historical, ecological or social themes. One example of a drama that might be developed centered around caretaking in an animal habitat. Other scenarios she developed for elementary age children involved the impact of changes due to technological advances: How does one fishing village confront the loss of their livelihood when a neighboring village upstream begins fishing with large nets instead of the old traditional ways? (Heathcote, 1997).

Drama themes are generated from the children's suggestions with minimal props and direction. Children playfully elaborate these dramas from their own knowledge and understanding. These methods have been particularly successful with elementary school-age children. Heathcote suggests that in initial phases of a dramatic interaction (or a play interaction), the teacher's interventions must be subtle. By taking a role that enables the teacher to speak indirectly about the unfolding play or drama, its context can be supported and shaped.

In the following example, the teacher, speaking as if she were a member of the hospital governing board whose office was located "upstairs," has taken a role that allows her to withdraw from direct involvement once the play interaction is underway (Scales, 1970). Another way the teacher remained available indirectly was by means of a prop such as a pretend telephone or intercom. She was thereby able to return if needed to help negotiate any breakdown in the interaction or expand upon a child-generated "problem." Adapting Heathcote's drama methods (Heathcote & Bolton, 1995; Heathcote & Herbert, 1985), here is how she intervened when shooting play had gotten out of hand in the playground of her school:

> Picking up a cell phone (made of a nearby unit block), the teacher called out, "We need a mobile ambulance unit to handle the wounded in the play yard!" In this manner, she temporarily stepped into the play frame by taking a "role" in order to reshape the context of the children's previously chaotic play quickly and indirectly. Following this intervention, the play took a more positive turn as many of the gunslingers stored their arms in the "armory" the teacher had created under the climber in order to enlist in the "medical units." Particular favorites were "Pharmacy" and "Intensive Care" scenarios, where children could prepare vials and bottles of brightly colored medications; dispense pills, bandages, and splints; and monitor IVs made of plastic tubing, funnels, and colored water. ✇

This expansion of the theme from random shooting play to hospital play engaged many more players. The theme of the play changed again on another occasion, when the teacher merely gave the children armbands marked with a red cross. Less mature players could be included now, and the older children could and did assume more complex roles in an elaborated play theme that entailed greater interactive challenge.

Later the teacher should also shift responsibility for advancing the play to the children. The teacher, who in the earlier example was only a member of the "hospital governing board," might now appear to be "helpless" to know what to do next or who is in charge. In this way, the teacher can subtly shift her "teacher power" and authority to invent over to the children (Heathcote & Bolton, 1995; Heathcote & Herbert, 1985).

> In the hospital drama, the teacher addresses Jason as a colleague: "Jason, have you been 'certified' by the governing board of the hospital to serve as its 'director' of emergency units?" After receiving assurance from Jason that he had been "certified" to serve and had "appointed Juan as his Chief of Staff," the teacher retreated from the play to set up a "disaster control center equipped with cell phones." Jason and his friend, Juan, began to man the dual steering wheels of the emergency truck and direct the flow of "casualties" to the "intensive care unit." ✇

Avoiding Some Pitfalls. The teacher in a "role" must not forget that it will be necessary to return to being the teacher—signaling this shift in relationships by a change of voice or posture—for it is inevitable that the children will have to go home, no matter how much fun they are having. Shoes and socks and jackets and sweaters must be found and projects stored and the school tidied for tomorrow. Hence, whatever part in the play teachers create for themselves, the roles must allow movement in and out of the play. Again, the teachers' roles should never be central ones; they should only allow them to be available when needed to support, guide, and sustain the play, but never to direct or dominate.

Moreover, in assuming their "role" in play, teachers must communicate clearly that the drama is part of the world of pretend, the world in which things are only make-believe. Otherwise, the children might become confused about the reality of their play.

Consider the teacher who failed to do this. After spending several days with a child constructing a robot out of cardboard boxes, tape, and wires, she was shocked when, on completion of the robot, her partner demanded that she "plug it in!" It is impossible to describe the look of disappointment on the child's face when told, "It's only make-believe." One can only speculate that the child's confusion arose because he thought he had entered the powerful world of adults, where things "really" happen, whereas the teacher felt she had entered the child's world of make-believe, where all things are possible because they are only pretend. The teacher had much to learn from this episode.

Story Dictation and Story Playing

Do you remember Patrick, the 3-year-old who dictated the story "I have lots of friends"? By encouraging a child to dictate stories to be acted out later by classmates, the teacher provides an outlet for the child's deeply felt needs—in Patrick's case, the need for friends. Furthermore, because of the urgency of the child's desire to communicate those needs, and because of the autonomy allowed by virtue of the child being the one to choose the subject, story, and players, the teacher establishes fertile ground for the development of literate behaviors.

The story dictation/story play curriculum, articulated largely by Vivian Gussin Paley (1981, 1986, 1992, 1999, 2004), recalls Sylvia Ashton-Warner's (1963) discovery that reading is mastered easily if the words to be used are autonomously chosen (for these are the words that have personal and emotional impact for the child). It is a literacy and play curriculum that lends itself to applications in prekindergarten, kindergarten, and elementary classrooms, allowing opportunities for children to move from dictating story plays to

At circle time a young storyteller selects actors to play the roles he has created.

eventually writing their own creative texts to be presented at a Readers Theater or Author's Chair (Dyson, 1997, 2003; Owacki, 2001).

The following are a few examples from the stories dictated to teachers in one school over the course of several years. In these teachers' classrooms, the story dictation and story play curriculum is quite simple. The opportunity to dictate a story is offered every day. A record of who has dictated and who has not is kept so that all may have a turn. Some first- and many second-grade children write their own stories and read them or enact them for their classmates (Dyson, 1997, 2003; Scales, 1997).

Minimizing the addition of props to enhance children's use of their imagination, the stories are acted out by the child-authors and others whom they select. For children who are not yet reading, the story can be read by the teacher and the acting spontaneously performed with a bit of minimal direction from the child-author and the teacher. A record of these stories, along with field notes on the dramatization, is kept in the portfolio of each child.

Laronda.   Laronda came from a large, hard-working, strict family where pretense was frowned upon. She differed from her peers in class who were, for the most part, offspring of university-based, academically oriented families. She dictated a number of story plays during her second year at preschool when she was 4 years old. An enthusiastic storyteller, she quickly grasped the conventions of storytelling and story playing.

Laronda was popular with her classmates, and her stories mention many of her friends by name. In content, the stories are tied to themes and activities of a devoutly religious home life, the world of work, and the domestic comings and goings of an extended family. Laronda's stories rarely mention play as an activity and incorporate few fantasy elements. Here is one of her many stories:

> Once there was a sister, and there was a pretty girl. The pretty girl got lost. Then their boyfriends caught them. Then they went home to eat dinner. After that they went over to their grandma's house. And then their daddy came home. Then their mother went to work. Then the sister had a cold. That's it. (February) ♉

From her field notes on other children's plays, the teacher noted that Laronda was called upon frequently by other children to play the role of "Queen" but never the "Princess." This, despite the fact that in some of her own stories Laronda created a "princess" role for herself, although one who "left because she had to cook." Apparently the children recognized something "adult" about Laronda's pragmatic world. There are few parties and no birthdays to celebrate there. There are domestic chores to be performed, and there is work to "go to" and "come home from."

Other children in this mostly middle-class group placed themselves at the center of the worlds they created, often being taken to the park to play, whereas the voice of Laronda was part of a choir of family voices. The teacher wondered about the impact of Laronda's group-oriented culture that discouraged too much focus on the self, play, and imaginative expression. How much of Laronda's intellectual energy in future schooling would be spent in managing and bridging two disparate worlds in this cosmopolitan university community (Giddens, 2000; Gonzalez-Mena, 1998)?

Jason. Jason, a kindergartner, is the only child of an adult-dominated household. His parents are adamantly opposed to gun play and vigilantly monitor his television viewing to minimize his exposure to violence.

During the year, Jason cautiously attempted to establish himself as a member of the peer group, particularly with a group of the more vigorous boys in the class. The first of the last two stories he dictated shocked his parents:

> Once upon a time, there was a dragon and he went home. And he went to his friend's house. And then he went to another friend's house. And then he saw a horse. And then he saw another horse and killed the horses. And then he went back home. And then he saw ten hundred million horses and killed them. And then he saw some people and he killed

them. And then he saw everything that's alive in the whole wide world and he saw all his friends and he killed them.

Building the dramatic momentum of this chronicle of devastation, Jason's dragon goes to "New York," where "he killed everything else." He then goes to school and kills his teachers, all his friends and the people at school, and "knocked down all the trees of the whole school."

Finally ". . . he knocked down the whole world and the whole sky and every plant. The End." ⌀

When Jason's alarmed mother queried him about this play, he turned to her with twinkling eyes and said, "I was a dragon, you know." This did not surprise the teacher, who already had seen in Jason's previous stories a little dragon shyly trying to show its face. She sensed that this story was Jason's declaration of independence. It unleashed the full power of his imagination, as well as his ability to express latent aggression in a literate, creative way.

Here is Jason's next (and final) story:

Once upon a time there was a Ghostbuster. And then the Ghostbuster went to his friend's house and instead of his friend there was a dragon. And then the dragon said, "Bye, bye. I don't want to play with you. I'm going to the park!" And the dragon went to the park and he got to the park and then when he was at the park he went on the swing. And then a girl came and she said, "What are you doing here?" And then the girl played on the slide. And then the dragon played on the slide. And the girl played on the swing. And then a spider came and then a spider found a web. And they both said, "How are you doing?" (Stage direction: One says it first and then the other.)

And then the dragon went home and he drank some tea. And when he was done he went to bed. And the robbers came in and they looked around and then they went out. And then the little girl played a little more and went home and ate dinner and went to bed. And when she went to sleep some robbers came in, and they looked around, and they stole everything that she had. And they went out. And they all woke up in the morning and ate their breakfast. And they all went to the park and had a party. (Stage direction: All the characters hold hands and begin their singing.) The End. ⌀

Here we see a competent and vigorous 6-year-old very much in command of the story writing conventions he has acquired. He uses a formulaic opening, "Once upon a time," and although most of the occurrences are physical, one represents a mental event: Jason indicates expectation in the second sequence when he says, "instead of his friend there was a dragon." Jason supplies stage directions to clarify and expand the story and presents a mixture of popular media characters (Ghostbuster, robbers), fairy tale characters (dragon, spider), and others, all using direct speech and reciprocal conversation. Sentences are complex and include subordinate clauses, such as "when she went to sleep."

Using these conventions with style and poise, Jason constructs a story that successfully integrates the strands of his life (e.g., going to bed or to places like a friend's house or the park) and incorporates expectations derived from his family and teachers (you eat dinner, then go to bed; the girl and dragon take turns on the slide). In the style of many traditional tales, all of his characters, good and bad, end up as friends; they all go to the park and have a party. Furthermore, by including such details as Ghostbusters and robbers, Jason incorporates the demands of his peer culture. He now has established himself as not only his own "person," but as a full-fledged "member" of the group.

The story dictation activity of the preschool evolves naturally into journal and booklet writing activities in the later elementary years. The motivating power of this activity is augmented by the social opportunity to share stories from an "author's chair," as in a second-grade class mentioned earlier in the chapter, or in a third-grade classroom's "author's theatre" described so powerfully by Anne Dyson (1995, 2003). Gretchen Owacki (2001), also using drama in the classroom, devotes a chapter to describing a primary school curriculum called "Readers Theatre."

As children think and talk about their experiences, they learn that what they talk about can be written and what can be written can be read. In doing so they begin to learn to listen, to speak to others, and thereby to learn the specifics of language and print conventions.

BALANCED OPPORTUNITIES FOR VARIED KINDS OF PLAY SUPPORT COMPETENCIES IN LANGUAGE AND LITERACY

Spontaneous sociodramatic play and guided play through story dictation/story playing and writing are by no means the only literacy activities to be emphasized in the play-based curriculum. Literate behaviors are best supported by a wide range of diverse classroom resources and activities that are balanced on a continuum from spontaneous to guided play. Careful consideration of time, space, materials, and staff provides a planning context for achieving diversity and balance.

Time for Language and Literacy in Play

First, does the program permit sufficient time for literate behavior in play? The pattern of the day should allow for long, uninterrupted periods of spontaneous play in all centers. If children are rushed and the day is chopped up with teacher-directed "inside time," "group time," "sharing time," "snack time"—that is, with too much teacher choice and teacher voice—the children will have little opportunity to integrate and contextualize their play themes through literate behaviors.

Space for Language and Literacy Learning

Is enough space provided for literate behavior in play? Work tables, writing centers, and play areas should be spacious enough to accommodate communication and be set up in such a way that the children can establish face-to-face engagement and visually share materials (i.e., draw on materials that serve as a source for a topic such as miniature toys, etc.), or comfortably share and exchange their knowledge of language and literacy with each other, as in Harriet's Booklet Writing Time.

Materials for Language, Literacy, and Reading and Writing in Play

Materials for language and literacy play include all kinds of writing and printed materials, such as books, catalogs, tablets, clipboards, sticky notes. Ample amounts of attractively displayed and maintained supplies of paper, crayons, and markers are needed. Books, paper, and writing materials should be in the reading or writing center, but also in the dress-up and home play corners, near the outdoor climber, in the block play area, and next to the fishbowl (to record the daily development of the cluster of baby snails!). With the teacher's help, items can be labeled, directional arrows drawn, and symbols and signs made to identify activities and projects. The inclusion of a well-balanced collection of factual and fantasy books, biographies, poetry, and alphabet books is a valuable resource for both teachers and children.

Guidance for Literacy in Play

In promoting literate behaviors, the staff should know when and how to join imaginatively, but not take over, the children's play, as well as when and how to withdraw. The teacher can help the children elaborate their play themes through language, from simple guidance involving help with the construction of a treasure map or an emblem on a superhero cape, to making signs for streets, the bus stop, airport, or house numbers for the cardboard box homes of miniature clothespin dolls.

STANDARDS FOR LITERACY: CALLS FOR ACCOUNTABILITY

Many early childhood teachers are experiencing pressure to implement standards for literacy and report on children's competencies. Special emphasis has been placed on early literacy skills. These assessments are based on a range of standards that vary from state to state (see "A Sampler of Standards" in chapter 6). Some teachers have found that in some cases these standards are in conflict with what they consider developmentally appropriate practice and may narrow the efficacy of a play-centered program. Others felt so much testing could be detrimental to the emotional well-being of children and erode their sense of self-esteem (Fein, Ardlila-Ray, & Groth, 2000; Wien, 2004). The guidelines in The Continuum of Children's Development in Early Reading and Writing in the joint position statement of the International Reading Association (IRA) and the National Association for the Education of Young Children (NAEYC) (1998) is a helpful tool in implementing standards. Response to current calls for accountability through standards and assessment has opened a dialogue among early childhood professionals and educators about ways to make sure that equity of opportunity to develop competencies in a broad range of literacy skills is available in the play-centered classroom (Fein, Ardlila-Ray, & Groth, 2000; Roskos & Neuman, 2005; Seefeldt, 2005).

The many anecdotes in this and other chapters illustrate how standards can be addressed in classrooms where the purposes of language are honored and supported by a language and literacy rich, play-centered environment. The motivating power of the story play curriculum for young English language learner Masha comes to mind. Matthew, a child with special needs, struggles to use language to interact in fast-paced fantasy play with peers. Three-year-old Patrick's introduction to early literacy with his "I Have Friends" story and Angela's compelling narrative reveal much for teachers. These stories reveal the agency and motivation in children's learning as well as demonstrating the acquisition of specific language and literacy competencies. In these vignettes we have seen an advance from the range of literacy learning displayed in the story play dictation of 3- and 4-year-olds, such as Patrick and Laronda, to that of the more sophisticated story play productions of kindergarten-age children such as Jason and Juan, in their enactment of a fantasy narrative in sociodramatic play, to the more sophisticated story plays of a kindergarten-age child such as Jason. In guided play with his primary-school teacher we saw Jomar integrate social knowledge about the conventions of writing as he "edits" his booklet writing. Emergent literacy was seen in Emilie and Vanessa's letter to the principal of their primary-grade school about the quality of the "pensiels" in their classroom. In these anecdotes we have seen the role the children's teachers play in supporting their advancing development. In large part, evaluation of children's progress in the early years has been based on compilations of documents the children produced and systematic recording of teacher observations. Educators are now involved in a new dialogue about how to establish accountability to assure equity of educational opportunity for all children (chapter 6).

Teachers know that children of any age function at varying levels along a continuum of emerging competencies in reading and writing. In Table 8.1, phases of development derived from the NAEYC and IRA's joint position statement (1998) provide an illustration of the range of expectations and suggested curriculum for young children.

Table 8.1
Expected Competencies in Reading and Writing

Expected Competencies	Examples	Teacher and Environmental Support
Phase 1: Awareness and exploration (goals for preschool). Children explore their environment and build the foundations for learning to read and write.	Children listen to stories and may pretend to read. They acquire book handling skills. They engage in drawing and scribble writing as they develop competency in using writing tools. Many begin to write their names and attempt other words such as favorites *rainbow, I love you,* and *Dear Mommy or Daddy.* Children enjoy labeling their paintings, drawings or photographs of family and pets. Many like Angela will want to dictate a narrative to go with their drawings.	Time, space, and materials for language and literacy are provided on a daily basis at multiple sites for storytelling and dictation. Many opportunities for spontaneous and guided exploration of book handling skills, scribble writing, and spontaneous letter formation are provided throughout the classroom.
Phonemic awareness developed through familiar songs, rhymes, and games.	Children begin to recognize their own names as well as those of their peers.	Group activities emphasize phonemic awareness and beginning and ending letter sounds.
Phase 2: Experimental reading and writing (goals for kindergarten). Children develop basic concepts of print and begin to engage in and experiment with reading and writing and continue to develop phonemic awareness as they engage in beginning reading. Children go from scribble writing to formal writing of words for notes, labels, and their own names.	May use invented spelling to enhance play such as "Don't shake the table," or a "kwyot plas" sign.	Formation of upper- and lowercase letters is introduced through models and templates; appropriately ruled paper is available for spontaneous use in a print rich environment A group activity of clapping on the syllables of children's names develops awareness of the beginnings and endings of words and syllables.
Phase 3: Early reading and writing (goals for first grade). Children begin to read simple stories and can write about a topic.	Children may read their own stories and story plays. Children begin to want to learn dictionary spelling of invented words such as Jomar's *SPASMANHEEIZFLIEEN.*	Opportunities are provided for writing in journals and booklets on a daily basis. Writing materials are made available throughout the classroom to support children's spontaneous writing.

Table 8.1
Continued

Expected Competencies	Examples	Teacher and Environmental Support
		Developmentally appropriate conventions of text construction, spelling, and writing are introduced at small group or circle time or to individual children in conference.
Phase 4: Transitional reading and writing (goals for second grade) Children begin to read more fluently and write various text forms using simple and more complex sentences.	Children may begin to create writing tasks for themselves such as a class newspaper or letters to parents or to others such as Vanessa and Emilie's letter to the principal about the "bad pensiels" in their classroom.	Writing continues to occur on a daily basis; abundant books for independent and directed reading are available every day. Guidance in conventions of text construction, spelling, and writing are presented in whole or small groups and in conference. Features of a written text, such as dialogue, are considered in activities such as the "Author's Chair" or in reading and discussions of the writing styles of familiar authors.

Source: National Association for the Education of Young Children & International Reading Association. (1998). *Learning to read and write: Developmentally appropriate practices for young children: A joint position of the International Reading Association (IRA) and the National Association for the Education of Young Children (NAEYC).* Washington, DC: National Association for the Education of Young Children.

WHEN TEACHERS TALK

Turning Negatives Into Positives Through Language

NEGATIVE TALK

Teachers often express concern about negative ways children use language, such as name calling and disrespect for adults. The worst is to say "I'm not your friend."

Some teachers thought children might be helped by being invited at circle or meeting time to brainstorm about ways to avoid using words that make others feel unhappy and consequently make the school an unhappy place. Children could be invited to help create a chart with columns. Listen and record the ways children express their feelings. Honor each contribution by writing it down in the "happy" or "sad" column. Discuss how we can change negative words to positive ones that make our classroom a happy place. Grownups call this "diplomacy," a competency we need throughout our lives (Mitchell, 1993).

RELATING TO CHILDREN WITH SPECIAL NEEDS

Teachers wondered how they could help children communicate in play with a child with a hearing loss. Some suggestions included asking the children to place their hands over their ears and try to communicate; inviting someone fluent in signing, particularly if the child can use sign language or read lips, to teach children to sing and sign. Wisely, the children themselves contributed nonverbal modes of communicating such as, "Look right at him" and "Talk with your hands and eyes."

Other problems arising out of an inability to communicate will be described in detail in a play vignette in chapter 11.

TRANSITION TIME

Teachers shared ideas about turning the inevitable transition times into guided play. As children waited to wash hands, one teacher used an activity that had a language arts component called "The Ship is Loaded With . . ." The teacher starts with something like "The ship is loaded with cheese" and children add rhymes "peas, teas and so on" (Seefeldt & Galper, 2001).

SUMMARY AND CONCLUSION

A play-centered language arts curriculum arises from a context that honors the purposes of children's communication and the responses they might evoke before it stresses isolated strategies for literacy learning. Literate behaviors, particularly in pretend and sociodramatic play and storytelling, are seen as precursors to a grasp of the concept of "story" or "narrative" and the necessary perspective-taking this implies. Such understanding emerges through play as, together, children talk, draw, and share their early attempts to write. In one classroom, the story play activity was a catalyst for second language learning and was a mirror of development in the case of one Russian-speaking child. Happily, in her case, advances in second language learning, socialization, and literacy moved as an integrated whole. Other patterns might emerge in other situations.

Through ample opportunities in guided and spontaneous play, children become participants in and authors and readers of their own stories. Reading widely and writing in many forms lead to an understanding of the many genres of authoring. They become motivated to begin to learn dictionary ways to spell words, develop phonemic awareness, acquire letter and sound recognition, utilize upper and lower case letter forms appropriately, and master the rules for capitalization and punctuation.

While a classroom that is rich in language and literacy is a powerful resource for children, sources, agents, and settings for learning language are not limited to teachers and schools. In many contemporary classrooms, children's classmates and their worlds beyond school are also resources that provide a broad sociocultural context. Through a play-centered language arts curriculum, we tap into the richness of the full range of diverse cultures and languages in our classrooms and communities.

SUGGESTED RESOURCES

Cook-Gumperz, J. (Ed.). (1986). *The social construction of literacy.* New York: Cambridge University Press.

This book provides a sociocultural perspective on the acquisition of literacy.

Dyson, A. H. (2003). *The brothers and sisters learn to write: Popular literacies in childhood and school cultures.* New York & London: Teachers College Press.

Dyson continues to bring us her inside view of the culture of America's increasingly diverse classrooms. She reveals the genius of children and acknowledges the work that teachers accomplish in their classrooms.

Genishi, C. (2002, July). Young English language learners; resourceful in the classroom. *Young Children, 57*(4), 66–70. Washington, DC: NAEYC.

For Genishi, young English language learners come to our classrooms with their language glasses already half full rather than being defined as "limited in English language proficiency" because by the time they have come to school they have already used language to connect with others and make sense of their world.

Heath, S. B. (1983). *Ways with words: Language, life, and work in communities and classrooms.* New York: Cambridge University Press.

Provides a sound ethnographic view of the influence of culture and communication on literacy learning and schooling.

Seefeldt, C. (2005). *How to work with standards in the early childhood classroom.* New York and London: Teachers College Press.

A comprehensive and essential guide for teachers. Seefeldt's wisdom and scholarship again provide practical as well as theoretically grounded leadership in an era of standards and assessment.

Wagner, B. J. (1999). *Dorothy Heathcote: Drama as a learning medium.* Portsmouth, NH: Heinemann.

This new edition of a seminal work on Dorothy Heathcote gives an in-depth look at her pedagogy of drama. Chapters on Using Role in Teaching, Nonverbal Drama, and Code Cracking Literature and Language will be particularly valuable to educators.

Science in the Play-Centered Curriculum

Rosa is playing with a boat at the water table under the shade tree. She slowly pushes the boat down and looks as the drops of water gradually fill it. She watches it sink, whispering, "Come up now!" She lifts it up. She collects small rocks and bark chips from the base of the tree and fills the boat with six large bark chips. "Here you go—Toot! Toot!" She adds three rocks and the boat slowly begins to take on water. Quickly, she piles on two more rocks and the boat sinks. The rocks go down with the ship, but the bark chips come floating to the top. "Pop! Pop!" Rosa pushes one of the chips down again and watches as it pops up as soon as she lets it go. ✆

Play at the center of the curriculum integrates science as well as language, art, mathematics, and social studies. It takes the trained eye of the educator to see the science processes, concepts, and content that the children are involved with as they play. Children are engaged in scientific processes whenever they are observing, comparing, and exploring. We often find young children involved in inquiry even though this is not the formal, analytical process of the scientist or older student. Let's take a brief look at Rosa's water play—an example of a typical activity in early childhood education programs.

How does this child's activity relate to science? When Rosa carefully pushes the boat down, she is investigating what will happen—a scientific process. She observes the water entering the boat. Observing is another basic scientific process. Scientific processes relate to her own actions and developing understandings of the physical world. Rosa is also extending her knowledge of scientific concepts or "big ideas" in science. She does not yet understand that objects that are heavier than their equal volume of water will sink, and those that are lighter will float. However, through activities such as this, Rosa extends her beginning understanding of weight. Rosa is also learning more about the content of science—factual knowledge about the properties of the bark chips such as their specific color, shape, and size. As we shall discuss, scientific processes, concepts, and content are key aspects of appropriate science curriculum for young children.

Why should an early childhood education curriculum emphasize science? Young children need to learn about the physical as well as the social world in order to consider the physical world as being understandable. In this way, science is a natural and necessary part of development. Children's attempts to learn about the world and how things work can be thought of as their science curriculum.

Science is an implicit part of the early childhood education curriculum that centers on play. However, many early childhood educators lack the background in science to bridge the play-centered curriculum that emerges from the children's own interests with standards-based science curriculum.

The focus of this chapter is different from the focus of most books on science activities for young children. Other books usually suggest ways for teachers to set up structured science activities. The teachers we talked to described many teacher-initiated activities, such as growing seeds and sorting autumn leaves, that they found in books on science education for young children. Some of these are excellent. Many teachers described investigative projects, themes, or units from science curriculum materials adopted by their districts or based upon state frameworks and national standards. Although we agree that excellent science programs can be found that are developmentally appropriate, they are not necessarily based on children's own expressed interests. In that sense, they represent only a small range of the science curriculum. They are good examples of teacher-planned activities.

To design a program with play at the center, we highlight activities that children initiate through their own exploration and play. As we noted in chapters 1 and 5, this does not mean that teachers are not involved. Emergent curriculum as well as teacher-initiated science curriculum then can be integral parts of a play-centered curriculum.

One purpose of this chapter is to demonstrate how science is already an integral part of the play-centered curriculum. Teachers then can identify it and also help parents, other staff, and administrators see how rich the traditional play curriculum is in the area of science. Considering play as the core of the curriculum, we will go on to address a second purpose: how teachers can extend the investigation of ideas and processes that arise within the context of children's play.

This chapter begins with a tour of the environment of an early childhood program, analyzing how different indoor and outdoor areas offer numerous opportunities for children to be involved in science. We then provide an introduction to the nature of science education. We discuss ways in which teachers can extend the themes that children use in their unstructured play to more structured activities that involve the children with science concepts, content, and processes. The chapter concludes with an analysis of the ways in which teachers can integrate other science curricula with a play-centered program. We use the continuum of intervention strategies presented in chapters 4 and 5. Throughout this chapter we address teachers' concern that their science curricula addresses program standards.

SCIENTISTS TOUR THE KINDERGARTEN

The integrated play curriculum is the basis for a developmentally appropriate science program for young children. As young children play, they are involved in many things that scientists would identify as "learning about science." If scientists toured your program, what would they find? This is what happened when several science professors toured a local kindergarten program. Marilyn is a biologist, Bob is a chemist, and Toni is a physicist. Although they made these observations in a particular kindergarten class, they could

Observing and describing are the foundations of science.

have made similar observations while visiting other play-centered preschool or primary programs.

Outdoor Area

Marilyn: I'm amazed at how much goes on in such a short time. I've seen a lot of activity related to the rain we had yesterday. Jerry was watching a snail move along the side of the sandbox. He commented on the silvery trail the snail made and then discovered the many trails already made all over the wooden side of the sandbox. He's involved in the scientific process of observing. He and Alicia organized a "snail race" with three snails. The road was the slide. They were watching the different speeds the snails traveled. In science, comparing is also a fundamental process. I was surprised that the children pointed out that the snails crawled up at an angle. Many adults wouldn't have discovered all that information about snail behavior.

Bob: Yes, I was also surprised at what I saw happening without any formal instruction. The sand in the sandbox is pretty wet and several youngsters were making "cakes." There was a lot of investigating going on to find out what they called the best batter, just the right amount of moisture to hold the shape in their cake pans. They had all kinds of ideas on how to improve the "batter," including adding more water and more coarse sand. Through the scientific process of experimenting, they were learning about the properties of materials. Several of the children worked on this for 30 minutes, about half a high school chemistry lab period. Their attention span and absorption in their activity impressed me.

As the children continued to play, Marilyn, Bob, and Toni pointed out many things they considered involvement with science concepts, processes, and content. For example, Soshi was trying to learn to pump on the swings. As she tried to figure out how the rhythmic rocking of her body would make the swing go higher, she was involved in learning more about cause and effect. Lisa and Peter were "fishing" in a puddle and found a large worm with many "rings" that the children called armor rings in their dramatic play. Learning about the particular characteristics of living organisms is important content in the field of biology.

The Block Area

Toni: This looks like "pre-architecture." I'm impressed with the children's understanding and use of shapes. Look at this repetition of triangular blocks here and the interesting example of symmetry there, an important concept in both science and mathematics.

Marilyn: It's been a long time since I've been in a kindergarten class. Aren't these blocks fantastic! Look at how Luis concentrates as he places that block on the tower. And how the children are experimenting, trying to figure out if the longer block or the two shorter blocks will work better . . . and how they try again . . . and, of course, look at the fun they're having.

Toni: There are so many opportunities for questions, for inquiry. I wonder if he will be able to figure out a way to make that block tower stand.

Marilyn: Yes, he just learned about the idea of buttressing . . . another important concept . . . and now, I bet, he's going to use it again over there.

They all fall silent for a moment, watching April and Tanisha build roads for small cars. The children use a block for an arch and several triangles to make a bridge. Tanisha puts a car at the top of the bridge and lets it roll down. April learns from her friend's solution and experiments by giving the car an extra push: "Sooo fast!"

The Art Area

Toni: There's a lot of play and science going on right here. Take a look at that clay table. What strikes me immediately is the way the children explore the properties of the materials. That "food" made out of playdough is not nearly as clearly defined as the food made out of plasticine. The kids have investigated the properties of these different kinds of clay and the limits of what one can do with the clay. Which clay is harder or softer? Which is smooth? I noticed one boy discover that the bridge he made with the playdough doesn't take much stress. The plasticine had more of the tensile properties he needed in a building material.

Marilyn: I'm enjoying watching that girl, Marcia, mix finger paints. She's trying to make a shade of green that matches the color of the paper. And she's quite precise about it. Look how she adds such a small drop of white. She's involved in the processes of observing, of comparing, and of experimenting. It seems like she's learning about concepts relating to shades of color.

SCIENCE IN THE EARLY CHILDHOOD INTEGRATED CURRICULUM

The visiting scientists observed as Soshi, Jerry, Alicia, and the other children followed their own interests through their play. In fact, in some of their activities, we see a curiosity about concepts that are milestones in the evolution of science itself: the laws of floating and of distance and velocity, and the physics of the buttress. These interests and the activities they stimulate are common among children. How can our observations of young children's natural interests as expressed through play lead us to the formation of a balanced science curriculum?

The Goal of Early Childhood Science Education

If we analyze the nature of science, we recognize that central to all scientific inquiry and discovery are important dispositions such as curiosity, a drive to experiment, and a desire to critically assess the validity of answers. We believe the goal of science education for early childhood education is to encourage and support these dispositions.

This is our rationale for seeing play as the core of the early childhood science education program. Children's spontaneous play shows us the children's interests, what they are curious about, and how they pose questions and solve problems.

We believe that a developmentally appropriate science program is based on the similarities between scientists involved in science and children involved in play—an interest plus the energy, knowledge, and skills to pursue that interest. In addition, we find that in both science and play, the interest is often social—shared by others at home or at school or provoked by the particular social context. Therefore, to infuse the early childhood program with the spirit of scientific inquiry, we need to acknowledge the vitality of the children's scientific interests as shown through their play. We can then incorporate these interests, and the social energy that accompanies them, into the curriculum.

This approach to early childhood science education addresses what we believe is the basic weakness of the traditional K–12 science curriculum. Our nation has contributed so much to scientific development and has prospered so much from its applications. Yet, today, many U.S. students graduate with a low level of science literacy which may hamper future scientific development. Most science curriculum programs are seriously flawed by their focus on science facts and routines. What these curricula lack is that which is central to scientific endeavor: the joy of finding out.

The child who asks why certain yellow flowers appear in some places in a spring meadow but not in others is a naturalist involved in inquiry. In contrast, the child who dutifully colors in the outline of spring flowers is doing something unrelated to the process of science. The first has put forward a problem to be solved, which at its core is scientific and for the moment is acting like a scientist. The second child has formulated an entirely different problem, which is how to respond to the teacher's lesson successfully.

In a play-centered curriculum, young children are not simply studying facts but are pursuing problems of interest and judging the adequacy of answers. For all children to develop the ability to engage in scientific inquiry, teachers must respect them as emergent scientists. In this way we encourage all children to see themselves as members of the scientific community. If this sense of community with science is not established in the early years, the prospects of attracting these children to science in adolescence and young adulthood are diminished. It is in these later years and not before that children become capable of participating in the more rigorous forms of scientific inquiry that we recognize as scientific thought.

Scientific Literacy for All Children. For decades, the American Association for the Advancement of Science has sponsored the work of scientists, science educators, and classroom teachers in an effort to foster programs that ensure that all students become literate in science, math, and technology. *Benchmarks for Science Literacy* is the report of the association's Project 2061 (1993). How is scientific literacy for children in kindergarten through grade 2 described?

> From their very first day in school, students should be actively engaged in learning to view the world scientifically. That means encouraging them to ask questions about nature and to seek answers, collect things, count and measure things, make qualitative observations, organize collections and observations, discuss findings, etc. Getting into the spirit of science and liking science are what count most. Awareness of the scientific world view can come later. (p. 10)

National associations of scientists and science educators such as the American Association for the Advancement of Science (AAAS) and the National Science Teachers Association (NSTA) underscore the importance of focusing on equity issues in science education. Children are curious and eager to learn about the physical world. Early childhood educators can play a critical role in providing equal support for girls and boys, as well as for children from all backgrounds, to define themselves as competent scientific investigators.

To develop an appropriate science curriculum, we draw upon what we know about the nature of science and the development of children. In analyzing the scientists' comments as they observed the kindergarten program, we see that they discussed scientific processes, content, and concepts, as well as dispositions such as curiosity. These are the very points made by the American Association for the Advancement of Science in Project 2061 (1993) as well as *Science for All Children,* authored by the National Science Resources Center (1997). This approach is also taken by national science curriculum projects such as Full Option Science System (FOSS), Great Explorations in Math and Science (GEMS), and the Education Development Council's *Young Scientist Series* (e.g., Chalufour & Worth, 2003, 2004) as well as the teacher resources developed by the National Science Resources Center (e.g., 1996, 1997). This is also the approach taken by science education books and texts for teachers, such as those by Althouse (1988), Cliatt and Shaw (1992), Doris (1991), Holt (1989), Kellough (1996), Koralek and Colker (2003), Seefeldt and Galper (2002), Starbuck, Olthof, and Midden (2002), and Wasserman and Ivany (1996).

As teachers, we can analyze the scientific nature of children's activities by asking ourselves: What scientific processes are involved? What scientific concepts are the children developing? What is the scientific content of their activity?

The Nature of Science

The following is a typical definition of the term *science:* "a study that deals with an area of facts or truths that are arranged systematically and demonstrate the operation of general laws."

Many early childhood educators and parents of young children recall memorizing a definition such as this one. Today the emphasis is on the importance of helping students gain competence in the processes of science through participation in meaningful scientific activities. A parallel emphasis is placed on the long-term development of an understanding of scientific concepts—the "big ideas" in science. Scientific content, the facts, is still a basic part of science education, but as American Association for the Advancement of Science, Project 2061 (1993) and other policy statements emphasize, learning scientific facts is not the primary goal of science education as it was in previous decades.

Scientific Processes.   In the early childhood years, scientific processes are the ways children seek answers to their questions. Young children can engage in various science processes by observing, describing, comparing, questioning, collecting and organizing data, communicating with others (e.g., discussing and recording information), interpreting results, and seeking answers to questions.

In a first-grade class, 6-year-old Mark and 7-year-old Gilian observed that earthworms have rings and some of them have a thickening near the front end. They compared several earthworms and found that both small and large worms have a lot of rings, but that "only the bigger ones have a lump near the front." They wanted to find out what the lump was and if the older worms, like trees, have more rings. With their teacher's help, they found the answer to their question about the lump in a high school biology text drawing of a worm. No information was given in the text on the number of rings, so they went back and counted. To do this, they found that they needed a magnifying lens because one worm was tiny and it was difficult to count its rings. Learning to use the tools of science is an important aspect of the development of science competencies. Mark and Gilian drew pictures of the worm, involving themselves in the scientific process of recording information.

Young children are capable of using many scientific processes. They are often careful observers and hone that ability when they examine the rings on a worm or the legs of a beetle. They are eager to engage in communicating their observations, another scientific process. Young children can compare objects; they can organize information; and they can record their data through drawings, photos, or videotapes. The availability of low-cost digital cameras offers children, as well as adults, opportunities to document change over time as they make their own books. Some books about changes can be created in a day, such as one about making and baking rolls. Children also begin to understand concepts of time through digital camera recordings of long-term projects, such as documenting the growth of beans planted in cups, pumpkins planted and harvested in the school garden, or the growth of Bun-Bun, the class rabbit.

Scientific Concepts. Scientific concepts are organizing principles of "what we know." For example, "cylindrical," "green," "hard," and "life cycle" are examples of concepts that we can apply in many content areas. For example, Ibrahim knows that green is a property that can refer to different objects: the tomato leaf, the harder tomatoes, and paint at the easel. Many basic concepts young children develop relate to the properties of objects. They learn to describe objects in terms of such properties as color, shape, size, and weight. Teachers can model science conversations that acknowledge children's love of long, unusual, and descriptive words such as transparency and minuscule.

As children grow older, they are able to understand more abstract, relational concepts such as ideas about motion, light and shadows, changes, and relative position. Children learn science concepts best when they encounter the same concept in different content areas. For example, Duckworth (2001) reminds us that "we see how early experience, only partially understood, overtime contributes to the construction of large ideas" (p. 185).

During their brief tour, the scientists observed the children dealing with a great many scientific concepts. For example, Tanisha and April were learning about concepts of distance and velocity, and Luis was learning about the concept of buttressing.

Science Content. Science content refers to the subject matter. Teachers who develop a balanced science curriculum comment that many science books and textbooks are science-content oriented. For example, a book on insects might include sections with facts about leafhoppers, aphids, dragonflies, mayflies, moths, and butterflies. Early childhood educators often provide rich opportunities for children to explore the world of nature. This is important, but it is also vital that we provide ample opportunities for young children to explore a wide range of science areas. For example, along with books on nature, we can provide books on machines, rocks and minerals, and weather.

In a balanced science curriculum, children learn science content within an organized framework of scientific concepts and through their involvement in scientific processes. In a balanced science curriculum that is play-centered, the particular scientific content, concepts, and processes that children explore at any moment are expressions of the children's own curiosity, interest, and creativity.

If we analyze the touring scientists' observations of this kindergarten in terms of science content, we find that some children were finding out about worms, some about sand, some about blocks, and some about different collage materials.

Observing plants and animals in the classroom can lead to a curiosity about nature.

Ibrahim's teacher has documented his involvement with gardening activities. He is one of several children who return to the garden each day. At 4 years old, Ibrahim has learned a lot about the tomatoes in the small garden outside his child care center. He knows that tomatoes can be yellow as well as red, and he can identify several varieties of cherry tomatoes and beefsteak tomatoes. He can also distinguish a tomato leaf by its shape, texture, and fragrance. He knows when the tomatoes are ripe and how to pick them carefully. Ibrahim's teacher shares her observations with his parents. She explains how his playful activities relate to specific state standards such as children's understandings of attributes of objects (e.g., color, shape, and size), as well as their understanding of the life cycles of plants. ✇

A consideration of the range of science content is important. It is important, as this example shows, for children to have the chance to return to favorite activities again and again. As children work with the same objects over an extended period, they enjoy their growing mastery of specialized science content.

The Nature of the Child

To promote a developmentally appropriate science education program, teachers continually learn more about the nature of science and also about the development of the children they teach. What are the interests shown by 4-year-old

Madison and 7-year-old Samuel? How can we describe their way of understanding the physical world around them?

The Child's Level of Development. In chapter 2, we briefly introduced basic principles of constructivist developmental theories. Other aspects of these theories are discussed in greater depth in chapter 13. In developing an early childhood education science curriculum, teachers find constructivist theories helpful in explaining children's responses, and their ways of interpreting their observations and experiences.

The work of Piaget and others demonstrates that young children do not carry out scientific processes such as experimenting in the same way that adults do (Piaget, 1965a). For example, children might experiment with yellow and blue paint to create a particular shade of green, but their experimentation will not be systematic. Rather than adding a bit more blue and mixing it well, they might add different amounts of different colors. Young children might try different ways to use a set of weights to balance a balance beam, but their efforts are trial and error rather than planned and comprehensive.

A close look at children's levels of cognitive development leads us to understand why young children will not be able to comprehend many scientific concepts despite well-intentioned instruction. One teacher became frustrated when teaching a lesson on gravity to 4-year-olds:

> Catherine dropped seven or eight objects. She explained to the children that the objects fell because there was a force of attraction between Earth and the object. She told them that the objects in a spaceship float around. After this demonstration and explanation, Catherine asked the children to explain why the objects fell when she dropped them. Their replies: "They like to." "They're attractive." "It gets pushed down." "It's falling." "Is it lunchtime?" ∅

Mature scientific thinking involves the ability to analyze, to form hypotheses, and to make inferences and deductions. Young children are not able to do this in the way adults do. The deductions and inferences made by young children do not have the generalized application found in the thought of most adolescents and adults. As the previous example illustrates, children's thinking is egocentric and perception-bound. They are not yet able to understand all aspects of sequences that occur over time.

In *The Child's Conception of Physical Causality,* Piaget (1965b) describes children's growing understanding of shadows. He found that young children believed that the objects themselves produced the shadows (e.g., that the shadow next to a book was like a substance coming from the book). Little by little, children came to understand that a relationship exists between the shadow and the source of light. Not until most children were in middle childhood did they understand that the shadow is an absence of light and that the light is being blocked by the object.

This does not mean that we should underestimate young children's abilities or ignore their interests. Shadows illustrate this point well. Many young children demonstrate their fascination with shadows in their spontaneous play. Skillful teachers find guided play as well as teacher-initiated activities that draw upon children's interests.

Science Learning and Social Contexts.

Around the world, children's development in science learning is also influenced by their social and cultural environments. Families, schools, and communities are important personal influences (Vygotsky, 1978). In some cultures, children have many experiences that support the development of particular scientific processes, concepts, and content. Parents and teachers in urban areas, for example, might focus on providing children with explorations with different types of building blocks. The children might tend to build cityscapes—apartment buildings, offices, factories, and freeways. In contrast, the parents and teachers of children who live on farms might stress content such as plants and animals, concepts such as "the life cycle," and observational processes such as observing whether plants are ready for harvest.

Children's understandings usually develop faster in subject areas in which they have greater experience with the physical world. These are also areas of knowledge in which they have greater experience with the social world, as important adults and peers share social knowledge with them. With time for further maturation and more interactions with the physical and social world, young children's manner of thinking changes. We need to build our science programs around children's present ways of thinking and provide the experiences that will foster future development.

Developing a Sense of Place.

Jaelitza, a teacher in a rural child-care center and school, reflects on outdoor adventures in her article "Insect Love: A Field Journal" published in *Young Children* (1996):

> Teacher Neil found a Promethia moth, a nocturnal moth, which had attached itself to a bottle in the pony shed. Brought into the light, it did not fly away, and so we were able to observe it very closely. Matt and Levi were very interested. Neil showed us its picture in the field guide and went on to answer the two boys' questions by referring to the moth as well as the text of the guide.
>
> Matt and Levi were interested in our new field-study materials—bug "houses" and a new magnifying glass. They were ready to set out immediately, and I followed. Turning over logs that demarcate the tepee garden patch, we found a ready supply of sow bugs, immature snails, worms, ants and spiders. . . . (p. 31)

Jaelitza (personal communication, 1996) and other teachers and naturalists express the concern that few of today's children have opportunities to develop a deep connection to the land, a sense of geographical place, through sustained opportunities to play outdoors in fields, woods, beaches, and even empty city lots (Greenman, 2005; Nabhan, 1997; Pyle, 1993; Rivkin, 1995, Starbuck, Olthof, & Midden, 2002).

This need for place is expressed beautifully in Nabhan and Trimble's (1994) *The Geography of Childhood*. Similarly, in the article "How Nature Shapes Childhood: Personality, Play, and a Sense of Place," Nixon (1997) reflects on the wisdom of naturalists and conservationists such as Pyle, Louv, and Nabhan, who have written about the need for children to have extended time in which to play and explore in their natural environments. Nixon introduces Pyle's compelling concept of the "extinction of experience" and discusses Louv's insight that today, just when more children are developing greater awareness, knowledge, and feelings about protecting the global environment, fewer children are having unstructured and direct experiences with nature in their local environments.

Helping Urban Children Develop a Sense of Place. Although play-centered curricula draw upon and reflect children's social contexts, it is critical that we not limit our expectations and curricula to these contexts. This principle is particularly important in science. The majority of Americans today live in urban areas. In cities and suburbs, and particularly in unsafe areas, we need to ask: How can we help urban children, their families, and ourselves develop a sense of place, an appreciation and ease with the outdoors, and a feeling of wonder about life?

In an article in *Science and Children,* Melben (2000), a teacher in an urban elementary school, views urban children's lack of outdoor nature activities as an example of inequities. She presents examples of efforts to develop science projects that followed the children's own interests and drew from their experiences. Her descriptions of projects with rainwater and pigeons amply illustrate that children's understandings of ecology and sense of wonder can be promoted in urban as well as more rural settings.

The urban children in Shelley's preschool program had been sloshing through the snow for weeks as they walked to their neighborhood school. Shelley first extended these activities by bringing snow and icicles inside in containers so that the children could have unhurried observations and chances to discuss the melting process. She then put water in an ice tray and took the tray out of the freezer throughout the morning so that the children could observe the changes. This led to a weeklong observation of the melting of a 50-pound block of ice that Shelley purchased from an ice company and placed in a baby bathtub. ✑

The Child's Interests

Observation of individual children's spontaneous play is central to discovering their interests. These interests are the children's bridge between play and science and home. As teachers committed to equality of opportunity, it is particularly important for us to consider the ways in which children's interests can lead all children to participate in science (Browne, 1991).

> Bee loves to observe the silkworms. She feeds them mulberry leaves, has arranged her own box, and is keeping a daily journal with descriptions and pictures. Her teacher discovers that Bee's grandmother comes from Laos and knows how to spin the silk from the cocoons into thread. Bee, her grandmother, and her teacher work together to plan a series of activities that are multicultural, playful, and scientific. ✄

> In her kindergarten, Alia has built a treasure box. This is an example of a teacher-initiated project that requires little knowledge of English while promoting continuous peer interactions. First, her teacher has the children draw a representation of their carpentry project. With some adult help, Alia carefully measures and cuts the wood. She learns about sanding, first using coarse sandpaper, then a finer grade. This activity is part of the ongoing science program that builds on children's interests and that promotes equity for all children. ✄

Meeting the Needs of Children Who Are English Language Learners

Throughout this chapter we provide examples of students who speak various languages who come to school with varied interests, experiences, and talents. Play-centered science curricula provide numerous opportunities for children to develop greater fluency in English as they explore the physical world and interact with their peers. When teachers make sure that the environment includes numerous familiar objects, including ones from children's home cultures, children know that they are welcome, can draw upon familiar experiences, and show their competencies. In this way, teachers reduce stressful situations and provide support for listening and speaking in engaging situations.

Through science activities, teachers take advantage of the many ways that the development of a new language parallels that of the first language. Central to first language development is a supportive social and physical environment. Similarly, early childhood educators create environments where children's learning of English can flourish (Genishi, 2002). As children explore, they wish to communicate their observations, questions, and desires. Playful science experiences provide opportunities for children's gestures to be understood in context, for a two-word phrase to convey ample meaning, and for simple sentences to contribute to conversations.

> From his first day at school, Carlos looked forward to experimenting at the water table. Initially, he spoke mostly with two other children who spoke Spanish as well as English. His teacher noted the complexity of his explorations. Recognizing his interests and level of ability, his teacher bought plastic tubing, funnels, and a series of graduated beakers so that Carlos and his friends would find many challenging problems to solve. ✆

Developing Inclusive Science Curriculum for Children with Special Needs

In inclusive programs, teachers plan play-centered science curriculum to meet the needs of young children whose needs have not yet been formally identified as well as those who are receiving special services. Just as the scientists toured the kindergarten with an eye toward opportunities for learning science, all teachers can tour their environment with an eye toward serving students with special needs. Such informal tours are even more useful in the company of early childhood special educators, occupational therapists, or speech therapists. The following questions can serve as an initial guide for the tour.

Do all children have easy access to materials? Are particular accommodations necessary for a child to be able to see or hear or use tools such as scales, magnifying lenses, or scissors? Are there quiet corners for a single child to focus on an exploration as well as open outdoor spaces for active exploration, climbing, and swinging? Are spaces set up so that children can play alone or with one other child without the stimulation of a larger group?

As they work with children with special needs, teachers remember that all children have particular strengths and interests. For example, Pat shared one of her treasured memories of a kindergarten child with autism who loved to play with blocks. She honored his joy and involvement with blocks rather than insisting that he "go to another activity first." After many weeks, it was there in the block area that, to the delight of all, he first engaged in parallel play and later spoke his first word.

EXTENDING THE SCIENCE CURRICULUM

How can teachers extend the science processes, concepts, and content that children deal with in their own unstructured play? How can we decide when to intervene and when not to? What best supports children's learning?

In chapters 4 and 5, we discussed principles that guide orchestration and presented a continuum of intervention strategies ranging from setting the stage to guiding play to teacher-initiated activities. When thinking about enriching the

Guided discovery extends the play-centered curriculum into the elementary grades.

science curriculum, we can think about strategies at all points along the continuum. In this section, we discuss strategies and their implications for extending children's involvement with science. Recognizing the key role of play in development, we plan the curriculum by focusing first on providing an environment rich in possibilities for spontaneous play. We then think about teacher-planned interventions. This contrasts with science programs that typically begin with particular activities and then consider opportunities for children to explore and create.

Setting the Stage for Learning About the Physical World Through Spontaneous Play

The basis for a play-centered curriculum is a well-planned environment. As described in the tour of the kindergarten, well-planned indoor and outdoor environments allow for multiple opportunities for spontaneous play. Developing an environment that is rich in opportunities for children is a great challenge for teachers. It takes careful planning to enable children to have the chance to work with a wide variety of materials in a great many ways. Different types of paints, clays, collage materials, blocks in different shapes and sizes, sand and water, climbing structures, plants, animals, and a great collection of objects, especially recycled ones, are a few of the many materials found in play-centered programs.

The play-centered environment is flexible, and the physical space can be rearranged as interests change. If a group of children is interested in working with large blocks, the teacher might decide to extend the space allotted for block activities, as well as provide additional materials. We observed children in one class making an impressive collection of blocks with milk cartons of different sizes fitted together. One fortunate class in a rural area had new possibilities open up when Russell's father brought in a truckload of coarse sand from the river and the parent group built a sand and gravel pit. The children became more involved in large vehicle construction play.

Encouraging Further Exploration of the Environment

After initially developing the environment, teachers then observe children in their spontaneous play in order to modify the environment so that children can extend their play. Like a dance, this involves the teachers themselves in a creative and playful process.

Using the kindergarten class that the scientists toured as an example, the teacher could add materials or offer assistance in the following ways to allow children to extend their observations and experimentations. Jerry and Alicia were interested in snails. What would they do if their teacher turned over a shovelful of soil to expose worms, sow bugs, and larvae? Other children were using blocks to build towers. What would happen if the teacher took this opportunity to introduce blocks of additional shapes? Perhaps a set of table blocks, such as pattern blocks, would lead to greater interest in different types of constructions.

Returning to the vignette at the beginning of this chapter, Rosa's teacher observed that Rosa continued to play at the water table for several days, experimenting with boats and cargo. Based on these observations, her teacher decided to place a box with an assortment of objects near the water table. She included objects of different sizes and materials such as metal, wood, plastic, and cork. She also added some large wooden objects that floated and small metal objects that sank. Rosa's teacher understood that she was providing new curricula opportunities for all the children, as well as individualizing the curriculum for Rosa.

In these examples, teachers observe the children, follow their lead, think of the many materials that might be added, and select one or more to add in a nonobtrusive way. This is an ongoing process of matching and extending. Another preschool teacher describes how digital photos allowed children opportunities to examine and talk about what they did and to generate ideas for extending their explorations (Hoisington, 2003).

Interacting with Children in Their Play

Taking the child's-eye view in science education often takes the form of wordless communication. A teacher's smile, returned to a child's questioning glance, is nonverbal communication. In the context of the child's attempt to balance one more block on a tower of blocks, it is a scientific conversation: "When you do it that way, they fall over." "Yes. I was surprised too."

During spontaneous play, teachers help children maintain their focus by assuming the role of the Artist Apprentice so that play areas remain less cluttered. In guided play, teachers might decide to take the role of Parallel Player, sitting side-by-side with children. If teachers enjoy exploring and playing with blocks or with sand or collage materials, their own sense of interest, wonder, and focused involvement through spontaneous play will be communicated. As long as the teachers' explorations and play involve them in experimenting and discovering new ways to do things or the enjoyment of familiar patterns, they can avoid the trap of producing static models that children might copy. Teachers model use of scientific language in the role of Spectator. What questions come to mind: "How can you build a tower with connecting turrets using table blocks?" "Can you build a tunnel under the sand pyramid you just constructed?"

Orchestrating Extensions for Play

In chapter 4, we discussed how teachers use the idea of the play continuum as they plan play-centered curriculum. Here we consider how teachers can make play central to the science curriculum. We begin with play-generated curriculum that emerges from the interests of the children.

Play-Generated Curriculum

In their play, Sarah, Dean, and Nellan expressed their interest in worms. John, their second-grade teacher, saw this as an opportunity to introduce different science experiences involving worms. He provided pieces of Plexiglas so the children could observe the movements of the worms in greater detail. When this proved a popular activity, John asked the children to find other wormlike animals. Within a week, there was an exciting collection of caterpillars, several kinds of worms, and insect larvae that Nellan brought in. This led to a conversation between Nellan and the other children about the differences between worms and insects, as well as the sequence of the insect life cycle. ✇

One teacher in a school-age child-care program enjoyed the enthusiasm that the children brought to their play with light and shadows. She extended this play by showing them how to outline each other's shadows with chalk on the walkway. This led to the question: "How long and how short does your shadow get?" In follow-up activities, they outlined their shadows on butcher paper several times during the day. The children and teachers had fun generating many researchable questions, for example: "Can you shake your shadow hand with someone else's?" "Can you make your shadow stand on someone else's shadow shoulders?" ⌀

Teachers turn to curriculum materials developed by science educators, as well. For example, FOSS and GEMS have units for young children that draw upon children's interests as expressed in their play. For example, in the Full Option Science System unit *Air and Weather* (2005), children construct and try out parachutes, make a balloon rocket system, and build kites and pinwheels.

In our selection of science-related activities, we, as teachers, reflect society's social and cultural values, as well as our personal interests. For example, when John asks the children to collect other wormlike animals, he is thinking about his state's science frameworks, which include a focus on living things and the life cycle for the primary level. Shelley related children's explorations with ice to the physical science strand of her state's frameworks that includes "states of matter" as an important concept. These are examples of ways in which teachers expand upon those aspects of the children's spontaneous play that are recognized by society as relevant to science learning.

Curriculum-Generated Play

In a play-centered curriculum, teachers constantly explore the ways in which the curriculum can lead to play. The connection is often seamless. This is seen most often when science curricula are cohesive and well-integrated, rather than a series of unrelated activities.

Although a teacher-planned science program can be an integral part of a play-centered program, it is critical to evaluate carefully the program's philosophy, format, and specific activities to assure that the entire program or specific activities complement a play-centered curriculum. Most importantly, teachers find that they can select or develop units involving activities with a variety of materials that draw upon children's interests and naturally lead back to children's spontaneous play while promoting an integrated curriculum. The Full Option Science System (FOSS) units *Balance and Motion* (2005) and *Air and Weather* (2005), and the Great Explorations in Mathematics and Science (GEMS) units *Treasure Boxes* (1997) and *Ant Homes Under Ground* (1996) often stimulate play in which children draw upon what they are learning. In *The Young Scientist Series*, Chalufour and Worth begin with opportunities for open exploration followed by suggestions for more focused explorations and extension activities (e.g., 2003, 2004). In *Serious Players in the Primary Classroom*, Wasserman (2000) describes how teachers can plan thematic science units so that children have opportunities to replay concepts and content they already have encountered in more structured lessons.

The following vignettes describe the ongoing thematic unit on arthropods and continued exploration and play of Jenny's kindergarten and first-grade children.

In September, Jenny teaches the children how to use bowls to collect insects and spiders in a wooded area near the kindergarten/first-grade classroom. She models tapping bushes or shrubs with a stick over a white plastic tub. Leaves, dirt, dust, and animals fall into the tub. Ned, Shawn, and Ashley crouch around the tubs eagerly narrating in careful detail the movements of the animals: "There's a tiny green spider. It's *so* small, wait, there's two. How many spiders do you have? Don't let it get out!"

Children's interest in spiders continues. Several weeks later, Ashley, Yumi, Eric, and Ned are on their hands and knees, carefully using sticks to lift and adjust the position of a metal, wheeled object. Eric lifts the entire object slowly, revealing red debris, dirt and many small insects. Suddenly Ashley yells, "Oh my gosh, a spider! A red spider! It has eggs." A large, rust-colored spider with a round, whitish abdomen is revealed. Quickly it burrows back into the debris and soil. Ned says quietly, "It's a mother spider. It's an egg sac. The white thing is an egg sac." Ashley declares, "It's red like the dirt." Over the next few weeks, the rust-colored spider appears in journals and drawings (such as in Figure 9.1). The children return often to the area to find the spider.

In January, the fourth and fifth graders join the kindergartners outdoors. Shawn walks to the white plastic tubs, chooses one from the wagon

Figure 9.1
Journal Entry About a Spider

We fownd a Spidove Thet
Was all Red ecSept for There
Was a big White Ovel Thing.
We Thingk it Was a Age Sac.
We Thingk it Was a Femall.

and finds a large stick on the ground. He walks with his fourth-grade partner to a bush and silently taps the bushes. He stops, places the bowl on the ground, crouches and looks inside the bowl. His partner watches him. Shawn stands, takes a step back to the bush and taps again, silently collecting more debris and animals. Again he places the bowl on the ground, squats and bends his head deeply over the bowl and looks. His fourth-grade partner mirrors his stance. ✑

Recasting the Curriculum in Play

When science curricula are appropriate for the development and interests of the students, teachers support ways for children to replay what they are learning. Kogan (2003) relates how kindergarten students in a bilingual (English) school in Mexico City recast a thematic unit about the human body in their play. When children told their personal stories about accidents and broken bones, their teacher tape-recorded the conversations during roleplay. Kogan describes the in-depth emergent curriculum in which children first drew "memory drawings" of their bones, then viewed x-rays, and examined chicken bones to compare with their drawings. The class visited a medical clinic where a child's grandfather worked. There they had a chance to talk with medical personnel about the x-ray machine and see how doctors checked x-rays on a computer monitor. The kindergartners even used laboratory microscopes to view slides with blood. Back in the classroom, children represented their growing knowledge in numerous ways, including play. Some represented bones, carefully considering what to use for the inside and outside. Others built a complex x-ray machine, considering how to control the light. These playful activities resulted in further inquiry: "What has bones?" "What bones do different animals have?" And so this inspiring Bone Project continued, involving children and teacher in the full continuum of play-centered curricular activities.

ADDRESSING STANDARDS IN THE PLAY-CENTERED CURRICULUM

According to the National Science Education Standards (1996),

> From the earliest grades students should experience science in a form that engages them in active construction of ideas and explanations that enhance their abilities to develop the abilities of doing science. . . . Students should do science in ways that are within their developmental capacities. (chapter 6, p. 1)

The National Science Education Standards statement emphasizes the importance of developmentally appropriate curriculum and constructivist teaching practices. Our review of national and state standards demonstrates that an integrated primary science curriculum with play at its center can address most national and state science standards and indicators. Indeed, many science strands and specific standards relate to the playful activities discussed in this chapter. In this section, we begin with an overview of some of the major science learning outcomes included in national and state standards. In Table 9.1 we draw upon examples from this chapter to illustrate how teachers address standards in ways that are developmentally appropriate and develop children's abilities to "do science."

As we have noted before, the numerous national and state standards can seem confusing and overwhelming. Teachers can simplify the process of addressing science standards. The National Science Education Standards (1996) and standards of many states emphasize the importance of integrated, extensive explorations of familiar environments and materials so that young children develop deeper understanding rather than superficial information that is often the result of unrelated activities planned to address unrelated, specific standards.

To examine your program's standards from an integrated perspective, it is important to identify the "big ideas" (i.e., what processes, concepts, and content are identified as the most important). At the national level, the K–4 standards address "science as inquiry" and focus on children's abilities to understand and engage in inquiry processes such as asking questions, observing, using simple tools, using data to construct explanations, and communicating their work to others. These are the very processes that we have emphasized throughout this chapter.

The national standards address scientific concepts as well as content in areas such as physical sciences, life science, earth and space science, health, technology, and environmental science. For example, standards for the physical sciences include children's developing understanding that objects can be described by their properties and that the position and motion of objects can be described. Most state standards for primary grade students are similar to these national standards, although the organization, detail, and illustrative examples may differ.

Most state standards for preschool include a similar emphasis on scientific processes: children's asking questions about their world, seeking answers, and communicating with others. The standards focus on "big ideas," concepts and content with most state guidelines providing examples of learning experiences that are developmentally appropriate. For example, children use wet and dry sand and talk about their experiences; children describe the rocks in their environment; children discuss and record their observations of the life cycle of butterflies. Table 9.1 illustrates how teachers can relate children's play-centered activities to science standards.

Table 9.1

Addressing Science Standards in the Play-Centered Curriculum

Example of Curriculum Standard	Example
Inquiry: Children develop their abilities to engage in scientific inquiry, e.g., observing, comparing, experimenting, and communicating.	At the water table, Rosa observes objects floating and sinking.
Young children engage in play as a means to engage in inquiry.	
Physical Science: Children develop an understanding of the position and motion of objects.	Luis builds a block tower.
Children will experiment with a variety of objects to determine when the objects can stand and the ways that objects can be balanced.	
Physical Science: Children develop an understanding of the position and motion of objects.	April and Tanisha roll toy cars down the bridge.
Children will explore and describe various actions that can change an object's motion such as pulling, pushing, twisting, rolling, and throwing.	
Science as Inquiry: Children develop their abilities to engage in scientific inquiry, e.g., observing, comparing, experimenting, and communicating.	Mark and Gilian observe earthworms using a magnifying lens. They seek further information to answer their questions
Children will ask questions about their environment; they will employ simple tools to extend the senses.	
Life Science: Children develop an understanding of the characteristics of organisms.	Ibrahim identifies tomato leaves by their size and shape.
Physical Science: Children develop an understanding of objects and materials.	Marcia mixes finger paints.
Children explore the properties of varied liquids and solids.	

The stated goal of the national standards and almost all state science standards is to support young children's curiosity, wonder, and engagement with their physical world and knowledge about it. Some state standards and indicators for early childhood programs are very general while others are carefully crafted to articulate with the state's primary science standards. These often appear more detailed. We find that teachers can address standards in an integrated, meaningful way when they emphasize play and exploration. In doing so, teachers consider children's interests and the knowledge they bring from home.

WHEN TEACHERS TALK

Developing Confidence in Teaching Science

Many teachers are concerned that they know too little about science to develop a rich science program. Unlike the scientists who toured the classroom, many people are aware that they have little expertise in the life sciences, physical sciences, or earth sciences. How can teachers who think that they have a weak preparation in this area develop a challenging, play-centered science curriculum? The following suggestions are useful guides for teachers:

1. Select science units or themes that promote in-depth engagement and understanding, along with a playful sense of inquiry. The National Science Teachers Association (NSTA) and the American Association for the Advancement of Science (AAAS) underscore the importance of focusing on children's depth of understanding rather than the "topic-a-day" approach to science.

   An in-depth, multifaceted approach is typified by the Reggio Emilia approach. Italian educators and parents, who have developed the Reggio Emilia approach to education, experiment in their curricula with the many ways that children can bring greater depth to their examination of experiences such as a broad jump event or a butterfly project. This approach also exemplifies how an emergent curriculum is dependent on teachers' close observations of and conversations with children (e.g., Edwards, Gandini, & Forman, 1993; Hendrick, 1997; Wurm, 2005).

2. Select units that include science processes, concepts, and content that the children can relate to their everyday lives, families, and cultures. The National Science Education Standards emphasize the investigation of authentic questions such as those encountered in daily life situations when considering issues of equity and access for all students: "The diversity of students' needs, experiences and backgrounds requires that teachers and schools support varied,

high-quality opportunities for all students to learn science" (National Academy of Sciences, 1995, p. 4).

Furthermore, the National Science Education Standards recommend that the central strategy for teaching science is the exploration of "authentic questions" (National Academy of Science, 1996, p. 30). We find that these explorations are most likely to be replayed in children's subsequent spontaneous play.

3. View yourself as one member of a community of playful investigators rather than as the expert. Think about the science-related activities that you enjoy so that your students will observe your curiosity and your sense of wonder. Become knowledgeable about the interests and abilities of your children and their families, as well as others at school and in the community. By recognizing the scientific expertise of others, you are serving as a good role model for your students.

Ferguson (2001) writes about Thomas, a 5-year-old in her class who appeared uninvolved with the other children, as well as uninterested in the classroom curriculum. This changed dramatically when, during a class discussion about snakes, Thomas hesitantly shared that he knew all about snakes, that he "has almost 100 snakes in his basement" (p. 6). Of course, he received quite a response. Ferguson describes how she extended this teachable moment into a lengthy inquiry project, although she felt uncomfortable around snakes. Thomas and his uncle Bob served as enthusiastic resource specialists to Ferguson and the other students. Uncle Bob brought in a large snakeskin. Thomas and several children took a trip to a pet store where they saw a huge snake. This was followed with related classroom activities that reflected the children's interests, including a collection of plastic reptiles that Ferguson placed in the manipulative area.

This example as well as others from this chapter, such as Bee's grandmother and the silkworm cocoons, illustrate that teachers need not feel that they have to be scientific experts. Teachers can enrich their science programs by turning to local resources provided by children, their families, and the community.

4. Support science literacy by surrounding children with science resource media. By showing your students that you, yourself, turn to science resources, you are helping students learn how scientists investigate. Many science books have been published for children with photos or accurate illustrations. Science films and videos abound, and nature films and videos are especially plentiful. In an environment that is rich in science resources, children and teachers continually extend their knowledge of the physical world and their opportunities for exploring it. Science books for children are readily available.

Each month, the journal *Science and Children* reviews science resources and computer programs. Each year it publishes *The List of Outstanding Trade Books for Children,* as well as a selection of recommended science trade books in Spanish. Numerous resources are now available on the Internet. (See chapter 12, "Toys and Technology.")

SUMMARY AND CONCLUSION

Young children are curious about the natural world. They are interested in finding out about their physical environment—finding out about how things work. A program based upon children's interests therefore includes an emphasis on science. As early childhood educators integrate the curricula with children's spontaneous play as the focal point, they begin to see the great extent to which children's activities involve science processes, concepts, and content. Like the scientists who toured the kindergarten, teachers begin to "see science" and see opportunities for additional science activities everywhere. The play-centered science curriculum provides the means to foster children's active engagement and address program standards at the same time.

Teachers can begin with an environment that invites children to explore their physical world through spontaneous play. Further exploration is encouraged through the addition of materials and through supportive teacher-child interaction. Drawing upon the children's expressed interests, teachers can introduce science activities related to children's play. Teachers' knowledge of guidelines for appropriate practices in addressing standards as well as their knowledge of the scientific processes and "big ideas" identified in national as well as local standards, can guide their curriculum decisions. Appropriate teacher-directed activities can be introduced that complement play-centered activities and lead back to play.

The early childhood years provide a rich and perhaps critical opportunity to draw the natural power and direction of children's reasoning into the community of science. If we incorporate these interests and energies into the early childhood education classroom, we will promote equity for all children and promote a scientifically literate generation.

SUGGESTED RESOURCES

The following texts are recommended as comprehensive science education resources for early childhood educators. Each promotes a deeper understanding of the nature of science education and recommends ways of planning developmentally appropriate, integrated science curriculum in science.

Chaille, C., & Britain, L. (2003). *The young child as scientist: Constructivist approaches to early childhood science education* (3rd ed.). Upper Saddle River, NJ: Longman/Allyn & Bacon.

Full Option Science System (FOSS) units for kindergarten through grade 3 are developed by the Lawrence Hall of Science, University of California, Berkeley, and distributed by Delta Education, Inc., Nashua, NH.

The FOSS curricula materials provide opportunities for children to explore and discover, as well as chances for teachers to take the lead in introducing scientific processes, concepts, and content. Many of the units involve materials and activities that are naturals for curriculum-generated play, such as *Balance and Motion,* and *Air and Weather.*

Harlan, J., & Rivkin, M. S. (2004). *Science experiences for the early childhood years: An integrated affective approach* (8th ed.). Upper Saddle River, NJ: Merrill/Prentice Hall.

Hill, D. M. (1977). *Mud, sand, and water.* Washington, DC: National Association for the Education of Young Children.

This book is a classic among preschool educators and includes many appropriate suggestions for using these child-proven materials with primary-grade children, as well. For students and teachers who have had few encounters with mud, sand, and water in their own educational experience, we recommend this book as another source of activities to "focus our thinking."

Koralek, D., & Kolker, L. J. (Eds.). (2003). *Spotlight on Young Children and Science.* Washington, DC: National Association for the Education of Young Children.

This is a collection of articles that appeared in the journal *Young Children* as well as articles written especially for this useful resource.

Nabhan, G. P., & Trimble, S. (1994). *The geography of childhood: Why children need wild places.* Boston: Beacon Press.

Nabhan and Trimble are respected contemporary natural history writers who are recognized for their beautiful prose and insightful reflections. This is a collection of essays in which they reflect on their own childhood experiences, their children's experiences, and the experiences of the world's children. Their descriptions will inspire readers to follow up on this vital topic.

National Science Resources Center. (1996). *Resources for teaching elementary school science.* Washington, DC: National Academy Press.

This book is the discovery science resource for teachers. Descriptive information is provided for science curriculum materials that include core materials, supplementary materials, and science activity books for all science content areas, as well as the NSRC evaluation criteria for curriculum materials, book lists and resource guides, and periodicals.

Rivkin, M. S. (1995). *The great outdoors: Restoring children's right to play outside.* Washington, D. C.: National Association for the Education of Young Children.

This inspiring book provides the means for teachers to support children's sense of place.

Science and Children

This monthly journal published by the National Science Teachers Association includes articles for teachers of young children, as well as children in the upper-elementary grades. As mentioned in this chapter, the recommended science trade books for children, both English and Spanish, and the reviews of media are excellent resources for parents, librarians, and families.

Seefeldt, C., & Galper, A. (2007). *Active experiences for active children: Science* (2nd ed.). Upper Saddle River, NJ: Merrill/Prentice Hall.

Starbuck, S., Olthof, M., and Midden, K. (2002). *Hollyhocks and honeybees: Gardening projects for young children.* St. Paul, MN: Readleaf Press.

The variety of ideas for gardening projects meet the needs of teachers who are inexperienced as well as knowledgeable in gardening with young children. Teachers from all settings—urban to rural—will find a wealth of information and creative ideas.

The books in the *Young Scientist Series,* developed at the Education Development Center, illustrate how teachers can develop an inquiry approach based on young children's interests in nature, blocks, and water.

Chalufour, I., & Worth, K. (2003). *Discovering nature with young children.* St. Paul, MN: Redleaf Press.

Chalufour, I., & Worth, K. (2004). *Building structures with young children.* St. Paul, MN: Redleaf Press.

Chalufour, I., & Worth, K. (2005). *Discovering water with young children.* St. Paul, MN: Redleaf Press.

The Arts in the Play-Centered Curriculum

As in an opera, 4-year-old Noah stands at the easel, reflects, and then declaims in song what he has playfully discovered about color:

> There is some colors which are red, blue, yellow
>
> There is a lot of colors
>
> And there is aqua, aqua,
>
> And there is blue, blue, there is blue, blue . . .
>
> and white and aqua
>
> There is white and aqua

Now he contemplates his palette and sings, "There is some colors," and names the primaries, "Red, blue, and yellow." He dips his brush into the blue: "And there is blue, blue, there is blue, blue," emphasizing blue perhaps because it is basic to aqua. Noah intends to create aqua and knows that one does not do that by starting with white. Finally, the white is celebrated, "and white and aqua," and Noah closes softly, "There is white and aqua." ✍

This delightful image of a child singing while painting accompanies the closing credits of Thelma Harms's classic film, *My Art Is Me* (1969).

What does the image reveal? It reveals the creative transformations in the flow of play that lie at the heart of children's art making. It also tells a lot about what Noah knows about color, and about what he doesn't know about color—there is a bit of green in aqua. And, importantly, it demonstrates how art (Noah's painting, poetry, and song) and problem solving (his creation of aqua) are intertwined in the context of play. The creativity involved in Noah's art making is close to the concept of intelligence, which in Piaget's view is synonymous with development (Furth, 1970). Close observation of children playing within the arts gives teachers sound content for a developmental curriculum. In this chapter, we focus specifically on what are called the visual and constructive arts, such as painting, drawing, collage, and block building. However, the foregrounding of play within all the arts is the critical issue. Throughout, we stress that all curricula in the arts should encompass a balance of play options. These range from opportunities to engage in directed and guided play in the arts such as often occurs at circle, project, and small-group time but, more importantly, making sure there is ample time, space, and materials for spontaneous play in all mediums.

The arts, in fact, are indispensable to a successful developmental curriculum. This is because children spontaneously turn art into play, and play is the young child's principal matrix for learning. Indeed, the most successful curricula put art to use at every turn—and, by art, we mean graphic art, construction, poetry, storytelling, music, dance, and drama—so that play and the arts curriculum are indistinguishable from each other. Play for the child, and a playful attitude in the adult, can transform what is mere craft into "art."

Now, the spontaneity with which children turn art into play does not mean that specific planning for art need not take place. Such planning embraces a number of considerations:

- When should arts activities be spontaneous? When should they be guided or directed?
- What can be learned from spontaneous engagement in the arts?
- What materials, tools, and resources do the children need?
- What technical homework should the teacher do?
- How can teachers and the environment encourage spontaneity?
- How should they provide guidance and direction?

Considerations such as the above are discussed next with particular attention to graphic art and construction but with references throughout to many of the other arts, such as music and drama.

PLANNING FOR THE ARTS IN THE PLAY-CENTERED CURRICULUM

An effective arts curriculum for young children is expressed through play, arises from within play, and is modified continuously by children to fit the circumstances of their play. Furthermore, since play occurs throughout the early childhood classroom, so too will the arts—going far beyond, for example, the "art corner" seen in many settings for young children. The issue in planning for the arts in the curriculum is not to ensure that play serves the arts (although that should occur too—Noah should discover that aqua has green in it) but, more importantly to this chapter, to ensure that the arts serve play. To see that this happens, the teacher must, from the very outset, enter the children's world of play and bring into that world the basic materials and props of art (Gee, 2000; Zimmerman & Zimmerman, 2000).

Entering the Child's World of Spontaneous Play

A teacher may enter the child's world of play by introducing a new play prop or by modifying a setting at points when play falters. Sometimes the teacher does this upon his own initiative and sometimes at the children's need or request. Furthermore, sometimes he discusses or demonstrates the new prop or setting directly, and sometimes he does not. Under what circumstances do these variations occur, and what, in the first place, impels the teacher to enter the spontaneous play world at all?

Since spontaneous play is often of a "pretend" nature ("I'm the mommy, you be the baby." or "Look at me, I'm a puppy!"), teachers fear that the supportive

Children learn through guided play experiences.

expertise required is that of theater or drama, an arena that few feel confidently prepared to engage in. But what if the teacher shrinks back and merely relies on the traditional environmental supports, those familiar play props so frequently seen in dress-up or home play corners? The setting may become too static. The sensitive teacher, having observed children's play patterns closely, knows that even simple modifications in props and settings will stimulate children to initiate more elaborate pretend play. She may pick up a play phone and in a play voice call for an "emergency crew." She may add to the available props an armband with a red cross on it, a badge with "police" written on it, or a few chiffon scarves or transparent curtains. In these cases, little needs to be said to the children. They are likely to pick up the indirect cues instantaneously and create scripts to integrate those props into the ongoing play. This method of indirectly shaping the context to suggest new or elaborated avenues for drama or dramatic play was utilized by British drama educator Dorothy Heathcote. Her approach is explored in detail in B. J. Wagner's (1999) *Dorothy Heathcote: Drama as a Learning Medium* and in a special edition of *Theory into Practice* by Lux (1985).

Routines may become static in the graphic arts, as well. The single easel set up in a corner of the classroom every day may get little more from the child than a perfunctory painting "for a teacher." To stimulate playful engagement and focus, the teacher might introduce novel painting tools. Sponges, for example, stimulate the creation of patterns and textures. Rollers invite children to paint over the entire surface of the paper rather than merely working in a cramped area in the middle.

Guiding play by introducing new props or tools is frequently necessary. By demonstrating how the paintbrush can be used to apply paint to the sponge or roller rather than dipping these tools directly into paint, the teacher helps children gain greater control and mastery over their productions. By modeling these somewhat sophisticated accessories, the teacher helps children, 4 years old and up, create a new world of pretend. In dramatic play, the teacher helps a child create his own superhero cape out of paper rather than pulling one from the costume box that he used when he was 3. By bringing constructive art to dramatic play, the teacher engages the child anew. He will make sure that materials for drawing, cutting, and scribbling are near to hand so that accessories to complement dramatic and fantasy play can be created quickly.

Sometimes children actively engaged in dramatic play will seek the teacher's help. It may be for new props: "We need things to make a hideout!" Blankets, old sheets, pieces of carpet, and large and small blocks will serve. Or it may be for technical assistance—help, say, in designing a network of tunnels in the sand. Indeed, a young child's technical requirements can become quite elaborate. "There's buried treasure in the sand pit, we need a pirate's map," may signal the need for the teacher as "artist apprentice" to help construct a network of lagoons, walkways, bridges, and highways, or to devise relevant graphics such as a skull and crossbones, DANGER, DETOUR, and other hazard signs.

Incorporating Artwork

Bringing artwork into the classroom environment is not difficult (Isenberg & Jalongo, 2006). For example, on some bright, sunny day, we may want to trace around children's shadows with the fat chalks we made by mixing plaster of paris and powdered tempera with water in Dixie cups (remembering, of course, to pour the dry mixture into the water, as well as safety concerns about use of powdered mediums). Later the children will wonder about why the chalk outlines of their shadows don't fit them when they return to capture them in the late afternoon.

Are the fat chalks still at hand for use on another day (wet and rainy this time) when there are no shadows at all? The children can use them to create beautiful red and blue and violet "expressionist" stains on the wet asphalt. Maybe this is the day that Noah will begin to construct his knowledge of color by discovering all the necessary pigments to make aqua. If the teacher is lucky, he may be able to share this epiphany by guiding Noah to notice the many tones of aqua on the pavement.

The arts, science, and play merge when children work on the skeletons they will hang in the haunted house. This artful play with bones will get its scientific accuracy from a chart from the school's encyclopedia or, better yet, from our visit to the biology department of a nearby college. Children may begin to get acquainted with their bodies: how they look and work and what's in them.

Are black paper and a clear plastic jar on hand to make a home for the worms dug up in the moist earth the day after it rained? In this seamless world, the teacher might wonder where art leaves off and science begins.

Indeed, constructive play with blocks alone involves art and math, often replicating architecture, whose interdisciplinary richness has earned it the title of queen of the arts. Blocks are a major accessory for pretend play, creating the context for elaborate fantasies for individuals, pairs, and groups of children. Blocks serve as an important adjunct to extend play. Cardboard box houses (see picture, p. 291) furnished with fabric, wallpaper, and rug scraps, and peopled by miniature clothespin dolls become a small city when blocks laid end to end become "Main Street." Curved units define a small park and provide other needed structures. Here we see several guided play projects evolving and being integrated into the children's spontaneous block play, a sure validator of a play-generating curriculum. Valuable insights into the child's developing intelligence, competence, and social awareness can be gained by teacher observations, notes, and photos of such play in block areas. (For a review of literature and new insights, see Frost, Wortham, & Reifel, 2005; Nicolopoulou, 1991; Reifel & Yeatman, 1991.)

THE ARTS: MIRROR OF DEVELOPMENT AND GUIDE FOR CURRICULUM DESIGN

Like archaeological remains, children's paintings, constructions, block building, assemblage and collage, and recordings of songs, stories, and dances mirror development and can be examined and diagnosed as documents of growth and development (DeVries et al., 2002; Griffin, 1998; Veldhuis, 1982). As such, they can be used to assess the effectiveness of the curriculum in supporting playful exploration of the arts.

Heidi's Horses: Documents of Change and Growth

Consider some of the drawings of horses made by one child over a period of about 5 years (Fein, 1984). Heidi's drawings, in Figure 10.1, mirror her particular interests but nonetheless follow the general developmental sequence of drawing schemes reported as characteristic of all children (Gardner, 1992, 2000; Isenberg & Jalongo, 2006; Kellogg, 1969; Lowenfeld, 1947). Heidi had many opportunities to playfully and deeply explore her own particular subject

2 Years: ALL OVER SCRIBBLES

Scribbles are scrubbed on, off, and through paper.

2 Years / 6 months:

CLUSTERS

Lines are more controlled and begin to be clustered in center of paper.

3 Years:
DIRECTIONAL MOVEMENT

Large arm movements order themselves into a circular mode around a central mark.

3 Years / 6 months:

SPIRALS

Directional movement develops to spiraling lines.

Spiraling lines separate themselves into coils.

4 Years:
THE CIRCLE

Coiling lines become deliberate circle configurations, continuous lines which start at one point and return to that point.

First Person;
Available Structures

Circle configurations are elaborated with additional circles and with lines radiating to and from their centers, creating a vertical-horizontal relationship at their intersection with the perimeter. These become representational: father, mother, dog, cat, house, birthday cake.

4 Years / 2 months:
THE FIRST HORSE:
RECTILINEAR
Multiple legs

The circular formation and vertical-horizontal lines permit formation of the first horse.

Figure 10.1
Heidi's Horses

Source: From *Heidi's Horse* by Sylvia Fein, 1984, Exelrod Press. Reprinted with permission.

Breadth and width;
Four legs spaced

Refinement: the horse receives four legs—only four.

4 Years / 10 months:
DEVIATIONS FROM THE RECTILINEAR
Slanting legs; Curved back line

First deviations from the vertical-horizontal are used for ears and legs in opposing diagonal directions. The new diagonals immediately unify head and neck and create a new shape.

5 Years:
UNIFICATION OF HORSE PARTS

The unification of the head and neck is applied to contain the whole horse within one unbroken outline.

5 Years / 3 months:
DEVELOPMENT OF THE UNIFIED HORSE
Sturdy shape

Problems of leg-spacing and length are solved.

The new diagonal directions of line allow the horse to run.

Body markings: blazes and dapples

A learning plateau provides time to consolidate, and to enrich the horse's gear and markings.

Heidi's last major construction before her sixth birthday is to extend the horse's head towards the ground, "so he can eat."

6 Years: **THE HORSE MORE POWERFULLY CONSTRUCTED**
The boxy shape is rounded

The rigid, box-shaped horse is transformed by fluid, calligraphic outline into a powerful horse with flexible stride.

Figure 10.1
Heidi's Horses (*continued*)

7 Years: THE HORSE IN ACTION
Cowboys and rodeo

Heidi shifts her interest to action-packed performances; the elegant single horse recedes.

As storytelling becomes more restrained, precision returns to the drawings, and the rider receives artistic attention.

8 1/2 Years: HEIDI: SELF-PORTRAITS
Queen Heidi, the very 1st

Heidi assumes importance second to the horse, and appears in favorable roles. She thinks of herself as a horse.

8 1/2 Years: TECHNICAL TASKS: OVERLAPPING

The rider's body turns partially to side view.

Overlapping begins. The horse has two legs on one side of his body, two on the other.

8 Years / 11 months: ADVANCES USING OVERLAPPING
The rider in profile

Overlapping possibilities are extended to arm and stifle joints.

Problems appear when the position of the horse's hind legs are reversed.

Two horses side by side

One horse overlaps another to show that they are standing side by side. Figure/ground relationships have become more complex.

of interest (indeed, passion) in a supportive environment that encouraged art making and allowed a free choice of subject matter. The drawings graphically illustrate that it is interest, intersecting with personality and intelligence, that fuels play and the development that results from play.

Often children's drawings and constructions are sent home from school with little thought, when compilations of paintings, drawings, or stories can provide a pivot in parent conferences or for assessment purposes for a better understanding of the trajectory of a child's interests, development, and competencies.

Staff and Environmental Support for Play in the Arts

An arts curriculum becomes established in the play-centered program through the modes of intervention described in chapters 4 and 5. In the sections that follow, we illustrate in detail how the establishment of a viable arts curriculum depends critically on specific manifestations of staff and environmental support.

First, in broad terms, it is important in the arts curriculum to provide support for a balance of spontaneous and guided play.

In specific terms, when adequate time, space, and well-managed materials are provided—and when teachers have done their technical and conceptual homework and the appropriate balance of spontaneous and guided play is struck—engagement in the arts can be explored deeply.

Time, Space, Materials, and Teacher Know-How

Time.   In ideal programs, ample time for spontaneous and guided play with arts materials is provided throughout the school day. A balance between the two is essential, however. Making child-structured play the only mode leads to fragmentation and chaos; on the other hand, an overabundance of teacher-directed or teacher-guided activities prevents children from integrating their knowledge by trying things out for themselves. A simple measure of the balance of play options can be achieved by examining the daily schedule and staffing pattern of programs to determine whether play options are sufficiently balanced and supported by adequate staff. If much of the day is devoted to teacher-directed group activity, it is likely that occasions for spontaneous play are being eroded. Research indicates that in early childhood the most effective learning occurs in small groups (four to six children) engaged in either spontaneous or guided play activities.

Space.   In well-planned programs, space is organized to encourage various configurations of children to engage in arts activities at multiple sites throughout the classroom and play yard:

- Clean, smooth work surfaces free of glue or paint residue from previous projects may be set up in several areas, with seating inviting the solitary play of an individual child or the collaborative or parallel play of pairs and groups. Small trays or Formica-backed blocks for individual work with clay and other wet mediums can be obtained (usually as scrap) from a local kitchen installer or lumber yard.

- Ideally, these areas will be relatively quiet and protected from the flow of fast-paced play but at the same time accessible to and visible from active play areas.

- Expectations for the kinds of play to take place are clearly cued by furnishings and accessories, which will distinguish areas where free exploration of materials and resources is expected, from those where teacher-guided activities or more structured projects will occur.

If monitored sensitively, both outdoor and indoor centers for drawing, scribbling, writing, dance, and music making can support engagement in the arts as an end in itself or as an adjunct to pretend play.

Pacific Oaks College has developed valuable guides for assessing the complexity of playground spaces, which also can be used to calculate the play potential of

Drawing can be available at the easel as well as the work tables.

music- and art-making centers (Kritchevsky, Prescott, & Walling, 1977). These guides help teachers achieve greater predictability in play patterns. And while management and predictability are important elements in any program, inflexible attempts to organize all aspects of arts activities lead to an inhibition and a dwindling of the children's creative expression. Conversely, too little organization in presentation and sequencing in arts activities can result in the tyranny of chaotic movement and environmental clutter. Both extremes undermine the children's chances for mastery, competence, aesthetic development, and understanding.

Materials.   Open-ended arts activities and construction materials ideally complement spontaneous play, providing the raw materials, resources, and accessories for the world of pretend. All the arts, including drama, song, and dance, often merge with and become indistinguishable from play. Not all materials, however, need to be open-ended. For example, older children can use templates for frequently called-upon images—stars, various animals, dinosaurs, vehicles, geometric shapes, and even numerals and letters. The use of these materials should be couched, however, in an atmosphere of free exploration, creativity, and problem solving, and they should be well balanced with an abundance of open-ended materials. Music and rhythm instruments fall into a similar category and might need some preliminary introduction in their appropriate use in order to enhance the quality of spontaneous play with such items when they are displayed at an open center in the classroom.

At a drawing and scribbling table set up for guided play (e.g., with scissors, markers, and plastic templates set out), 4-year-old Toby uses the bus template turned on its side to represent a wind-filled flag fluttering from the main mast of his ship. By tracing the curved edges of the multiple wheels of the bus, he represents the rippling fabric perfectly. Several children immediately seize upon the novel potential in the templates, creating flags for their own drawings.

Teacher Know-How.   In doing their technical homework, early childhood teachers will want to equip themselves with technical information. For example: What colors make pleasing blends? How do primary and secondary colors blend? Knowing this, the teacher can set up the palette at the easel, so that colors that are contiguous blend pleasingly as in Figure 10.2. Teachers also should be familiar enough with art materials to be able to answer the following questions from their own experience:

- What are the characteristics of paint, paper, and clay?
- How much starch or extender should be added to the paint? The color should not look transparent, watery, and washed out. A creamy texture that flows off the brush pleasingly rather than clumping in globs is desired.

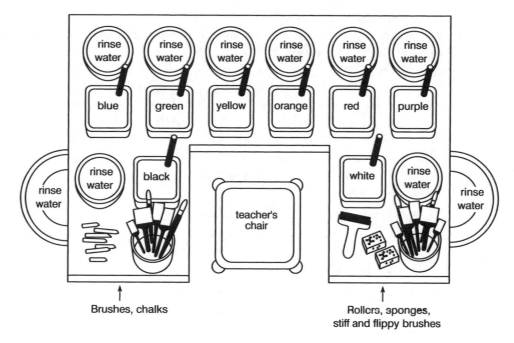

Figure 10.2
Berkeley Child Art Studio Group Palette for Painting Class.

Source: From *The Berkeley Child Art Studio* by M. deUriarte, 1978, unpublished manuscript.
Berkeley, CA. Reprinted with permission.

- What kind of clay would be best—a low-fire white clay that takes a glaze or acrylic paint nicely when it is fired, or a rich-toned red clay that is handsome in itself when fired, but that might stain children's clothing if aprons are not worn?
- Have safety concerns for use of mediums such as glue, powdered pigments, wheat paste, etc., been addressed and children's allergies known to all staff (Isenberg & Jalongo, 2006)?

Teachers will want to have a good grasp of the children's own peer culture, which emerges in play in their classrooms. On another level, they will want to know something about the cultural, historical, and aesthetic traditions not only of their own heritage, but of other cultures, as well. What kinds of music or recorded materials are suitable for young children for use during active class time, in or out of doors? What about during nap time and during the late afternoon in after-school care?

Presentation of Art Making and Constructive Play Materials

In addition to the nature and use of art resources and materials, we are concerned with their presentation, accessibility, maintenance, replenishment, and

imaginative selection. Children will not use an item spontaneously if they cannot see it, if they do not have some basis for imagining its potential, or if it
doesn't work. Therefore:

- Items should be displayed at eye level. If possible, use movable shelves
  as well as some storage units that are equipped with sturdy wheels; this
  provides flexibility to display materials where they will be used or needed. Musical instruments, movement accessories such as scarves and
  headbands, and recorded music could be stored and displayed for use
  indoors or out in such a movable unit.

- Crayons should be kept clean and sorted by color with the paper peeled,
  so a real choice of color can be made.

- Tempera paint should be of a good consistency and tempera paint
  blocks should be clean. Each medium should be presented in a skill-
  appropriate choice of colors.

- Water color pans should be clean, and set up in a skill-appropriate
  choice of colors, and in a self-help set-up.

- Paint set-ups should evolve, starting with (1) primaries, (2) secondaries
  and tertiaries, (3) black and white, and (4) tints.

- Brushes, rollers, and sponges should be introduced as appropriate.

- Appropriate paper for each medium should be available.

- Felt markers should mark, scissors cut with ease, and masking tape is
  readied for use in small strips on a block or two. All items should be displayed in a self-help set-up.

- Make sure that provocative new items are available from time to time
  along with a continuous flow of novel "found" treasures and recyclables
  such as the dots from the paper punch, various stickers, or old greeting
  card pictures and colorful paper scraps. Even the inevitable "anony-
  mous" easel paintings can be recycled into beautiful collage material.
  Cut into strips or random shapes, they provide incentive for creating
  new inventions and accessories for fantasy play—headbands, bracelets
  and belts—at spontaneous drawing and crafts tables.

The teacher's respect for the child's expression is reflected in the quality
of materials available and the care taken in their presentation. Sometimes
the most expensive materials are not always the best. In cases of more costly
materials, consider how they might possibly be obtained. For example, while
newsprint or recycled computer paper may be adequate for the drawing and
scribbling table, it is poor support for tempera applied with a young child's
vigorous strokes. With resources parsimoniously husbanded through such

activities as the recycling of crayons and diligent scrounging of paper ends from local printers, perhaps a very good quality easel paper (ideally 80#) could be affordable.

Blocks.   Some practical pointers involve support for the use of blocks for constructive engagement in spatial problem solving. The following anecdote illustrates some of the points we make:

> At a staff meeting to discuss ways that teachers could combat violence and fighting in play, several teachers brought up the issue of combative kinds of play that seemed to occur frequently around the large dinosaurs. At this school, these accessories were located in both a block building area and outside in a large sand area. One teacher reported that on a visit to another school, he had seen an alternative dinosaur display; both large and small dinosaurs were located in a carpeted area within the science center. The area also included attractive books and materials that provided pictorial information on dinosaur habitats from the prehistoric age. In this way the science area was expanded and enriched, and the block area was liberated for constructive play. ✆

- Both large and small unit blocks should be made available indoors and outdoors, both with and without props. Block-shaped templates on shelves aid access and storage.
- Stacking blocks too neatly and storing them out of the way or in the same place at all times will diminish children's expressive use.
- Heaping blocks in a box or basket is not recommended, because dumping them out can breed chaos rather than construction, as well as an indifference to the care of the environment.

In arranging materials for block play, the problem solving and spatial reasoning required to erect and stabilize a structure can be foregounded when props are absent. The child's imaginative fantasy still will be involved and possibly liberated to be expressed more fluently without props. This is especially true because many accessories frequently reference stereotypic scenarios derived from commercial media (Seiter, 1995).

On another more general note, constant vigilance is needed to ensure that the children's display areas do not become usurped for teacher or project storage, or become catchalls, thereby losing their effectiveness as a support for "choice." This is a particularly pernicious problem when there are multiple users, such as occurs in the necessary rotation of morning and afternoon staffs or when different age groups must be served.

Monitoring the Quality and Challenge of Play in the Arts

Physical knowledge experiences found in water play, finger painting, and work with playdough have a universal appeal. At least initially, children find the tactile/sensory aspects engrossing. Knowledge of the physical properties of materials is often assumed to be acquired through children's free manipulation of such media. The ease with which finger paint and playdough can be transformed through manipulation also recommends them as valuable adjuncts to fantasy and functional play. Children frequently will create songs and stories as they work with these materials.

Standards for Competencies in the Arts.   Teacher know-how also includes a knowledge of standards of developmentally appropriate competencies in constructive arts, drama, music, and movement and dance, so all children's advances may be extended and supported through guided as well as spontaneous play. Teachers will want to acquaint themselves with the National Art Education Association's (1999) standards for the arts so children in the classroom have opportunities to integrate their knowledge and express deep feelings and meaningful ideas through the arts (Isenberg & Jalongo, 2006). See Table 10.1 for samples of standards and suggested curriculum in the arts.

Immersion in the Languages of Art

Six-year-old Jason attends a child art studio on Saturday mornings. His mother, a primary-school teacher, has stayed to observe the first day. She has subsequently adapted what she calls "total art immersion" for her own first-grade class. Aware of the needs of the custodian at her school, she conducts this guided play activity in the semi-shelter just outside her classroom door. She asks parents to donate old shirts or smocks to cover the children's clothing for the activity.

The first phase of the activity involves finger painting to music and movement. Children begin by choosing two colors of finger paint. Jason and the other children are encouraged to spread the paint with hands and fingers as far as they can reach on the large sheet of paper which covers the whole table. Today eight children, their teacher, and one parent volunteer are involved. Jason has been willing to put on one of his father's old shirts with sleeves rolled but is very tentative about touching the paint. However, when the music sets up a marching beat and children are encouraged to go around the table using fingers to draw lines, Jason falls in as all march around the table singing in time to the music.

Within a few minutes, the finger paint has covered most of the table. Tools for mark-making, such as twigs, old combs, and toothbrushes, are made available. The teachers announce, "We're making rivers and mountains and snakes that ripple and wiggle and squiggle around the

Table 10.1

Addressing Some Standards for Visual and Constructive Arts

Standards	Examples
Children will become responsible users of art media and tools.	Noah spontaneously experiments with mixing colors to make "aqua" at a well-organized painting center where he has learned routines for independent use of materials.
	Special tools, such as a paint roller, help him relate to the whole pictorial space rather than one small area only.
Children should have opportunities to gain mastery of a variety of techniques and processes.	In guided play activities Noah and his classmates begin to learn about volume by constructing tunnels out of clay for miniature animals.
Children will become aware of and be able to talk about line, texture, color, and space.	In a special multimedia finger painting activity, Jason begins to learn about line, texture, space, and color. In a feedback session about the group piece, Jason comments on the textured collage sections when he declares he "likes the bumpy parts best."
Children will be able to recognize their own work and that of peers.	At snack time children discuss their paintings that have been displayed for the monthly art show. Later they will design invitations for parents and act as docents for an "opening" at "pick-up" time later in the day.
Children will develop control and be able to dance and execute rhythmic movement in concert with music.	Masha's mother makes headbands and waistbands for use in the movement and dance center. Tucking colorful scarves into the waistbands and headbands, Masha teaches other children her "Fly Horse" dance.
	At daily music time, some children learn and use a simple notational system to indicate a pattern of long and short accents and rests in a three-line composition for rhythmic hand clapping.
Children will become acquainted with and share in the classic genres of their own and other cultures.	Isabella interprets a Matisse painting in her own way in her K–1 art class. Matisse is her favorite painter. Her brother, Adrian, prefers the special African masks they have learned about in his second-grade class.

Sources: Based on *Purposes, Principles, and Standards for School Art Programs,* by National Art Education Association, 1999, Reston, VA: Author; and *How to Work with Standards in the Early Childhood Classroom,* by C. Seefeldt, 2005, New York: Teachers College Press.

table." Now a snowstorm comes as small scoops of dry tempera are sprinkled into the wet and children use their hands to make beautiful blended smudges.

But soon a rainstorm comes up. As mark-making tools are gathered, small brushes and trays of liquid tempera are provided. It's raining faster and faster and faster, and teachers and children create patterns of raindrops all over the table with spatters and splashes of raindrops. As trays of liquid are removed, seeds are sprouting and plants are growing more lines.

By now the paper is quite wet. Torn and crushed strips and pieces of crepe paper and shiny pieces of gift wrap are distributed for children to press into the wetness to create textures and new patterns. The crepe paper makes multicolored stains, turning red and blue to violet. Finally, confetti is offered, and Jason delightedly integrates his bits into the group's composition.

The handsome piece is allowed to dry as the children clean up. Later it is hung and at snack time they view their work. As they talk about their composition, they begin to learn the names of the processes they have used; color, line, texture, and space are just a few. Jason liked the bumpy parts the best. ✑

Cultural Enrichment in the Arts.   In some school districts, primary grade teachers and art specialists have adapted an arts curriculum that enhances cultural and aesthetic literacy. Children are introduced to the styles of artists from different periods and cultures and then invited to replicate a style in their own drawings or paintings. Isabella vividly emulates the style of Matisse, who became her favorite artist, in a painting she made in her K–1 art class (Figure 10.3).

Through this same program, other older children noted parallels in the African masks they were making and the drawings they had rendered in the styles of Modigliani or Picasso.

Preschoolers at another school create and mount a spectacular display each year of African figures in what their teacher, Berta, describes as a Gallery of Cultures in their classroom. Their teacher assists them by helping in the preparation of an armature for each figure out of a wooden dowel or paper towel spool mounted on a base of heavy cardboard. The heads and hands of the figure are made of bakers clay. Pipe cleaners inserted into the spool provide flexible arms. An array of swatches of brightly colored African textiles, such as kente cloth, along with ample amounts of tape and glue, is the inspiration for the creation of stunning costumes for the figures. Many books from the library with illustrations of traditional costumes influence the children's choices.

Figure 10.3
Isabella's "Matisse"

The cultural richness of children's communities is illustrated by the following:

Karen, an artist and parent who creates dolls depicting characters drawn from traditional African stories, began sharing her dolls and stories in her sons' preschool class. She now shares them throughout the primary school classrooms in her school district. Other families enjoy the presentation of her characters and storytelling through the education program at a major museum located in a nearby community. ⌀

Integrating the Curriculum Through the Arts.   How art-making materials and activities not only serve aesthetic development, but support learning in mathematics and development in logical and spatial knowledge, is illustrated in the following example of curriculum-generating play.

In a Head Start classroom, children were introduced to pattern duplication and pattern extension during small group time. The teacher discussed and demonstrated the difference between patterns and designs. On the same day, one of the children spontaneously generated her own pattern sequence at the painting easel by creating a page full of small, multicolored triangles and circles arranged in an original pattern with accurate extensions. Other children followed suit, and the teacher created a display for the school corridor of the products children created that involved the concept of patterning. ⌀

A kindergarten teacher helps children learn the features of geometric figures—triangles, rectangles, and squares—through a guided play activity using toothpicks and clay balls to construct models of the figures. ⌀

Because children's intuitive math is going on "everywhere," including in arts activities, it is the teacher's responsibility to note and support these competencies when and where they occur. In this way, teachers in play-centered programs can feel more confident that all children are assured of equitable access to the kinds of knowledge that will serve them throughout their schooling (Scales, 2000). (See chapter 7 for more on mathematics and play.)

While manipulation of many arts materials is intrinsically satisfying, at some point the teacher must be sure to ask in what ways these spontaneous tactile/sensory activities lead to more challenging experiences that advance all aspects of development (see chapter 1 on how play serves the curriculum). As noted in the previous anecdote, constructive play with art-making materials is an ideal context for engaging children in early activities involving competencies in aesthetic development, storytelling, science, and mathematics. A number of questions can be raised:

- Does the activity have an educational rationale? How much learning does it really promote?

- Does it link up with goals for the group curriculum and/or with a learning plan for individual children?

- Does it support extension into pretend play with peers? Does the activity have a balanced emphasis on not only aesthetics and the narrative aspects of sociodramatic play, but on its potential to support children's growth in other areas, such as early math and science? Can we be sure that the curriculum, particularly for the kindergartner and older child, is a rich one? In mixed-age groupings, are too many aspects of the curriculum overly challenging for the youngest? Or are we "dumbing down" the curriculum for the older children? Is the activity related to standards for expected level of development of children?

Guided and Directed Play in the Arts

We know that young children learn most effectively through play, and educational strategies often rely on guided or directed play. In the role of play tutor—for example, at the clay table—teachers might show the children how to model basic clay shapes (as precursors to developing concepts of volume).

To build the children's repertoire of three-dimensional sculptural forms, teachers might show them how to hollow out a ball of clay to make a dinosaur's cave; or how to extend the hollow to make a tunnel where the hands of two friends meet; or how to make clay coils, slabs, and seriated balls. In one preschool program, Wade integrated knowledge about clay modeling when he proceeded to add teeth to the jaws of his hollowed-out clay form. Sylvie, a second grader, using slabs of clay that she had rolled out smoothly, cut and shaped a beautiful rectangular jewelry box (complete with a fitted lid) for her grandmother's birthday.

A play-generating curriculum was introduced to children making their first transition from home to school. It involved creating a special room. (See photo on page 291 showing two boys with their "rooms.") To start, a shoe box was provided to each child, along with bits of wallpaper, tile, fabric, wood, and carpet pieces, with an invitation to create a replica of a room for themselves. Child-made models from previous years might be provided at the initiation of this project. Aurora, learning English in her bilingual classroom, emulating labels on classroom furnishings, asked that labels in both English and Spanish be placed on the items in her "room."

Music and Movement in the Play-Centered Curriculum

In many programs, teachers present the music and movement curriculum as a directed or guided experience for the whole group as a part of each day's routine. New and traditional movement and music material as well as ethnic songs and rhythms can be introduced in this way. One teacher discovered that the movement group became more cohesive and inclusive when boys were asked to pick a girl to sit beside in movement class. In this way, when paired for folk-dancing routines, the option for cross-gender as well as same-gender dancing became possible. Within the framework of teacher-guided play, the following are some other familiar possibilities:

Call and Response and Improvisational Routines.   Call and response routines, improvisation, and ensemble playing with instruments and voice enhance children's listening skills and perception of pattern and rhythm.

Alternating a single child's improvisation on an instrument such as a xylophone, drum, or triangle, with ensemble playing and singing, as in the next example, where the teacher rotates turns of improvisation by placing a hat on the head of a child she selects to improvise after others sing and play:

Baker's hat, just your size,
When it's on your head you improvise.

Similar improvisation with instruments and singing can be utilized around traditional favorites with a strong, simple rhythm, such as "Noah's Ark." Perhaps one would alternate voice and instruments with the children singing unaccompanied at first:

Who built the ark, Noah, Noah.
Who built the ark, Noah did.

and then continue with both voice and rhythm instruments:

Here come the animals, two by two.
If I were there I'd come along too.

This is particularly effective when accompanied by various percussion instruments, such as those utilized in the Orff-Kodaly curriculum (Alper, 1987; Isenberg & Jalongo, 2006). If the teacher has a piano and can play, this helps children maintain the rhythm and pitch.

Simple echo routines involving rhythmic patterns of hand clapping, finger snapping, knee slapping, and other sound making, with or without rhythm instruments to accompany patterned movement or dance, can be thoroughly satisfactory activities.

At the level of guided play, a well-organized listening center for two or more children, stocked with a diversity of recorded music, could be provided. These recordings can include cards with salient information about the music written out so that the guiding teacher can point out aspects of it to the children. For older children who are beginning to read, the cards can be filed in the listening center for direct use. As many teachers know, spontaneous songs and dances are created constantly by children as they play, and these songs could be recorded and enjoyed at the listening center as well (Veldhuis, 1982).

Although much of this chapter deals with graphic and constructive play in the arts, music is an important avenue for the development of children's thinking and aesthetic sensibilities and, therefore, deserves to be carefully integrated into the curriculum.

Orff-Kodaly Method.   Familiar songs and games can be integrated into a more systematic, guided play framework such as that developed in the Orff-Kodaly method (Alper, 1987; DeVries et al., 2002; Isenberg & Jalongo, 2006; Wheeler & Raebeck, 1985). The general objective of this approach is to refine the senses so that the child gains knowledge of and appreciation for various aspects of music such as rhythmic patterns and tonal discrimination. Furthermore, because the emphasis is on making and enjoying music as a group activity rather than as individual performance, the method has a positive social value and does not emphasize competitiveness.

Furth (1970) echoes the Kodaly approach when he writes,

The opportunity can be given to children to express facets of their personalities that go along with their developing intelligence in the medium of music. To play in rhythm, to control intonation and intensity of tone, to construct musical phrases over time, to symbolize all these things in musical notation, as well as to interact with others and submit one's activity to the group task—all this is part and parcel of human intelligence. It is for this reason the music teacher can justifiably rely on intrinsic motivation. His goal is musical thinking, with the accent on thinking. He is not concerned with turning every child into a professional . . . musician. (pp. 140–141)

To play and enjoy music together as a group without emphasizing competitiveness has a positive social value.

Counting and pattern-making skills can be developed in music activities when a notational system derived from Orff-Kodaly is used to mark accented beats and rests. One first-grade teacher encouraged children to compose their own three-line songs in this way. Children then clapped the pattern of fast and short beats and rests in unison as they were indicated on a blackboard by each child composer.

Music promotes auditory discrimination and phonemic awareness through rhyming words and segmentation (Seefeldt, 2005). Participating in music involves abstract thinking important to mathematics. Music contributes to social skills and, of course, it can lighten a tense moment and ease transitions.

Diverse Musical Traditions Enrich the Classroom Culture

When preparing the environment, some teachers use culturally and linguistically diverse selections of recorded music to accompany children's dance and movement. Often, parents are a rich resource that can be called upon to enhance this diversity. In one class, a Chinese family provided a recording of popular contemporary Chinese children's songs. These became instant favorites because of their particularly catchy and appealing rhythm. In this same classroom, a Russian parent interested in dance provided accessories in the form of child-sized, elasticized headbands and waistbands decorated with bright ribbons and sequins. With these, children needed no teacher assistance to create their own dance costumes by merely tucking a selection of brightly colored scarves into the headbands and waistbands. This contribution helped her Russian-speaking daughter establish early communication with other children in dance and movement. (See chapter 8, "Language, Literacy, and Play.") Once such activities are launched with a small group of children, teachers might be able to withdraw but closely monitor from a distance. In this way, they can help ensure that the music and movement experience will remain focused and evolve as musical play without deteriorating into random tag, rough-and-tumble, or chasing games.

Music can enhance the affective tone of an environment. However, musical activities that merely distract or entertain, although possibly useful as "management strategies," cannot be justified as developmental curricula.

In guided play in the arts, care should be taken to avoid undue focus on the virtuosity of a teacher rather than the particular needs of children. Such performances might well be enjoyed by and be interesting to children, but they fall into the category of directed play. As such, they should be balanced with opportunities for free improvisation with music.

In addition—and this point is crucial—in high-quality programs, no teacher-guided play or directed circle time activity should be mere preparation for something else. Introduction of materials is important; however, nothing in the early childhood arts curriculum should be simply a "dry run." Every single arts activity should make sense in the context of the children's lives at school, and each step in an art sequence should be intrinsically interesting.

Working Within the Zone of Proximal Development.   When guided/directed play in arts activities is linked in some relevant manner to children's fantasy play, or if the teacher can play parallel to children (as suggested in chapter 5), then such play is protected from becoming merely work disguised as play. The teacher can then stay in touch with the child's developmental needs. In this manner, the teacher participates in what Vygotsky (1967) referred to as the zone of proximal development, that area where children experience their own future, more advanced, self through stimulation and challenge in the context of interactive play with peers or with an adult.

Children with Special Needs: Guiding for Mastery and Competence

Consider Jerry, an active and often unfocused child:

> Four-year-old Jerry jumps from the jungle gym and dashes across the yard yelling, "Rocket launch! Rocket launch!" Within seconds, he reaches the sand pit, jumps in, and plows through Andre's and Peter's sand towers. Taking Jerry gently by the hand, his teacher productively redirects this explosive energy. "You seem to know a lot about rockets," she says. "How about drawing one with me?" ✆

Through drawing she engages the child in a vivid and expressive rendering of his fantasy. The recognition Jerry may have been seeking in spontaneous play with peers might be accomplished more easily through guided, creative expression. Such expression will serve him better until linguistic ability and his competence in interacting with others advance to meet the need he feels to share his powerful fantasies.

Creating some segments of a cartoon strip about rockets might help Jerry. When the teacher labels aspects of his vigorous but seemingly meaningless scribbles by using words in bubbles and arrows that highlight and clarify important information—"here is the launching pad, here is the rocket's nose"—Jerry is led to experience himself as a more effective communicator.

More ambitiously, Jerry's drawings and words might become a "movie" when taped together and attached and wound onto the take-up spindles of the paper movie machine a parent made for the classroom. As Jerry's movie is unreeled and narrated for the class, the teacher demonstrates sequence as a feature of a narrative while sharing Jerry's word images.

Guided play often provides opportunities for the teacher to observe closely and learn how the competencies, interests, and personality of a child complement or conflict with the social challenges of the group setting. For example, in a prekindergarten conference with a kindergarten assessment team, Sara, an art therapist, made the suggestion that active and unfocused children often may be helped to gain control by working not with fluid materials such as finger paints or water-based media, but with more resistant materials. Stitchery, when presented on a frame or an embroidery hoop, is an example of a material that can give structure and boundaries. Clearly defined patterns might be included as guidance. A simple pattern of a rocket ship might be motivating for a child like Jerry. In addition, she noted that children with perceptual problems may need not only more form, but activities that provide a calming effect derived from doing what they are good at. The issue here is to allow the child to experience control rather than lack of control (Wasserman, 2005).

> Lisa frequently has difficulty sharing the available supply of playdough. Learning this about Lisa's needs, the teacher might ask her to assist in the preparation of a new batch of dough to be shared with others, thereby helping Lisa manage her needs, emotions, and impulses in the group setting. ⌀

Enhancing Children's Membership in the Group.   Guided play with art-making materials affords many opportunities for language use and social and cultural sharing and, again, gives the teacher an opportunity to observe quietly. Often the group project is stimulated directly by the children: "I want one like Martha has!" "So do I!" With the help of the teacher, the paper earrings that Martha just made are studied. The required materials are set up at a table so that Martha can teach the others to make earrings of their own.

In the primary grades in particular, projects that enhance group membership may sometimes be ongoing and involve long-range goals. Even so, every step toward the project goal is ideally play-centered and intrinsically satisfying. Making a group book, a class poem, a quilt, a mural, or decorations for a school party—all can support the child's growing ability to plan, to look forward, and to share socially. For example, in the first-grade classroom we discussed in chapter 8, a group of children created a newspaper for all the members of the class. It involved several weeks of research and planning before the first and only edition was published. Group projects such as this can provide valuable opportunities for children to learn about and participate in the cultural richness of many of today's classrooms.

Children's Play Interests Reflected in a Play-Centered Curriculum

Children's playful engagement in the arts frequently provides us with ideas for new curricula. This is reflected vividly in myriad ways. The monsters of one year's pretend play give way to Robin Hood the next. The prince and princesses in this year's group book become the daddy and mommy dinosaur in next year's. So, too, with the paintings and constructions any class creates; each year the genre is different. Musical interludes can become a part of children's spontaneous story play dictation, or they can become part of an "author's theatre" in later elementary school. Once introduced as a genre, children will incorporate songs they know, such as nursery rhymes or contemporary media songs, into their plays.

British drama educator Dorothy Heathcote (Heathcote & Bolton, 1995) often used child-generated songs and chants in her drama work with children (see chapter 8 for some discussion of drama as one of the literary arts). Children's guided play experience in music at one preschool led to the appropriation by novice players of the following strategy for achieving entrance into superhero play.

A group of 4-year-old boys playing superheroes are blocking the entrance to the climber for two girls, Yolanda and Shani. Randall steps to the top of the slide and asserts: "I'm the red one and nobody except superheroes can come."

Their teacher, taking a leaf from Paley's (1992) *You Can't Say You Can't Play*, initiates negotiation by asking, "What do they have to do to play? Randall and Alex, you know we agreed at our meeting that we can't hit and we can't say 'You can't play.' Tell them what they can do. How do they have to act to be part of it?"

Alex steps forward and strikes a pose with crossed arms poised for karate chops. "They have to do this!"

> *Teacher:* "Could you superheroes have a meeting with Yolanda and Shani and teach them what to do? They already know the superhero song."

Yolanda begins to sing the song the boys taught at music earlier in the day.

> *Teacher:* "Could they come up and guard the back platform?" (The climber has multiple platforms, the back being a bit less desirable.)

Randall: "OK, but I am guarding the slide and Alex is guarding the pole."

Yolanda and Shani clamber up the slide. ✆

Children also create their own curricula. Guided activities in which peers exchange and share experiences through paintings and drawings are a case in point. Mikka originates "rainbow belts" for "rainbow superheroes," and the superhero group becomes gender inclusive. In another class, children seize upon Toby's bus-on-its-side template to create flags of their own, thereby making Toby's problem-solving experience theirs.

Integration of Children's Experiences and Feelings Through Play in the Arts

Spontaneous play allowed Noah to integrate his new knowledge about colors—he used this growing grasp of color to start creating aqua. Such integration and recasting of experience and the application of knowledge in new contexts also can occur in guided play.

Consider Jason:

Jason's only painting for the monthly art show revealed much. His intense interest in depicting trains and the intersecting lines of railroad

In play, children recast their knowledge of the world in new ways.

tracks revealed the cognitive and representational competence of a 5-year-old. It also related to his new, spontaneous interest in writing his name and making signs to designate areas of play for himself and his 4-year-old friend, Wesley.

In this particular classroom, a problem arose when Wesley, as a young 4-year-old, did not share Jason's interest or capabilities in writing. Wesley felt left out, and his mother asked the preschool teacher not to stress writing. ⊘

As we can see, life in the zone of proximal development is not always fun, nor does it always flow smoothly, but it certainly challenges children as well as their teachers!

A special dictated letter with a picture "for mom" or an e-mail may be called for when distressing experiences, such as the birth of a baby brother or Mom's too abrupt departure, occur.

In another case, Lonnie, a formerly abused child currently healing in his adoptive home, needed to include multiple masking tape "band-aids" in the many self-portraits he produced. ⊘

A Balanced Arts Curriculum

Throughout this book and in this chapter, we stress the need to balance curriculum offerings across the continuum of directed, guided, and spontaneous play. When play is at the center, the arts as well as other options will be examined carefully to ensure that the balance between spontaneous and guided or directed play is optimal for the group served. In determining the appropriate balance of arts activities, we must always consider:

- The cultural, social, and developmental needs of both the group and individual children
- The dynamic of the group
- The quality and size of the physical environment
- The number of staff and length of program day

Table 10.2, at the end of this chapter, provides a generous, but by no means exhaustive, listing of some basic arts activities, showing their positions along the play intervention continuum. Some individuals and groups will need more structure and fewer options, or more complexity with an increase in guided or even directed play; others will need less complexity with more opportunity for spontaneous play. In each case, we can select from the basics to create a menu of activities that enhances potential for play.

WHEN TEACHERS TALK

Respect for Art Materials

Questions arose about children's misuse of materials and lack of respect for property such as what to do about excessive paint spills and drips from unsteady hands and the muddying of colors in paint cups when a brush is returned to a different cup than the one from which it was drawn. One teacher suggested rubber grips that are color coded to match their paint cup. Another teacher, who had full-inclusion children in her program, remarked that such grips originally were designed for children with impaired motor skills, but she found they served many others, as well.

It was noted that, when children are allowed to help set up new materials and observe the teacher's excitement about the potential of clean, fresh new items, they will develop a respect for the environment. Children's independence and autonomy can be supported when clear steps in a process are communicated and children are given a part of the responsibility for maintaining the quality of the art space. They become enthusiastic supporters of the environment as they save, sort, and recycle various materials.

MASTERY OF ROUTINES

Another teacher, currently volunteering in a child art studio program at a nearby museum, demonstrated to the group how children can learn the steps to load their paintbrushes carefully to avoid drips, apply paint, and then rinse and return them to the proper containers. Also, painting on large pieces of paper on a flat surface with an individual palette of paint blocks gives children greater control than work at an easel (Smith, Fuciano, Kennedy, & Lord, 1993).

WHAT CAN WE LEARN FROM CHILDREN'S DRAWING AND PAINTING?

Teachers noted that they were encouraged to use samples of children's art work to make authentic assessments of development. What should they look for? Much information is available on universal features of the development of drawing schemas in such works as Lowenfeld (1947), Goodnow (1977), and Kellogg (1969). Much less information is available on the features of development of drawing by children with emotional, perceptual, or developmental disabilities.

WARNING SIGNS IN CHILDREN'S ART

Sara, an art therapist working on a kindergarten assessment team, noted that certain features of children's drawings provide early "warning signs." Some of these are a sudden regression to scribbling stage in drawing schemes, drawings that show lesser competence in the execution of some features, the repetition of an obsessively recurring theme, or drawings with all lines leaning in one direction (Wasserman, 2005).

In the course of this discussion, a cautionary anecdote was submitted: In one teacher's class, a smaller than average child consistently painted at the bottom edge of the paper at the easel. Teachers thought this child possibly had a perceptual problem. When they encouraged the child to elevate himself by standing on a large block while painting at the easel, his paintings began to fill the pictorial space.

Table 10.2

Arts Activities on the Play Continuum

Activity	Spontaneous Play	Guided Play	Directed Play
Drawing and scribbling	Free use of markers, pencils, chalk, crayons, scissors, punches, assorted papers	Teacher sets up environment; little monitoring required	
Collage	Selecting and arranging	Teacher sets up environment; children learn from each other	Help with cutting and pasting initially
Painting			
Tempera	Free application of paint to paper; free to select content	Teacher sets up environment and monitors from a distance until rituals are learned	
Easel	Free application of paint to paper; free to select content	Teacher sets up environment, helps establish routines for use of paint, and monitors from distance	May demonstrate textures and techniques through use of rollers and sponges
At table	Free experiment with primaries plus black and white	Monitors from a distance once rituals learned (e.g., obtaining a supply of clean water and paper, etc.); teacher available to discuss work	Sets up environment and introduces materials and palette

Table 10.2
Continued

Activity	Spontaneous Play	Guided Play	Directed Play
Group palette	Free experiment and free content	Teacher discusses application, choices children make (see Figure 10.2)	Sets up environment, presents palette, and guides selections of paint and brushes
Watercolor and Payons (water-soluble crayons)	Same as above	Monitors from a distance	Introduction to materials and routines
Clay	Free expression with ample amount of clay	Monitors from a distance—teaches further skills only as interest arises from work	Teaches initial skills, such as use of cutting wire to obtain clay, use of slip and powdered clay; models rolling out a slab, making a ball (snakes), etc.
Playdough or bakers clay	Free exploration with or without tools	Sets up environment, monitors from a distance, prepares dough of good consistency, presents different types	
Printmaking (relief)	Free selection of some materials—is never self-directed	Guidance in making plate; teacher presents appropriate materials	Inking and printing of plate—younger children require guidance
Silk screen	Selecting elements from torn or cut paper	Guidance in placement to ensure registration on paper	Inking and printing
Wood gluing	Can be self-directed once skills are learned and area for use is set	Presentation of materials	Guidance initially in gluing

(continued)

Table 10.2
Continued

Activity	Spontaneous Play	Guided Play	Directed Play
Woodworking	Can be self-directed for one or two, once skills are learned and appropriate area for use is established; seen as possible adjunct to spontaneous play	Usually necessary to have teacher guidance or close monitoring	Skills in use of tools taught: hammer, nails, vise, chisel, screwdriver, handsaw, etc.
Special events; holidays, T-shirts, or group works such as murals, quilts, greeting cards, invitations, decorations, calendars	Various intrinsically interesting steps may often be incorporated into play	Some steps can be monitored from distance	Teacher has goal, presented in a sequence; sequence and goal clearly presented
Diagnostic self-portraits			
Collage portraits	Children construct; interpretation of how to do it left up to child	Monitors from a distance, replenishes materials	Teacher provides elements and describes activity; eyes, ears, mouth, nose, egg shape or circle for head
Drawing (from mirror or free)	Same	Children may be provided with a life-size cutout of a head and shoulder shape	Teacher describes activity
Whole body painting	Same	Sets up materials	Teacher describes activity
Music, movement, drama, storytelling and story playing			

Table 10.2
Continued

Activity	Spontaneous Play	Guided Play	Directed Play
Music and instrument—teacher modeling	Not spontaneous play	Guides, as in finger plays, simple songs, such as ABC song and songs involving letter-sound recognition; teacher or child composed patterns and rhythms	Teacher directs
Music and instrument—improvisation	Children improvise; open center	Musical environment—Teacher monitors, might model some music or instrument ability or set a pattern of accented beats	
Story dictation and writing	Content usually open—not spontaneous play; might influence child's later sociodramatic or private play	Teacher available one on one—or for small group doing one story or poetry, may probe for narrative elements	Variously directed, various goals; takes dictation or gives direct assistance to writers; might aid invented spelling or simple letter-sound correspondence as warranted
Drama conventions such as use of a "play" voice	Can be used to facilitate spontaneous play	Teacher monitors when it is drama for *understanding;* helps children reflect and take perspective without disrupting play	Teacher-directed play when *production* for an audience becomes the goal
Story playing	Spontaneous play interpretations of roles, events, or stories	Teacher reads text and guides story playing	Teacher writes dictated story play or assists child in doing so

SUMMARY AND CONCLUSION

In this chapter, we have based our rationale for an arts curriculum in early childhood on the following premises:

A curriculum in the arts for early childhood at the preschool level and in the early elementary grades finds its center in the necessity for children to play. It encompasses not only graphic arts, but drama, music, dance, movement, and all forms of constructive play. It should be a play-generating curricula in which children's autonomy and interests are supported. It can take several forms, being orchestrated along a continuum that supports both guided and spontaneous play.

However, the effectiveness of an early childhood arts program will be measured by the degree to which we observe that children are able to enter into sustained, effective, self-directed play. Is guided or directed art the only form we see? Do we see knowledge gained in guided arts activities being integrated as it is reapplied in spontaneous play?

In summary, the major question to ask is: What *are* the quality and quantity of children's spontaneous play within the arts curriculum?

An important task for the teacher is to balance the options for kinds of play in the arts program. By ensuring the child's independent choices in play, the teacher is supporting development and engaging the child's interest and authentic expression. Although implementation of developmentally appropriate standards is an important priority that provides equitable access to educational and cultural resources for all children, it is best to remember that children learn most effectively through play and are unable until middle childhood to perform work in the adult sense (Alward, 1995). (This issue is discussed more fully in chapter 13.)

In conclusion, when teachers find the source for their curricula in play, they link it to child development and discover its validation. In the early years, the arts are core subjects, as important as English, mathematics, or any other subject, and are integral to the entire curriculum. Much of the child's development is revealed most vividly through the documents children produce in the arts and constructive play. When these are shared with the child, in addition to her parent, the child becomes a witness to her advancing competence and grows in self-esteem.

SUGGESTED RESOURCES

deUriarte, M. (2006). *Mira arte: Artistic development in alternative spaces.* Retrieved January 1, 2006, from www.miraarte.org.

This site summarizes deUriarter's 26 years of research on stages of composition and graphic development in children's art, across cultures, and illustrates the provision of alternative spaces for art making and exhibition of children's art.

Dyson, A. H. (1989). *Multiple worlds of child writers: Friends learning to write.* New York: Teachers College Press.

In this book Dyson stresses the connection between children's drawings and their oral and written composing and the impact such activities can have on their social worlds. Children's portraits demonstrate the power of the arts to transform relationships, lives, and classrooms. These are inspiring "must reads."

Goodnow, J. (1977). *Children drawing.* Cambridge, MA: Harvard University Press.

One of several good surveys of the stages of children's drawings.

Isenberg, J., & Jalongo, M. R. (2006). *Creative thinking and arts-based learning: Preschool through fourth grade.* Upper Saddle River, NJ: Merrill/Prentice Hall.

A veritable handbook on creative expression across the curriculum. Includes sections in each chapter on the environment, activities, and standards as well as safety and special needs.

Piaget, J., & Inhelder, B. (1967). *The child's construction of space.* New York: Norton.

Chapter II, titled the "Child's Conception of Elementary Spatial Relationships in Drawing Pictorial Space," is a basic but rather technical piece. However, it provides teachers with an opportunity to read a primary source. The children's interviews that are included in the chapter nicely illuminate the more theoretical portions.

Smith, N. R., Fuciano, C., Kennedy, M., & Lord, L. (1993). *Experience and art: Teaching children to paint* (2nd ed.). New York: Teachers College Press.

A now classic work on children's painting with many art activities that are well-grounded in the experience of its authors.

Wagner, B. J. (1999). *Dorothy Heathcote: Drama as a learning medium.* Portsmouth, NH: Heinemann.

This new edition of a seminal work on Dorothy Heathcote gives an in-depth look at her pedagogy of drama. The chapters titled "Using 'Role' in Teaching," "Nonverbal Drama," and "Code Cracking Literature and Language" will be particularly valuable to educators.

Zimmerman, E., & Zimmerman, L. (2000, November). Art education and early childhood education: The young child as creator and meaning maker within a community context. *Young Children, 56*(6), 87–92. Washington, DC: National Association for Education of Young Children.

Informative overview of major approaches to children's art in preschool and the early primary years.

Play and Socialization

Andrew lopsidedly heads out the door of his preschool classroom with his mother's large, leather briefcase slung over one shoulder. Despite being encumbered by the briefcase, he insists upon carrying it wherever he goes. His destination today is the swing at the rear of the play yard. He recently has become willing to set the briefcase on a bench nearby when he uses the swing. However, if anyone goes near it, stormy protests can be expected.

Andrew is 3 years and 1 month old and a newcomer to this 4-hour program. Separation from his mother has been difficult. To ease Andrew's adjustment, his teacher invited his mother to remain at school until a reasonably amicable separation could be achieved. Andrew's mother, on leave from her part-time job, has been able to accommodate his need. Since Andrew played happily while his mother was present, she anticipated this interval would be brief. The interval, however, began to stretch into weeks, and his mother's leave from her job was nearly over. Andrew, even if engaged, continued to insist on leaving with his mother. Finally, Andrew's mother and his teacher devised a strategy to allay his anxiety: His mother was to leave her large, leather briefcase on the bench near the door as a reminder that she would be returning at some predetermined time. First, she stayed away until snack time; then she was to return at story time, and so on for longer periods of time each day.

Andrew's mother was always meticulous about returning at the promised times in the preschool day, and eventually Andrew was able to stay for the full 4 hours of the program—not without a catch, however; the briefcase must stay behind to ensure his mother's return. It was many weeks before Andrew allowed the briefcase to be tucked away safely by his teacher into his cubby, and it was not until the second half of the school year that it did not come to school with Andrew at all. ⌀

SAYING GOODBYE TO PARENTS

For some theorists, separation from parents is a major milestone for children, and their research on this subject suggests that the character of this achievement is an important indicator of secure or insecure attachment to the parental figure. Attachment theorists assert that when unusual conflict or anxiety surrounds separation from the parent or caregiver, the child may develop significant other problems in relating to others (Ainsworth, Bell, & Stayton, 1974; Balaban, 1985, 2006).

A naturalistic study looking at children's patterns of separation on entrance to preschool, followed by a study of their attempts to enter into play with other children, was conducted by Tribble (1996). Findings from this study indicate that children who had difficulty separating from or rejoining their primary caregiver also had subsequent difficulties in persevering in and/or varying their attempts to initiate in spontaneous peer play.

This chapter focuses on the teacher's role in thinking about and guiding children's socialization. We show how careful observation of children's talk and interactive behavior is one of our best guides in determining children's social and communicative competence. Many of the illustrations presented are drawn from teacher anecdotes and teacher research. They raise many questions, show some of the dilemmas teachers face, and suggest some solutions.

The ability to initiate and maintain effective play with peers will be referred to frequently in this chapter as one of the major indicators of a needed social competency. The following anecdote illustrates how complex the effect of separation from a parent or caregiver can be and suggests ways it may impact relations with peers.

From Separation to Integration: John's Fire Hydrants

This vignette is about a $4\frac{1}{2}$-year-old named John, who appeared to teachers to be socially isolated from his peers (Scales, 2005). They felt this may have arisen from the intersection of several factors; a reluctance to separate from his father, a new baby brother in the home, and his first experience in a preschool class consisting of children with established relationships from the previous year.

John arrived at school with his father in September. John was dressed in a long yellow raincoat, black boots, and a black fire helmet. Rain or shine, John wore this attire for the next six months. To help with John's transition, his father spent the better part of each morning at the school's drawing and writing table with his son and several girls. This pattern continued for many months.

Comfortable entry into school is an important transition.

Figure 11.1
John's Earliest Fire Hydrant and One with a Loose Cap That Is Leaking

John and his father, Greg, studied the fire hydrants they saw on their walk to school. They took photographs and compiled many small books on fire hydrants. John's father drew many models of fire hydrants as he became a fixture with John at the drawing and writing table. John also drew fire hydrants. He also painted fire hydrants (Figure 11.1) and dictated stories about fire hydrants. John used an adult-like style in his speech and storytelling, and preferred the company of either his father or other adults in the program with whom he talked at length about fire hydrants. Shy offers of fire hydrant pictures by one of the girls at the drawing table were ignored. ✐

Once established, this intense interest fire hydrants continued unchanged for many months. In enacting his stories at circle time, John always took the role of the fire hydrant with few parts allotted to others, except for the girls who were "regulars" at the drawing and writing table.

An analysis of his stories and paintings over time revealed that a major change occurred in December, when John depicted his fire hydrants with faces (Figure 11.2). At this time, he introduced the character of a "walking, talking" fire hydrant in his dictated narratives. Here is a "walking, talking" fire hydrant story:

Figure 11.2
A "Walking, Talking" Fire
Hydrant

December 13 Story

Once there was a fire hydrant and it was a walking, talking fire hydrant. Then another hydrant came and it was the newest one that John the walking, talking fire hydrant had ever seen. The very new hydrant fell down and broke one of its caps!! The cap was made of cast iron; it was old but the model number was new. Then another hydrant came and another hydrant came and then another. Then the hydrants got broken. They did not put out water anymore. Then there was a very, very, very old fire hydrant came and rewinded the camera that they were using. Then a ball popped out of a hose hookup. Than a block came out of the other hookup. ✄

The fire hydrant pattern in painting, drawing, and storytelling persisted until spring. But finally in a story dictated in May a major advance was made. To his teachers this story indicated a shift in John's gradual socialization. He dictates a story about, and takes the role of, a very silly firefighter. (There is no fire hydrant present in this story.) Here we see John abandon his adult-like narrative style for what seems to be "baby talk." Is John emulating what he reads as the language of his peer group and the rough-and-tumble play of the boys in the class? Not accidentally, his awareness of the context of the classroom is indicated in his reference to the fence of the school. The fence surrounds the playground and is near where many of the more active boys congregate in the play yard.

May 1 Story

An Entire Fireman . . . . Once there was a fireman and he fell in a puddle and got his suit all wet. And then he got in front of the big hookup and the garbage truck went over his legs! And he went to the hospital and he got da-da yocky-not medicine. He felt much, much, much better. And then they went to the ba-ba fence and jumped in puddles (and the ba-ba fence is the fence near the child-care center). ✄

Additional evidence of John's growing interest in the classroom environment is seen in the paintings he produces around this same time (Figure 11.3).

Although John has not abandoned the fire hydrant theme, he has begun to depict fire hydrants that have an Asian look, with pagoda-like appendages and Asian-looking calligraphy in the pictorial space. Is this a reflection of the school's multicultural curriculum, an awareness of the multilingual signs that had recently been affixed to learning centers and cubbies? Or was it the Japanese calligraphy and cultural objects celebrating Boys' Day and Girls' Day (Japanese holidays)? Is he responding to the art work created by his one friend, a Japanese girl who is also a "regular" at the drawing table?

But it is his final story, dictated in June, that indicates a great leap in socialization for John.

Figure 11.3
Fire Hydrants with Asian-appearing Pagodas and Calligraphy

June 5 Story

Firefighters from all over the city came to a really big fire. There were not enough fireplugs close by. So the firefighters had to take their small hoses and hook them up to each truck. There were 7 trucks. And then they got their monitors but there was not enough pressure! (Monitors are the big nozzles on top of the trucks.) They saved a very, very, very tall building from danger of the fire. The end. ✐

In this story John has created many roles. There are seven firefighters and seven fire trucks; well over half the class has been included. He allocates the superordinate roles of firefighters to boys and the subordinate roles of trucks to girls. He does not place himself in a central role as a hydrant, and when asked about this, he replied, "I wanted to be among the firefighters." John's integration into the classroom culture seems to have been facilitated by the storytelling, story-acting curriculum at his school. However, it comes at a cost. In his selection of choice roles for boys and lesser roles for the girls, we see that John has incorporated the gender stereotypic indicators of power that are often seen in group settings (Cook-Gumperz & Scales, 1996; Nicopoulou, Scales, & Weintaub, 1994). The sequence of stories and paintings in John's portfolio gave a vivid picture of his social adjustment to school. In addition, it revealed the very unique way in which John, over the school year, had constructed his own form of social integration.

DIVERSITY CREATES ENRICHMENT AND CHALLENGE FOR TEACHERS

The culturally diverse classrooms of today, with mixed-age groups, and a policy of including children with physical impairments and other identified special needs, can provide great enrichment for its members. However, open-play settings can also represent a challenge to social integration. In the anecdote that follows we demonstrate the added complexity that such diversity may bring to interactive play:

"Little Dragon"

After a celebration of the Chinese New Year and the children's astounding creation of a dragon, 3-year-old Christopher began emulating the actions of a dragon. He rigidly strode through the play yard, imaginatively breathing fire while stalking some of the older boys in the class. At about the same time, Christopher's mother noted that she began receiving an unusual number of "Ouch Reports" (see Figure 11.4) for Christopher (Alkon et al., 1994).

Christopher's mother wondered what was going on. As a Chinese American, was it possible that he was becoming a target of abuse by the "rough," older boys in the class? She began to wonder if she had made a mistake in enrolling Christopher in this integrated, university-based preschool. Perhaps she would have been wiser to place him in the new Chinese language school that was opening in a nearby community. Christopher's descriptions of events in the "Ouch Reports" indicated that it was often Alex, the oldest, largest, and most popular child in the program, who had chased him.

Following this, the teacher surveyed the "Ouch Reports" and found that Christopher did have a few more reports of bumps, falls, and scrapes than other children his age. The implications of these findings were discussed in a staff meeting in relation to Christopher. Teachers were also able to reference the set of ongoing observations on this particular child that had been compiled. In the early days of the program, Christopher had spent most of his time near his early morning teacher, but now he had begun to spend more time in the active outdoor play areas of the school. Teachers noted that when Christopher pretended to be a dragon, the older boys chased him with cries such as "Here comes the bad guy!" Teachers' attempts to reason with Christopher and the older boys about this pattern would end the chasing temporarily by the 4-year-old boys. Three-year-old Christopher, however, always tearfully insisted that he wished to continue to be a dragon. He seemed to have little interest in integrating himself by taking on a character from the play scenarios of the older boys. The moment the teacher's attention was averted, he would approach the group again as a dragon, with the same consequences.

Christopher seemed enchanted with his ability to obtain the attention of the older boys. When conflict arose or when he fell while fleeing from the "superheroes," he seemed developmentally unable to comprehend the teacher's admonitions about the consequences of this entry strategy and the need to thematically coordinate his play with others.

Luckily, around the time of spring break, a new child of about Christopher's age was admitted to the program. His favorite play persona was

University of California   Child Care Services

OUCH REPORT

Child's Name: _John Doe_   Teacher's Name: _Jane Doe/Teacher_

Today's Date: _7_/_25_/_97_ Time of Accident _4_:_40_ a.m/p.m.

Location of Event: _Far yard_

Contributing Factors: _"I hurt myself right on the leg._
I was being chased and I bumped."

Type of Injury: **Location of Injury:**

_ Cut
✓ Scrape
_ Bump or Bruise
_ Mouth injury
_ Crush injury
_ Human Bite
_ Insect bite/sting
_ Injury by foreign object
  (splinter, sand in eye etc.)
_ Hair pulled
_ Other _____

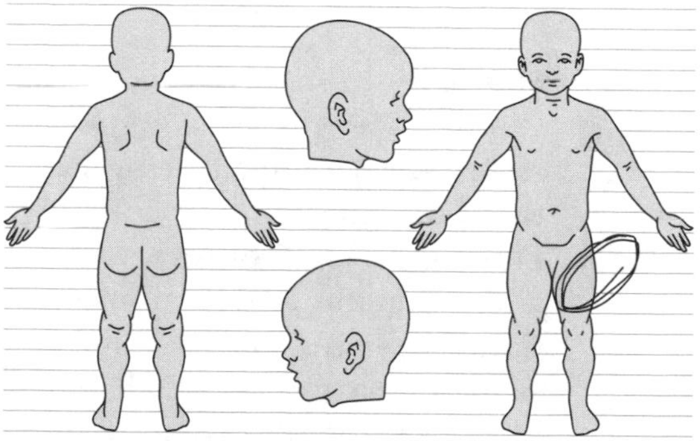

Type of Treatment Given: **Recommended Follow-up:**

— Cleaned injured site
✓ Ice pack applied   _He seems great - he was_
_ Band–Aid or dressing applied   _a little shaken by_
✓ Child rested or laid down   _hurting himself._
✓ Given comfort
_ Antiseptic applied
_ Other _____

Head Teacher (initial/date) _BR_

Figure 11.4
Ouch Report

Source: Adapted by University of California Head Teacher Rebecca Tracy for classroom use.

Tyrannosaurus rex. Not surprisingly, the two formed a union and soon became the magnet for a small but cohesive group of younger children. When this group was granted a special dragon territory on one of the smaller play structures, they were able to rant and rage with each other powerfully but be protected from forays by older "superheroes" in search of "bad guys." ✆

Inclusion of Children with Special Needs

In the move toward inclusion, play-centered classroom teachers must be realistic about the goals they set for all the children, including those with special needs, and the availability of resources to implement them. Underfunding, along with failure to establish agreement on goals and a time frame for their achievement with all concerned, can hamper a successful inclusion program (Wasserman, 2005). Some of these diverse factors might have been a barrier to the successful inclusion in play of a child with a speech impairment in the vignette that follows.

Matthew

Matthew, a large, slow-moving child (age 6 years and 5 months) with a severe speech impairment, has entered the sand play area where two active boys, Greg, an unusually aggressive child (5 years and 1 month), and François, a child of African American heritage (4 years and 9 months), after a lengthy and tenuous negotiation, have established a play interaction. They are making "quicksand" by pouring water and sprinkling dry sand into a trench which has been dug by the teacher. Matthew has jumped to a mound nearby and stands opposite Greg, looking down into the "quicksand." As they face each other, Matthew attempts to enter the play not by speaking, but by kicking a tire embedded in the sand above the trench. Recently he has been attempting to play and interact more frequently with other children. Greg responds by jumping across the trench and pushing Matthew into the sand. ✆

Previously, Matthew relied solely upon the teachers to interpret his needs. His teachers, however, still closely monitor his play with peers because of his rather limited physical skills (Scales, 1989, 1996). In this, Matthew resembles many children with special needs, who rely greatly on adults to provide them with support in the interpretation of their needs (Erwin, 1993; Newcomer, 1993). The manner in which Matthew attempts to enter the play between Greg and François (by kicking a tire as an initiating act) is somewhat typical of other children with special needs. According to van der Kooij (1989b), some children with special needs respond to their environment in a single way, either nonverbally or verbally, which also makes it difficult for them to enter play situations.

"Quicksand"

The following excerpt from a longer text indicates what happens when Matthew attempts to enter the play with Greg and François:

Greg:	Take this, Matthew.	Greg jumps to a mound near Matthew and shoves him over.
Matthew:	(unclear utterance)	Matthew picks up a handful of sand and throws it at Greg.
Greg:	Take this.	Greg shoves Matthew again and jumps over trench.
François:	Ya! Ha!	François returns to the sandpit.
Greg:	[Help me], François.	
Greg:	Get him.	The two boys begin to attempt to push Matthew into the trench.
François:	Hi ya!	
Greg:	Push him over. Shove.	Both boys are pulling Matthew.
François:	Are we pushin' him in the quicksand?	
Greg:	No, push him right down here.	Greg points to center of trench.
François:	Now you come here, Matthew. I've got something to show you.	François stands up, moves to Matthew.
Matthew:	I know what you're going to do. I saw it.	(Matthew's speech is understandable as he points to François.)
François:	Come! Help me lift big boy up. Fat mouth. ⌀	Both boys tug at Matthew.

At the beginning of this sequence, shortly after Greg pushes Matthew, two teachers intervene. One attempts to encourage Matthew to use his language to tell Greg his objections to being pushed into the sand. A second teacher moves to assist and redirect Greg. She first acknowledges the good aspects of what Greg and François have made together, but also warns that it might need "special attention" because it could be "dangerous." Thus, she signals the boys that they can expect closer monitoring from teachers. Despite this warning, the two boys continue to attempt to push Matthew down into the sand.

Again, a teacher arrives to alter the direction the play has taken. "Are you playing the game with them, Matthew?" he asks. Without waiting for Matthew to respond, Greg and François chime in. They define the game as one that involves ". . . tryin' to push him [Matthew] down there." They say that Matthew has said "Yes," he wishes to play. At this point Matthew speaks up clearly, saying, "No," indicating he does not wish to play.

When the boys persist in pushing Matthew into the quicksand, the teacher again restrains them and informs them that if they continue, they will have to leave the sandpit: ". . . I say again there's no throwing sand here. I wouldn't let sand get in your eyes." Following this warning, Greg and François resume their play around the theme of making "quicksand."

Somewhat later, Matthew makes another attempt to enter the play with Greg and François. This time, he has modest success when he relatively clearly assures the two boys, "I know what we can do, put sand on top." Having affirmed the theme of the play, he is not bothered further and sits quietly nearby, observing the pit of quicksand.

François returns to the sand area with more water.

Matthew:	I know what we can do.	Sitting on mound above the trench watching, Matthew clearly addresses Greg and François.
François:	What?	
Matthew:	[. . . put sand on top.]	
François:	You're right, Matthew.	François affirms Matthew's contribution.
Greg:	Then when people walk here, they'll sink in [and go in quicksand] Kaboom! ∅	

The teacher in this anecdote was unsure how to intervene. Should he interrupt it by attempting, probably unsuccessfully, to help Matthew enter the play? The teacher wondered if he should protect or encourage Matthew to enter this fast-paced, rough-and-tumble play with two unpredictable partners. This example illustrates the social difficulties that children with special needs may experience with peers during play.

Although reciprocity is a salient feature of effective social play, many young children with special needs do not demonstrate this skill (Koplow, 1996; Newcomer, 1993; Wolfberg, 1999). Many are unable to incorporate another peer into shared play. According to Newcomer, some are overly inhibited and "extremely wary of play situations," tending to rely on adults. On the other hand, children with too few inhibitions might be reluctant to delay gratification of their impulses (Newcomer, 1993; van der Kooij, 1989b). Because reciprocity may be problematic in children who have special needs, teachers must be especially aware of play situations that involve these children and encourage them to share in interactions with their peers (Kostelnik et al., 2002; Odom, 2002).

In the previous vignettes we have illustrated the various factors that may impede children's ability to establish and maintain interactive play with peers in the classroom; the first two involved issues of separation, the third concerned the inability of a younger child to take the perspective of others, and the final episode involved three children attempting to play together. One, Matthew, was a child with special needs; a second was François, a child who was culturally different from his classmates; and the third was a child who often acted out aggressively. From these examples we see that it is not always easy to know precisely how to support play.

TRADITIONAL RESEARCH AND PRACTICE

In the past, teachers who turned to research with questions related to play and socialization found relatively few answers. Researchers were sometimes even uncertain that play was really taking place. They were not always able to identify its boundaries. This made it difficult to determine who was playing "what and with whom," and so they were reluctant to intervene directly in children's play.

Smilansky's (1968) recommendation (derived from her research) that intervention support elaborated dramatic play is one notable exception. Teachers were aware, however, that the nature of children's play and social interaction was affected by quality and character of the physical environment. In order to lend more rigor to play intervention through the modifications of settings, they have employed various checklists and rating scales to assess environmental features such as boundaries and links between areas, as well as level of play complexity (Harms, Clifford, & Cryer, 1998; Kritchevsky, Prescott, & Walling, 1977). These methods verify the presence or absence of desired features in classrooms and play yards. However, they do not reveal how these elements in themselves might act to generate social and cooperative behavior.

CURRENT PRACTICE ILLUMINATED BY RESEARCH

Starting in the 1970s, this issue was studied in detail by a number of researchers working in a sociocultural tradition (Cook-Gumperz & Corsaro, 1977; Dyson, 1997; Reed, 2005). Many were collaborating closely with teachers or were teachers themselves (e.g., Cochran-Smith & Lytle, 1993; Cook-Gumperz & Scales, 1996; Corsaro, 1997; Erickson, 1993; Gallas, 1998; Perry, 2001; Reifel & Yeatman, 1991; Scales, 1996; Tribble, 1996). Drawing on this research, our knowledge of the specific ways that play interactions contribute to socialization has increased (Sawyer, 2001).

Many of these were naturalistic, observational studies which looked at peer play and communication as it unfolded. These studies demonstrated how children develop the skills to monitor the varying social and cultural contexts they encounter. Some studies showed how school practice constrains or complements the development of essential features of social competence (Cook-Gumperz & Corsaro, 1977; Cook-Gumperz, Corsaro, & Streeck, 1996; Corsaro, 1985, 1997; Corsaro & Schwartz, 1991). Other research brought to light the complex issues involved in the gender socialization of boys and girls (Dyson, 1994; Goodwin, 1990; Nicolopoulou, Scales, & Weintraub, 1994; Scales & Cook-Gumperz, 1993).

Differences in Boys' and Girls' Play and Socialization

A year-long study of children's narratives by Nicolopoulou and Scales (1990) found that preschool boys' and girls' stories differed in both content and form. In their stories, boys were inclined to pile powerful or violent images one upon

Children synchronize their play with action and sound.

another, with little apparent order or sequence. Girls, on the other hand, tied their stories to the rhythm of the home. For example, children get up and have breakfast, have birthday parties, go to the park, come home, and go to bed.

For girls, the family romance was paramount, with marriage, family relationships, or the frequent themes of arrival, losing, or finding of babies. Boys, on the other hand, rarely spoke of any relationship other than that of a "friend"—a friend with whom they more than likely battled as a culminating feature of their stories. These gender differences emerged early and persisted despite teachers' efforts to broaden the repertoires of both boys and girls.

"Tough Guys." The following anecdote reveals a previously hidden, gender-related, social hierarchy in the allocation of roles in children's storytelling (Scales, 1996).

> Near the end of the day at a university-based preschool, 28 children are seated around a square taped on the carpet. This is "the stage" where they will enact stories dictated to a teacher earlier in the day. At this particular moment, however, the proceedings have stalled: The child-author's original choice of an actor for the part of a blue Power Ranger has refused the role. The children are becoming restless and inattentive. The teacher, hoping to get things moving again, whispers a suggestion: "Why don't you pick Max? He really wants a part in your play!"
>
> "Oh no," responds the author. "He can't be it! It has to be one of the tough guys."
>
> The stalemate was resolved when it was suggested that Max could "pretend" to be a "tough" guy. ✄

Suddenly, a previously unseen aspect of the social life of this classroom has become transparent. We knew that for the girls, "princess" roles were highly prized tokens of social favor, argued for and parceled out in play and story acting. Now, a once-hidden social hierarchy in the boys' world was revealed as well.

When stories such as this and the power relationships they reveal are merely suppressed in "gender-neutral" classrooms, they go unnoted as a hidden curriculum. However, through story playing in preschool and what Dyson (1995) called an "author's theatre" in the elementary classroom, such issues can become accessible for negotiation and dialogue about who "gets in" and who "gets left out," who owns which social roles, and who has power in the play life of the classroom (see also Scales, 1996, 2005).

As teachers and researchers are aware, not only do the themes and characteristics of boys' and girls' stories differ, but so, too, does their willingness to engage in play usually associated with members of the opposite sex. As far back as 1977, Garvey and Berndt noted that boys were reluctant to play roles, such as a "prince," that are commonly associated with girls' stories or play. Teachers report that this is still the case in today's classroom.

Paley (1984), a teacher and writer, examined the differences in the play of preschool boys and girls. She found that when time for spontaneous play was lengthened, boys became more willing to engage in quiet table activities, more typically favored by girls. She also recommended that teachers respect children's role choices as an important part of their self-concept. In addition to Paley's work, further observation, reflection, and dialogue by teachers about their classrooms can contribute to greater understanding of how to mediate gender equity.

"Neighbors."   An observational study of one classroom conducted by Cook-Gumperz and Scales (1996) revealed that the social dynamics of group settings alone may sometimes aggravate the occurrence of gender stereotypic behaviors. Cook-Gumperz and Scales collected a set of observations of two groups playing adjacent to one another in the block area of the classroom. One group consisted of boys, the other of girls. When the group of boys moved to play more closely to the girls, the girls' play interactive communication changed markedly. They began to enact roles of helpless mommies and babies who were in danger. Roles in their previous play had involved grooming and feeding miniature animals. In addition, during this time the boys' play became more assertively aggressive and "macho" as they circled around the girls, ostensibly to obtain blocks from a shelf to the rear of the girls (Cook-Gumperz & Scales, 1996).

In a contrasting observation collected during a brief interval midway through this long play event, the constellation of boys marched noisily out of the classroom. One boy remained behind and began inching near the girls' play space, making "strange clucking sounds." A brief conversation between the lone boy and one of the girls in the group ensued when she commented on his strange noises. In this exchange, it was notable that no stereotypic forms were used as they addressed each other as "neighbors." The two appeared to be attempting to negotiate the boy's entrance into the girls' play space. However, the noisy return of the larger group of boys to the block area disrupted this negotiation, and the would-be neighbor was drawn into the larger configuration. At this point, the assertive behavior accelerated and included loud singing and chanting. The noise finally aroused the attention of a teacher, who attempted to settle the matter by redirecting the children back into segregated groups to "share" the blocks. The attempt by the two to play together as "neighbors" (an inspired solution) went unnoticed (Cook-Gumperz & Scales, 1996).

In order to avoid conflict rather than any attempt to scaffold possible cross-gender play, the teacher opted for a management strategy alone. Because group size appears to contribute to the invocation of gender stereotypes, guided play opportunities with a teacher in smaller configurations of mixed gender groups might help children develop repertoires of non-stereotypic play discourse. On the discourse boundaries between genders, teachers can help support children's efforts to define themselves and their relationships in new ways (Dyson, 1993; 2003; Tobin, 2000).

Children's Negotiations Create a Dynamic Context for Play

Working closely with teachers, Corsaro, a sociologist, and his colleague Cook-Gumperz (1977), studied the ways children negotiate and achieve their own self-generated social objectives in play through their conversations. Cook-Gumperz, Corsaro, and Streeck (1996) found that play interactions are shaped by and, in themselves, shape children's understanding of the social and environmental expectations of situations.

In studying the ways children communicate with each other in play, we find that children's lives in preschool are embedded in a particular social context, whose impact cannot be ignored without neglecting children's interest, self-direction, and motivation (Scales, 1997). The social work that children engage in as they play has been largely unexamined by practitioners whose valuing of play has its roots in early childhood's psychodynamic heritage. Constructivists such as Piaget and Vygotsky have had an important impact on our view of children's development. Both researchers and teachers have been stimulated by Vygotsky's reference to the "zone of proximal development." Many recent articles, however, have made too narrow an interpretation of the "zone of proximal development" and failed to note that Vygotsky also asserted that play in itself is the source of development and creates the zone of proximal development (Nicolopoulou, 1996b).

To illustrate this point, consider the following descripion of an open activity period in a primary school classroom where the play roles that four elementary-age children set for themselves reflect their developing social competency.

Newspapers

At midyear, 6-year-olds Clay, Zoe, Randall, and Michelle have decided they will use their daily activity period to make a class newspaper. In this language- and literacy-rich classroom, they have had many opportunities to examine and play with different kinds of writing, such as letters, articles, books, lists, and signs. Their teacher, Harriet, wisely helps them develop traditional competencies in handwriting, spelling, and letter sounds on a daily basis. So Zoe, Clay, Randall, and Michelle did not come to their play project uninformed.

Their interest in the newspaper project extended over several weeks and involved much research and many revisions, additions, and reviews by their teacher and classmates. News articles as well as jokes and cartoons were collected and included in the final comprehensive version. Although only one "edition" was published, every child in the classroom received a copy (Morrison, 1985a). In this primary-grade classroom, daily activity time, during which children have ample choices of things to do, provides a "zone of proximal development," or what Newman, Griffin, and Cole (1989) would call the "construction zone."

In the play that occurs in the free interaction among peers involved in the activity period, children are provided with an opportunity to experience the "give and take," or reciprocity, that is a salient feature of effective social play, where shared needs, interests, and competencies can be mediated. This reciprocity also provides the context for moral, social, and ethical development, as well. "This reciprocity is rarely achieved between children and adults, but in play it is the rule rather than the exception" (Alward, 2005, pp. 1–2).

Research on Play and Socialization Within Special Education. Researchers have also focused on play and socialization within special education and integrated classrooms (Erwin, 1993; Hanline & Fox, 1993; Hartmann & Rollett, 1994; McEvoy, Shores, Wehby, Johnson, & Fox, 1990; Ostrosky, Kaiser, & Odom, 1993). Young children with special needs have exhibited an increase in socialization skills after interacting with peers in a play environment. Researchers have found that children with severe disabilities in integrated sites spent more time engaging in activities with their classmates than in unoccupied behavior, which broadened their base of social support (Erwin, 1993). A recent publication by Frost, Wortham, and Reifel (2005) contains a comprehensive section titled "Play and Children with Disabilities." These authors surveyed the considerable research and technology that culminated in much greater access to play opportunities for young children with disabilities. Additionally, new play designs for equipment and toys are greatly enhancing the potential of inclusive classrooms. Play in inclusive settings has the potential to enhance social competence for these children. However, it is not easy to achieve.

Parents Take an Active Role in Supporting Inclusion. Belkin (2004) wrote about the experiences of the parents of a boy with cerebral palsy. It is an inspiring story that chronicles their persistence and fortitude in ensuring their child's inclusion in a kindergarten classroom. Such determination is often necessary to navigate the bureaucratic barriers to attaining access to resources for children with special needs. Many lessons were learned by these parents, not the least of which was about possibilities for inclusion in a typical classroom set up for pairs or small groups of four at low tables or on the floor. A seemingly simple thing in the context of their many problems was the inability to locate a wheelchair scaled to the height of Thomas' kindergarten peers when they were seated on the floor or at low tables. Such a wheelchair would have facilitated his being able to establish eye contact with his peers, an important component of interaction, particularly since Thomas was both speech- and mobility-impaired (Isenberg & Jalongo, 2006; Milligan, 2003).

PLAY PROVIDES A BRIDGE BETWEEN THEORY AND PRACTICE

We have discussed some of the ways in which our examination of children's play interactions and storytelling provide a bridge between theory and practice. As demonstrated in the anecdotes we present, our broad constructivist view of child development does not confine us to relying on any single, rigid, theoretical approach. Classical Piagetian theory can serve us well in the study of individuals, but we also look to Vygotsky when examining how the social dynamics of the classroom intersect with individual development.

Rather than taking a top-down approach—that is, bringing only a selected theory to bear—teachers might find greater explanatory power in analyzing their own records and observations. This has been described as an interpretive approach. Such an approach looks closely at specific play interaction and takes an insider's view rather than that of the detached outsider. It grounds these explanations in contexts well known to participants. By this means, findings can be corroborated and discrepant cases identified and explained (Cochran-Smith & Lytle, 1993; Erickson, 1993, 2004; Gaskins, Miller, & Corsaro, 1992; Packer & Addison, 1989; Perry, 2001; Sawyer, 2001).

The Interpretive Approach

The value of an interpretive approach, which draws on multiple theoretical perspectives, is demonstrated by the "tough guy" anecdote cited earlier in this chapter. Remember that the child author first resisted letting Max play the role of a Power Ranger, saying he was not a "tough guy." Subsequently, he changed his mind when it was suggested that Max could pretend to be a tough guy. Max's acquiescence to the teacher's suggestion could be analyzed from a number of perspectives. A classical Piagetian point of view might suggest that the class of actors pretending to be Power Rangers could be analyzed to consist of tough and non-tough guys, that is, in terms of class inclusions and coordinations, or of conservation and identity.

Developmental issues, such as classification and the ability to conserve, certainly were involved. However, these analyses do not account for all of the child's reasoning and do not account for his agency and motivation. Here an interpretive perspective, with its sociocultural orientation, broadens constructivist thinking to provide further explanatory power (Alward, 2005; Scales, 1996). From a sociocultural perspective, the context of the story-acting activity presented the child with a conflict and an ambiguity that needed to be resolved, and the teacher, as mentor, offered an alternative that helped him find a solution with-in the collaborative construction of the "play."

At the individual level, from a Piagetian perspective, it might be consid-ered to be a disequilibrating situation that helped the child advance to a high-er level of thinking. With respect to the social dynamics of the classroom, this is the kind of negotiation of power roles that Dyson (1995) refers to in her work on urban classrooms. When teachers take an interpretive approach, they discover that children actively contribute to their own socialization and a sense of themselves as social entities, and to the production and reproduc-tion of the children's culture (Gaskins, Miller, & Corsaro, 1992; Corsaro, 1997). In play-centered curriculum, teachers have a potent opportunity to observe how, as children insert elements from the larger culture into their play world, they are forced to make sense of both their real and fantasy worlds (Nicolopoulou, 1996b).

In discussing ethnographic and linguistic research on children's narra-tives, Dyson has noted that individual children assume the voices of others, both past and present, as they use the linguistic forms they have appropriated from teachers, parents, and peers to construct a text (Dyson, 1995, 2003; Dyson & Genishi, 1994).

Dyson also found, however, that when addressing present-day events, such as the ambiguity surrounding gender, the text is, in and of itself, trans-formative. That is, it transforms the child's perception of the past and the future. For example, when today's child uses a past expression of gender (e.g., "princess"), she is not merely miming in some frozen way an outmod-ed social attitude. Rather, because the old-fashioned expression is now em-bedded in the different social context of today's world, it brings about change or transforms by giving rise to ambiguities the child must resolve through dialogue with others. If we merely drive gender expressions under-ground as a hidden curriculum, we fail to provide any occasion for this transformative mediation to occur as the child struggles to reconcile the tension between gender conventions of the past and emerging ones of the present (Dyson, 1995).

Teachers Take a Research Stance: Views from the Inside

Teachers can take a research stance by systematically observing play communi-cation to see how the classroom social environment is being "read" by chil-dren. For example, the teachers' videotaped observation of the interactive strategies of the three children in the "quicksand" episode gave them impor-tant information about how to guide their interactions and later reconfigure the play environment of the sand pit in order to support more players (see Figure 11.5).

Children's Interactive Strategies

The interactive strategies that children utilize provide clues to their ability to understand the views of others. Situational strategies children employ also reveal how actions and speech are coordinated and synchronized to conform to a mutual understanding of the unfolding interaction. Such behaviors are essential to prosocial behavior. Children can be provided with opportunities to learn needed skills at "turn taking" in play interactions with peers. The notion of taking turns may arise in play at the swings on the playground, or when children put their name or mark on a waiting list for a turn at the water table or computer. The wise adult makes sure the child gets a turn; children need to be able to trust the "marks" on those lists.

In most early childhood classrooms, turns at games can start early in cooperative dyads. If groups are not too large or too formally structured, the understanding of a conversational turn can be demonstrated in talk at circle time. Small games, such as lotto, and familiar songs can contribute, as well. And, of course, children need to be given ample opportunity to practice their skills at turn taking in spontaneous play.

Social coordinations occur in play.

Central to this approach to understanding children's socialization is the notion that the play context is dynamic. As they play, children develop their understanding of the unfolding activity (Cook-Gumperz & Gumperz, 1982). For example, when negotiating a theme such as "home play," children come to understand that to successfully enter into play, one must be "on topic."

Research tells us that to maintain social cooperation, children, like adults, constantly signal their mutual understanding of unfolding interactive themes. Mutual understanding is signaled when children initiate a play episode or topic or when a topic is changed; play partners will often be observed to affirm the change with a "right." "We're making soup, right?" "Right!" "And it'll have alphabets, OK?" "OK!" (Corsaro, 1979, 1997, 2003; Gumperz & Cook-Gumperz, 1982; Sawyer, 2001).

While this is usually expressed in a co-player's "right" or an "OK", affirmation also can take a nonverbal form. For example, a co-player may express uptake of a theme of cooking by an appropriate gesture, such as beginning to stir a bowl of "sand soup."

Turn Taking and Children with Special Needs. The notion of turn taking is especially important for those with special needs who have difficulty cooperating with peers. For example, in general, "one will observe the mutual influence of individuals upon each other" (van der Kooij, 1989b). However, with regard to some children with special needs, "egocentrism" might block such "mutuality." Opportunities to practice skills such as turn taking are important for these children, so they can learn to interact effectively in play with other children (Koplow, 1996; Odom, 2002; van der Kooij, 1989b; Wolfberg, 1999).

STUDYING THE SOCIAL ECOLOGY OF A PRESCHOOL CLASSROOM

Most of the observational material cited in this chapter has been drawn from naturalistic studies of preschool or early primary settings for 3- to 6-year-olds. The basic method of analysis was pioneered in conversational studies conducted by Gumperz (Jaworski & Coupland, 1999). It was adapted for work with young children by sociologists Corsaro and Cook-Gumperz (Cook-Gumperz & Corsaro, 1977; Corsaro, 2003).

Contrasts in Social Ecologies

Researchers Cook-Gumperz and Corsaro analyzed four episodes that were drawn from videotapes of a preschool classroom (1977). In this section, we discuss and contrast these episodes in order to demonstrate how the social and ecological cues of settings influence children's play and socialization.

In the Home Play Center: Rita and Bill.   The first episode involved two children, Rita and Bill, playing husband and wife. It demonstrates how little negotiation is required to establish play themes in the home play center because children bring what the researchers call "conventionalized expectations" to this site (Cook-Gumperz & Corsaro, 1977).

For Rita and Bill, the most difficult portion of their interaction involved their attempt to ward off the incursion of two unruly "kitties," who attempt to enter the playhouse. Corsaro and Cook-Gumperz noted that once a play episode is underway, children are protective of their interactive space.

Knowing that children's interactions are fragile, teachers will respect ongoing interactions by helping potential intruders such as the "kitties" become established at a site nearby or involved with others who are not engaged already. In this case, Rita and Bill handled the problem themselves by dismissing the "kitties" to the "backyard."

The Sand Table: Constructing a Play Fantasy.   In the second episode, a four-sided sand tray was the site for more inventive and well-coordinated play themes. It challenged children's use of their linguistic and communicative skills to construct a unique collective play fantasy because at this site scenarios were not conventionalized as they are in home play centers. The collective fantasy opened with a "rainstorm." Then a small sand mound was elaborated into a "home for freezing bunnies." The players coordinated the changes of theme and did so again as the sand mound became a final safe haven from "lightning" in a "B . . . I . . . G steel home."

In contrast to the first episode, the children at the indoor sand tray were required to structure their activity creatively as it emerged. They could not rely on conventional expectations, such as those in home play centers. Rather, they had to depend on their own communication to collectively create and sustain the order of their talk about their spontaneous and novel fantasy.

Although the home play center is ideal for the neophyte communicator, more open settings (such as the sand tray with miniatures) also are needed to provide challenge for older children. At such sites, children stretch their communicative strategies as they cue each other to the meaning of unfolding play events they are collaboratively creating. Such strategies include some of the following:

1. Using special linguistic cues to signify the fantasy (e.g., taking the role of the bunnies).

2. Using repetition to acknowledge some feature of a previous utterance (such as echoing and repeating key words and phrases like *freezing, rain,* and *lightning.*

3. Tying new material to previous thematic content. For example, using the word *and* plus a phrase containing new material allows an opening for another child to interact. In one episode, a child named Sabrina said, "I'll take the baby to the store." Her friend Sarah added, ". . . and the big sister will drive the car; and I'll be the big sister."

4. Using an ongoing verbal description of behavior as it occurs; for example, saying "Help, we're in the forest, and it's beginning to rain," while visually manipulating miniature toys.

Settings That Constrain Peer Talk and Interaction.   Cook-Gumperz and Corsaro (1977) analyzed a third episode, which occurred at a work table. The teacher attempted to engage the children in a guided-play activity involving the creation of pictures with paint-filled squirt bottles. The teacher inhibited the children's language use and development of interactive skills because she did most of the talking, controlled the flow of talk, and initiated most topics.

With a greater awareness of the importance of the need for children to exercise their interactive skills in self-directed play, teachers might consider how they can include plenty of opportunity for spontaneous talk among peers at the project table. In this way, teachers can attain their instructional goals in guided play and still maintain the value that comes through interactive peer talk.

An Undefined Context.   In a fourth episode, the setting also constrained interaction. It involved what Corsaro and Cook-Gumperz referred to as an undefined context. Here conflict and confusion in play resulted from the ambiguous cues that the teacher inadvertently set up. Children did not know whether they were at a teacher-dominated site or a child-dominated site.

In the school where this episode occurred, the researchers observed that work tables usually cued "school" kinds of behaviors. In contrast, play in the home corner or at the sand tray was much less constrained by teacher models, and peer talk flowed freely.

On the day that this episode was observed, a teacher had casually placed a work table near the home play corner, inadvertently confusing cued expectations for interactive play. Three children were seated at the table. However, a singular lack of coordination existed in their short-lived play interaction. Two were playing "teacher" and one was playing "police." The informed teacher alters contexts only with an awareness of possible unforeseen consequences. Sometimes mixing environmental cues can produce interesting and positive transformations in children's play, but it also can result in failed interactions or disaster.

SOLITARY AND PARALLEL PLAY REEXAMINED

We can sometimes be misled about children's social skills when we classify play solely on the basis of what we hear. Children do not place speech in the foreground of their communication. Instead, they use all modalities of communication, such as gesture, rhythm, and intonation, to achieve their interactive goals.

> Three children, Andrea (age 3 years and 2 months), Celine (age 3 years and 4 months), and Peter (age 3 years and 4 months) were playing with pots and pans at an outdoor sand table. Andrea and Celine were busy chatting about what the "baby" would eat for breakfast, while Peter silently stirred a bowl of sand nearby. ∅

Pam, their teacher, observed their play and assessed Peter's silent engagement as an example of solitary or parallel play. However, her later analysis of a videotape recording of this episode provided evidence for Peter's more active participation in the group interaction.

Though close at hand, Pam failed to take note of the role that Peter had been assigned. Only at the end of the episode was she made aware that she and Peter had been filling the roles of "baby" and "babysitter," respectively. This was revealed to her when Andrea, the "mommy," emphatically pointed her finger and said to Pam: "Baby, you—I'm goin' out to the woods." Then gesturing toward Peter, Andrea said: "You stay here with the babysitter."

Later, when shown the videotape of the episode, Peter confirmed his knowledge of his role. However, he seemed disinterested in informing Pam exactly how or when he became the "babysitter." Presumably for him it was an obvious "given" (Scales & Webster, 1976).

Whether Peter's play was solitary, parallel, or collaborative was not easily determined. However, close analysis of the videotape revealed that even without speech, Peter was a significant participant in this interactive play.

For the older child, language plays a more important role. Older children do not rely to such an extent on environmental cues to guide understanding. With their increasing linguistic ability, they are able to detach play from its situational context. Should play be disrupted, older children are more capable of re-establishing it and also are able to maintain interactive play across various sites through use of language alone (Scales, 1997).

Teacher Support for Play Interactions

In this chapter, we have attempted to show that initiating or entering play is a complex matter and involves more than mimicking adult formulas, such as "Hello, may I play with you?" Such an opening probably would be greeted with a resounding "No," particularly among 4-, 5-, and 6-year-olds. Within the children's culture, distinctive forms of communication are constructed.

Research shows that children develop their own particular strategies for making an entrance into an already established play episode. One successful tactic children use involves circling about the site of the play event until the players make an overture to them (Corsaro, 1997, 2003). Teachers (in the role of gatekeeper), noting a child's desire to enter a play episode, can assist by helping the newcomer find an activity or role that complements the play event. The teacher also might set the newcomer up nearby with similar props.

An example of a unique solution to a gate-keeping problem occurred when two girls barred the entrance of a third to the playhouse. The teacher's repeated suggestions of possible roles for the entering child had been rejected again and again.

Squabbling and howling continued for some time until one of the rejecting pair had a marvelous idea: The newcomer could be the "door." This role eminently suited Mia, the newcomer, who on other occasions often took the role of gatekeeper, excluding others herself. She immediately barred the entrance with widespread arms and legs.

Children Grant Warrants for Play

Sometimes play is established around action alone, as in the game of tag. However, close observation reveals that even such seemingly simple play involves the natural history of an activity, what Cook-Gumperz and Corsaro, (1977) called the granting of a "warrant." Think of a warrant as permission to establish a new play theme.

A typical example of the granting of a warrant occurred in connection with the quicksand segment presented earlier. Greg and François agreed that an area in the sandpit was quicksand. However, François, seeing that the water poured into the sand created a froth, referred to it as "chocolate milk." This constituted an attempt to get a warrant for a new theme. This elaboration was quickly rejected by Greg, who said, "You remember, we're makin' quicksand." François affirmed by a cheery "Oh, right, right," and the previous warrant was re-established.

Negotiations around the granting of warrants go on continuously in children's interactions. These warrants provide a thread to link sequences of activities. When a warrant has been granted, close observation of the play interaction reveals this as a focal point where communicative modes, both verbal and nonverbal, converge. Teachers can observe that children's rhythm and posture, gesture and action, are well-coordinated. These focal points are evidence that a mutually satisfactory interaction is taking place.

On further observation, teachers will also note sequences of maximal divergence or transition points. At these times, the children do not share a mutual understanding of the context and, therefore, have different views about the ongoing interaction. This lack of mutual understanding will even be evident in lack of coordination in the children's body language and posture.

In the following segments of the "quicksand" interaction, because the event consists largely of rough-and-tumble play, most of the transition points involve a teacher intervention. Two of the boys, François and Greg, seem to want to engage in rough-and-tumble play and play fighting (as indicated by their laughter). The third child, Matthew, does not, signaled by the fact that he is not laughing (Perry, 2001; Reed, 2005).

At such transition points, teachers may wish to intervene as peacemakers to clarify and reorient the players to a mutually acceptable focus. However, if teachers are not observing closely, they may sometimes intervene at the wrong point or make an irrelevant suggestion, thereby disrupting rather than supporting the interaction. Even a teacher's well-meaning reinforcing behavior, such as registering approval of children's cooperative play, sometimes serves only to disrupt the play and distract players.

"Quicksand" Revisited.   We return now to an earlier segment of the "quicksand" episode. Our purpose here is to consider in detail the initiating and sustaining of play. In this segment, we also learn about some of the problems that can arise in multidialectical play interactions. François, a child of African American heritage, speaks Black English as well as standard English and a form of English one might hear a TV speaker use. Unfortunately, most of François's teachers generally speak only standard English. His play partner, Greg, uses standard English and also a form of English used by TV speakers.

At the beginning of the episode, Greg is in the center of the sandpit at the intersection of the three pathways that had been configured by teachers. Greg stationed himself there as soon as he arrived at the beginning of the school day. Only three interactions occur in the sand on this day, and all involve the negotiation of a warrant with Greg in order to gain access to the sandpit (see Figure 11.5).

In environmental terms, an obvious feature of this particular sand "curriculum" was that the physical setup of the sandpit constrained play because the arrangement of intersecting passageways gave dominion over a large area to Greg, the one child who stood at the intersection. It also limited the possibilities for the types of play interactions that could go on. The steep slopes and narrow passages of the pathways invited very close physical contact. They tended to generate virtually a single possibility: rough-and-tumble play.

First Attempt to Establish a Warrant for Play
François enters the sandpit and addresses Greg with "Hi ya, Greg."

Figure 11.5

Greg responds, "Hi ya, François." Then François jumps to a mound of sand near Greg as the episode begins:

François:	Let's see what time it is. Oh, yeah, it's time for one by two by two.	Speaks rapidly, using style, rhythm, and tone of Black English
Greg:	No. No.	
François:	OK—well one by two by two, one by two, by two—ooda do da doo, one by two by two—me and my two by two—one by two by two—one by two by two is over.	François wrestles with Greg. Both boys are laughing.
Greg:	OK, François.	
François:	OK, Fatso.	François moves away.
Greg:	Here you go. Take this!	Throws a handful of sand at François. Boys now begin to throw sand at each other. ✂

In this sequence, François has attempted to establish a warrant with Greg for a play fighting game called "one by two by two." François addresses Greg in what is recognized by linguists as Black English because of its rhythm, intonation, and other features (Labov, 1972).

As the two children tussle about in the sand, François continues to address Greg in a kind of rhythmic, songlike manner, saying: "Oh, I'm gonna catch you." The teacher begins to monitor more closely. As the children begin to throw sand at each other, the teacher moves in to intervene. The sand throwing, though a prohibited activity, is well coordinated and is not a transition point. However, as a prohibited activity, the teacher cannot permit it. A transition that disrupts this interaction occurs when the teacher is required to enter.

Second Attempt to Establish a Warrant

François falls into the trench. Greg moves over and they tussle and toss sand about.

François:	Oh, oh, my goo goo.	
Greg:	Why—I'll get rid of your shirt if you do that again. I'll take your shirt off and I'll tear your shirt right off. That's the first thing I'd do.	Greg moves on mound above trench; turns to look at François.
François:	Tear you [inaudible] come back.	Greg and François tussle about in the sand.
Greg:	(laughs) ∅	

In this second attempt to establish a warrant, François again has used intimate Black English, addressing his friend as if Greg were a member of François's culture. The attempt ends with the boys tussling in the sand and the predictable entrance of the teacher.

At this point, Greg's complaint to the teacher, "I don't wanta play this," constitutes a rejection of François's second bid for a warrant for play. At this transition point, the teacher attempts to help the children find a more suitable focus.

Third Attempt to Establish a Warrant

Speaking in deeper tones and switching to a TV hero voice, François stands on the mound above Greg and initiates another warrant.

François:	I'm at the cliff of the mountain.	François takes a new posture on the mound.
Greg:	You won't get me, François.	Greg moves from François and the intersection.
François:	You won't get me either. Try to tear me apart. ⊘	François moves out upper-left exit. Greg follows.

This warrant is more to Greg's liking, and a well-coordinated game of tag is launched. The warrant attempt has succeeded. The play interaction, though primarily gross motor in nature at this point, is well-coordinated and cohesive.

The episode just described is noteworthy because one of the children speaks Black and standard English, as well as TV English, and shifts from one to the other midway through the episode. We see here that the demand is greater in this setting for the African American child to adapt his linguistic style to his play partner's speech style. François's initial overtures to establish a play warrant by utilizing Black English were not successful (Labov, 1972).

However, because he is multidialectical, François switched first to a form of TV English and then to standard English. Teachers analyzing this data do not consider it an accident that when he employed the alternative strategy of changing dialects to initiate his next two play warrants, François was successful. One was a game of tag, and the other centered around the theme of "making quicksand." Not unpredictably, as we noted in the beginning of this chapter, François and Greg, the now cohesive pair, later tried to exclude Matthew. As Corsaro (1997) has noted, children often will vigorously resist the entry of others in their play, fearing the disruption and breakup that such entry often inflicts on their fragile interactions.

The challenge in this play episode for Greg, François, and Matthew was to find a common language. Situations such as this provide an interesting challenge to the skills of teachers in creating a supportive play environment that responds to the diverse social needs of all children.

Spatial Arrangement Supports Interactive Play

At the environmental level, teachers facilitate cohesive interactive play by defining various zones in the classroom and play yard. Dividers and other spatial markings or arrangements protect interactive space so that players are not easily distracted and play is not disrupted. An example of this is seen when teachers arrange the environment so that block building or other floor play does not occur in the middle of pathways.

Teachers can establish spaces that bring children into proximity to each other, like around a rectangular sand tray or table. Then, for example, if two children are playing and a third enters, a side of the table can accommodate the newcomer. The visual array of toys shared by all informs the entering child about the play theme in progress and suggests a possible role to be taken up. Such spaces also help establish "face engagement" for those along the sides. In this case, the basics of communication are ensured, as well as a shared understanding of the theme of the unfolding play (Goffman, 1974, 2000).

Such configurations provide what has been called "defensible space" (Cook-Gumperz, Gates, Scales, & Sanders, 1976). Each child has a territory (his side of the table), so that entry into interaction with another in this situation places everybody on equal footing. Such a space also provides for two pairs of children playing side by side in parallel play. This opens up the possibility that the play of two pairs may become socially more coordinated as a foursome.

Children with Special Needs and the Environmental Context.   The environmental component is also critically important in early childhood special education classrooms and inclusive classrooms. The engagement of children with special needs can be influenced especially by the following: physical arrangement of the classroom, the appropriateness of materials and activities, and the interactions of the people in the environment. Added complexity occurs when the classroom environment must accommodate the needs of users of wheelchairs or those with limited mobility. As was noted in an earlier anecdote, disparity in height of seating for a wheelchair user may inhibit eye contact necessary for social interaction. If the child with special needs is also hearing-, speech-, or sight-impaired, added accommodation must be provided.

STANDARDS AND ASSESSMENT IN EARLY CHILDHOOD PROGRAMS

While the activities we have been describing represent socialization to the classroom culture, more and more pressure is being felt by teachers to include more emphasis on and assessment of formal academic curriculum standards. The broad area of socialization covers children's ability to interact with peers, and dispositions to learn and what, in later schooling, is called social studies. Social Studies as a discipline encompasses a wide array of subject areas representing content from a variety of academic fields of knowledge. Areas of knowledge for social studies identified by the National Council for Social Studies (2000) are:

- Time, continuity, and change
- People, places, and environments
- Production, distribution, and consumption
- Civic ideals and practices

WHEN TEACHERS TALK

Social Science For Young Children

A primary-school teacher who had recently returned from London reported on a project that she thought might be adapted for use as a part of a social science curriculum for young children. This interesting curriculum involved a set of mini museum displays titled "Suitcases and Sanctuaries" at the Immigrant Museum in London in 2005. Children working with artists, poets, and drama educators created "Letters Home" from immigrant children. Other younger children crafted objects and created a display of what immigrants from a diaspora following a disaster such as the Irish potato famine might have brought with them in their battered luggage. Many teachers could, of course, envision ways this curriculum could be adapted as a way to address anxieties in the face of more recent disasters.

Many of the social studies content areas can be addressed in concrete ways in a play-centered curriculum grounded in children's day-to-day interactions with one another in the community life of the classroom. This community has its own culture and involves sharing of the social resources of the classroom by participants and, in this sense, is a microcosm of the wider community of adults. Sharing, reciprocity, fairness, and democratic processes are necessities in the child's world as well as ours. Most standards for socialization involve dispositions, such as empathy for others, the ability to interact effectively with peers, and respect for the diversity of others. As this chapter amply illustrates, these attributes are best acquired by children as they engage in interactive play in the community of a caring classroom. Their assessment is best derived from systematic records of observations of the interactive behaviors of the children in guided and spontaneous play.

SUMMARY AND CONCLUSION

This chapter assumes that a major way children develop socially is through the exercise of their communicative skills in play and interaction with peers. Adult modeling of verbal skills and interactive strategies is not enough. The child's application of given strategies is not only developmentally determined, but also requires the child to interpret the situated character of meaning in unfolding play events. When teachers take over this interactive work, they rob children of opportunities to develop their own strategies. This makes close observation by teachers a critical factor in providing relevant support, particularly for mixed-age and/or inclusive groups or in ethnically and linguistically diverse play settings. Such observation allows teachers to:

1. Examine play through its communicative features to assess how contexts interact with social expectations to influence children's play.

2. Make and test judgments about the effectiveness of play settings.

3. Utilize their knowledge of the classroom context with its interplay of environmental and social expectations to create new curricula for play and socialization.

4. Assess children's achievement of developmentally appropriate standards through systematically recorded observations of guided and spontaneous play and examination of children's products such as drawings, paintings, journal writing, and storytelling.

Categories of play, such as parallel, solitary, or collaborative, have served us well over the years, as has our heritage from the psychodynamic and constructivist traditions in early childhood education. This heritage has been augmented by new technologies, analytic methods, and the fresh theoretical orientation of the sociocultural school of Vygotsky and others, which has begun to influence our thinking on issues of identity, social equity, acquisition of cultural resources, and the impact of globalization in our classrooms (Anderson, 1995; Corsaro, 2003; Jaworski & Coupland, 1999; Swartz, 1997).

Through new theoretical approaches we can now design and implement curricula that support socialization in much more relevant and specific ways. Through observation and analysis of play in its sociocultural context, our strategies can relate to local and previous experiences, such as problems with separation, individual and special needs of particular children, and the cultural and linguistic diversity of classrooms and play situations.

SUGGESTED RESOURCES

Corsaro, W. A. (2003). *We're friends, right: Inside kids' culture.* Washington, DC: The Joseph Henry Press.

Drawing on ethnographic research in nursery schools, Corsaro demonstrates particular strategies children employ to accomplish their social goals and examines cross-cultural aspects of play from an interpretive perspective.

Jaworski, A., & Coupland, N. (Eds.). (2000). *The discourse reader.* London: Routledge.

A selection of seminal readings in the field of discourse collected in one volume with judicious guides. Essential for an interpretive approach to analysis of interactions in the classroom.

Koplow, L. (Ed). (1996). *Unsmiling faces: How preschools can heal.* New York: Teachers College Press.

An informative collection of essays and articles from teachers regarding special needs and therapeutic issues.

Paley, V. G. (1992). *You can't say you can't play*. Cambridge, MA: Harvard University Press.

Paley, V. G. (1984). *Boys & girls: Superheroes in the doll corner*. Cambridge, MA: Harvard University Press.

These two works give teachers an inspiring new approach to play intervention. One gives insight into differences in the play patterns of boys and girls, and the other helps teachers challenge children to think of ways to avoid the exclusion inherent in saying, "You can't play." It involves negotiations with children in ways that respect their intentions. *Boys & Girls* suggests a modification of the play environment to accommodate differences

Reed, T. L. (2005). A qualitative approach to boys' rough and tumble play: There is more than meets the eye. In F. F. McMahon, E. E. Lytle, & B. Sutton-Smith (Eds.), *Play: An interdisciplinary synthesis* (Play and Culture Studies, Vol. 6). Lanham, MD: University Press of America.

Reed sees rough-and-tumble play as a form of affiliation, and as an expression of affection between boys.

Richner, E. S., & Nicolopoulou, A. (2001, April). *The narrative construction of differing conceptions of the person in the development of young children's social understanding*. (Special issue: Language Socialization and Children's Entry into Schooling; Guest editor: Nancy Budwig). *Early Education and Development*, 393–432.

Provocative findings from a theoretically sound report of the authors' microanalysis of story play material.

Seefeldt, C., & Galper, A. (2000). *Active experiences for active children: Social studies*. Upper Saddle River, NJ: Merrill/Prentice Hall.

An excellent resource for teachers. Sound theoretical rational and a host of meaningful activities and projects, including sample assessment forms and letters to parents enlisting family support for curriculum activities.

Play, Toys, and Technology

To begin their Night Sky project, kindergarten teachers Suzanne, Christa, and Margaret orchestrate their annual Friday sleepover at school, which is accompanied by sky watching through a telescope. They follow this with a mural that over time acquires children's renditions of objects that move in the sky. This includes objects they read about—such as planets, moons, stars, galaxies, black holes, and aircraft—as well as imaginary creatures and objects such as unicorns, aliens, and fairies. The children research their drawings and paintings on the Internet, in books from the library, and resources contributed by families of children in the three classrooms.

In the next phase, children build a spaceship from a large cardboard box, complete with a mission control constructed in the playhouse area that includes a pretend microwave oven. They use walkie-talkies and pretend computers to orchestrate play landings on planets and moons, and begin to construct a space ABC word wall that will later become a book for their kindergarten library.

Third graders who visit the kindergarten present a provocation; they say that the kindergartners don't have the right number of moons for Saturn on their mural! So the kindergartners plan a pretend space mission to Saturn to count the moons. They create characters for their spaceship crew on the Saturn mission. Each day, a new episode is imagined at group time. Their crew includes paper-doll representations and histories for each character. For example, there is Princess Squirty Cupcake Pumpkin, the crew photographer, who on Earth is a full-time princess, 30 years old, and when in space, takes pictures of planets, aliens, and stars. Another character is Sonic Timor, who lives in Japan in a tent, is 65 years old, has five children, and builds electrical things for fun. His mission-control job is radio monitor. ⌀

Toys are objects that represent tools for stimulating children's imaginations and skills with communication. They are the concrete objects that children use to fashion their experiences with sensorimotor play, constructive play, dramatic play, and games with rules. As we see in the example just given, children use toys such as blocks and cardboard to construct settings and tools for their pretend play. They use replicas of objects from our adult world, such as microwave ovens and radios to carry out their pretend scripts. Children may even use computers, either as they were designed to be used or as accessories to their own dramatic purposes in which they represent the social uses of technology in their play.

However, the toys are not the only ingredient of children's play. We also need to examine the cultures and social interactions that are the context for the use of toys and technology.

In the curriculum project on the Night Sky, a positive aspect of children's relationship to technology is depicted. The project evolved from earlier in the school year when children studied underwater life. The questions generated about what lives on the earth, in the sea and in the sky stimulated the Night Sky project. Technology related to space travel is represented by the children in their projects and in their dramatic play. The teachers use tapes of the soundtrack from the movie *Apollo 13* as part of the mission-control environment for dramatic play and walkie-talkies to simulate the landing of the kindergarten spacecraft during their space journey. Details of their mural are researched using the Internet, and overhead projectors are used to project images for the space simulations. To celebrate the return from their mission, families are invited to come to school after dark to view Saturn through the telescope of a local amateur astronomer.

In this chapter, we look at both toys and the use of technological media that influence children's play. We invite you to consider how the objects themselves and the social contexts in which children and adults use those objects shape children's play in early childhood settings. We explore the issues surrounding media-based play and toy marketing as well as the role of the Internet in play-centered projects.

TYPES OF TOYS

The category of toys is large and composed of many subcategories. Purely sensorimotor toys give rise to repetitive activity and the joy of making things happen with an object. Bouncing balls, shaking rattles, spinning tops, rocking horses, and monkey bars are a few familiar examples. Representational toys look like other objects in the culture or in nature. Miniatures of animals, toy vehicles, houses, utensils, furniture, and dolls are familiar examples. Construction toys can be manipulated and used to create new objects. Bristle blocks, wooden blocks, Legos, and Tinkertoys are examples we see in classrooms for young children. Locomotion toys include tricycles, bicycles, skateboards, scooters, and wagons (Hewitt & Roomet, 1979; Wolfe, 2002).

Toys affect development in profound and sometimes subtle ways. For one thing, they orchestrate both individual and social activity. Toys have a "logic of action" that suggests how the toy is to be used. For example, a toy telephone suggests or cues particular forms of motor, representational, and social behavior.

Some toys are specific in their cues. Legos and pattern blocks cue children for constructive play. Action figures, dolls, stuffed animals, and toy vehicles cue for dramatic play. Game boards suggest games with rules. Toys also cue teachers for specific play expectations. The toys that teachers designate as math manipulatives might include collections of miniature animals, vehicles, or furniture for children to arrange in sets and thus construct logical-mathematical relationships. Manipulatives might also include pattern blocks or Cuisenaire rods for similar purposes. In the case of miniature objects, experience with logical-mathematical thinking is linked to children's dramatic play accessories. In the case of patterning materials, these relationships are linked to constructive play.

In playing with representational objects, children explore their culture.

Another common "teacher category" for classroom toys is fine and gross motor toys. Pegboards, pattern boards, and puzzles aid in developing fine motor coordination, whereas trikes, scooters, swings, and climbers help children develop large muscle skills. Materials for sensorimotor play in the classroom include raw materials for art and construction such as sand, water, paint, mud, and playdough.

No matter how adults classify toys and raw materials for play, the key point is that children will use toys in their play in ways that suit their own agendas, not necessarily those of adults. The essential question is "How does the child see the play potential of a given toy or material?"

Along these lines, Griffin (1988) suggests that teachers categorize toys by the effects they have on children's inner feelings and social interactions, rather than by the intellectual concepts and skills the toys are thought to develop. Some toys suggest active group play, such as blocks, housekeeping toys, and art materials. Others—such as pegboards, puzzles, miniature animals, and books—cue for quiet, solitary play. Griffin notes that toys that are self-correcting in nature, such as bead strings and pegboards, are soothing to children because they give children an opportunity to create order and control in their physical environments. They are calming in the same way that gardening might be for adults. Many of Montessori's self-correcting toys have this appeal for young children (Montessori, 1936).

Toys such as miniatures and books in a solitary context encourage flights of imagination without the burden of negotiating pretend play with others.

Children can use miniatures to represent emotionally laden experiences, thus allowing them to process confusing or troubling experiences at a more comfortable distance. For example:

> Sean had trouble separating from his mother at the start of the preschool day. Each day for the first few weeks of school, after a tearful good-bye, Sean took out the tiny family dolls and a small, plastic playhouse. "Bye Mommy," he said as he walked the little boy doll into the house. "I love you," he whispered, as he put the Mommy doll into a toy car and "drove" it away. He then brought the Mommy doll back to the house and said, "It's time to go home now. Did you have a good day?" as he put the Mommy and little boy into the car. 𝄞

This kind of play allows children to project their feelings onto toys without having to play just one role. It also allows them to control the situation from the outside. Accordingly, Griffin suggests that classrooms have an ample supply of toys that are potentially "charged" for children: baby bottles and high chairs, spiders, dragons, capes, magic wands, and hats. Sensorimotor "raw" materials such as water, mud, paint, glue, and collage materials also help children establish emotional equilibrium in their play because they are so pleasing to the senses and afford opportunities for mastery and control.

TOYS AND DEVELOPMENT

As development proceeds, we see a change in children's primary uses of toys. The best toys for young children have the quality of "play-ability," which allows children to adapt the toy to their individual needs and stages of development over an extended period of time. Blocks are a good example of a toy with high play-ability. A 2-year-old might experiment with stacking and falling blocks, repeating the process over and over in sensorimotor play. Three- to 7-year-old children might use the blocks to construct objects they have seen ("This is the dolphin pool at Marine World") or as a prop in dramatic play (a telephone or walkie-talkie). Finally, blocks might serve as the pieces for a game with rules, as children stand blocks on end and "bowl" them down with a pitched tennis ball, giving points for each "hit."

In addition to providing toys with high play-ability, teachers also might want to provide toys that meet specific needs at particular developmental stages. For example, the process of symbolic distancing described in chapter 3 calls for sensitivity on the part of the teacher to provide toys that are a good match of structure to the child's developing symbolic concepts. Structure is the degree to which a toy or other object resembles the object that the child is symbolizing. For example, in order to scaffold their play scripts, 2- and 3-year-olds might require high structure in their toys, such as replicas of tools, vehicles, or housekeeping accessories. Play may easily break down in disputes over who gets to talk on the toy telephone or use the toy fire engine, so teachers might want to have multiple sets of realistic toys available. Having multiple sets of replica toys also allows children to explore similar interests or roles.

As we discussed in chapters 2 and 3, older children, 4- to 8-year-olds, are more likely to use "unstructured" toys such as blocks, marbles, or sticks in their play. The representational abilities of older children have developed to the point that meaning exists in their own imaginations rather than depending primarily on the characteristics of the objects themselves. For example, an older child might appropriate a block to stand for a sandwich, a helicopter, a wallet, and a cup of coffee, all within the course of a single play episode.

Teachers who carefully observe children's sociodramatic play can ascertain the levels of symbolic distancing in role play and in play with objects. Then they can provide an array of toys ranging from structured replicas to unstructured objects for children to use.

Games with Rules

As children move from early childhood into middle childhood, games with rules become increasingly evident in their play. Board games and games of motor skill—such as hand games, jump rope, soccer, hopscotch, and tetherball—have long been favorite games with rules for children in primary grades. Most of us have vivid childhood memories of ball and rope games, and clapping and chanting games played spontaneously on our school playgrounds or neighborhood streets.

Some games with rules such as hopscotch or tic-tac-toe require no special equipment and can be played in a variety of settings. Others, such as jump rope or soccer, require some purchased materials. In contemporary society, we have an increasing variety of commercial toys in the category of games with rules. These range from traditional board games such as Candy Land or Monopoly to video and computer games with rules. These games have in many ways supplanted the pervasive outdoor motor games of earlier decades and replaced them with games that rely on visual acuity and fine motor coordination to carry out winning moves.

Planning for Development in Game Play.   Whatever the form—board game, computer game, or playground game—teachers need to be sensitive to the cognitive leap represented by children's entry into the play stage of games with rules. In dramatic play, children construct the cognitive and social basis for their emerging understanding of the nature of rules. In the dramatic play of preoperational thought, children's fantasies are explicit and frequently articulated: "Let's pretend that it's raining today so we had to get our umbrellas" or "You have to be the big sister that's going to the store." Rules of dramatic play are implicit and are negotiated as the fantasy unfolds. Comments such as "Puppies sound like this" or "Cowboys run this way" accompany children's verbalization and enactments of fantasy story lines.

As children enter into the play stage of games with rules, usually beginning at about the age of 6 years old, we see a shift in the relationship of rules to fantasy. Now the fantasy becomes implicit or taken for granted by the players, such as the "as if" frame of reference for Candy Land or Monopoly. The rules are explicit, formulated by the manufacturer, and often are negotiated further by the players before the play begins. Verbal discussion shifts from "Let's pretend . . ." to "The rule says. . . ."

Games need to honor this developmental progression. Games with rules marketed for preschool and kindergarten children need to be used with caution and sensitivity by teachers. Board games and sports equipment have their place in the early childhood classroom, but should not be used in place of the more appropriate constructive and dramatic play materials for this age group. Instead, sensitive teachers will encourage children who use balls and bats, jump ropes, board games, and computer programs to create their own rules and construct their own understandings of winning and losing (DeVries et al., 2002).

Selecting Appropriate Games for Young Children.   Understanding the development of play is only one aspect of selecting appropriate games for young children. Other features of game design are important when choosing games for children to play in early childhood classrooms. As children develop the competencies to understand games with rules, electronic games are increasingly appropriate. Good games include simple graphics and a sense of engagement in the "as-if" world created through technology. Simulations and roles that children can identify with are characteristics of this engagement. Good games have defined goals, but uncertain outcomes. Levels of challenge that escalate as children play repeated rounds and solve problems with more variables and create alternative strategies engage children's minds and creative capacities. Another quality of good games, whether they are traditional board or dice games or electronic ones, is the option of interaction among players. In this sense console games frequently provide more options for multiple players than computer games. Young children enjoy collaborating and discussing their problem solving and their pretend landscapes in computer play, and teachers and researchers believe that this enhances the cognitive and social value of these electronic games (Scarlett et al., 2005; Singer & Singer, 2005).

Toys That Limit Development

As potential tools of the imagination, good toys range from pebbles, sticks, and feathers found in nature to "classic" commercial toys such as balls, blocks, and clay. Ideally, these unstructured toys invite children to incorporate their own fantasies, images, roles, and scripts into their play. However the commercial exploitation of play is rapidly eclipsing the freedom inherent in many of these "classic" toys. A walk down the toy aisle in most stores shows the profusion of electronic and "do everything" toys on the market. In order to develop abstract concepts and the capacity for imagination, we have to give young children opportunities to apply their own meanings and actions to toys. Toys that have only one use do not provide children with the flexibility they need to use their imaginations in alternative ways (see Oravec, 2000; Singer & Singer, 2005).

An action figure whose role or behavior is narrowly defined by the toy's features or a doll whose body movements and talk are produced by the machine inside stifles children's emerging imaginations. Such toys can interfere with the development of distancing strategies that underlie abstract thinking. These one-use-only toys make millions of dollars for toy manufacturers, but they are not conducive to children's play development. In fact, the limiting characteristics of some toys not only affect the development of cognition and imagination for young children, but also limit development in other areas. For example, some of the highly detailed toy weapons available for children suggest only violent play, and some of the media character dolls are packaged to persuade children that each character performs only one role or function in play, often a gender-stereotyped role (Carlsson-Paige & Levin, 1990; Levin, 2005; Levin & Carlsson-Paige, 2006; Seiter, 1995).

Frequently even unstructured constructive play toys such as Lincoln Logs, Legos, or animal action figures now come with templates for using the toys in specific arrangements or are marketed in "kits" with only the pieces for a particular model pictured on the package included. Such marketing practices limit development as children become accustomed to the models they are expected to imitate rather than the use of toys to fulfill possibilities in their own imaginations (Linn, 2004). Legos now come not only in these kits that circumscribe creative products but are marketed in pastels for girls and primary colors for boys, with the accompanying packages that show gender-typed models for construction.

Commercial partnerships, such as McDonald's with Play-Doh, result in kits that frame playdough creations as a Big Mac and fries rather than the objects that children invent on their own. With the growing national concern about child obesity, the pervasiveness of fast food marketing in the toy industry is also of notable debate. When we examine more structured toys such as dolls and "action figures," the messages regarding gender stereotyping, violence, and precocious sexuality are even more insidious (Kline, 1995; Linn, 2004).

TOYS AND THE MARKETPLACE

In considering developmental stages of play and the structure of children's games, teachers inform themselves about what play materials are most appropriate for their classrooms. By doing so, teachers may ameliorate the fact that children and parents, as well as teachers, are continually under siege from the toy industry to purchase toys and games that might not be in the best interests of children or appropriate to the development of their imaginative play concepts. Much of what is marketed to children is not only developmentally inappropriate but also exploits the very vulnerabilities that encompass childhood, such as the desire to be more grown up, have more power, and have friends. This is not accidental, as Schor (2004) and Linn (2004) point out in their recent books on consumerism and children. Marketers of toys rely heavily on the media portrayal of childhood in which socially constructed phenomena such as the coveting of toys to love, or accessories to become glamorous or "cool," become part of the assumptions about typical children's development in the United States.

Characteristics of Gender Identity

A major developmental milestone for preschool, kindergarten, and primary-grade children is the establishment of a positive gender identity—feeling good about oneself as a boy or a girl in our society. With their emerging concepts of

Play with concrete materials supports children's imagination and pretense.

classification in full sail, children eagerly classify information from their parents, teachers, peers, and the popular media into categories of "boy behavior" and "girl behavior." In our culture, many behaviors are "boy-or-girl" behaviors. In the same way that the "good-guy/bad-guy" distinctions appeal to children because of their concrete qualities, children also look for the concrete indicators for gender classification, such as haircuts or clothing (Cherney, Kelly-Vance, Gill Glover, Ruane, & Ryalls, 2003; Cortés, 2000; Tobin, 2000). Once an object or a behavior has been classified as boy-like or girl-like, then the reasoning continues: "If I am a boy, I must do boy-like things and play with boys' toys" or "If I am a girl, I must behave as girls do and own girls' toys."

Like racial stereotyping, gender stereotyping limits the range of experiences that children have in their play and the concepts and skills development associated with those experiences. Teachers can use similar techniques to address the presence of all forms of stereotyping in classrooms with young children.

Leslie, a K–1 teacher, has purposely selected a wide range of play materials for her classroom. "I want both boys and girls to develop the fine motor skills, such as the cutting, pasting, and using a paintbrush, that accompany art play," she comments. "I want both genders to develop large motor skills in climbing, running, sliding, and riding. A wide range of toys helps both the boys and the girls in my group to develop spatial reasoning and the bodily kinesthetic intelligence associated with constructive play. Building a spaceship of Legos or a fort of blocks enhances these experiences for all children. To encourage this, we as teachers need to consciously arrange for children to move beyond stereotyped conventions of what boys and girls do and try new activities." ✇

Gender, Toys, and the Media

Teachers across the country report marked differences in the play of boys and girls in their classrooms and discuss the possible influences of "boy toys" and "girl toys," particularly those that represent media characters. Boys battle and vanquish bad guys. They rescue and escape, climb and fall, pursue and are pursued. Girls are most frequently engaged in domestic play themes and nurturing roles, and create situations where they must be rescued (Cortés, 2000; Dyson, 1997; Seiter, 1995; Singer & Singer, 2005).

Boys are more likely to dramatize these themes using toy weapons, vehicles, and superhero and GI Joe dolls. Girls are more apt to select Barbie dolls, My Little Pony, house accessories, and toy cosmetics. Has it always been like this? Yes and no. Before the 1960s and 1970s, toys were stereotyped regarding the adult occupations of men and women. Boys might play at being firemen or doctors; girls pretended to be mothers or nurses. Both boys and girls, however, participated in the active adventures of riding the range as Dale Evans joined the ranks of Hopalong Cassidy and the Lone Ranger as adventurers.

In the 1970s, parents and educators made concerted efforts to diminish the gender stereotypes promoted in children's literature, television, film, and toys. These efforts were somewhat successful as girls, particularly, began to cross gender lines in their play. It became more acceptable for boys to be sensitive and nurturing and for girls to be assertive and independent. In the 1980s though, much of this ground was lost as deregulation of commercials shown during children's programming allowed toy manufacturers to specifically target children's interest in conforming to social perceptions of gender identity in order to sell more toys (Linn, 2004; Schor, 2004; Singer & Singer, 2005). Current research indicates that although girls play with gender-stereotyped toys, they are more flexible in their choices, while boys are more set in their stereotyped choices (Fabes, Martin, & Hanish, 2003; Singer & Singer, 2005).

Toys That Promote Growing Up Too Fast

One of the marketing strategies to emerge in recent years is the concept of "age compression" in which gender-related products designed for older children or teens are heavily promoted for younger children (Levin, 2005; Schor, 2004). For example, Barbie dolls are now more popular with preschool age groups than with the older girls they were originally designed for. The marketing of Barbie in 2002 involved the doll packaged with sexy lingerie and stiletto heels. Another marketing concept is the image of "edge," which Schor (2004) describes as a version of "coolness" with peers associated with teen music and sexuality. The Bratz dolls, ostensibly marketed for preteen girls, are also on the wish list for many 5- and 6-year-old girls. The sexually provocative Bratz dolls give the messages that fashionable clothing is the key to success as a girl "at the top of her game." (The baby Bratz doll targeted for ages 4 and up is characterized as having a "passion for fashion.") More disturbing is the sexual "edge" implied by such dolls as the Bratz Twinz with differing "fashion personalities; one girl is wild and dangerous, the other's as sweet as can be" in the description of the product on the Web site of a large toy chain (Linn, 2004; Schor, 2004).

A related phenomenon is the "kids rule" approach of such corporations as Nickelodeon. As Corsaro (1985, 2003) first noted over two decades ago, one aspect of status in the peer culture for young children is the defiance of adult authority. Television and video that portray adults as foolish and boring at best and frequently stupid as well exploit this developmental phenomenon. Products define their desirability by opposition to adult authority. Schor (2004) provides examples such as Nickelodeon's "Slime the Principal Contest" in recent years and the popularity of the "Jumbo Prank Kit" designed to annoy adults.

Toys That Portray Power Through Violence

Toys marketed to young boys have an increasing focus on violence and bullying. For example:

> Four-year-old players Jeremy, Seth, and Mark were playing Teenage Mutant Ninja Turtles in and around the outdoor play structure. Their play was based on the cartoon, action figures, and increasingly, the videogame marketed to younger children. The play involved martial arts moves, such as strikes and karate kicks, interspersed with sounds like "Ooph!" and "Whaaa!" as they pretended to fight. Plant stalks used as swords supplemented the fighting gear. Mark pointed out the pinecone he wielded was "one of those spiky things" that kill the robots.
>
> The robots in this scenario are the bad guys, and the boys argued with Shane, their teacher, that "we aren't really hurting anyone. They are just machines!" when he tried to intervene in their increasingly frenetic and violent moves. Shane remarked that the most troublesome thing about the play is that since no one wanted to "be the bad guy" the boys coerced younger, less-powerful players to be the robot victims of their violence. ⊘

A particularly insidious example of toys that promote violence and stereotypes is the Forward Command Post marketed in 2002 in the wake of war in Iraq. The catalog copy for J.C. Penney for winter of that year depicted a dollhouse that appears to have been bombed and is populated by a soldier in battle fatigues carrying an assault rifle. Other toys in the same vein for that year were the GI Joe Long Range Army Sniper, and a collection of either white- or dark-skinned military action figures (Foss, 2002).

The organization Teachers Resisting Unhealthy Children's Entertainment (TRUCE) is a good resource for teachers who are faced with this kind of frenzied, violent, and stereotyped play in their settings. See resources at the end of chapter 5 for contact information and publications.

MEDIA-BASED PLAY

In chapter 5, we presented scenarios related to dilemmas that teachers face at this time in history—the link between play and media. The most obvious culprit here is television, although tapes, DVDs, video games, and computer software have become increasingly problematic.

Television and Children's Play

Critics of television for young children have long argued that television viewing deadens children's imaginations and social interaction skills in two ways.

First, the process of television viewing puts young children in a passive role, absorbing the products of others' imaginations in full color and sound, rather than stimulating the children's imaginations. Second, if children weren't watching television, they would be playing. In that play they would develop their own symbolic concepts, extend their capacities for problem solving and creativity, and increase their abilities to negotiate and cooperate with others (Levin, 1998; Singer & Singer, 2005). Research bears this out. In 1997, Hofferth & Sandberg conducted a survey of the daily activities of children, finding that playtime has declined and television time increased from 1981 to 1997. For 3- to 5-year-olds, play time and TV time are nearly equal (17 hours playing; 13 for TV); for 6- to 8-year-olds, TV time outstrips play time (13 hours to 11 hours per week). Television viewing varies by income, parental education, and race. Homes with lower incomes and lower levels of parent education are characterized by more TV viewing by younger children (Schor, 2004).

Critics of television also argue that the stereotyped and often violent content of children's programming is detrimental to their play and future development (Anderson & Bushman, 2001). The media influence on children's play takes several forms, one of which involves the characters and plots that children create for their play narratives. This influence is particularly insidious because young children are just learning to develop their sense of story. Bruner (1986) describes character and action as the first "landscapes" of the human capacity for narrative. When these formative landscapes are filled with violent and destructive characters and action, they could have pervasive and long-lasting effects on development. The imaginative process involves playing and replaying images from life experiences (including images from media) and organizing these images into scripts for ascertaining and expressing meaning. When much of the content of this imagery is violent, it may lead not only to "desensitization" for violence but to a preference for violent imagery that "normalizes" and justifies one's own violent behavior (Ackerman, 2002; Huesmann, Moise-Titus, Podolski, & Eron, 2003; Katch, 2001). Some researchers contend that violent imagery in video games is even more insidious than TV because of the disposition developed that violence is the most important way to gain personal power (Elmer-DeWitt, 1993).

Although characters such as Luke Skywalker and Princess Leia from the *Star Wars* trilogy or Peter Pan represent positive forces, they repeatedly resolve conflicts through violent actions. Characters such as Darth Vader represent villains that might help children define their understanding and resolution of good and evil, but again, the resolution of evil influences is achieved by violence. Children watch these characters enthusiastically kill and injure others. Because young children are very literal in their thinking, they understand that "this is how we do things." The battles that ensue between the positive and negative forces in Star Wars, Batman, or Harry Potter films influence children's emerging beliefs about the manner in which good vanquishes evil. Unfortunately, most media examples convey the message that violence is acceptable as long as the motive is good.

Fortunately, positive role models are also available and illustrate alternative possibilities. Mr. Rogers, Barney, Dora the Explorer, and Steve and Blue on *Blue's Clues* are characters whose attraction for young children rests on their warmth, humor, and caring behavior. They resolve conflicts without violence. Teachers need to talk to children about the personalities and powers of their heroes and heroines and help them imagine nonviolent alternatives to resolving conflicts between good and evil.

Action is the second "landscape" in Bruner's model for the structure of narrative. In this aspect of narrative, children construct plots and themes for their play. At worst, the action in television/video-derived play is limited and repetitive, as well as violent. Children imitate with great attention to detail the characters, events, and actions they have seen, and resist creative alternatives to imitated scripts, giving rise to what Singer and Singer (2005) describe as "imitative" imagination rather than creative imagination. This limited play often is accompanied and exacerbated by commercial accessories that have explicit detail and cue children to use them in only prescribed ways, as we have described in the section on toy structure and commercialism.

ADVOCATING FOR CHILDHOOD IN AN AGE OF CONSUMERISM

Although there are limited federal regulations on children's programming, teachers should alert parents and discuss with children the television toy commercials they see, and the television shows that promote certain toys as characters. Ironically, regulations that prohibit unrealistic and unsafe depictions of toy usage placed on toy advertisements do not apply to the television shows that depict the character toys, and have given rise to "copycat" dangerous play (Schor, 2004). Young children do not have a well-developed sense of what is fantasy and what is reality, particularly when confronted with the special effects of audiovisual media. Nor do children have the life experience or self-reflective concepts needed to make wise consumer choices.

Children who have experienced "television/media literacy" lessons that help them understand how special effects are created on film have been found to engage in less violent behavior than children who have not had such instruction (Singer & Singer, 2005). Hobbs and Frost (2003) report that older children who received media literacy training improved in reading comprehension, writing, and critical thinking compared to children not receiving such instruction. Robinson and colleagues (2001) studied the effects of reduced television viewing among 8- to 10-year-olds in a community in California. Children whose viewing declined made 70 percent fewer toy requests of their parents than those in the control group whose viewing patterns remained the same.

Certain questions need to be discussed with children to counteract the effects of toy and media exploitation, such as the following: Will it last? How much would I use it? Am I being manipulated by commercials? One first-grade teacher found her daily sharing time to be a good avenue for consumer education. She helped children discuss the features of toys they liked and focus on the play alternatives for a particular vehicle, action figure, or doll rather than on their plans to collect them just for the sake of collecting. Other teachers use children's books on the topic of alternatives to television as springboards to teach media literacy in preschool (Hesse & Lane, 2003).

Encourage Good Children's Programming

Most young children spend hours watching television each day. The previous limitations on the length, type, and number of commercials during children's programming that were present in the 1960s and 1970s were suspended by government actions in the 1980s. This deregulation has resulted in a rash of television commercials disguised as children's cartoons, whose major purpose is to convince children that they can't "play" the themes they see on television without purchasing all the toys. Each character in the line of toys, such as GI Joe, Power Rangers, or Barbie, has specific features so that children are led to believe they have to own the complete set (Levin, 1998; Levin & Carlsson-Paige, 2006; Linn, 2004; Schor, 2004). In addition to talking to children, we as teachers can advocate for good programming for children by actively supporting the efforts of such organizations as Action for Children's Television and informing parents about their efforts. See suggested resources at the end of this chapter for organizations and contact information.

The Potential of Video to Enhance Imaginative Play. A key principle in the development of creative thought lies in the ability of children to dwell in the realm of possibility, to take the here and now of objects, people, and situations and entertain possibilities of what might be. As raw material for creative thought, images from electronic media have the potential to contribute to a rich store of imagery for playing with ideas. They also have potential to help adults and children create common play scripts, characters, and themes that may guide play. In a recent project inspired by school-readiness research and policy, Singer and Singer report results from guided play training with preschoolers, their parents, teachers, and care providers using videotapes of common play scripts such as restaurant or store. This play tutoring increased readiness scores in the assessment areas of imagination, social skills, persistence, self-help, independence and number, shape, color, and letter recognition (Singer & Singer, 2005).

COMPUTER PLAY AND YOUNG CHILDREN

We have discussed the topic of computer play throughout this chapter, taking the view that computers in classrooms for young children should be treated much like any other tool or material for children's play. In fact, this was the view of computers set forth by Seymour Papert (1980), creator of Logo, in his now-classic work *Mindstorms*. In discussing the potential for the graphics program Logo to influence education, Papert referred to computers as "powerful objects to think with" and predicted that they would revolutionize classroom practices.

However, this view was not embraced easily by early childhood educators. When computers were first introduced into the educational marketplace, many educators were skeptical of the value they would have for young children's play. Early critics of computers for young children seriously questioned whether the abstract medium of computer graphics was appropriate for young children. Along with others, they also expressed concerns that the computer did not foster active exploration and play in the same ways that open-ended toys such as blocks, Legos, tricycles, sand, paint, and water play might. They feared that the direct experiences that come through children's play with real objects are so central that the foundation for logical-mathematical thinking would be "short-circuited" by the abstract quality of computer images. Another pervasive fear was that computer play put the machine in control of the child rather than the child in control of the machine (Haugland & Wright, 1997; Skeele & Stefankiewicz, 2002).

Now that computers are being used in most early childhood classrooms, many educators, including Papert (1993), acknowledge that the educational revolution once predicted has not occurred. Nor have computers harmed development as the early critics predicted. Rather, teachers tend to design computer activities and choose software that reflects their own instructional strategies. Teachers who emphasize drills tend to use computers as "tutors" for skill-oriented tasks—such as matching shapes, letters, or numbers. However, many of these skills, such as learning vocabulary for directionality (above, below, right, left), are learned more appropriately in the context of active play with concrete objects.

In contrast to the "computer-as-tutor" approach of animated workbooks, teachers who value play tend to choose "computer-as-tool" and the "computer-as-tutee" types of software, which offer children more opportunities to control computer play. Haugland (1992) reviews the effects of computer software on child development, indicating factors that foster development, as well as those that might even reduce the development of creativity.

Tool Software

A variety of software is available for young children that provides the same tools that we use, but with more child-friendly user interfaces. As young children begin to read and write, they can use some adult software such as e-mail programs successfully, as well. Art/graphics programs, word processing, and multimedia programs that combine the child's written words with images, sound, and sometimes animation, are readily available (Haugland, 1999, 2000; Murphy, DePasquale, & McNamara, 2003; von Blanckensee, 1999).

Children use these programs in the context of their play to create and illustrate stories; make books, greeting cards, and gifts of their creative work; or, in the same way as "real" drawings or paintings, to express their artistic inclinations. Whether children use multimedia programs to integrate images with words or use graphics programs alone, it is important to apply the same standards as with traditional art materials. Children always should be encouraged to create original artwork rather than rely on clip art or electronic coloring books.

Older children can make wonderful mentors and role models when they assist with computer play in the early childhood classroom.

Maria is a fifth-grade mentor who helps in Andrea's kindergarten computer center twice a week. On this day, Joshua has been playing with a graphics program. He has made a line drawing of a bunny, and Maria has taught him how to fill in the area with different colors. After several minutes, Josh frowns. "I don't want this bunny for my story. I want that bunny," he says, pointing to the painting he had made earlier. Maria, who recently learned to use a scanner for her own work, asks the teacher if she can take Joshua to the school library to scan his painting. Later, he dictates his story using the scanned image of his bunny. When Joshua's writing is printed with his scanned drawings, the result looks much like a printed book. ✆

Although we as educators should focus our attention on the processes of children's play, not their products, it is also important to think about both process and product from the child's view. Some researchers have found that young children's self-esteem increases more over time in classrooms with computers than in classrooms without them. Many teachers believe that children feel more competent and important when they use computers because they view computers as adult machines (Clements, Nastasi, & Swaminathan, 1993; Haugland & Wright, 1997).

E-mail is a wonderful communication tool for children's play. The speed of sending and receiving e-mail makes it especially exciting for children who have a hard time waiting for a response by "snail-mail." Teachers often find that children write more, write in greater detail, and correct their writing more when they use computers to write for a real audience as in using e-mail (Bernhardt, 1997; Salmon & Akaran, 2001).

In Nancy's first-grade class, students have same-age e-mail buddies at another school, adult e-mail buddies through a corporate partnership, and fifth-grade buddies at their own school. The children have partners in their class and, together, they write to their e-mail buddies. Nancy finds that the children not only benefit by helping each other, but enjoy the social aspect of composing written language together.

When the computer sounds to signify that a new e-mail message has arrived, a child rushes to the computer and announces that Lily and Brian have e-mail. They head for the computer and find a message from their adult e-mail buddy. The children love getting mail and want to write back right away. In response to their question, their buddy has written about her pets and asks, "Do you have any pets?"

Twenty minutes later, Brian and Lily send off the following message:

1. I have a gol fis. My gol fis is bubbles.
2. I have a dog. My dog is very ol.
3. Do you like gol fis?
4. Do you like hres?
5. Do you like cows?
6. Do you have a cow?

Nancy finds that the students write differently to their different buddies. They write quickly and informally to their same-age buddies. They try hard to correct mistakes when they write to their adult buddies. Because their fifth-grade buddies come to class to read to them, they usually write with a purpose, asking for a particular book or commenting on a book that has been read. Although participating in e-mail is always a matter of choice, most children rush to answer their messages and wait with expectation for a response. ✒

Guiding Play with Computers as Tools

Teachers can guide children's play with computers by scaffolding its use as children explore its features and begin to use it for their own imaginative ends. For example, Cochran-Smith, Kahn, and Paris (1990) note that word processing can serve to free children's imaginations from the constraints imposed by handwriting. The 5- and 6-year-olds they studied were often sidetracked from the goal of creating text by difficulties in handwriting. Their attention would shift from the story line to the production of letter forms.

Word processing frees children to compose more connected text. They can use their mental energy to compose story lines and construct concepts about letter-sound relationships in invented spelling. The formation of letters no longer claims the lion's share of their attention. The teacher helps children review what they have written and plan more complex texts by asking questions such as "How did the mom feel about that?" The teachers also help children coordinate their invented spelling with finding letters on the keyboard. (See chapter 8 for a further discussion of acquisition of literacy skills.)

Another computer-based tool for literacy that is found in classrooms for young children is text-to-speech. This tool supports children as they develop the concept of letter-sound correspondences as they play. Von Blanckensee, in her book *Technology Tools for Young Learners* (1999), describes children using text-to-speech tools:

> Nina is sitting at my Macintosh lap computer in the library of her school. She is 4½ years old, one of the youngest students in her kindergarten class. She types a string of letters and tells me that she is writing a story. I ask her if she would like the computer to read it to her. She watches me highlight the letters and select "speak selection" from the tools menu. She laughs with glee as the computer voice pronounces "slifmefmaemf."
>
> We do this several times, changing the voice on the computer. This produces more laughter, until Nina has an idea. "Let's hear it say my name," she says as she starts to search for the *N*. After some effort, she has typed her name—the only word Nina currently knows how to write.
>
> Now the computer says "Nina." Nina's laughter turns to sheer joy . . . after several replays of her name, she wants to try my name. She is already thinking about the words she will write. (p. 52) ✍

In research on text-to-speech, Casey found gains in reading and writing fluency among young children using this technology. This is not surprising given the immediate auditory feedback and freedom for exploration and play that this tool provides (cited in von Blanckensee, 1999).

As these examples illustrate, teachers' guidance of children as they shift focus among the various tasks of writing composition, such as taking the perspective of one's audience, and transcription serve as an example of children and teachers working within what Vygotsky called the *zone of proximal development*. Such guidance helps children construct patterns of their own and eventually will lead them to coordinate independently all aspects of the writing process.

Computer Simulations, Games, and Books

"Tutee" software for young children also offers opportunities to control play with the computer. Some of these are simulations in which children enter as characters into the play and control characters' actions on the screen. Others allow children to manipulate objects in interesting ways. One program, for example, allows children to create buildings and towns and then change their perspective gradually, as if they were able to fly overhead like a bird. Other forms of computer programming software, such as Logo, were developed especially for young children. In these types of software, children encounter challenging problems to solve that are built into the software design. Forman (1999) believes that when children use computer simulations to augment real materials such as blocks, the program's ability to replay the previous actions allows children to reflect on and improve their problem-solving strategies.

The availability of interactive books, generally on CD-ROMs, is another popular form of tutee software. A quality interactive book begins with a good story that is worth reading again and again. Children control the story by clicking on objects to begin animations, hearing the story in different languages, turning off the "reader" altogether, and, in some cases, choosing alternative events and endings. Some interactive books are available on the Internet, but at this time, the pictures generally load slowly, even with fast Internet connections.

Computer simulations, games, and books are attractive to children and offer many opportunities to develop problem-solving strategies and creative thinking. Teachers need to be diligent in applying the same criteria in their selection as with other books or games (i.e., gender equity, nonviolent content, sensitive awareness to culture and ethnicity, child-centered and developmentally appropriate, etc.). Educators have expressed concerns about the gender stereotyping of computer play. Many teachers fear that, like mechanical toys in the past, computers will become part of the "boys' toys" category and be avoided by girls. Not only does stereotyping limit the developmental opportunities of young children, it also sets the stage for limiting imagination opportunities and children's ideas about what they might like to do when they grow up (Clements, 1994; Derman-Sparks & Ramsey, 2005; Sarama & Clements, 2002).

Integrating Technology

Teachers increasingly view computers as simply another valuable part of the young child's environment, rather than as a panacea for all learning or a threat to social play (Haugland, 1999, 2000; Murphy et al., 2003; Sarama & Clements, 2002; von Blanckensee, 1999). From this view, the ways that the computer fits into the culture of the classroom and children's play within that culture become the important issues to consider. The social context and manner in which children come to use computers as objects for play determine their comfort level with this aspect of technology in their lives. When computers are used to serve children's imaginative purposes, this process is enhanced.

Play with computers that allows the child to be in control fosters attitudes of competence and flexibility. It humanizes the machine through a playful stance rather than allowing the machine to dehumanize the child in situations where only the machine has the "right" answers and the child must struggle to produce them (Andersen, 2000. Jungck, 1990).

Recognizing that appropriate use of technology fosters learning and self-esteem in young children, the National Association for the Education of Young Children (NAEYC) developed a position on technology in 1996. NAEYC recommends that educators:

- Apply the principles of developmentally appropriate practices (Bredekamp & Copple, 1997) in choosing and using technology.

- Integrate technology as one of many options available to children in the learning environment.

- Be conscious of promoting equal access to technology to all children, including children with special needs.

- Take responsibility for avoiding software that includes stereotypes or violence, especially if the violence is controlled by the child. Software selection, like selection of other materials, should reflect the diversity of today's world.

- Take responsibility for working with parents in choosing appropriate software.

- Use technology in their own professional development, such as using e-mail as a tool to collaborate with other educators and to access educational resources on the Internet.

We agree with these recommendations and also emphasize the following: Teachers should encourage children to play with technology in ways that are open-ended, allowing children to determine the outcome of their play. Additionally, when teachers use the Internet to research children's questions, they serve as role models for teachers as learners.

To help teachers choose instructional activities that are technology-based, von Blanckensee (1999) designed the following scale: Choosing Technology-Based Activities for Young Children, Ages 3–7. (See Table 12.1 for an adaptation.) These include activities that use audio recorders, cameras, video recorders, computer simulations, games and books, and e-mail. This rating scale includes three issues for teachers to consider when evaluating the appropriateness of an activity: (1) content/method, (2) technology design issues, and (3) computer software design issues. The items used for ratings help teachers ensure that they use technology in ways that reflect individual needs, promote gender equity, and respect cultural diversity.

Table 12.1
Choosing Technology-Based Activities for Young Children

Ratings: 0 = poor 1 = adequate 2 = good 3 = excellent
Teachers may want to redesign or avoid activities that are poor on any criteria.

Content/Method

The activity supports learning objectives which are developmentally appropriate and consistent with the curriculum. The activity:

- relates to the child's direct experiences.
- is integrated into the curriculum through connections to other hands-on activities which support the same learning objectives.
- is interesting and challenging to students at a wide range of ability and skill levels.
- is open-ended, allowing children to learn through their own playful investigation.
- supports language development either directly, through interactive use by children in groups, or through extensions of the activity.
- is appropriate to children with varied learning styles.
- can involve two or more children working cooperatively.
- positively addresses or is sensitive to issues of multiculturalism.
- positively addresses or is sensitive to issues of gender equity.
- positively addresses or is sensitive to issues of individual differences.
- has nonviolent content, in the case of computer games and simulations.

Technology Design Issues:

- The child can learn to physically operate the technology independently.
- The technology is safe for the age level intended.
- The technology is chosen and set up to minimize the risk of breakage.
- The technology can be adapted, if necessary, for students with special needs.

Computer Software Design Issues:

- The menu is uncluttered, and uses picture clues with words for menu choices.
- The child can navigate through the software easily, go back to the main menu, or exit the software at any time.
- The program provides help. The child can escape and/or get help at any time.
- The design is attractive to children: It may include colorful graphics, sound, animation.
- The program can be used in more than one language.
- The program can be used by students with special needs.
- Children can print and save their work.

Source: Copyright 1997 by Leni von Blanckensee. Reprinted by permission.

Choosing Computer Software

Because new software becomes available constantly and existing software is upgraded frequently, we have avoided recommending specific software in this book. Rather, teachers need a framework for judging software themselves or access to software reviews that share their point of view. The rating scale in Table 12.1 provides an excellent framework for considering the many issues involved in selecting software that we have mentioned throughout this section. The scale takes into consideration technical and interface design; issues of diversity, equity, and nonviolent content; and whether the software supports constructivist learning in ways that are age-appropriate.

Teachers also can turn to ratings of software based on criteria that are in keeping with NAEYC guidelines. The Haugland Developmental Software Scale (Haugland, 1997) is well known and has been used to evaluate a wide range of current software. The scale includes the following criteria: age appropriateness, child control, nonviolence, clear instructions, expanding complexity, independence, process orientation, real-world models, and the quality of technical features. Evaluations of children's software are available through many Web sites, some of which are listed in resources at the end of this chapter and may also be reviewed using the Haugland and Gerzog Developmental Scale for Web Sites (1998).

Other sources of information about high-quality software are state departments of education. Many states provide a variety of resources on the Internet, accessible to teachers anywhere. For example, the Internet site of the Northwest Educational Technology Consortium has a searchable database of software for grades K through 12, rated by teachers (www.netc.org). Additional information also might be available through county offices of education or local school districts. When choosing software rated by others, teachers will want to make sure that the criteria used for rating are philosophically consistent with a play-centered curriculum.

Using Computer Technology to Extend Play and Projects

In the example that begins this chapter, the kindergarten program embarked upon a month-long project on space travel, using sources on the Internet to view images of planets, stars, and space journeys. Internet sites especially designed for children abound. See resources at the end of this chapter for some suggestions.

Children can also use the computer to create representations of their play and projects. Wong, Kedson, and Herzog (2004) describe the benefits of K–1 children creating their own PowerPoint presentations. Impetus to reflect on children's own interpretations of content and collaboration with others develops perspectivism and creates the context for the zone of proximal development. Wang and colleagues contend that the use of PowerPoint technology can be very effective in bringing children more fully into the self-reflective

In pretend play, children explore technology from daily life.

aspects of documentation assessment, a prominent feature of play-centered curriculum and projects. In this study teachers used Kidspiration to help children write or dictate concept webs and Kid Pix to create drawings for their presentations about their class project on measurement in their community. The PowerPoint presentations began with prompts from teachers about what children found most important about the concept of measurement and expanded to children's reflections on field trips, visits by "experts," and their own exploration and play with measurement tools. (To view examples go to www.uiuc. edu/ups/curriculum2002/measure/index.shtml).

Some early childhood teachers have become enthused about using digital imagery to record and revisit experiences in the curriculum and children's creations. Such revisitation affords children opportunities to reflect on their learning with more depth and detail (Forman, 1999; Murphy et al., 2003).

In Toronto, teacher-researchers Pelletier, Halewood, and Reeve (2005) enhanced their traditional journaling process with the use of digital photos. They combined the use of a database called Knowledge Forum with photo journals in a class of kindergarten students. For example, in one class, children kept electronic journals complete with digital photos as they were investigating the topic of simple machines.

> The students had been doing experiments in class with pulleys and levers. They were using Knowledge Forum to comment on photos of our experiments. At recess one day, the children became very excited when they discovered a shovel that had become wedged between the shed and the fence. They suggested that I could take a picture of it and to put it in our Machines view in Knowledge Forum. The children then decided that the question to go along with the photo would be, "How do we get it out?" The ensuing ideas and debate were quite lively—someone suggested putting tape on the end of a stick to retrieve the shovel. Someone else said that a lever might work. Yet another student wrote "uusrhns" (use your hands). Ultimately, the shovel came out in a river of water once the snow melted and the children had gone on to other investigations. It is still a lovely example of how children's ideas inform and direct the learning in a meaningful way. (C. Halewood, personal communication, October 8, 2005)

Structuring the Physical Space for Computers

If computers are to be used as a tool for children's play, they must be part of the classroom rather than isolated in a computer lab. Physical placement in the room becomes an important consideration. First, there are health and safety issues for the children and the computers. The computer needs to be placed near a grounded electrical outlet, away from water, other potential spills, and food. A surge protector is recommended to protect the hardware and to provide additional outlet space if necessary. The computer center also needs to be far enough away from rigorous physical activity to avoid potential accidents. When positioning the computer, avoid places where direct sunlight creates glare on the screen.

A second consideration is creating an optimal environment for children's play. We suggest a table large enough for two to three children to work together, with space on both sides of the computer for children to place materials related to their computer play. A printer should also be connected to the computer so that children can keep the products of their play.

WHEN TEACHERS TALK

Concerns About Media and Stereotypes

Many teachers express concern about children's words and behavior regarding race, culture, and gender that they find unsettling, sometimes offensive. Teachers also wonder how to respond when parents look to them for advice. Fortunately, as our population is becoming more diverse, an increasing array of resources is available to teachers to use in developing anti-bias, multicultural curriculum (Derman-Sparks and the A.B.C. Task Force, 1989; Derman-Sparks & Ramsey, 2005; Levin, 1998; Ramsey, 1998).

STEREOTYPES AND GENERALIZATIONS

What are stereotypes and generalizations? Cortés (2000) discusses the differences between stereotypes and generalizations, but emphasizes that no clear, easy distinctions exist. Generalizations help us know what to expect. Most people from South America speak Spanish. Many Korean foods are spicy. People from Sweden have blond hair. However, not all South Americans speak Spanish, not all Korean foods are spicy, and not all Swedes are blond.

In contrast to generalizations, stereotypes about group members are usually inflexible, unsubtle, and portray group members as alike and homogeneous, rather than as people having various interests, looks, and abilities. Cortés (2000) writes, "Generalizations provide *clues* to individuals who belong to different social groupings, but in stereotypes, those clues tend to become assumptions" (p. 150).

Teachers might find that young children are most vulnerable to developing stereotypes or being injured by stereotypes when they have few experiences with people from a given group or are, themselves, one of few children of a given race or ethnicity in a school or community (Tobin, 2000).

Cortés (2000) warns us that we cannot assume that children have no knowledge of particular groups. He recounts the story of a fourth-grade teacher who decided to teach a unit about the Rom (Gypsies). Even though a large Rom population was located nearby, none of the children knew anyone. Instead, they had negative stereotypes about the Rom, many drawn from media texts.

INVISIBILITY CAN SUPPORT STEREOTYPES

Invisibility also can support stereotypes. For example, Seiter (1995) notes that ads for children's toys show few children of color, and they are rarely the center of action. "Children of color and girls of all races are dispersed to the sidelines as mascots, companions, victims" (p. 7). How does this absence or invisibility influence children's sense of themselves and others?

Teachers and parents are concerned about the role that children's media and toys have on children's assumptions about social groupings. Cortés (2000) argues that media products do, indeed, function as "public textbooks" in our society. How do children "read" Barbie? Aladdin? Mulan? Pocahontas? GI Joe dolls? What about the characters largely missing from these "textbooks"—people of color in commercials, Latinos and Asians in movies and on prime-time television, and, especially, persons of color who are female? We also need to examine the context in which characters interact. Is the media and toy world a segregated one? Who plays with whom? Who is rich or poor? Who is violent? Who shows emotion?

In *"Good Guys Don't Wear Hats": Children Talk About the Media,* Tobin (2000) points out that to understand the complex influence of the media, it is important to do more than simply analyze the content. We must look at the interaction of the media text with particular children and their particular environments. Thus, the same movie or television program will be understood differently depending on the viewer and the context. Children from different families living in different communities will interpret images and behaviors derived from popular media in different ways.

In his work in Hawaiian classrooms, Tobin found, for example, that Hawaiian-born children of Native Hawaiian and Asian ancestry understood a "Japanese pirate" character differently than a newly arrived Caucasian child who had had few previous experiences with Asians or Polynesians.

However, this does not mean that the stereotypes of race, gender, or ethnicity conveyed through toys and the media are benign for any child. A major developmental milestone for preschool, kindergarten, and primary-grade children is the establishment of a positive identity. We believe that another important milestone is the establishment of positive feelings toward those in other groups. During these years, the multiple aspects of "who I am" as well as "who they are" are further differentiated, and they often turn to the popular characters in toys, films, and television (Dyson, 1997, 2003; Seiter, 1995).

How do young children make sense of the portrayal of gender, race, ethnicity, and differing needs as portrayed in images they encounter? How can we make sense of their play, which often seems to reflect stereotypes rather than generalizations?

The strategies we discussed in the section "Responding to Violent Play" (chapter 5) are useful here: Observe play carefully, look beneath the surface of play, and ascertain children's purposes in play. In addition, communication with families about stereotypes observed in children's play and advocacy for appropriate content in children's media continue to be important.

SUMMARY AND CONCLUSION

In this chapter, we have looked at toys and games for young children and explored some of the issues that confront educators when selecting materials for children's play. We have looked at cognitive and social development as reflected in children's play materials, and have discussed issues of stereotyping by gender, race, and ethnicity. We have considered the effects of media-based play on children's development, and outlined strategies that teachers might use to control the influences of popular media culture on the play in their classrooms.

Finally, we have looked at the influences of technology on children's play in early childhood classrooms, and explored some of the interactions we see in materials for play and the social contexts in which play occurs. Like book literacy, computer literacy occurs in a social context, nested in the culture of the classroom, the school, the community, and society at large. The same might be said of "television literacy" or "video literacy" in that by expressing literacy in any medium, we exercise the skills and knowledge that are approved by others in the social contexts we value (Emihovich, 1990; Greenfield, 1984, 1999).

These literacies are in turn affected by what children bring to school from home, as well as what they experience in their classrooms (Genishi & Strand,

1990). Perhaps "toy literacy" is stretching the concept, but socially approved ownership and behaviors with toys are of great importance in the peer culture of young children. Toy ownership and familiarity with scripts from TV, video, or books are the "cultural capital" of the peer culture in classrooms for young children. In this sense, cultural capital represents the knowledge and skills that give some children status with their peers, such as knowing the plot of Robin Hood, having the latest media superhero toys, or understanding the strategies needed to succeed at a computer game (Dyson, 1997; Emihovich, 1990; Gumperz & Cook-Gumperz, 1982). For example:

> Nate, a kindergartner whose fine and gross motor skills were poor, and who spoke with a lisp and was difficult to understand, was not a popular play companion in his classroom. However, learning to use several computer programs made him the expert to whom other children came for advice and helped him carve out a niche of competence for himself within the classroom culture. ✐

We see toy and computer literacies in this broad view as "an encounter between thought and reality, between desire and possibility, that takes place in the symbolic realm and thereby vastly multiplies human capacity to process, analyze, criticize and reinvent experience" (Easton, 1980, cited in Emihovich, 1990, p. 230). From this perspective, all toys in the classroom—from the blocks to the computer, from lotto games to superheroes—contribute to children's emerging literacy in our culture as they find ways to express themselves and communicate with others through play.

SUGGESTED RESOURCES

Carol Gossett's Kindergarten Connection: A Network of Educational Resources and Materials (www.kconnect.com)

> Carol is a former president of the California Kindergarten Association and a veteran teacher. Her expertise in science curriculum is apparent on this Web site full of suggestions for activities in all subject areas and a feature reviewing children's books.

Children's technology review available by subscription online at www.childrenssoftware.com

Edupuppy—Everything for Early Childhood Education—Preschool to Grade 2 (www.edupuppy.com)

> This site is useful to teachers and families. We found nearly 50 resources for many of the curriculum topics listed here. Resources for advocacy for young children are also listed.

Haugland, S., & Wright, J. (1997). *Young children and technology: A world of discovery.* New York: Allyn & Bacon.

This book reviews research on the development of young children and computers and offers strategies for integrating computer technology into the classroom. It includes examples of developmentally appropriate software, criteria for evaluating technology, and frequently asked questions regarding technology and young children. Web sites that review software for children abound. Following are some places to start:

Kathy Schrock's Guide for Educators (http://school.discovery.com/schrockguide)

This site is outstanding, with a wealth of curriculum projects posted by teachers. For example, in selecting the topic "animal habitats," over 20 user-friendly entries came up. It also includes clip art and a puzzle maker.

The Kids on the Web: Children's Books (www.zen.org/~brendan/kids-lit.html)

This Web site offers links to children's literature sites and includes poetry and on-line books. There are features that children may use to post their own work, and links to children's authors' homepages.

Levin, D. E. (1998). *Remote control childhood: Combating the hazards of media culture.* Washington, DC: National Association for the Education of Young Children.

In this comprehensive resource for teachers, Levin presents research findings and anecdotes that illuminate the pervasive influence of popular media on children's play. She offers concrete strategies for counteracting the effects of media violence in classrooms and for working with families and advocating on behalf of young children.

Levin, D. E. (2005). So sexy, so soon: The sexualization of childhood. In C. Olfman (Ed.), *Childhood lost: How American culture is failing its children.* Westport, CT: Greenwood/Praeger.

This article addresses a lot of relevant issues regarding girls and popular culture and the focus of so many of their toys on sexiness and appearance. Anecdotes from teachers and parents and suggestions for guidance and advocacy make this an important source.

Linn, S. (2004). *Consumer kids.* New York: The New Press.

Linn provides many examples and insights into the social, political, and psychological consequences of the marketing of toys, media, and food to children. Her description of the marketing industry and her own background as a psychologist make for an interesting and informational read.

Schor, J. B. (2004). *Born to buy: The commercialized child and the new consumer culture.* New York: Scribner.

Schor addresses many of the same issues regarding toy and marketing that Linn describes and frames them in the context of a social order based on consumerism that permeates the lives of families in the United States.

Singer, D. G., & Singer, J. L. (2005) *Imagination and play in the electronic age.* Cambridge MA: Harvard University Press.

For decades, Dorothy and Jerome Singer have studied the effects of media on the imaginations of children. In this recent book, they discuss both the benefits and dangers associated with all types of electronic media, including television, video games, and computers on the creative and imaginative processes of children.

Skeele, R., & Stefantkiewicz, G. (2002) Blackbox in the sandbox: The decision to use technology with young children with annotated bibliography of Internet resources for teachers of young children. *Educational Technology Review* (online serial) *10*(2), 79–95.

These authors provide a useful overview and annotated review of Internet sites and resources for early education. Some of our favorites include:

Starbright Foundation (www.starbright.org) and ERIC Clearinghouse on Disabilities and Gifted Education (http://ericec.org) are both useful resources for adaptive technology for children with special needs.

Technology and Young Children—National Association for the Education of Young Children Technology and Young Children Interest forum provides many links to sites that review technology along with research and policy sources on technology. Online at www.techandyoungchildren.org

von Blanckensee, L. (1999). *Technology tools for young learners.* Larchmont, NY: Eye on Education.

A comprehensive resource for teachers using a variety of technology tools, including digital photography, multimedia, graphics, the Internet, and e-mail. The author emphasizes putting children in control of "grown-up" tools in the context of play.

Conclusion: Integrating Play, Development, and Practice

Two boys and a girl are walking up a hill. Four-year-old Charlie shudders and throws his arms up in quick staccato movements, making explosive sounds interrupted with calls for help. "I need your help; the Klingons are surrounding me."

Jerry, wearing a baseball cap, shouts acknowledgment and comes to the rescue. "It's OK, they're gone. Let's go." They link arms and descend.

Sheila follows. "I have to go to the bathroom."

The two boys look around. "The bathroom's over there," one says and points to a concrete building buried in the shadow of trees.

"Come with me." Her request is ignored, and the boys commence another episode. "I'll be Zelda," she says as she joins the play, but her body reminds her of other needs, and she descends toward the picnic tables. She later returns, holding her father's hand. They head toward the bathroom. Having addressed her own and her parent's concern for safety in unfamiliar places, she returns and reenters the play with an assertion of her competence. "I was right. That is the bathroom."

A few hours later, the children chase Jerry's father across the field. He turns and gently tosses his son to the ground. The chase continues, out past the concrete bathrooms, down to the beach, back up the hill. The two boys temporarily drop behind and plan their attack. "Listen, all we have to do is. . . ."

As the chase ends, they huddle and plot the afternoon's play. Sheila is excluded. Some distance away she sits down on the hillside, pulling at weeds. Shortly afterwards, she and Jerry begin walking together. She has a long face. "You weren't nice to me," she says.

Charlie comes toward them, yelling, "Jerry, wait up! Wait up! There isn't a bee in it. I got it out (of the Coke can)." Sheila and Jerry wait for Charlie to catch up. The three old friends are again one. ✑

Look at all that is occurring in this simple vignette. These 4-year-olds are cooperating, collaborating on common themes that are agreed to and adhered to. They are imitating and reproducing elements of their culture. They are using language to guide their play and to provide its content. They display practical knowledge, as in recognizing the bathroom, as well as understanding when parental protection is needed. Sheila is able to express her feelings of exclusion and to reinstate herself in the triad after her temporary absence. Lastly, Charlie figured out how to get a bee out of a Coke can.

We see in play the expression of intelligence, the management of needs and emotions, the elaboration of common themes and efforts, and the reproduction of culture. We see the give and take of cooperation. The evolution of social consciousness and of sexual identity also is evident. The world of childhood and the world of play are inseparable. Play is evident from infancy through adulthood and unquestionably occupies a central role in human development. Our purpose is to put play at the center of classroom curriculum. In this concluding chapter, we revisit in somewhat broader terms the theoretical basis for our faith in the value of play as a focal point in curriculum planning and classroom management.

CONSTRUCTIVISM AND DEVELOPMENT

The term *constructivism* is used to express the belief that development is not simply maturation or biological unfolding, nor is it the result of the environment or experience imprinting itself on the developing mind, through, for example, reinforcement. The term is derived from the word *construct* and is meant to suggest that the child plays an active role in constructing that which is developed. Constructivism is a theme in education that resulted from an interpretation of Jean Piaget's work on child development.

What Is Developed?

Each of the main theorists who have written about child development could tell us something different about what is going on in the opening vignette. Piaget could help us understand the representational methods and coordination of concepts used in the play. Mead could help us understand the way in which this play affects the developing sense of self in these three children. Vygotsky could show us how the collective activity of the children is creating a context for their own understanding. This context is a micro-culture developing among the children with its own history. Their play also relates to the broader culture and history that the children share. Freud could help us understand how the play addresses deeper emotional themes associated with the control of instinctive forces. Erikson would show us the development of trust and autonomy represented in the play. For example, notice how Sheila asks the boys to escort her to the bathroom and how she comfortably tells Jerry he wasn't nice to her. Dewey might point out the competence and industry represented here.

Even in the simplest scenes of spontaneous and unguided play, development is occurring in all areas of human growth. For the sake of summary, we identify these areas as intelligence, personality, competence, and social consciousness/sense of self. We believe that each of these is developed by the child through spontaneous and self-directed activity within social, cultural, and historical contexts. This is the meaning of the constructivist view of development. Development does not result from the unfolding of genetically predetermined potentials, nor as the direct result of social experience in the form of education or selective reinforcement. Intelligence, personality, competence, and sense of self are constructed by the child through self-regulated activity embedded in social, historical, and cultural contexts. We maintain that this view is consistent with the theorists just mentioned, and believe that without play, no development would occur.

Our position can be summarized with five points:

1. Play is the primary context in which the four domains of intelligence, personality, competencies, and social consciousness are developed and integrated.

*Play and development are
inseparable.*

2. These four domains are inseparable from social experience within cultural/historical contexts.

3. Self-directed activity is necessary for development in these domains and is aligned closely with play.

4. These four domains are functionally interdependent and are each involved in all forms of play.

5. Each domain is constructed through means-ends coordinations.

Means-Ends Coordinations and Development

Another way to view constructivism is to think about the ways by which the child constructs the means of achieving desired goals. This is called means-ends coordinations, and it concerns, for example, how a reorganization of old means can be used to achieve new ends or, conversely, how new means can be constructed to reach old ends. This is similar to evolutionary biology where old structures are transformed to serve new functions; that is, old means change to serve new ends, and old ends are met through new means. For example, old "means," fish gills, served an early "end" of oxygenating fish blood. New "means" such as lungs evolved to serve this earlier "end." At the same time, a bone in the gill of fish, an early "means," evolved into a middle ear bone in mammals, making modern hearing possible. Hence, an old means serves a new end. The development of intelligence, personality, competence and sense of self also develop through shifts in means-ends coordinations.

Intelligence is the area of development most closely associated with Piaget's means-ends analysis. The fact that intelligence develops through the dynamics of means-ends coordinations establishes the common tie between intelligence and constructivism. In Piaget's view, intelligence is not a measurable trait such as IQ, nor is it how smart one is nor one's factual knowledge. For Piaget, intelligence implies human reason or adaptive understanding. Piaget perceived the development of reason to be an evolution in the child's adaptation to the environment that subsequently leads to understanding. This evolution occurs because early understandings ultimately are challenged by the environment. When new experiences are inconsistent or incompatible with earlier ways of understanding, change ultimately results. For example, basing an understanding of quantity on how things look will yield less consistent interpretations of the world than understanding that quantity is a composition of units. For example, knowing that rearrangement of a number of objects does not change their number, is a universal understanding that occurs for all children in all cultures, but takes most of early childhood to evolve. This evolution is a result of construction rather than learning, genetic unfolding, or social imitation and instruction.

Personality also entails means-ends relations and is constructed. Personality might be thought of as our unique means of maintaining acceptable emotional states while at the same time satisfying goals. Personality begets emotional stability while its owner is carrying out daily goal-directed activity. In a sense, personality is the constructed means by which individuals develop emotional self-regulation. Everyday acts—such as playing with friends, doing what others expect of you, going to school, solving disputes, or negotiating turns on a swing—entail emotion. The way these emotions are managed is a reflection of personality.

Those who have been around young children often are impressed with the range of differences between them. Even at birth, some children are calm, some are more active, some accept changes in routines, and some do not. Although such temperaments occur early and sometimes remain into adulthood, the issue of personality is more complex and tied in direct and subtle ways to a child's experiences and to the deep emotional substrata that underlie all human activity. Personality, like intelligence, is constructed and not given at birth.

Competencies are the things that we can accomplish reliably—the abilities that allow us to function in the world. Competencies are largely fashioned through intelligence, but cannot be separated from other areas of development. Like intelligence and personality, competencies also are tied to means-ends relationships because they are either the means of reaching goals or the goals themselves. Thus, a competency can be instrumental in achieving a goal, such as when social competencies allow one to play effectively with others, or a competency can be a goal itself as when one tries to fashion the means of entering into play with others. Competencies always involved emotions because we have feelings about what we do. Emotions are also competencies in the sense, for example, of being able to relate our feelings to the feelings of others as well as in the competencies implied in the self-regulation and control of emotions.

Social consciousness is a term we use to understand the child's evolving sense of self and how the self is related to the other "selves" it comes in contact with in the course of daily life. Social consciousness is inseparable from intelligence, personality, and competency and, like these other areas, is constructed through the coordination of means-end relations. Here, however, the means-end coordinations are related to social causality, or how people affect one another. The sense of self is fashioned through an understanding of two types of causality. One is linked to an objective understanding of ourselves, and the other is linked to understanding how we affect others and how social conditions, in turn, affect us. For example, a stable understanding of ourselves must take into account how others see us or how others affect us. We are affected by the actions and perceptions of others, and we, in turn, create the same conditions for others. Understanding this requires a reflection on the means-end relationships that occur in social causality; that is, how am I affecting others and how do others affect me?

CONSTRUCTIVISM AND SOCIAL-CULTURAL THEORIES OF PLAY

Two major developmental psychologists who were contemporaries of each other and whose theories were introduced in chapter 2, are Jean Piaget and Lev Vygotsky. Although Piaget and Vygotsky both were constructivists, they had differing views on childhood development. It's important that we understand some of the issues that divide and unite these important thinkers.

Jean Piaget (1896–1980)

People have posed the question of what it means to be human since the beginning of human understanding. Historically, this question has been left to theology and philosophy, but in the twentieth century, it increasingly has become the province of developmental psychology. Jean Piaget, the Swiss biologist, is probably the single most recognized person in developmental psychology. His work spans most of the twentieth century and transformed our understanding of human rationality and mental development.

Piaget, born in 1896, was a biologist interested in evolution. He made the startling discovery that some of the most basic of our understandings are not obtained or learned through cultural transmission or even by direct physical experience. The construction of knowledge, according to Piaget, occurs as a series of predictable and universal stages unfolding as a function of a slowly elaborated form of internal consistency in the mental coordination of actions that relate first, to sensory motor patterns of action, and later to internal mental representations of actions. His theory assumes that this sequence of stages is universal, occurring in a similar way for all humans who are healthy and active. Piaget's famous conservation experiments provide examples of predictable stages of understanding. The child first conserves number, understanding that rearranging a set of objects does not change the quantity of the set. This typically occurs toward the end of early childhood. It is years later before the child understands that changing the shape of something does not change its weight (i.e., the conservation of weight). It is later still that the child can conserve volume, understanding that changing the shape of a substance does not change its volume.

Development is viewed by Piaget as changes in patterns of action within the individual which result in increased internal mental consistency. This concept of development gives a completely new twist to the nature/nurture controversy. Piaget believed that developing children are not simply maturing according to a genetic program (nature), or the product of environmental influences (nurture), but rather, are the active constructors of their own nature. For Piaget, the child's development follows from the laws of activity and means-ends coordinations, in the same way that thermodynamics or the movement of objects follow laws. The specific course of development is viewed as common to all people because the laws of activity and means-ends coordinations are common to all people, not because people share the same experiences or the same genetic makeup.

Teachers might find it difficult to derive practical curriculum from Piaget's theory because of his focus on autonomy and self-directed activity, and because his theory says little about how social interactions affect development. In fact, Piaget did not address in depth the problems of education and curriculum. In spite of this, pedagogical theory throughout the United States and much of the world has been influenced by Piaget. The theories of Vygotsky, however, prompt us to think about what Piaget has left out of his formulations, and many educators today look to him for direction on how to structure the social elements of the classroom to achieve curriculum goals (Bodrova & Leong, 1996; Nicolopoulou, 1991).

Lev Vygotsky (1896–1934)

Lev Vygotsky was born in Russia in 1896, the same year Piaget was born in Switzerland. Both were part of the new modernism that was influencing continental thought. Darwin's theory of evolution, Freud's theory of the unconscious, and Einstein's theory of relativity were all part of the modernism of the late nineteenth and early twentieth centuries. It was a time of great intellectual and social change. Karl Marx's theory of economics and social institutions, in fact, provided a foundation for the Russian revolution.

Vygotsky was largely influenced by the social theory of his time and by the changes accompanying the Russian revolution. He was interested in how social interactions affect individuals, and how individuals and society are influenced by history and culture. Vygotsky greatly influenced Russian psychology and argued that conceptual activity cannot be separated from social experience. Further, this experience unfolds within a cultural-historical context. This was an extension of his belief that the regulation of conscious activity can take place only within a social context (Davydov, 1995).

Vygotsky believed that all activity happens in a social context and begins as social experience that is later internalized. Because Vygotsky died in 1934, before Piaget published his most significant works, it would have been impossible for him to know how Piaget ultimately handled the issue of individual development and social experience.

Connecting Piaget's and Vygotsky's Theories

Those who attempt to understand the relationship between development and education will benefit from understanding how Piaget's and Vygotsky's theories complement one another. Many assume that Piaget is an individualist, believing that development occurs independently of social experience, and that Vygotsky is an environmentalist, believing that learning occurs as a function of the social-cultural-historic environment. In fact, both Vygotsky and Piaget are constructivists, believing that learning is neither a direct function of social activity or individual activity, but rather, an interaction between both forces. For example, Piaget believes that true conceptual activity, by which he means rational thought, can not proceed without the use of a referential system that is tied to and dependent upon social agreement. Rationality is impossible without language, words, and mathematical symbols embedded in social contexts, where people must coordinate their points of view with those of others and come to agreements and disagreements. Rationality is impossible when the world is viewed only from one's own perspective because a single perspective cannot take into account all points of view (Piaget, 1954, 1962b, 1995; Vygotsky, 1978).

Understanding this position is critical to understanding Piaget's work. He is concerned primarily with how humans establish logically necessary and objectively verifiable knowledge. Objective knowledge concerns our ability to think logically about spatial relationships: time; relationships among time, motion, and distance; geometric relationships; quantitative relationships such as number, volume, length, and weight; laws of causality; and chance. His theory holds that the attainment of objective knowledge is the result of a gradual "decentering" process. This process involves a progressive development from a state in which the child's ability to represent is limited to what is immediately available or "presented" to the senses, to a later period in which "presentation" is still tied to the child's own experiences but less so than before. Eventually, after early childhood, the young adult can give a representation that is freed entirely from specific sensation and experience and is socially coordinated with others through the use of arbitrary signs such as words (Piaget, 1962b).

A CLOSER LOOK AT PIAGET AND CONSTRUCTIVIST THEORY

Piaget is the primary architect of constructivist theory. In the following section, we take a closer look at his ideas, expanding upon and reviewing those introduced in chapter 2.

Schemes: Assimilation, Accommodation, and Play

The concept of "action scheme" is important to Piaget's view of intelligence. A scheme is a pattern for action that can be repeated, like a program in a computer. The reflexes of the newborn are the first schemes. Blinking, grasping, sucking, turning the head, moving the tongue, and opening and closing the mouth are examples. By 3 years of age, more elaborate schemes, such as catching a ball or putting on a shirt, have evolved out of a coordination of simpler schemes. This elaboration of schemes continues throughout development and yields at each stage the possibility of more complex and adaptive activity (Piaget, 1963a).

Human development is driven by adaptation to the environment and consists of the twin processes of assimilation and accommodation. Assimilation is an incorporation of the environment into the child's own patterns of action or schemes. In a sense, the child uses already-developed competencies to understand new events. Accommodation takes place when schemes or competencies are inadequate and create contradictory results. Accommodation is a change in schemes as they are modified to fit new circumstances and occurs as a result of interactions with the environment. For example, an amount can be changed by adding or subtracting substance. At some point in children's development, they sense the contradiction between this understanding and the belief that an amount can change even when no additions or subtractions have been made. This feeling of contradiction will contribute to the development of an understanding of conservation of quantities.

Assimilation distorts and changes things because it modifies the world according to the child's schemes. Accommodation, on the other hand, is a process of bending to the pressure of reality. Piaget identifies play with assimilation. This reflects the link between assimilation and the distorting quality of play, where pretense and fantasy make the world what the child wishes it to be. When the child turns the living room furniture into a spaceship, the nature of the furniture has been distorted in the child's mind and turned, for the moment, into components of the rocket ship (Piaget, 1962b).

Piaget identifies accommodation with imitation because in reproducing reality (imitating), the child's action schemas are accommodated to reality. When a child imitates the sounds of a horse while pretending to be a horse, the child is accommodating to the sounds made by horses.

Although Piaget associates pure assimilation with play, assimilation and accommodation cannot be entirely separated. Children's play develops from a coordination between assimilative and accommodative activity. As children develop, so does their play. Play themes become more elaborate, symbols become more evolved, and social coordinations become more complex and cooperative. Although some believe that Piaget contends that play is an expression of assimilation, it is more accurate to say that play and assimilation share the subjugation of the world to the child's immediate interests.

How Do We Know Intelligence Is Constructed and Lawful?

The universal ways that children interpret experience are evidence that the construction of reality reflects developmental laws. For example, all children at some point over-generalize language rules for marking time and number ("I played and I goed to the store" or "I put the shoes on my foots"). As another example, all children at some point in their development, reason that a part is larger than the whole—that, for example, the vase contains more roses than flowers, even though only some of the flowers are roses. All children at some point believe that a quantity changes even if only its appearance has changed. They believe that pouring a liquid into a different-shaped container will change its amount, or that rearranging a pile of blocks will change the number of blocks. These ways of interpreting events are constructed and not copied from experience.

Stages of Development and Play

Because play is inseparable from all facets of development, play itself must develop. The first 2 years of life are called the sensorimotor period, because during this phase, the child's understanding of the world is tied to direct physical, rather than mental, assimilations and accommodations. Play consists of physical actions that are combined and repeated for the simple pleasure of mastering new combinations. During this period, the child gradually develops the ability to mentally represent the world. This development entails six distinct stages, beginning with birth and the exercise of sensorimotor reflexes and ending with the beginning of representational functions, such as imitation, pretense, and language, which emerge at around 2 years of age.

Sensorimotor play lacks the symbolic or pretend quality of later play, because pretense requires representation, which is achieved only at the end of this period. During the early stages of this development, infants cannot construct the symbolism and imagery that are needed to support pretend activity, like picking up a piece of grass and pretending to eat it.

The second major developmental period, the pre-operational period, begins with the onset of representation or the ability to form images of objects or events that are not immediately available to the senses. The emergence of representational thought is the result of an advance in the coordination of assimilation and accommodation. Assimilation and play are now capable of giving meaning to symbols produced by accommodation and imitation. The ability to create symbols has a profound effect on children's play in terms of its themes, the symbols used to support the play, and the means of communicating the purpose and manner of the play. The play of this period does not replace sensorimotor play, but rather joins sensorimotor play to create a more diverse palette of possible action (Piaget, 1962b).

During the preoperational period, children form early concepts that are limited in stability. Comprehension of everything, from the concrete and familiar (e.g., mommies and daddies, brother and sister) to the abstract (e.g., number, time, movement, measurement), is unstable and in constant risk of contradiction because young children reason from particular to particular rather than understanding how particular cases relate to the whole set of possible cases. For example, at one moment, mommies might be people who help you, even though not all who help you are mommies and not all mommies help. At another moment, a mommy might be anyone with a baby, even if the relationship is not maternal (Piaget, 1966).

Piaget has elaborated on the fact that during the pre-conceptual stage, play is the primary and most suitable way for children to express themselves as well as modulate or understand their emotions. The medium of play allows a direct expression of emotions and allows the child to defuse and explore unpleasant emotional experiences, even to the point of changing reality to his or her liking (Piaget, 1962b).

A third period, the concrete-operational period, begins at about the age of 6 or 7 years and is characterized by the emergence of consistent concepts. The emergence of true conceptual reasoning is brought about by an increasingly reversible coordination between assimilation and accommodation. This, in turn, is facilitation by social coordinations made possible through language and other representational systems that allow for agreement and disagreement with others. These integrations allow the child to decenter from direct sensory data, such as imagery, perception, emotion, and practical behaviors.

This decentering allows the formation of concepts that have a generalization and application that goes beyond individual experience and idiosyncratic symbols (Alward, 1996, 1997a, 1997b; Piaget, 1962b, 1995).

Play is still necessary to development, but because of the achievements during this period, the play of 6- and 7-year-olds is directed increasingly toward social coordinations and successful reproductions of reality. This might be seen in formal games with rules or an interest in constructing models.

Because of the new mental power provided by conceptual reasoning, the 7- to 8-year-old child is more easily able to express, regulate and understand emotions through the use of words and concepts rather than pure play. However, play, pretense, and fantasy remains a critical component of emotional self-regulation.

A fourth major period, the formal-operational period, begins with the elaboration of hypothetical or theoretically possible interpretations and the elaboration of scientific or logical means of deciding between competing hypothetical propositions. All the earlier forms of play remain a part of the young adolescent's life, but during the formal operational period, play also incorporates the complex refinements that characterize work. Youth group activities, with real tasks of working with others, and making things "that really work" are examples of play-related activity at this stage. Here emotions can become the focus of reflective activity with a gradual expanding of insight into the nature of human experience.

The Construction of Reality

The construction of reality entails gradual progress in the reliable and logical interpretation of experiences and their emotional content. This allows the prediction of unexperienced outcomes. For example, we know that pouring a liquid from one container into another does not change its amount. We know, without carrying out the activity, that if we were to pour the liquid back into the original container, it would occupy the same amount of space.

As noted earlier, Piaget was interested in how we construct an objective or rational understanding of time (the temporal succession of events), objects (the differentiation of sensation into discrete entities), space (the relative movements and positions of objects), and causality (the attribution of necessary links between events). In each of these areas, human intelligence eventually fashions an objective understanding. Moreover, these understandings successively deepen from those of the infant to those of the most advanced scientific theorists. Modern science is, after all, a continuing quest to understand the nature of objects, time, space, and causality. This quest never will be finished because each new understanding sets the conditions for further questions.

By 2 years of age, most children have constructed a limited, yet reliable, understanding that objects are permanent entities, organized in space and

Emotions, intellect, and social life are drawn together in play.

time, and linked in causal relationships. Even this seemingly simple under-standing is constructed gradually. Imagine a child of 14 months sitting on the floor. His mother, whom he's been watching, approaches on his right and pass-es behind him. The infant turns to his left, anticipating seeing his mother reappear. This behavior suggests that objects, time, and space are becoming organized into a whole where objects continue to exist even though they ap-pear and disappear over time; the child realizes that they exist in a space where, for example, the same target can be reached by different routes. He anticipat-ed his mother's trajectory in space and intersected that point not by visually following her, but by taking an alternative route.

This simple understanding takes many months to develop and is a precursor to a more complex mental organization, characterized by logical-mathematical coordinations. Finding objects hidden within or under other objects, finding one's way around the house, knowing that throwing the ball over the fence will be an obstacle to the dog with whom he's playing fetch, and being able to reach the same place by different routes all speak to a spatial understanding in which placements (position in space) are coordinated with displacements (changes in position). The ability to coordinate positions with changes in position is an early form of logical-mathematical thought. It makes possible the problem solving in near space, which we observe in children toward the end of the sensorimotor period. Understanding that objects continue to exist as they appear and disappear marks the first conservations where, in the context of changing sensations, something remains unchanged. It is the reversible coordinations of sensorimotor action that make the first constructions of space, time, causality, and object permanence possible (Piaget, 1954). This cognitive achievement has effects on the whole child and can be seen, for example, in the onset of separation anxiety which coincides with the emergence of object permanence.

During the early school years, we see advances in the child's understanding of reality. Children begin to understand that reality can be ordered in a variety of ways; for example, things can be ordered in a series from least to most. This may be reflected in the understanding of time and numbers (e.g., history, age, the calendar). Coordination of part-whole relations is beginning, where the child understands that wholes are composed of parts, that a whole can be broken into parts, and that parts can be reassembled into wholes. This can be seen in the child's understanding of words ("There are more children in the classroom than there are boys, because some of the classmates are girls") and beginning arithmetic ("Seven is bigger than 4 because if you take 4 from 7, you have 3 left over").

As understanding becomes logically organized, we refer to the child's thinking as operational, meaning that the internal mental coordinations carried out by the child are organized in a system of reversible operations that allow concepts to remain stable and, further, to obtain the status of objective reasoning. An example of operations is seen in the reversible coordination of part-whole relations and in order relations. For example, two parts can be combined to yield a third $(A + B = C)$, and a whole (C) can be divided into its parts $(A$ and $B)$. The fact that development tends toward these operational organizations shows that it is lawful and universal.

SOCIAL EXPERIENCE AND THE CONSTRUCTION OF REALITY

As discussed above, Piaget endeavored to show that the construction of reality, expressed in what may be called objective knowledge, is constructed through the internal regulations of the child. Because the laws of these internal regulations are assumed to be universal, a communality of knowledge exists among all people. However, Vygotsky believed that all conceptual knowledge is encountered first in social interactions. If development is dependent upon social experience, one might expect people from different cultures and different social experiences to develop differently. We believe, that Piaget and Vygotsky complement rather than contradict one another by showing how inter- and intra-individual forces shape development.

Piaget believed that two developmental themes exist, each consisting of coordinations that eventually lead to stable concepts. One is the internal regulations of the child, and the other is cooperation with others. Social coordinations are essentially the conditions that allow us to agree or disagree with another or to cooperate or compete with others. Piaget asserts that these two processes are inseparable and are simply different sides of assimilation and accommodation. Further, he believed that both aspects of development follow a lawful course. Social actions, like mental actions, tend to become organized in logical-operational systems. Social experience provides the possibility of differing points of view—agreeing and disagreeing, understanding and not understanding. Each of these affects the accommodations of our thinking. The corresponding and, at times, conflicting intelligence of others participates in the development of our own intelligence (Alward, 1997a; Piaget, 1995).

The child's evolving ability to think rationally is tied to social life. The child's capacity for reason eventually must detach from the child's own perspective and incorporate the perspective of others. This process of agreeing and disagreeing with others depends upon a means of representing reality that is free of the individual means of representation (practical knowledge, images, sensations, perceptions, emotions, dreams, unconscious symbols). It depends on a socially agreed-upon system of representation such as that provided by language (Piaget, 1962b).

A child might have developed certain mental operations, but it does not follow that this same child is necessarily competent in the particular cultural forms of knowledge that require these operations. For example, most 8-year-olds throughout the world have developed the operations necessary for understanding simple addition. However, only some of these children know how to respond to the equation $4 + 9 = $ ___. For individuals' intelligence to be applied or expressed in particular cultural forms, individuals must have experience in those forms and express their understanding as a competency in those forms. This is the job of schooling and other informal mechanisms of social transmission. The untutored mind can develop the intelligence to understand something, but without an encounter with the cultural form, the child will not be able to demonstrate or express the understanding.

What we learn cannot be separated from social experience. Experience occurs only within the embrace of a particular historical-cultural moment; within the envelope of particular values and patterns for work and play; and with the use of particular, largely cultural, representational means. So, although intelligence might proceed by a lawful unfolding coordination of schemes, what are coordinated are actions and representations, and these are inseparable from social experience. Thus, people in differing cultural and historical settings might develop through the same basic developmental stages and yet have different ways of expressing their intelligence in daily life. This is because the demands of daily life differ across cultures, societies, and periods in history. Furthermore, much of human knowledge is not subjected easily to the rigors of logically mathematically governed discourse and is, therefore, subject to complex disagreements. Science, for example, is an attempt to bring common interests into a discourse setting governed by laws of logic and mathematical reasoning, and even as such, science proceeds through a complex process of argument, disagreement, critique, review, and revision.

PLAY AND DEVELOPMENT

We've emphasized throughout this book that play is a central source of children's development. In the following sections, we summarize the relationship among play and four domains of development.

Play and the Development of Intelligence

The natural activity of the child feeds the self-regulated development of intelligence. Natural activities in the early years are almost exclusively play-bound, because the character of non-play activity requires a way of understanding and a way of directing one's activity that has not yet developed in the young child. During the early childhood years, the child's intelligence is marked by a lack of coordination between the two functions of intelligence: assimilation and accommodation. The child is constantly understanding the world in ways that engender contradictions and fluctuations. The resulting modifications in understanding and behaviors are never complete enough to ward off continued vacillations and contradictions. The ongoing and constant modification of the child's intellectual structures is marked by a progressive coordination or equilibrium among assimilation, accommodation, and social coordinations, but it is not until the end of early childhood that this equilibrium is stable enough to yield a conceptually consistent and logically ordered world. Prior to this, the child constantly is processing contradictory information. A big block cannot fit into a small hole, but a big Santa Claus can fit down a small chimney. The examples are as numerous as the beliefs of children.

Until this equilibrium is achieved, the child's intellectual activity is always bound within the larger domain of play because, not being able to form an objective, reliable, and stable view of the world, there is always a subordination of the world to the child's immediate view. In a sense, because children make of the world what they wish, we say that children are bound by play, where work and practice are tied to pretense, fantasy, and imitation.

In short, intelligence develops through the child's self-directed and natural activities, which are always play-bound because all of a young child's activity tends toward the subordination of reality to the ego. Lacking the means of true work—where assimilation and accommodation are reliably coordinated, and where intelligence is coordinated with others—the child is forced into a playful mode. In this mode, goal-directed activity slips into fantasy, efforts to grasp reality give way to pretense, and attempts to reconcile diverse perspectives slip into a subordination of reality to the child's immediate interests or perspectives. Hence, it is a truth about intelligence that the child, of necessity, must play in order to one day be able to work. It is practice at play and not work that will one day produce the intelligent worker.

Play and the Development of Personality

The entire range of children's needs and emotions is arranged and expressed in play. Their play themes deal with abandonment, death, power, acceptance, and rejection. Emotions are practiced and linked to needs, but with pretense as a buffer between the real fear of abandonment, for example, and the fantasy expressed in the play, "Let's say our mothers died and we're all alone."

Play, personality, and intelligence, all support each other, are inseparable and are all related to emotions. Play is not simply one of the possible activities in which a child might engage; it is more accurate to say that play is an expression of the child's personality, intelligence, and feelings.

Personality and intelligence are similar in some ways too, and it is here that we find the powerful relationship between the development of a healthy personality and the healthy expression of play. One of the tenets of constructivism is that as the child attempts to understand the world, intelligence becomes more structured, more consistent, better organized, and more powerful. However, sometimes personality and its regulation of emotions remains undeveloped, poorly formed, and maladaptive. For some, the process of living results in the development of adaptive, well-structured, healthy personalities. For others, the early and incomplete personality of childhood remains throughout life.

A process called "reflective abstraction" is inevitable and necessary in the case of intelligence but not inevitable in the case of personality and the regulation of emotions. Piaget created the concept of reflective abstraction to describe the way in which intelligence bootstraps itself up the developmental ladder. In reflective abstraction, the child brings into recognized forms, through representational activity, the unrealized or unrecognized relationships that make practical behaviors possible. That is, a natural, regulative process advances intelligence simply through the activity of bringing unrealized ideas into representational focus (Piaget, 1977).

As adults, we experience the power of reflective abstraction when, for example, we teach others. Teaching requires us to find a way of representing to others what we already know. The regulations underlying our practical knowledge are abstracted when we transform them into a representational form. In development, we might find a child, for example, who understands the conservation of discrete quantities (such as pennies) but who does not yet understand that pouring a liquid from a vessel into a different shaped vessel does not change the amount of the liquid. While still confused with the problem of conserving liquids, the child may be able to see that if a jar of pennies is poured into another jar, the number of pennies does not change. In this example, the child's ability to reflect upon an earlier understanding assists the shift from the disequilibrium of an earlier stage to the relative equilibrium of a later stage resulting in understanding the conservation of liquids.

A process similar to reflective abstraction is necessary to the development of personality and its regulations of emotions. A child's personality develops toward an equilibrium between psycho-emotional needs and possible interactions within the world. This process is furthered when the child can represent latent needs and emotions consciously. In the case of intelligence, reflective abstraction is inevitable because the child attempts to formulate goals and orchestrate means to reach those goals. It forces the child to represent goals and the links between possible actions and the realization of goals.

For example, in trying to put a necklace of beads into a paper cup, an 18-month-old child might imagine (represent) what is happening when the necklace, draped over the edge of the cup, knocks the cup over. The child might succeed by bunching the necklace into a ball and dropping it into the cup. In doing so, the child represents to himself the goal (getting the necklace into the cup), the obstacle (the necklace knocks the cup over), and the solution (bunching the necklace into a ball). In the case of personality, on the other hand, the inner self can remain unconscious, repressed, and fixated in patterns of action that can remain unconscious and not reflected upon throughout life. For example, a child might develop a certain personality as a way of fitting into or resolving conflicts within the family. Although this development might be a coping mechanism, its origins can be repressed and unavailable to the child for reflection.

The parallel between intelligence and personality is established by the common process of means-ends coordination and reflective abstraction. For personality to continue to develop, it needs to be embedded constantly in reflective activity. Symbolic play is the way the child represents emotional needs and concerns, as well as how these needs and concerns are resolved. Adults might depend upon therapy, analysis, ritual, art, or work, but the child depends upon play for the development of personality. This process points to the critical and necessary role that play occupies in the lives of children. Through the free and unconstrained process of play—unrestrained because it is freed from inhibition and bends the world to immediate needs and interests—the child brings into represented forms the unconscious and inner psycho-emotional self.

Play and the Development of Competencies

During the early childhood years, children develop an astonishing array of intellectual, physical, social, and emotional competencies. The infant at birth is helpless, lacking in all but the most rudimentary reflexive sensorimotor competencies, such as sucking, grasping, or looking at objects. The simplest of human competencies, such as removing a blanket from the face or purposefully grasping an object, are not present at birth.

By the time they reach preschool, children have acquired control over their bodily functions; can feed themselves; can dress themselves; can jump, crawl, and run; and have acquired a language and a wide range of representational skills. They can initiate social interactions, have begun to learn how to regulate emotions and express needs and feelings, have learned something about what is acceptable and unacceptable behavior, and have developed a problem-solving intelligence. In short, the preschool child has developed the unmistakable qualities of being human. Older children are more competent in how they feed and dress themselves. They can skip as well as jump. They can use language not only to initiate, but also to sustain interactions and solve complex emotional issues with others. The origins and the continued development of these competencies are tied closely to play.

Many competencies are sensorimotor schemes, integrating the senses with the use of muscles. Obvious examples might be eating, dressing, running and skipping, or even talking, which is a complex sensorimotor activity. Other competencies are not sensorimotor, but instead involve internal representations of possible actions, and are representational and abstract. The ability of children to think, problem solve, and coordinate their play with others are examples. Whether the competencies are sensorimotor or representational, their development is dependent upon play in a number of ways, the most obvious of which is functional practice. All acquired schemes, whether sensorimotor or not, are repeated. The repetition of newly acquired skills gives pleasure. Children play at making the sounds of their native language, play at large- and small-motor activities such as skipping or dressing, and, in general, enjoy exploring and practicing new intellectual powers.

Play, in addition to providing the functional practice for competencies, provides their contextualization and meanings. Children embed their emerging competencies in play activity, often with others, thereby refining not only their articulation, but also their meaning. For example, doll play might contain maternal and family themes, or block play might contain themes of construction and destruction. Outdoor play might involve games that define conditions for running, jumping, and skipping. Much of this contextualized meaning making involves the fantasy and pretend elements of play and, therefore, might be thought of as symbolic play. In play, the child is either creating a symbol (for example, by using a plate of sand to stand for a plate of food) or creating a tapestry of meaning in which a variety of symbols are woven into a meaningful whole.

Another role of play concerns the socialization of competencies. In some cases, they are themselves social, as in the ability to initiate and maintain interactions or a dramatic play theme. In other cases, the competencies are not in themselves social but can be brought together to meet social needs. For example, competencies for large-motor activity, language, problem solving, and considering the needs of others might be brought together in a playground chase game with hero figures taken from the culture.

The ability to form social relationships in which common goals can be established and activities between members of the group are coordinated to achieve these goals, is an exceedingly complex competency and slow to unfold. It begins with children playing together in proximity only, to eventually playing with each other but without common themes or purposes. Then it proceeds to attempt to establish and sustain common purposes, but with constant changes in direction, manner, and roles. Finally, social relationships develop into sustained and coordinated play with agreed-upon purpose, direction, manner, roles, and sustained emotional compatibility. This broad competency is almost synonymous with socialization and is at its core an evolution of the child's play.

In summary, competencies are the manifestations of intelligence and personality in the presence of emotions. They represent children's ability to control means-ends relationships within the context of needs and emotions, and to develop the means of participation within their culture. Their development is from the beginning tied to play, which provides (1) functional practice, (2) contextualization and meaning, and (3) socialization.

Play and the Development of the Social Self

We are individuals from birth, if not from conception, and yet our identity, our sense of self, must be constructed, developing gradually and passing through many stages. During the first few months, infants cannot distinguish themselves from their surroundings because they lack the intentional ability to interact with the world. For example, infants are limited in their ability to purposely cause effects on objects or others because they cannot distinguish between what they are causing and what others are causing (Piaget, 1954). Without an awareness of what one causes, no real sense of self is possible. So it is that the child will pass through the stages of intelligence, slowly moving from an undifferentiated beginning to a gradual recognition of the self as both the cause of effects and the effect of causes.

Because the awareness of self is, by necessity, tied to this reciprocal causality, the self being both a cause and an effect, its development takes two paths, each with its own ends, and yet, due to their common origin, ends that are inseparable.

On the one hand is the developing sense of what one can do or who one is (that is, an awareness of one's intelligence, personality, and competence). On the other hand is the gradual understanding of how the actions of others affect us and how we affect others. In the first, the end point of development is the objective self, a sense of self that progresses through a gradual shedding of its egocentric cloak, approaching an undistorted and objective stance where one's sense of self increasingly corresponds to how others see us. It is in the context of play that children learn to incorporate the viewpoint of others into their own sense of self. In the second, the end point of development is the generalized self, a sense of self as one social object among others, where the reciprocities between "self" and other are understood such that what is true for one must be true for others, and vice versa (Mead, 1934).

The sense of self is perhaps the most interesting and profound aspect of human development because its end is not just the self, but rather a social consciousness capable of generating the ethical, moral, and even spiritual conditions that make the human experience possible. It is because of the sense of self and its inexorable tie to the development of a social conscience that we come to understand the necessary links between social experience and the conditions that foster healthy development and a healthy social order. The development of a sense of self is, from its inception, bound to play, where one's own efficacy is explored, where one's own view is coordinated with that of others, and where problems of social coordination are encountered and resolved every day. Play is at the foundation of humankind's most profound and necessary ability—the weaving of the individual spirit into a social fabric.

THE MEANING OF PLAY IN CHILDHOOD AND SOCIETY

How does play contribute to children eventually becoming full members of society? We believe that the world of childhood and the world of play are inseparable and that play is critical to social, emotional, and intellectual development. At the same time, we are aware that, if left to play, children would not develop the essential capacity to operate within the adult world. How is it that play rather than work, that play rather than conformity to adult models, and that play rather than compliance with authority, is the major force in child development?

Play and the Work of Society

We distinguish between the work of childhood and the work of society. The first includes the many instances where the child formulates ends and means, such as when an infant uses a stick to retrieve an object, when a toddler works at solving a puzzle, or when a school-age child works at understanding the rules

Work and pretense are blended in play.

of a game. The second consists of the many instances in which the purpose and desired ends, as well as the means and even the success of the work, are determined from outside.

Although both forms of work are important and often merge, they have different status in the child's development. Because we view children's work as self-directed activity, it is by definition autotelic, or containing within it its own direction and purpose. The work of society, which also must be faced by the child, is heterotelic, having a direction and purpose imposed from outside. Although the child might engage in both forms of work, autotelic activity is essential to development because the dynamics of development involve accommodations or modifications brought about by resistances that the world presents to the child's understanding. In a sense, the child treats the world according to what he or she knows; with that often being inadequate, what the child knows must be modified. This is assimilation and accommodation. When, for example, children find their goal thwarted, it is within their inner experience that the goal, the obstacle, and the possible means of overcoming the obstacle are synthesized.

The dynamic interplay between the child's assimilations of the world and the corresponding accommodations is, by its very nature, autotelic because the understandings, the perceived sense of their inadequacy, and the willingness to make the necessary modifications are intrapersonal (within the child) rather than interpersonal (outside the child). We assert the primacy of play over work as a source of development because the development follows from the autotelic work of childhood, which, in the early childhood years, is bound to and subordinate to play.

In the schooling of children, we must seek a blend between the work of childhood and the work of society. We must find the balance that allows children to experience fully the inner tensions between what they presently know and the challenges of new experiences. We use the term *play* to characterize the context in which this balance is best achieved. This does not mean that we should not define the expected learning outcomes for the children in our care. It does, however, mean that in doing so, we must never lose sight of the developmentally driven energies and interests of the child. Accordingly, we endeavor to place the issue of academic standards, for example, within the sphere of developmentally appropriate practice within integrated and holistic school environments.

Autonomy as the Context for Development

The child lives in two inseparable, yet irreconcilable, social worlds: the world of adults and the world of peers. The adult society imposes itself on youth, creating a heteronomous rather than autonomous condition where codes of behavior are sanctioned by adults and derived by forces totally outside of the child's control or comprehension. For example, a teacher might tell a child to play fairly, but this does not mean that the child necessarily understands why being fair is important or how to be fair.

The social world of peers, on the other hand, constitutes a condition of autonomy rather than heteronomy. Here children elaborate their own rules and codes for behavior, deciding among themselves what is fair, just, and appropriate to the immediate setting. In this world, they test the extension of their own wills, and they orchestrate their campaigns against adult constraint.

Piaget made a strong argument that it is autonomy rather than heteronomy that creates the context for social, moral, and ethical development. Autonomy is essential to true social coordination, that is, the coordinations of one's own activities and needs with those of others (Piaget, 1965d). Such coordinations require a reciprocity in which members of the social group are on an equal footing, addressing shared needs and shared frames of reference. The relationships between children and adults achieve this reciprocity only partially because children never can be on a truly equal footing with adults. We must wonder how it is that children, through their autonomous pursuits, eventually will obtain the adult traits that now separate them from this world. We can offer three answers that support the belief that autonomy among children has an important place in curriculum.

First, children work and play at accomplishing what they believe they will (or must) become. The classroom constitutes a micro-culture that exemplifies a blend between the child's present level of development and the expectations of the adult world. Nothing is more important to children than participating in the adult world, of having its interest, attention, protection, and acceptance. Therefore, even when left to explore their own interests, children in large measure pursue the interests that correspond with our expectations.

Second, autonomy is necessary to development because social coordinations (and all shared knowledge is a social coordination) are, in fact, dependent upon autonomy. Each party of the coordination must take the other party into account. They must operate under rules that are particular to their own purpose, understood by the participants and not imposed from without.

Last, social autonomy creates the zone of proximal development. We presented Vygotsky's concept of the zone of proximal development (ZPD) in chapter 2. Vygotsky used the concept of the ZPD to characterize the social space where the disequilibrating perpetrations of the world are close enough to the child's level of development that the child can profit developmentally from these disturbances. It is in the zone of proximal development that formal and informal teaching take place because it is only within this zone that what takes place "out there" can affect what takes place "in here" (Vygotsky, 1967). Autonomy in social relations creates a zone of proximal development. Peers share a common level of development, focus, and interest and, therefore, feed one another's development. The perpetrations that originate in peer relationships fit into the zone of proximal development, where problems and tasks that arise in activity between peers present appropriate stimuli to development.

Development, Developmentally Appropriate Practices (DAP), and Play

Historically, early childhood education in the United States has not been a universal experience. In the mid-1960s the U.S. Congress determined that any national effort to break the cycle of poverty would be effective only if it included preschool education. This was the beginning of Head Start, which nearly half a century later continues to provide quality early childhood education to a diverse national population. Additional social forces such as an increase in the number of working mothers contributed to a push to introduce growing numbers of children to early educational experience.

As part of the national move to provide early childhood education to increasing numbers of children, the National Association for the Education of Young Children (NAEYC) was founded. One of its early presidents, Millie Almy, was also one of the first United States educators to study with Piaget. Almy conducted studies with United States children replicating Piaget's work on Swiss children, showing that, indeed, the thinking of young children is qualitatively different from the thinking of older children, that is, different not just in how much is known, but different in the nature of what is known and how that knowledge is used (Almy, 1967).

As the NAEYC took on an increasingly larger role in representing the educational needs of young children, it began to fashion the specifications for developmentally appropriate educational practices. It also defined "early childhood" as the period from birth to 8. This was not an arbitrary choice. Piaget's work shows that, even though schooling begins in many countries with children who are 6 or 7 years of age, children of this age are just beginning to reliably use conceptual reasoning to interpret experience. For example, the coordination of concepts such as "some and all," "more and less," "same and different" are still only partially formed in the early childhood years. Consequently, children of this age do not have a very clear understanding of numbers, time, space, causality, history, geometry, geography, classification, seriation, etc. While there are critics of Piaget's theories, there is no question about the universal difficulty that children have with these concepts in the early childhood years. The NAEYC believes, as do we, that the character of early childhood development requires specific concerns for the character of early childhood educational practices. These concerns are codified by NAEYC as Developmentally Appropriate Practices.

We embrace developmentally appropriate practice but go further in expressing our belief that play is the central force in early childhood development and that play provides an ideal foundation for the articulation of an integrated and holistic early childhood curriculum. By "integrated" we mean a curriculum where learning outcomes, such as literacy, are embedded throughout the curriculum. By "holistic" we mean a curriculum which addresses the whole child in terms of social, emotional, and intellectual development and the development of competencies and sense of self. The fact that the early childhood years overlap with the early schooling years does not dissuade us from our belief in the importance of play as an armature for curriculum. We believe that spontaneous play and autonomous activity is critical in the preschool and kindergarten years and that a blend of guided, spontaneous and autonomous play is a valuable curriculum through the early primary grades.

Expectations for Ourselves and Our Children: Academic Standards

Over the last two decades there has been a nationwide effort to develop academic standards for public education. The major focus has been on the K–12 school years, but more recently this effort has pushed down into the early childhood years. The stated goal has been to provide quality educational experiences for all children. As such, it is a continuation of many of the same forces that ushered in Head Start and other early intervention programs.

Standards are seen as a way of establishing clarity of curriculum content, raising expectations for the achievement of all children, and ensuring accountability for public education (Kendall & Marzano, 2004). We see the push for standards as another potentially great moment in the quest for quality education for all of the children in our care. However, as with many opportunities, there are risks as well.

The biggest risk is that many in the educational community will find it challenging to hold onto traditional early childhood educational values and at the same time be accountable to the expectations for academic standards. In particular, how do educators who recognized the value of a play-centered curriculum assure the various stakeholders that they can also satisfy the attainment of academic expectations? Honoring children's choices and interests in an integrated and holistic curriculum can be threatened by demands that teachers didactically teach isolated facts and concepts. This threat can take on draconian proportions in settings where the allocation of resources and the possibilities of a job are tied to accountability in rigid and over-determined terms. As one teacher recently said regarding "high stakes" tests, "Under No Child Left Behind, test scores can result in a 'restructured' school. This means the staff is fired. We give a 7-year-old a No. 2 pencil and a test booklet. The bubble sheet determines our fate. This is an astounding burden to place on a 7-year-old" (Brown, 2005).

We share this concern and have witnessed many situations where individuals, schools, and even communities have not fared well under the academic standards movement. As noted in chapter 1, Wien (2004) has provided an account of how eight Canadian teachers faced the imposition of academic standards on their early childhood curriculum. Only two of the eight were able to create an integrated curriculum where they were able to demonstrate having achieved expected outcomes (Wien, 2004).

These successful classrooms were very similar in character to what we have proposed as a play-based curriculum. According to Wien (2004), they were characterized by:

1. Ample time for children and teachers to explore and discover
2. Curriculum content embedded in social activity with maximum opportunities for peer-peer and teacher-child interactions
3. A climate of psychological safety
4. A sense of community
5. A quality of intellectual curiosity and quest for discovery
6. A teaching process that supported complex multiple contexts for learning
7. An openness to emergent processes

Wien also noted that the ability to create these integrated classrooms required the support of the school culture as well as opportunities for teachers to maintain and pursue professional literature and relationships. Wien concludes somewhat pessimistically, that "unless teachers have had some powerful intervention beyond traditional basic education background (such as early childhood education, a professional development group or a powerful mentor or colleague)" it may prove too difficult to overcome a linear segmented curriculum, with classroom time managed as a production schedule, with requirements for grading and report cards, and with a prescriptive, mechanistic school culture (Wien, 2004).

Seefeldt (2005) offers a more optimistic view that, although standards could become a barrier to implementing an integrated curriculum, they in fact almost require a total, integrated curriculum as well as authentic methods of assessment. "If standards are to have a lasting impact on the field of early education, it may be because of this focus on integration" (p. 43). She claims that standards contribute to an implementation of integrated curriculum in at least four ways:

1. Standards grew out of a support for curriculum integration
2. The large number of standards requires an organization and unification of the curriculum
3. The "big ideas" identified by standards provide a framework for creating an integrated curriculum
4. Teaching for thinking and problem solving is common to nearly every set of standards

We believe that the standards movement offers an increased opportunity to insure universal quality education and to increase the articulation of an integrated curriculum. In addition, in many instances state educational standards have specified the nature of ideal educational practices and thus give educators guidance in how to provide quality education. However, there will be efforts in some communities and schools to place the burden of accountability on the shoulders of children with the use of standardized measures of isolated facts and demonstrations of knowledge. We believe that such an approach is misguided and potentially harmful in the early childhood years. As Wien (2004) notes, "grades are unfitting metaphors for young children's learning . . . a linear, segmented curriculum in particular shows no knowledge of the rhythms of living of young children" (p. 150). We believe it is our responsibility as early childhood educators to show that a play-centered curriculum can achieve the developmentally appropriate goals we set for our young children. We believe that this is the best articulation of the meaning of play in childhood and society.

SUMMARY AND CONCLUSION

Play is a dominant activity from birth through early adolescence. It is part of all areas of social, emotional, and intellectual growth. Play is a way of understanding the world and of comforting the self. It takes its material from the social world of the child, as well as from the child's inner emotional needs. When we acknowledge the primacy of play, we recognize the primary vehicle in the child's early development.

A privileged relationship exists between autonomous activity and development. Self-directed activity, as opposed to other-directed activity, is essential to development because the dynamics of development involve modifying existing ways of behaving or interpreting in order to adapt to new challenges. This process of assimilating experience to already established patterns and modifying these to accommodate surprises cannot take place outside the felt needs, tensions, and the intuitively directed groping of the child. Hence, activity that is directed by the child is primary in development.

The issue of social autonomy is similar. The social conditions and regulations that children establish outside of adult authority are the necessary and primary conditions for social development. This, too, follows from the constructivists' position that social development is an evolution of social coordinations where children are increasingly able to align their respective goals to become partners in joint activity. This coordination and the ensuing reciprocities (how you treat me, I treat you) require autonomy rather than heteronomy (authority imposed from without) because reciprocity requires that the players be on an equal footing.

The work of developmentalists such as Vygotsky, Piaget, Erikson, and Mead make it clear that if children were not self-directed and engaged in autonomous social alliances, they would not develop. This does not mean, however, that adult guidance is not critical to the intellectual, emotional, and social development of the child. As we come to understand the constructivist point of view, we recognize that the guidance we provide must be a condition for growth, and growth in the early childhood years is indistinguishable from play itself.

We end with an optimistic belief that a play-centered curriculum is ultimately the best integrated curriculum for young children and that it can be articulated to meet whatever reasonable and developmentally based standards might be put forward for young children. We must ask ourselves as we put forth our academic expectations and set our classroom practices whether we are truly engaging and enhancing within our students their intelligence, their personality, their emotions, their competencies, and their sense of self. If we are creating an environment that can accomplish these ends, then we can be assured that whatever standards are applied to evaluating our effort, we will be judged to be successful.

Play at the Center of the Curriculum articulates the practical connections between play and our academic, social, and emotional goals for young children. We have treated in detail the possible links between play and traditional curriculum domains such as the visual and performing arts, language and literacy, mathematics, science, and socialization. In each of these chapters we've addressed the features of a play-based curriculum and the kinds of learning one can expect from such a curriculum. We have also devoted a chapter to the use of play in assessing whether children have achieved the goals we have set for them.

In our view, it is meaningless to talk about a developmentally based curriculum without implying a curriculum based on play. Teaching in a play-based and developmentally based curriculum requires knowing what the child knows, where the child's interests and energy lie, and where the child is going. It requires knowing how to engage the child so that the teacher's understanding of the child and the curriculum is developed along with the child's progress in understanding and acquiring skills. Entering into the child's play, by direct or indirect means, allows the teacher to see what the child knows and where the child is headed. Orchestrating play allows the teacher to support the child's progress through further manipulations of the play and non-play environments. The teacher, rather than being the guardian and administrator of the curriculum, becomes the gardener and architect of the environment, using play as its nutrients and structure.

SUGGESTED RESOURCES

Bodrova, E., & Leong, D. J. (1996). *Tools of the mind: The Vygotskian approach to early childhood education.* Upper Saddle River, NJ: Merrill/Prentice Hall.

This book presents a thorough look at the Vygotskian approach to early childhood education.

DeVries, R., & Kohlberg, L. (1987). *Constructivist early education: Overview and comparison with other programs.* Washington, DC: National Association for the Education of Young Children.

This is a good sourcebook that provides a comprehensive overview of Piagetian approaches to education with a comparison of other approaches.

Fosnot, C. T. (Ed.). (2005). *Constructivism: Theory, perspectives, and practice.* New York: Teachers College Press.

In this second edition edited work, numerous authors, in sum, provide a very thorough review of the history and theory of constructivism and its implications for educational practice.

Moll, L. C. (Ed.). (1990). *Vygotsky and education: Instructional implications and applications of sociohistorical psychology.* New York: Cambridge University Press.

A comprehensive, edited volume with numerous chapters authored by widely known authors. Introductory chapters familiarize the reader with Vygotsky's life and times, and to aspects of his work that are of particular relevance to educators. A number of the chapters describing research and applications of sociohistorical psychology focus on early childhood development and education.

Paley, V. G. (2004). *A child's work: The importance of fantasy play.* Chicago: University of Chicago Press.

Paley is a master kindergarten teacher who has written volumes on her classroom experiences. Everyone who works with young children should be familiar with her work, which expresses better than any theory the value and meaning of play in the classroom. This most recent book is a strong policy statement for the importance of fantasy play in children's lives.

Vygotsky, L. S. (1978). *Mind in society: The development of higher psychological processes.* Cambridge, MA: Harvard University Press.

An excellent resource for upper division and graduate students who seek a deeper understanding of Vygotsky's work.

Wadsworth, B. J. (1996). *Piaget's theory of cognitive and affective development: Foundations of constructivism* (5th ed.). White Plains, NY: Longman.

This resource emphasizes the inseparable relationships between cognitive and affective aspects of Piaget's theory. Several generations of upper division and graduate students have found that Wadsworth's text offers a clear introduction to Piaget's comprehensive theory.

References

Ackerman, D. (1999). *Deep play*. New York: Random House.

Adams, S., & Wittmer, D. (2001). "I had it first": Teaching young children to solve problems peacefully. *Childhood Education, 78*(1), 10–16.

Ainsworth, M. D., Bell, S. M., & Stayton, D. J. (1974). Infant-mother attachment and social development: "Socialization" as a product of reciprocal responsiveness to signals. In M. M. Richards (Ed.), *The integration of a child into a social world*. London: Cambridge University Press.

Alkon, A., Genevo, J. L., Kaiser, J., Tschann, J. M., Chesney, M. A., & Boyce, W. T. (1994). Injuries in child care centers: Rates, severity, and etiology. *Pediatrics, 94*(16), 1043–1046.

Alkon, I. (2004). The chicken and egg project. *Early Childhood Research and Practice, 6*(2), 1–19. Retrieved October 15, 2005, from http://ecrp.uiuc.edu/v6n2/index.html

Allen, B. N., & Brown, C. R. (2002). Eddie goes to school: Facilitating play with a child with special needs. In C. R. Brown & C. Marchant (Eds.), *Play in practice: Case studies in young children's play* (pp. 123–132). St Paul, MN: Redleaf Press.

Almy, M. (1967). *Young children's thinking: Studies of some aspects of Piaget's theory*. New York: Teachers College Press.

Almy, M. (1984). *Applying Piaget's theory in the early childhood classroom: Resource report*. Chicago: WorldBook-Childcraft.

Almy, M. (2000). What wisdom should we take with us as we enter the new century? *Young Children, 55*(1), 6–11.

Almy, M., & Genishi, C. (1982). *Ways of studying children* (rev. ed.). New York: Teachers College Press.

Alper, C. D. (1987). Early childhood music education. In C. Seefeldt (Ed.), *The early childhood curriculum: A review of current research* (pp. 211–236). New York: Teachers College Press.

Althouse, R. (1988). *Investigating science with young children*. New York: Teachers College Press.

Alvarado, C., Derman-Sparks, L., & Ramsey, P. (1999). Reflecting on the work of anti-bias educators. In C. Alvarado, L. Burney, L. Derman-Sparks, E. Hoffman, L. I. Jimenez, J. Labyzon, P. Ramsey, A. Unten, B. Wallace, & B. Yasui (Eds.), *In our own way: How anti-bias work shapes our lives* (pp. 183–210). St. Paul, MN: Redleaf Press.

Alward, K. R. (1995, June). *Play as a primary context for development: The integration of intelligence, personality, competencies, and social consciousness*. Poster presentation at the Annual Meeting of the Jean Piaget Society, Berkeley, CA.

Alward, K. R. (1996, April). *Piaget's implicit social theory: Play dreams and imitation revisited*. Paper presented at The Association for the Study of Play (TASP), Austin, TX.

Alward, K. R. (1997a, April). *Piaget, rationality and play*. Paper presented at The Association for the Study of Play (TASP), Washington, DC.

Alward, K. R. (1997b). *Top down/bottom up play based curriculum: An informal look at Piaget and Vygotsky*. Paper presented at the Jean Piaget Society, Santa Monica, CA.

Alward, K. R. (2005, June). *Construction of gender in the doll corner: Thoughts on Piaget's implicit social theory*. Paper for the Annual Meeting of the Jean Piaget Society, Montreal, Quebec, Canada.

American Association for the Advancement of Science, Project 2061. (1993). *Benchmarks for science literacy*. New York: Oxford University Press.

Andersen, G. T. (2000). Computers in a developmentally appropriate curriculum. *Young Children, 55*(2), 90–94.

Andersen, S. R. (1998). The trouble with testing. *Young Children, 53*(4), 25–29.

Anderson, C. A., & Bushman, B. J. (2001). Effects of video games on aggressive behavior, cognition, aggressive affect, physiological arousal, and prosocial behavior: A meta-analytic review of the scientific literature. *Psychological Science, 12*(5), 353–359.

Anderson, W. T. (Ed.). (1995). *The truth about truth.* New York: Jeremy P. Tarcher/Putnam.

Ardley, J., & Ericson, L. (2002). "We don't play like that here!" Understanding aggressive expressions of play. In C. R. Brown & C. Marchant (Eds.), *Play in practice: Case studies in young children's play* (pp. 35–48). St. Paul, MN: Redleaf Press.

Ariel, S. (2002). *Children's imaginative play: A visit to Wonderland.* Westport, CT: Praeger.

Ashton-Warner, S. (1963). *Teacher.* New York: Simon & Schuster.

Astington, J. (1993). *The child's discovery of the mind.* Cambridge, MA: Harvard University Press.

Axline, V. (1969). *Play therapy.* New York: Ballantine.

Azuma, H. (1994). Two modes of cognitive socialization in Japan and the United States. In P. Greenfield & R. Cocking (Eds.), *Cross-cultural roots of minority child development* (pp. 275–284). Hillsdale, NJ: Erlbaum.

Bahktin, M. M. (2000). The problem of speech genres. In A. Jaworski & N. Coupland (Eds.), *The discourse reader* (pp. 123–140). London: Routledge Press.

Balaban, N. (1985). *Starting school: From separation to independence.* New York: Teachers College Press.

Balaban, N. (2006). *Everyday goodbyes: Starting school—a guide for the separation process.* New York: Teachers College Press.

Ballenger, C. (1999). *Teaching other people's children: Literacy and learning in a bilingual classroom.* New York: Teachers College Press.

Barbour, A. C. (1999). The impact of playground design on the play behaviors of children with differing levels of physical competence. *Early Childhood Research Quarterly, 14*(1), 75–98.

Barnes, E., & Lehr, R. (2005). Including everyone: A model preschool program for typical and special needs children. In J. P. Roopnarine & J. Johnson (Eds.), *Approaches to early childhood education* (4th ed., pp. 107–124). Upper Saddle River, NJ: Merrill/Prentice Hall.

Baroody, A. J. (1987). *Children's mathematical thinking: A developmental framework for preschool, primary and special education teachers.* New York: Teachers College Press.

Baroody, A. J. (2000). Research in review: Mathematics instruction for three- to five-year olds. *Young Children, 55*(4), 61–69.

Baroody, A. J., & Wilkens, J. M. (1999). The development of informal counting, number, and arithmetic skills and concepts. In J. V. Copley (Ed.), *Mathematics in the early years* (pp. 48–65). Reston, VA: National Council of Teachers of Mathematics; Washington, DC: National Association for the Education of Young Children.

Bartolini, V., with Lunn, K. (2002). "Teacher, they won't let me play!": Strategies for improving inappropriate play behavior. In C. R. Brown & C. Marchant (Eds.), *Play in practice: Case studies in young children's play* (pp. 13–20). St Paul, MN: Redleaf Press.

Basche, K. (Writer/Producer). (1995). *Respecting how children learn through play* [Videotape]. Van Nuys, CA: Child Development Media, Inc.

Basile, C. G. (1999). The outdoors as a context for mathematics in the early years. In J. V. Copley (Ed.), *Mathematics in the early years* (pp. 156–161). Reston, VA: National Council of Teachers of Mathematics; Washington, DC: National Association for the Education of Young Children.

Bateson, G. A. (1976). A theory of play and fantasy. In J. S. Bruner, A. Jolly, & K. Sylva (Eds.), *Play: Its role in development and evolution* (pp. 119–129). New York: Basic Books.

Beardsley, L. (1991). *Good day, bad day: The child's experience of child care.* New York: Teachers College Press.

Beaty, J. J. (2005). *50 early childhood strategies.* Upper Saddle River, NJ: Merrill/Prentice Hall.

Belkin, L. (2004, September). Is there a place in class for Thomas? What a year of "immersion" can do for a boy—and everyone around him. *New York Times Magazine,* 40.

Bennett, N., Wood, L., & Rogers, S. (1997). *Teaching through play: Teachers' thinking and classroom practice.* Philadelphia, PA: Open University Press.

Bergen, D. (1994) *Assessment of infants and toddlers: Transdisciplinary team approaches.* New York: Teachers College Press.

Bergen, D. (2001). Learning in the robotic world: Active or reactive. *Childhood Education, 77*(4), 249–250.

Bergen, D. (2002). Finding the humor in children's play. In J. L. Roopnarine (Ed)., *Conceptual, social-cognitive, and contextual issues in the fields of play. Play and culture studies,* (Vol. 4, pp. 209–222). Westport, CT: Ablex Publishing.

Bergen, D. (2002). The role of pretend play in children's cognitive development. *Early childhood research and practice, 4*(1), 2–15. Retrieved February 16, 2005, from http://ecrp.uiuc.edu/v4n1/bergen.html

Bergen, D. (2003). Perspectives on inclusion in early childhood education. In J. P. Isenberg & M. R. Jalango (Eds.), *Major trends and issues in early childhood education* (2nd ed., pp. 47–68). New York: Teachers College Press.

Bergen, D., & Mauer, D. (2000). Symbolic play, phonological awareness, and literacy skills at three age levels. In K. Roskos & J. Christie (Eds.), *Play and literacy in early childhood: Research from multiple perspectives* (pp. 45–62). Mahwah NJ: Erlbaum.

Berk, L. E., & Winsler, A. (1995). *Scaffolding children's learning: Vygotsky and early childhood education.* Washington, DC: National Association for the Education of Young Children.

Berkeley Learning Technologies. (1992). Bailey's Book House. [Computer software]. Redmond, WA: Edmark.

Berkeley Learning Technologies. (1992). Millie's Math House. [Computer software]. Redmond, WA: Edmark.

Bernhardt, V. L. (1997). *Second annual evaluation report of education first demonstration schools, Pacific Bell and Pacific Bell Foundation.* (Unpublished).

Berry, J., & Allen, E. (2002). Faces to the window: "The construction project." *Early Childhood Research and Practice, 4*(1), 1–13.

Bettelheim, B. (1989). *The uses of enchantment.* New York: Random House.

Blake, I. K. (1994). Language development and socialization in young African American children. In P. Greenfield & R. Cocking (Eds.), *Cross-cultural roots of minority child development* (pp. 167–196). Hillsdale, NJ: Erlbaum.

Blurton-Jones, N. G. (1972). Categories of child-child interaction. In N. G. Blurton-Jones (Ed.), *Ethnological studies of child behavior* (pp. 97–129). New York: Cambridge University Press.

Bodrova, E., & Leong, D. (2003). Chopsticks and counting chips: Do play and foundational skills need to compete for the teacher's attention in an early childhood classroom? *Young Children, 58*(3), 10–17.

Bodrova, E., & Leong, D. J. (1996). *Tools of the mind.* Upper Saddle River, NJ: Prentice Hall.

Bornstein, M. H., Haynes, O. M., Azuma, H., Galperin, C., Maital, S., Ogino, M., Painter, K., Pascual, M. G., Rahn, C., Toda, S., Venuti, P., Vyt, A., & Wright, B. (1998). A cross-national study of self-evaluations and attributions in parenting: Argentina, Belgium, France, Israel, Italy, Japan, and the United States. *Developmental Psychology, 34*(4), 622–676.

Bowman, B. (2005). Play in the multicultural world of children: Implications for adults. In E. Zigler, D. Singer, & S. Bishop-Josef (Eds.), *Children's play: The roots of reading* (pp. 125–142). Washington, DC: Zero to Three Press.

Bredekamp, S. (1987). *Developmentally appropriate practice in early childhood programs serving young children birth through age 8.* Washington, DC: National Association for the Education of Young Children.

Bredekamp, S. (2004). Play and school readiness. In E. Zigler, D. Singer, & S. Bishop-Josef (Eds.), *Children's play: The roots of reading* (pp. 159–174). Washington, DC: Zero to Three Press.

Bredekamp, S., & Copple, C. (Eds.). (1997). *Developmentally appropriate practice in early childhood programs* (rev. ed.). Washington, DC: National Association for the Education of Young Children.

Bretherton, I. (1984). *Symbolic play: The development of social understanding.* New York: Academic Press.

Broderbund. (1999). Kid Pix Studio. [Computer software]. Novato, CA: Broderbund.

Bronson, M. (2000). Research in review: Recognizing and supporting the development of self-regulation in young children. *Young Children, 55*(2), 32–37.

Bronson, W. (1995). *The right stuff for children from birth to 8: Selecting play materials to support development.* Washington, DC: National Association for the Education of Young Children.

Brown, C. R., & Marchant, C. (Eds.). (2002). *Play in practice: Case studies in young children's play.* St Paul, MN: Redleaf Press.

Brown, L. K. (1986). *Taking advantage of media: A manual for parents and teachers.* Boston: Routledge & Kegan Paul.

Brown, P. W. (2005, October 6). Assessing kids' progress at school: Testing isn't teaching. *San Francisco Chronicle*, p. B9.

Browne, N. (Ed.). (1991). *Science and technology in the early years: An equal opportunities approach.* Philadelphia: Open University Press.

Bruner, J. S. (1963). *The process of education.* Cambridge, MA: Harvard University Press.

Bruner, J. S. (1976). The nature and uses of immaturity. In J. S. Bruner, A. Jolly, & K. Sylva (Eds.), *Play: Its role in development and evolution* (pp. 28–64). New York: Basic Books.

Bruner, J. S. (1986). *Actual minds, possible worlds.* Cambridge, MA: Harvard University Press.

Bruner, J. S. (1990). *Acts of meaning.* Cambridge, MA: Harvard University Press.

Bruner, J. S., Jolly, A., & Sylva, K. (Eds.). (1976). *Play: Its role in development and evolution.* New York: Basic Books.

Burkhour, C. (2004). Introduction to playground. Chicago, IL: National Center on Physical Activity and Disability. Retrieved October 12, 2005, from www.ncpad.org/fun/fact_sheet.php?sheet=9&view=all

Bushman, B. J., & Anderson, C. A. (2001). Media violence and the American public: Scientific facts versus media misinformation. *American Psychologist, 56,* 477–489.

Cadwell, L. B. (1997). *Bringing Reggio home: An innovative approach to early childhood education.* New York: Teachers College Press.

Carini, P. (2000). Prospect's descriptive processes. In M. Himley & P. Carini (Eds.), *From another angle: Children's strengths and school standards* (pp. 8–21). New York: Teachers College Press.

Carlsson-Paige, N., & Levin, D. E. (1990). *Who's calling the shots?* Santa Cruz, CA: New Society Publishers.

Carlsson-Paige, N., & Levin, D. E. (1998). *Before push comes to shove: Building conflict resolution skills with young children.* St. Paul, MN: Redleaf Press.

Carol Gossett's kindergarten connection: A network of educational resources and materials. (2005). Retrieved September 25, 2005, from www.kconnect.com

Casey, B. (2004). Mathematics problem-solving adventures: A language-arts-based supplementary series for early childhood that focuses on special sense. In D. H. Clements & J. Sarama (Eds.), *Engaging young children in mathematics: Standards for early childhood mathematics education* (pp. 377–392). Mahwah, NJ: Erlbaum.

Casey, J. M. (1997). *Early literacy: The empowerment of technology.* Englewood, CO: Libraries Unlimited.

Cazden, C. B. (1983). Adult assistance to language development: Scaffolds, models and direct instruction. In R. P. Parker & F. A. Davis (Eds.), *Developing literacy: Young children's use of language* (pp. 3–18). Newark, DE: International Reading Association.

Chaille, C., & Britain, L. (2003). *Constructivist approaches to early childhood science education: The young child as scientist* (3rd ed.). Boston: Allyn & Bacon.

Chalufour, I., & Worth, K. (2003). *Discovering nature with young children.* St. Paul, MN: Readleaf Press.

Chalufour, I., & Worth, K. (2004). *Building structures with young children.* St. Paul, MN: Readleaf Press.

Chalufour, I., & Worth, K. (2005). *Discovering water with young children.* St. Paul, MN: Readleaf Press.

Chen, J. (Ed.). (1998). *Project Spectrum: Early learning activities* (Vol. 2). New York: Teachers College Press.

Chen, J., Krechevsky, M., Viens, J., & Isberg, E. (1998). *Building on children's strengths: The experience of Project Spectrum* (Vol. 1). New York: Teachers College Press.

Cherney, I. D., Kelly-Vance, L., Gill Glover, K., Ruane, A., & Ryalls, B. O. (2003). The effects of stereotyped toys and gender on play assessment in children aged 18–47 months. *Educational Psychology, 23*(1), 95–106.

Children's technology review. (2005). Retrieved September 25, 2005, from www.childrenssoftware.com

Christie, D. J., Wagner, R. V., & Winter, D. D. (2001). *Peace, conflict, and violence: Peace psychology for the 21st century.* Upper Saddle River, NJ: Prentice Hall.

Christie, J. (1995). *Linking literacy and play.* Newark, NJ: International Reading Association.

Clawson, M. (2002). Play of language minority children in an early childhood setting. In J. L. Roopnarine (Ed.), *Conceptual, social-cognitive, and contextual issues in the fields of play: Play and culture studies* (Vol. 4, pp. 93–110). Westport, CT: Ablex Publishing.

Clayton, M., & Forton, M. B. (2001). *Classroom spaces that work.* Greenfield, MA: Northeast Foundation for Children.

Clements, D. (1994). The uniqueness of the computer as a learning tool: Insights from research. In J. Wright & D. Shade (Eds.), *Young children: Active learners in a technological age.* Washington, DC: National Association for the Education of Young Children.

Clements, D., Nastasi, B., & Swaminathan, S. (1993). Research in review. Young children and computers: Crossroads and directions for research. *Young Children, 48*(2), 56–64.

Clements, D. H., & Sarama, J. (2003). Young children and technology: What does the research say? *Young Children, 58*(6), 34–40.

Clements, D. H., & Sarama, J. (Eds.). (2004). *Engaging young children in mathematics: Standards for early childhood mathematics education.* Mahwah, NJ: Erlbaum.

Cliatt, M. J. P., & Shaw, J. M. (1992). *Helping children explore science: A sourcebook for teachers of young children.* Upper Saddle River, NJ: Merrill/Prentice Hall.

Clyde, J. A. (1994). Lessons from Douglas: Expanding our visions of what it means to "know." *Language Arts, 71,* 22–33.

Cochran-Smith, M., & Lytle, S. L. (1993). *Inside/outside: Teacher research and knowledge.* New York: Teachers College Press.

Cochran-Smith, M., Kahn, J., & Paris, C. (1990). Writing with a felicitous tool. *Theory into Practice, 29*(4), 235–244.

Cole, M., Cole, S., & Lightfoot, C. (2005). *The development of children* (5th ed.). New York: Worth.

Cook-Gumperz, J. (1986). *The social construction of literacy.* New York: Cambridge University Press.

Cook-Gumperz, J., & Corsaro, W. (1977). Social-ecological constraints on children's communication strategies. *Sociology, 11,* 412–434.

Cook-Gumperz, J., & Gumperz, J. (1982). Introduction: Language and social identity. In J. Gumperz (Ed.), *Language and social identity* (Vol. 2, pp. 1–2). Cambridge, UK: Cambridge University Press.

Cook-Gumperz, J., & Scales, B. (1982). *Toward an understanding of angel's hair: Report on a study of children's communication in socio-dramatic play.* Unpublished manuscript.

Cook-Gumperz, J., & Scales, B. (1996). Girls, boys and just people: The interactional accomplishment of gender in the discourse of the nursery school. In D. Slobin, J. Gerhardt, A. Kyratzis, & J. Guo (Eds.), *Social interaction, social context, and language* (pp. 513–527). Mahwah, NJ: Erlbaum.

Cook-Gumperz, J., Corsaro, W., & Streeck, J. (Eds.). (1996). *Children's worlds and children's language.* Berlin: Mouton de Gruyter.

Cook-Gumperz, J., Gates, D., Scales, B., & Sanders, H. (1976). *Toward an understanding of angel's hair: Summary of a pilot study of a nursery play yard.* Unpublished manuscript, University of California, Berkeley.

Cooney, M. (2004). Is play important? Guatemalan kindergartners' classroom experiences and their parents' and teachers' perceptions of learning through play. *Journal of Research in Childhood Education, 18*(4), 261–277.

Copley, J. V. (Ed.). (1999). *Mathematics in the early years.* Reston, VA: National Council of Teachers of Mathematics; Washington, DC: National Association for the Education of Young Children.

Copley, J. V. (2002). *The young child and mathematics.* Washington, DC: National Council for the Education of Young Children; Reston, VA: National Council of Teachers of Mathematics.

Corsaro, W. A. & Miller, P. (Eds.). (1992). Interpretive approaches to children's socialization. In W. Damon (Chief Editor), *New directions for child development* (Issue 58). San Francisco, CA: Jossey-Bass Publishers.

Corsaro, W. A. (1979). We're friends, right? Children's use of access rituals in a nursery school. *Language in Society, 8,* 315–336.

Corsaro, W. A. (1985). *Friendship and peer culture in the early years.* Norwood, NJ: Ablex.

Corsaro, W. A. (1997). *The sociology of childhood.* Thousand Oaks, CA: Pine Forge Press.

Corsaro, W. A. (2003). *We're friends, right: Inside kids' culture.* Washington, DC: The Joseph Henry Press.

Corsaro, W. A., & Elder, D. (1990). Children's peer cultures. *Annual Review of Sociology, 16,* 197–220.

Corsaro, W. A., & Schwartz, K. (1991). Peer play and socialization in two cultures: Implications for research and practice. In B. Scales, M. Almy,

A. Nicolopoulou, & S. Ervin-Tripp (Eds.), *Play and the social context of development in early care and education* (pp. 234–254). New York: Teachers College Press.

Cortés, C. (2000). *The children are watching: How the media teach about diversity.* New York: Teachers College Press.

Cowan, P. A. (1978). *Piaget with feeling: Cognitive, social and emotional dimensions.* New York: Holt, Rinehart & Winston.

Creasey, G. L., Jurvis, P. A., & Berk, L. E. (1998). Play and social competence. In O. N. Saracho & B. Spodek (Eds.). *Multiple perspectives on play in early childhood education* (pp. 116–143). Albany, NY: SUNY Press.

Csikszentmihalyi, M. (1993). *The evolving self: A psychology for the third millennium.* New York: HarperCollins.

Cuffaro, H. K. (1995). *Experimenting with the world: John Dewey and the early childhood classroom.* New York: Teachers College Press.

Curran, J. M. (1999). Constraints of pretend play; implicit and explicit rules. *Journal of Research in Childhood Education, 14*(1) 47–55.

Curry, N. E. (1971). Consideration of current basic issues on play. In N. Curry & S. Arnaud (Eds.), *Play: The child strives toward self realization* (pp. 51–62). Washington, DC: National Association for the Education of Young Children.

Curtis, D., & Carter, M. (2003). *Designs for living and learning: Transforming early childhood environments.* St Paul, MN: Redleaf Press.

Davidson, J. (1998). Language and play: Natural partners. In D. Fromberg & D. Bergen (Eds), *Play from birth to twelve and beyond: Contexts, perspectives, and meanings* (pp. 175–184). New York: Garland.

Davydov, V. V. (1995). The influence of L. S. Vygotsky on education theory, research, and practice. *Educational Researcher, 24*(3), 12–21.

Delgado-Gaitan, C. (1994). Socializing young children in Mexican American families: An intergenerational perspective. In P. Greenfield & R. Cocking (Eds.), *Cross-cultural roots of minority child development* (pp. 55–86). Hillsdale, NJ: Erlbaum.

Delpit, L. (1995). *Other people's children.* Boston: Harvard University Press.

Derman-Sparks, L., & ABC Task Force. (1989). *The antibias curriculum: Tools for empowering young*

children. Washington, DC: National Association for the Education of Young Children.

Derman-Sparks, L., & Ramsey, P. (2005). A framework for culturally relevant, multicultural, and antibias education in the twenty-first century. In J. P. Roopnarine & J. Johnson (Eds.), *Approaches to early childhood education* (4th ed., pp. 107–124). Upper Saddle River, NJ: Merrill/Prentice Hall.

Desjean-Perotta, B., & Barbour, A. C. (2001). The prop box: Helping preservice teachers understand the value of dramatic play. *Journal of the National Forum of Teacher Education, 12*(1), 3–15.

deUriarte, M. (1978). *The Berkeley child art studio.* Unpublished manuscript. Berkeley, CA.

deUriarte, M. (2006). *Mira arte: Artistic development in alternative spaces.* Retrieved January 1, 2006, from www.miraarte.org

DeVries, R. (1997). Piaget's social theory. *Educational Researcher, 26*(2), 4–17.

DeVries, R., & Kohlberg, L. (1987). *Constructivist early education: Overview and comparison with other programs.* Washington, DC: National Association for the Education of Young Children.

DeVries, R., & Zan, B. (1994). *Moral classrooms, moral children: Creating a constructivist atmosphere in early education.* New York: Teachers College Press.

DeVries, R., & Zan, B. (1996). Assessing interpersonal understanding in the classroom context. *Childhood Education, 72*(50), 265–268.

DeVries, R., & Zan, B. (2005). A constructivist perspective on the role of the sociomoral atmosphere in promoting children's development. In C. T. Fosnot (Ed.), *Constructivism: Theory, perspectives, and practice* (2nd ed., pp. 132–149). New York: Teachers College Press.

DeVries, R., Zan, B., Hildebrandt, C., Edmiaston, R., & Sales, C. (2002). *Developing constructivist early childhood curriculum: Practical principles and activities.* New York: Teachers College Press.

Dewey, J. (1971). *The child and the curriculum: The school and society.* Chicago: University of Chicago Press. (Original work published 1915)

Dominick, A., & Clark, F. B. (1996). Using games to understand children's understanding. *Childhood Education, 72*(5), 286–288.

Doris, E. (1991). *Doing what scientists do: Children learn to investigate their world.* Portsmouth, NH: Heinemann Boynton/Cook.

Doyle, A. B., & Connolly, J. (1989). Negotiation and enactment in social pretend play: Relations to social acceptance and social cognition. *Early Childhood Research Quarterly, 4,* 289–302.

Duckworth, E. (1996). *"The having of wonderful ideas" and other essays on teaching and learning* (2nd ed.). New York: Teachers College Press.

Duckworth, E. (2001). *"Tell me more": Listening to learners.* New York: Teachers College Press.

Dyson, A. H. (1993). *Social worlds of children learning to write in an urban primary school.* New York: Teachers College Press.

Dyson, A. H. (1994). *The ninjas, the X-men, and the ladies: Playing with power and identity in an urban primary school* (Technical Report No. 70). Berkeley, CA: University of California, National Center for the Study of Writing.

Dyson, A. H. (1995, April). *The courage to write: The ideological dimensions of child writing.* Paper presented at the Annual Meeting of the American Educational Research Association, San Francisco, CA.

Dyson, A. H. (1997). *Writing superheroes: Contemporary childhood, popular culture, and classroom literacy.* New York: Teachers College Press.

Dyson, A. H. (2003). *The brothers and sisters learn to write: Popular literacies in childhood and school cultures.* New York: Teachers College Press.

Dyson, A. H., & Genishi, C. (Eds.). (1994). *The need for story: Cultural diversity in classroom and community.* Urbana, IL: National Council of Teachers of English.

Edmiaston, R., Dolezal, V., Doolittle, S., Erickson, C., & Merritt, S. (2000). Developing individualized education programs for children in inclusive settings: A developmental framework. *Young Children, 55*(4), 36–41.

Edupuppy—everything for early childhood education: Preschool to grade 3. (2005). Retrieved September 25, 2005, from www.edupuppy.com

Edwards, C., Gandini, L., & Forman, G. (Eds.). (1993). *The hundred languages of children: The Reggio Emilia approach to early childhood education.* Norwood, NJ: Ablex.

Egan, K. (1988). *Primary understanding: Education in early childhood.* New York: Routledge.

Einarsdottir, J. (2000). Incorporating literacy resources into the play curriculum of two Icelandic preschools. In K. Roskos & J. Christie (Eds.), *Play and literacy in early childhood: Research from multiple perspectives* (pp. 77–90). Mahwah, NJ: Erlbaum.

Eisert, D., & Lamorey, S. (1996). Play as a window on child development: The relationship between play and other developmental domains. *Early Education and Development, 7*(3), 221–235.

Elgas, P. M., & Peltier, M. B. (1998). Jimmy's journey: Building a sense of community and self-worth through small-group work. *Young Children, 53*(2), 17–21.

Elkind, D. (1990). Academic pressure—too much, too soon: The demise of play. In E. Klugman & S. Smilansky (Eds.), *Children's play and learning: Perspectives and policy implications* (pp. 3–17). New York: Teachers College Press.

Elkind, D. (2003). Thanks for the memory: The lasting value of play. *Young Children, 58*(3), 46–51.

Ellis, M. (1988). Play and the origin of species. In D. Bergen (Ed.), *Play as a medium for learning and development* (pp. 23–26). Portsmouth, NH: Heinemann.

Elmer-DeWitt, P. (1993, September 27). The amazing video game boom. *Time,* pp. 54–59.

Emihovich, C. (1990). Technocentrism revisited: Computer literacy as cultural capital. *Theory into Practice, 29*(4), 227–234.

Engel, B. S. (1995). *Considering children's art: Why and how to value their works.* Washington, DC: National Association for the Education of Young Children.

Ensign, J. (2003). Including culturally relevant math in an urban school. *Educational Studies, 34*(4), 414–423.

Epstein, A., Schweinhart, L., DeBruin-Parecki, A., & Robin, K. (2004, July). *Preschool assessment: A guide to developing a balanced approach.* New Brunswick, NJ: National Institute for Early Education Research.

ERIC Clearinghouse on Disabilities and Gifted Education. (2005). Retrieved September 25, 2005, from www.ericec.org

Erickson, F. (1993). Foreword. In M. Cochran-Smith & S. L. Lytle (Eds.), *Inside/outside: Teacher research and knowledge.* New York: Teachers College Press.

Erickson, F. (2004). *Talk and social theory: Ecologies of speaking and listening in everyday life.* Malden, MA: Blackwell.

Erikson, E. (1950/85). *Childhood and society.* New York: Norton.

Erikson, E. (1977). *Toys and reasons.* New York: Norton.

Erwin, E. J. (1993). Social participation of young children with visual impairments in specialized and integrated environments. *Journal of Visual Impairment & Blindness, 87*(5), 138–142.

Fabes, R. A., Martin, C. L., & Hanish, L. D. (2003). Young children's play qualities in same-, other-, and mixed-sex peer groups. *Child Development, 74*(3), 921–932.

Fagot, B., & Leve, L. (1998). Gender identity and play. In D. P. Fromberg & D. Bergen (Eds.), *Play from birth to twelve and beyond: Contexts, perspectives, and meanings* (pp. 187–192). New York: Garland Publishing.

Fantuzzo, J., Sutton-Smith, B., Coolahan, K. C., Manz, P. H., Canning, S., & Debnam, D. (1995). Assessment of preschool play interaction behaviors in low income children: Penn Interactive Peer Play Scale. *Early Childhood Research Quarterly, 10*, 105–120.

Farver, J. (1992). Communicating shared meaning in social pretend play. *Early Childhood Research Quarterly, 7*(40), 501–516.

Fein, G. (1995). Toys and stories. In A. Pellegrini (Ed.), *The future of play theory: A multidisciplinary inquiry into the contributions of Brian Sutton-Smith* (pp. 151–164). Albany, NY: SUNY Press.

Fein, G. G. (1981). Pretend play in childhood: An integrative review. *Child Development, 52,* 1095–1118.

Fein, G. G., Ardeila-Ray, A., & Groth, L. (2000). The narrative connection: Stories and literacy. In K. Roskos & J. Christie (Eds.), *Play and literacy in early childhood: Research from multiple perspectives* (pp. 27–43). Mahwah, NJ: Erlbaum.

Fein, S. (1984). *Heidi's horse* (2nd ed.). Pleasant Hill, CA: Exelrod Press.

Ferguson, C. (2001). Discovering, supporting, and promoting young children's passions and interests: One teacher's reflections. *Young Children, 56*(4), 6–11.

Fischer, M., & Gillespie, C. (2003). Computers and young children's development. *Young Children, 58*(4), 85–91.

Fisman, L. (2001). Child's play: An empirical study of the relationship between the physical form of school yards and children's behavior. Retrieved September 18, 2005, from www.yale.edu/nixon/research/pdf/LFisman_Playgrounds.pdf

Flavell, J. H. (1963). *The developmental psychology of Jean Piaget.* Princeton, NJ: Van Nostrand.

Forman. G. (1998). Constructive play. In D. P. Fromberg & D. Bergen (Eds.), *Play from birth to twelve and beyond: Contexts, perspectives, and meanings* (pp. 393–400). New York: Garland.

Forman, G. (1999). Instant video revisiting: The video camera as a "tool of the mind" for young children. *Early Childhood Research and Practice, 1*(2), 1–8.

Forman, G. (2005). The project approach in Reggio Emilia. In C. T. Fosnot (Ed.). *Constructivism: Theory, perspectives, and practice* (2nd ed., pp. 212–221). New York: Teachers College Press.

Forman, G. E., & Kaden, M. (1987). Research on science education for young children. In C. Seefeldt (Ed.), *The early childhood curriculum: A review of current research* (pp. 141–164). New York: Teachers College Press.

Forman, G. E., & Kuschner, D. S. (1977). *The child's construction of knowledge: Piaget for teaching children.* Belmont, CA: Wadsworth.

Fosnot, C. T., & Dolk. (2001). *Young mathematicians at work: Constructing number sense, addition, and subtraction.* Portsmouth, NH: Heinemann.

Fosnot, C. T., & Perry. R. S. (2005). Constructivism: A psychological theory of learning. In C. T. Fosnot (Ed.), *Constructivism: Theory, perspectives, and practice* (2nd ed., pp. 8–38). New York: Teachers College Press.

Foss, K. (2002, November 23). All I want for Christmas is a bombed-out dollhouse. *Globe & Mail/Canada.* Retrieved September 22, 2005, from www.commondreams.org/views02/1123-01.htm

Fromberg, D. P. (1999). A review of research on play. In C. Seefeldt (Ed.), *The early child curriculum: Current findings in theory and practice* (3rd ed., pp. 27–53). New York: Teachers College Press.

Fromberg, D. P. (2002). *Play and meaning in early childhood education.* Boston, MA: Allyn & Bacon.

Fromberg, D. P., & Bergen, D. (Eds.). (in press). *Play from birth to twelve and beyond: Contexts, perspectives, and meanings* (2nd ed.). New York: Routledge.

Frost, J., Shin, D., & Jacobs, P. (1998). Physical environments and children's play. In O. Saracho

& B. Spodek (Eds.), *Multiple perspectives on play in early childhood education* (pp. 255–294). Albany, NY: SUNY Press.

Frost, J., Wortham, S., & Reifel, S. (2005). *Play and child development* (3rd ed.). Upper Saddle River, NJ: Merrill/Prentice Hall.

Full Option Science System (FOSS). (2005). *Air and weather.* Hudson, NH: Delta Education, Inc.

Full Option Science System (FOSS). (2005). *Balance and motion.* Hudson, NH: Delta Education, Inc.

Full Option Science System (FOSS). (2005). *Pebbles, sand, and silt.* Hudson, NH: Delta Education, Inc.

Furth, H. G. (1970). *Piaget for teachers.* Upper Saddle River, NJ: Prentice Hall.

Gallas, K. (1994). *The languages of learning: How children talk, write, dance, draw, and sing their understanding of the world.* New York: Teachers College Press.

Gallas, K. (1998). *Sometimes I can be anything: Power, gender, and identity in a primary classroom.* New York: Teachers College Press.

Gallas, K. (2003). *Imagination and literacy: A teacher's search for the heart of meaning.* New York: Teachers College Press.

Gandini, L., Hill, L., Cadwell, L., & Schwall, C. (2005). *In the spirit of the studio: Learning from the atelier of Reggio Emilia.* New York: Teachers College Press.

Ganzel, C., & Stuglik, J. (2003). *The llama project: Early childhood research and practice.* Retrieved February 16, 2005, from http://ecrp.uiuc.edu/v5n2/Ganzel

Garbarino, J. (1996). *Let's talk about living in a world with violence.* Chicago: Erikson Institute.

Gardner, H. (1992). *Frames of mind: The theory of multiple intelligence.* New York: Basic Books.

Gardner, H. (1999). *Intelligence reformed: Multiple intelligences for the 21st century.* New York: Basic Books.

Garvey, C. (1990/1977). *Play.* Cambridge, MA: Harvard University Press.

Garvey, C., & Berndt, R. (1977). *Organization of pretend play* (JSAS Catalogue of Selected Documents in Psychology, Manuscript 1589). Washington, DC: American Psychological Association.

Gaskins, S., Miller, P., & Corsaro, W. (1992). Theoretical and methodological perspectives in the interpretive study of children. *New Directions in Child Development, 58,* 5–23.

Gee, K. (2000). *Visual arts as a way of knowing.* York, ME: Stenhouse Publishers.

Geist, E. (2001). Children are born mathematicians: Promoting the construction of early mathematical concepts in children under five. *Young Children, 56*(4),12–19.

Genishi, C. (Ed.). (1992). *Ways of assessing children and curriculum: Stories of early childhood practice.* New York: Teachers College Press.

Genishi, C. (2002, July). Young English language learners: Resourceful in the classroom. *Young Children, 57*(4), 66–72.

Genishi, C., & DiPaolo, M. (1982). Learning through argument in preschool. In L. C. Wilkonson (Ed.), *Communicating in the classroom* (pp. 49–68). New York: Academic Press.

Genishi, C., & Dyson, A. H. (1984). *Language assessment in the early years.* Norwood, NJ: Ablex.

Genishi, C., & Dyson, A. H. (2005). *On the case: Approaches to language and literacy research.* New York: Teachers College Press and National Conference on Research in Language and Literacy.

Genishi, C., & Strand, E. (1990). Contextualizing logo: Lessons from a 5-year-old. *Theory into Practice, 29*(4), 264–269.

Ghafouri, F., & Wien, C. A. (2005). Give us privacy: Play and social literacy in young children. *Journal of Research in Childhood Education, 19*(4), 279–291.

Giddens, A. (1993). *New rules of sociological methods.* Palo Alto, CA: Stanford University Press.

Giddens, A. (2000). *Runaway world: How globalization is reshaping our lives.* New York: Routledge.

Giffin, H. (1984). The coordination of meaning in the creation of a shared make-believe reality. In I. Bretherton (Ed.), *Symbolic play: The development of social understanding* (pp. 73–100). New York: Academic Press.

Ginsburg, H. P., Inoue, N., & Seo, K. H. (1999). Young children doing mathematics: Observations of everyday activities. In J. V. Copley (Ed.), *Mathematics in the early years* (pp. 88–100). Reston, VA: National Council of Teachers of Mathematics; Washington, DC: National Association for the Education of Young Children.

Ginsburg, H. P., Klein, A., & Starkey, P. (1997). The development of children's mathematical thinking: Connecting research with practice. In I. Sigel & A. Renninger (Eds.), *Handbook of child psychology* (Vol. 4), *Child Psychology and Practice* (5th ed.). New York: Wiley.

Goffman, E. (1974). *Frame analysis.* New York: Harper & Row.

Goffman, E. (2000). On face-work: An analysis of ritual elements in social interaction. In A. Jaworski & N. Coupland (Eds.), *The discourse reader* (pp. 306–320). London: Routledge.

Goleman, D. (1995). *Emotional intelligence.* New York: Bantam Books.

Golomb, C., Gowing, E. D., & Friedman, L. (1982). Play and cognition: Studies of pretense play and conservation of quantity. *Journal of Experimental Child Psychology, 33,* 257–279.

Goncu, A. (1993). Development of intersubjectivity in the dyadic play of preschoolers. *Early Childhood Research Quarterly, 8,* 99–116.

Gonzalez-Mena, J. (1998). *The child in the family and the community.* Upper Saddle River, NJ: Merrill/Prentice Hall.

Goodnow, J. (1977). *Children drawing.* Cambridge, MA: Harvard University Press.

Goodwin, M. (1990). *He-said-she-said: Talk as social organization among black children.* Bloomington, IN: Indiana University Press.

Gowen, J. W. (1995). Research and review: Early development of symbolic play. *Young Children, 50*(3), 75–83.

Graue, E. (2001). Research in review: What's going on in the children's garden? Kindergarten today. *Young Children, 56*(3), 67–73.

Graue, E., & Diperna, J. (2000). Redshirting and early retention: Who gets the "gift of time" and what are its outcomes? *American Educational Research Journal, 37*(2), 509–534.

Great Explorations in Mathematics and Science (GEMS. (1996). *Ant homes under ground.* Berkeley, CA: Regents, University of California, Berkeley.

Great Explorations in Mathematics and Science (GEMS. (1997). *Treasure boxes.* Berkeley, CA: Regents, University of California, Berkeley.

Greenfield, P. (1999). Cultural change and human development. In E. Turiel (Ed.), *Development and cultural change: Reciprocal processes. New Directions in Child Development, 83,* 37–60.

Greenfield, P. M. (1984). *Mind and media: The effects of television, video games, and computers.* Cambridge, MA: Harvard University Press.

Greenfield. P. (1994). Independence and interdependence as developmental scripts: Implications for theory, research, and practice. In P. Greenfield & R. Cocking (Eds.), *Cross-cultural roots of minority child development* (pp. 1–40). Hillsdale, NJ: Erlbaum.

Greenman, J. (2005, May). Places for childhood in the 21st century: A conceptual framework. *Young Children, Beyond the Journal.* Retrieved September 16, 2005, from www.journal.naeyc.org/btj/200505/01Greenman.asp

Griffin, E. (1998). *Island of childhood: Education in the special world of the nursery school.* Troy, NY: Educators International Press.

Griffin, S. (2004). Number worlds: A research-based mathematics program for young children. In D. H. Clements & J. Sarama (Eds.), *Engaging young children in mathematics: Standards for early childhood mathematics education* (pp. 325–342). Mahwah, NJ: Erlbaum.

Guberman, S. R. (1999). Cultural aspects of young children's mathematical knowledge. In J. V. Copley (Ed.), *Mathematics in the early years* (pp. 30–36). Reston, VA: National Council of Teachers of Mathematics; Washington, DC: National Association for the Education of Young Children.

Gumperz, J. J., & Cook-Gumperz, J. (1982). Introduction: Language and the communication of social identity. In J. J. Gumperz & J. Cook-Gumperz (Eds.), *Language and social identity* (pp. 1–21). Cambridge, UK: Cambridge University Press.

Gustafson, S. C. (2000). *Educating for peace and nonviolence in early childhood.* Unpublished manuscript.

Hand, H., & Nourot, P. M. (1999). *First class: Guide to early primary education.* Sacramento, CA: California Department of Education.

Hanline, M. F., & Fox, L. (1993). Learning within the context of play: Providing typical early childhood experiences for children with severe disabilities. *The Journal of the Association for Persons with Severe Handicaps, 18*(2), 121–129.

Harlan, J., & Rivkin, M. S. (2004). *Science experiences for the early childhood years: An integrated affective approach* (8th ed.). Upper Saddle River, NJ: Merrill/Prentice Hall.

Harms, T. (1969). *My art is me* [Motion picture]. Berkeley, CA: University of California Extension Media Center.

Harms, T., Clifford, R. M., & Cryer, D. (1998). *Early childhood environmental rating scale* (rev. ed.). New York: Teachers College Press.

Harris, I. (1999). Types of peace education. In A. Raviv, L. Oppenheimer, & D. Bartal (Eds.), *How children understand war and peace* (pp. 299–320). San Francisco, CA: Jossey-Bass.

Hartmann, W., & Rollett, B. (1994). Play: Positive intervention in the elementary school curriculum. In J. Hellendoorn, R. van der Kooij, & B. Sutton-Smith (Eds.), *Play and intervention* (pp. 195–202). Albany, NY: SUNY Press.

Haugland, S. W. (1992). The effort of computer software on pre-school developmental gains. *Journal of Computing in Childhood Educators, 3*(1), 13–30.

Haugland, S. W. (1997). *The developmental scale for software.* Cape Girardeau, MO: K.I.D.S. & Computers.

Haugland, S. W. (1999). What role should technology play in young children's learning? Part 1. *Young Children, 54*(6), 26–31.

Haugland, S. W. (2000). What role should technology play in young children's learning? Part 2. Early childhood classrooms in the 21st century: Using computers to maximize learning. *Young Children, 55*(1), 12–20.

Haugland, S. W., & Gerzog, G. (1998). *The developmental software scale for web sites.* Cape Girardeau, MO: K.I.D.S. & Computers.

Haugland, S. W., & Wright, J. (1997). *Young children and technology: A world of discovery.* Boston: Allyn & Bacon.

Hazen, N., & Black, B. (1984). Social acceptance: Strategies children use and how teachers can help children learn them. *Young Children, 39*(6), 26–60.

Heath, S. B. (1983). *Ways with words: Language, life and work in communities and classrooms.* New York: Cambridge University Press.

Heath, S. B., & Mangiola, L. (1991). *Children of promise: Literate activity in linguistically and culturally diverse classrooms.* Washington, DC: National Education Association.

Heathcote, D. (1997). *Three looms waiting.* Berkeley, CA: University of California Media Center.

Heathcote, D., & Bolton, G. (1995). *Drama for learning: Dorothy Heathcote's mantle of the expert approach to education.* Portsmouth, NH: Heinemann.

Heathcote, D., & Herbert, P. (1985, Summer). A drama of meaning: Mantle of the expert. *Theory into Practice, 24*(3), 173–179.

Helm, J. H., & Beneke, S. (2003). *The power of projects: Meeting contemporary challenges in early childhood classrooms—strategies and solutions.* New York: Teachers College Press.

Helm, J. H., Beneke, S., & Steinheimer, K. (1998). *Windows on learning: Documenting young children's work.* New York: Teachers College Press.

Helm, J. H., & Katz, L. (2001). *Young investigators: The project approach in the early years.* New York: Teachers College Press.

Henderson, F., & Jones, E. (2002). "Everytime they get started, we interrupt them": Children with special needs at play. In C. R. Brown & C. Marchant (Eds.), *Play in practice: Case studies in young children's play* (pp. 133–146). St Paul, MN: Redleaf Press.

Hendrick, J. (1997). *First steps toward teaching the Reggio way.* Upper Saddle River, NJ: Merrill/Prentice Hall.

Hendrickson, J. M., Strain, P. S., Trembley, A., & Shores, R. E. (1981). Relationship between a material use and the occurrence of social interactive behaviors by normally developing preschool children. *Psychology in the Schools, 18*, 500–504.

Hesse, P., & Lane, F. (2003). Media literacy starts young: An integrated curriculum approach. *Young Children, 58*(4), 20-26.

Hewitt, K., & Roomet, L. (1979). *Educational toys in America: 1800 to the present.* Burlington, VT: The Robert Hill Fleming Museum.

Hill, D. M. (1977). *Mud, sand, and water.* Washington, DC: National Association for the Education of Young Children.

Himley, M., & Carini, P. (Eds.). (2000). *From another angle: Children's strengths and school standards.* New York: Teachers College Press.

Hinitz, B., & Stomfay-Stitz, A. (1998, November). *Infusion of peace education in the early childhood/elementary education classroom: Setting the agenda for a humane world.* Paper presented at the Annual American Educational Research Association, New Orleans, LA.

Hirsch, E. S. (Ed.). (1996). *The block book* (3rd ed.). Washington, DC: National Association for the Education of Young Children.

Ho, W. C. (Ed.). (1989). *Yani: The brush of innocence.* New York: Hudson Hills Press.

Hobbs, R., & Frost, R. (2003). Measuring the acquisition of media literacy skills. *Reading Research Quarterly, 38*(3), 330–355.

Hoisington, C. (2003). Using photographs to support children's science inquiry. In D. Koralek & L. J. Kolker (Eds.), *Spotlight on young children and science* (pp. 21–26). Washington, DC: National Association for the Education of Young Children.

Holmes, R., & Geiger, C. (2002). The relationship between creativity and cognitive abilities in preschoolers. In J. L. Roopnarine (Ed.), *Conceptual, social-cognitive, and contextual issues in the fields of play* (pp. 127–148). *Play and Culture Studies* (Vol. 4). Westport, CT: Ablex.

Holt, B. G. (1989). *Science with young children.* Washington, DC: National Association for the Education of Young Children.

Holton, D., Ahmed, A., Williams, H., & Hill, C. (2001). On the importance of mathematical play. *International Journal of Math Education in Science and Technology, 32*(3), 401–415.

Honig, A. (1998). Sociocultural influences on gender role behaviors in children's play. In D. Fromberg & D. Bergen (Eds.), *Play from birth to twelve and beyond: Contexts, perspectives, and meanings* (pp. 338–347). New York: Garland Publishing.

Houck, P. (1997). Lessons from an exhibition: Reflections of an art educator. In J. Hendrick (Ed.), *First steps toward teaching the Reggio way* (pp. 26–41). Upper Saddle River, NJ: Merrill/Prentice Hall.

Howes, C. (with Unger, O., & Matheson, C.). (1992). *The collaborative construction of pretend: Social pretend play functions.* New York: SUNY Press.

Howes, C., & Wishard, A. (2004). Revisiting shared meaning: Looking through the lens of culture and linking shared pretend play through protonarrative development to emergent literacy. In E. Zigler, D. Singer, & S. Bishop-Josef (Eds.), *Children's play: The roots of reading* (pp. 143–158). Washington, DC: Zero to Three Press.

Huesmann, L., Moise-Titus, J., Podolski, C., & Eron, L. (2003). Longitudinal relations between children's exposure to TV violence and their aggressive and violent behavior in young adulthood 1991–1992. *Developmental Psychology, 39*(2), 201–221.

Hughes, F. (2003). Sensitivity to the social and cultural contexts of the play of young children. In J. Isenberg & M. Jalongo (Eds.), *Major trends and issues in early childhood education: Challenges, controversies, and insights* (2nd ed., pp. 126–135). New York: Teachers College Press.

Hutt, C. (1971). Exploration and play in children. In R. E. Herron & B. Sutton-Smith (Eds.), *Child's play* (pp. 231–251). New York: Wiley.

Infinite potential through assistive technology. (2005). Retrieved September 25, 2005, from www.infinitec.org/play/outdoor/playgrounds

Inhelder, B., & Piaget, J. (1964). *The early growth of logic in the child.* New York: Norton.

International Reading Association (IRA) and the National Association for the Education of Young Children (NAEYC). (1998). *Learning to read and write: Developmentally appropriate practices for young children: A joint position statement of the IRA and NAEYC.* Washington, DC: NAEYC.

Isenberg, J. P., & Jalongo, M. R. (2001). *Creative expression and play in early childhood.* Upper Saddle River, NJ: Merrill/Prentice Hall.

Isenberg, J. P., & Jalongo, M. R. R. (2006). *Creative thinking and arts-based learning: Preschool through fourth grade.* Upper Saddle River, NJ: Merrill/Prentice Hall.

Jackowitz, E. R., & Watson, M. W. (1980). Development of object transformations in early pretend play. *Developmental Psychology, 16,* 543–549.

Jaelitza. (1996). Insect love: A field journal. *Young Children, 51*(4), 31–32.

Jambor, T., & Palmer, S. D. (1991). *Playground safety manual.* Birmingham, AL: Injury Prevention Center, University of Alabama.

Jarrell, R. H. (1998). Play and its influence on the development of young children's mathematical thinking. In D. P. Fromberg & D. Bergen (Eds.), *Play from birth to twelve and beyond: Contexts, perspectives, and meanings* (pp. 56–67). New York: Garland Press.

Jarrett, O. S. (2003). Recess in elementary school: What does the research say? Retrieved February 19, 2006, from www.ericdigests.org/2003-2/

recess.html (ERIC Document Reproduction Service No. ED466331)

Jaworski, A., & Coupland, N. (Eds.). (1999). *The discourse reader.* London: Routledge.

Johnson, J. (2003). *Early literacy assessment systems: Essential elements.* Princeton, NJ: Educational Testing Services.

Johnson, J., Christie, J., & Wardle, F. (2005). *Play, development, and early education.* Boston: Allyn & Bacon.

Johnson, J. E., Ershler, J., & Lawton, J. (1982). Intellective correlates of preschoolers' spontaneous play. *Journal of General Psychology, 106,* 115–122.

Jones, E. (1973). *Dimensions of teaching-learning environments: Handbook for teachers.* Pasadena, CA: Pacific Oaks College.

Jones, E. (2003). Viewpoint: Playing to get smart. *Young Children, 58*(3), 32–37.

Jones, E., & Cooper, R. (2006). *Playing to get smart.* New York: Teachers College Press.

Jones, E., & Reynolds, G. (1992). *The play's the thing: Teachers' roles in children's play.* New York: Teachers College Press.

Joshi, A. (2005). Understanding Asian Indian families: Facilitating meaningful home-school relations. *Young Children, 60,* 75–79.

Jungck, S. (1990). Viewing computer literacy through a critical ethnographic lens. *Theory into Practice, 29*(4), 283–289.

Kamii, C. (1982). *Number in preschool and kindergarten: Educational implications of Piaget's theory.* Washington, DC: National Association for the Education of Young Children.

Kamii, C. (Ed.). (1990). *No achievement testing in the early grades: The games grown-ups play.* Washington, DC: National Association for the Education of Young Children.

Kamii, C. (with DeClark, G.). (2000). *Young children reinvent arithmetic: Implications of Piaget's theory* (2nd ed.) New York: Teachers College Press.

Kamii, C., & DeVries, R. (1980). *Group games in early education.* Washington, DC: National Association for the Education of Young Children.

Kamii, C., & DeVries, R. (1993). *Physical knowledge in preschool education.* New York: Teachers College Press. (Original work published in 1978)

Kamii, C. (with Housman, L. B.) (2000). *Young children reinvent arithmetic: Implications of Piaget's theory* (2nd ed.). New York: Teachers College Press.

Kamii, C., Miyakawa, Y., & Kato, Y. (2004, September). The development of logico-mathematical thinking in a block building activity at ages 1–4. *Journal of Research in Childhood Education, 19*(1).

Katch, J. (2001). *Under deadman's skin: Discovering the meaning of children's violent play.* Boston: Beacon Press.

Kathy Schrock's guide for educators. (2005). Retrieved September 25, 2005, from http://school.discovery.com/schrockguide/

Katz, L. (1999). Balancing constructivist and instructivist curriculum goals in early childhood education. *Journal of the California Kindergarten Association,* 71–83.

Katz, L., & Chard, S. (2000). *Engaging children's minds: The project approach* (2nd ed.). Stamford, CT: Ablex.

Katz, L., Evangelou, D., & Hartman, J. (1990). *The case for mixed age grouping in early education.* Washington, DC: National Association for the Education of Young Children.

Kellogg, R. (1969). *Analyzing children's art.* Palo Alto, CA: National Press.

Kellough, R. D. (1996). *Integrating mathematics and science for kindergarten and primary children.* Upper Saddle River, NJ: Merrill/Prentice Hall.

Kendall, J. S., & Marzano, R. J. (2004). Content knowledge: A compendium of standards and benchmarks for K–12 education. Aurora, CO: Mid-Continent Research for Education and Learning (McRel). Retrieved February 11, 2006, from www.mcrel.org/standards-benchmarks

The Kids on the Web: Children's Books. (2005). Retrieved September 25, 2005, from www.zen.org/~brendan/kids-lit.html

Kim, S. (1999). The effects of storytelling and pretend play on cognitive processes, short-term and long-term narrative recall. *Child Study Journal, 29*(3), 175–191.

King, N. (1992). The impact of context on the play of young children. In S. Kessler & B. Swadener (Eds.), *Reconceptualizing the early childhood curriculum* (pp. 43–61). New York: Teachers College Press.

Klein, A., & Starkey, P. (2004). Fostering preschool children's mathematical knowledge: Findings from the Berkeley Math Readiness Project. In D. H. Clements & J. Sarama (Eds.), *Engaging young children in mathematics: Standards for early childhood mathematics education* (pp. 343–360). Mahwah, NJ: Erlbaum.

Kline, S. (1995). The promotion and marketing of toys: Time to rethink the paradox? In A. Pellegrini (Ed.), *The future of play theory: A multidisciplinary inquiry into the contributions of Brian Sutton-Smith* (pp. 164–186). Albany, NY: SUNY Press.

Klugman, E. (Ed.). (1995). *Play, policy, and practice.* St. Paul, MN: Red Leaf Press.

Kogan, Y. (2003). A study of bones. *Early childhood research & practice, 5*(1). Retrieved July 28, 2005, from www.lecrp.uiuc.edu/vol5/no1/kogan-thumb.html

Kohn, A. (2001, March). Fighting the tests: Turning frustration into action. *Young Children,* 19–24.

Koons, K. (1991). A center for writers. *First Teacher, 12*(7), 23.

Koplow, L. (Ed.). (1996). *Unsmiling faces: How preschools can heal.* New York: Teachers College Press.

Koralek, D., & Kolker, L. J. (Eds.). (2003). *Spotlight on young children and science.* Washington, DC: National Association for the Education of Young Children.

Kostelnik, M., Onaga, E., Rohde, B., & Whiren, A. (2002). *Children with special needs: Lessons for early childhood professionals.* New York: Teachers College Press.

Kranor, L., & Kuschner, A. (Eds.). (1996). *Project exceptional: Exceptional children: Education in preschool techniques for inclusion, opportunity-building, nurturing, and learning.* Sacramento, CA: California Department of Education.

Krechevsky, M. (Ed.). (1998). *Project Spectrum: Early learning activities* (Vol. 3). *Preschool assessment handbook.* New York: Teachers College Press.

Kreidler, W., & Wittall, S. T. (1999). *Adventures in peacemaking* (2nd ed.). Cambridge, MA: Educators for Social Responsibility.

Kritchevsky, L., Prescott, E., & Walling, L. (1977). *Planning environments for young children: Physical space* (2nd ed.). Washington, DC: National Association for the Education of Young Children.

Kroll, L., & Halaby, M. (1997). Writing to learn mathematics in the primary school. *Young Children, 52*(4), 54–60.

Kupetz, B. N., & Twiest, M. M. (2000). Nature, literature, and young children: A natural combination. *Young Children, 55*(1), 59–63.

Labov, W. (1972). *Language in the inner city: Studies in Black English vernacular.* Philadelphia: Pennsylvania University Press.

Lalonde, C. E., & Chandler, M. J. (1995). False belief and understanding goes to school: On the social-emotional consequences of coming early or late to a theory of mind. *Cognition and Emotion, 9,* 167–185.

Lancy, D. (2002). Cultural constraints on children's play. In J. L. Roopnarine (Ed.), *Conceptual, social-cognitive, and contextual issues in the fields of play* (pp. 53–62). *Play and Culture Studies* (Vol. 4). Westport, CT: Ablex.

Landreth, G. L. (2002). *Play therapy: The art of the relationship* (2nd ed.). New York: Brunner-Routledge.

Leavitt, R. L., & Eheart, B. K. (1991). Assessment in early childhood programs. *Young Children, 46*(5), 4–9.

Lederman, J. (1992). *In full glory early childhood: To play's the thing.* Unpublished manuscript.

Levin, D. E. (1998). *Remote control childhood? Combating the hazards of media culture.* Washington, DC: National Association for the Education of Young Children.

Levin, D. E. (2003a). Beyond banning war and superhero play: Meeting children's needs in violent times. *Young Children, 58*(3), 60–64.

Levin, D. E. (2003b). *Teaching children in violent times—building a peaceable classroom* (2nd ed.). Cambridge, MA: Educators for Social Responsibility; Washington, DC: National Association for the Education of Young Children.

Levin, D. E. (2005). So sexy, so soon: The sexualization of childhood. In C. Olfman (Ed.), *Childhood lost: How American culture is failing its children.* Westport, CT: Greenwood/Praeger.

Levin, D. E., & Carlsson-Paige, N. (2006). *The war play dilemma: What every parent and teacher needs to know* (2nd ed.). New York: Teachers College Press.

Levin, D. E., & Linn, S. (2003). The commercialization of childhood: Understanding the problem and finding solutions. In T. Kasser & A. Kanner (Eds.), *Psychology and consumer culture: The struggle for a good life in a materialistic world.* Washington, DC: American Psychological Association.

Lewis, C. C. (1995). *Educating hearts and minds: Reflections on Japanese preschool and elementary education.* New York: Cambridge University Press.

Lieberman, J. N. (1977). *Playfulness: its relationship to imagination and creativity.* New York: Academic Press.

Lillard, A. S. (1998a). Playing with theory of mind. In O. Saracho & B. Spodek (Eds.), *Multiple perspectives on play in early childhood education* (pp. 11–33). Albany, NY: SUNY Press.

Lillard, A. S. (1998b). Ethnopsychologies: Cultural variations in theory of mind. *Psychological Bulletin, 123,* 3–33.

Lillard, A. S., & Curenton, S. (1999). Do young children understand what others feel, want, and know? Research in review. *Young Children, 54*(5), 52–57.

Linn, S. (2004). *Consumer kids.* New York: The New Press.

Locke, P. A., & Levin, J. (1998). Creative play begins with fun objects, your imagination, and simple- to-use technology. *The Exceptional Parent, 28,* 36–40.

Lovsey, K. (2002). *Play entry strategies of autistic children.* Unpublished Master of Arts thesis, Rohnert Park, CA: Sonoma State University.

Lowenfeld, V. (1947). *Creative and mental growth.* New York: Macmillan.

Lux, D. G. (Ed.). (1985, Summer). *Theory into Practice, 24*(3).

Lynch, S., & Warner, L. (2004). Computer use in preschools: Directors' reports of the state of the practice. *Early Childhood Research and Practice, 6*(2). Retrieved August 13, 2005, from http://ecrp.uiuc.edu/v6n2/lynch.html

Ma, L. (1999). *Knowing and teaching elementary mathematics.* Hillsdale, NJ: Erlbaum.

Macmillan, A. (1998). Pre-school children's informal mathematical discourses. *Early Child Development and Care, 140,* 53–71.

Manning, K., & Sharp, A. (1977). *Structuring play in the early years at school.* London: Ward Lock Educational.

Marsden, D. B., Meisels, S. J., Jablon, J. R., & Dichtelmiller, M. L. (2001). *The work sampling system* (4th ed.). Ann Arbor, MI: Rebus.

Marvin, C., & Hunt-Berg, M. (1996). Let's pretend: A semantic analysis of preschool children's play. *Journal of Children's Communication Development, 17*(2), 1–10.

McCay, L., & Keyes, D. (2001). Developing social competence in the inclusive early childhood classroom. *Childhood Education, 78,* 70–78.

McCune, L. (1985). Play-language relationships and symbolic development. In L. C. Brown & A. Gottfried (Eds.), *Play interactions* (pp. 38–45). Skillman, NY: Johnson & Johnson.

McCune-Nicolich, L. (1981). Toward symbolic functioning: Structure of early pretend games and potential parallels. *Child Development, 52,* 785–797.

McEvoy, M., Shores, R., Wehby, J., Johnson, S., & Fox, J. (1990). Special education teachers' implementation of procedures to promote social interaction among children in integrated settings. *Education and Training in Mental Retardation, 25*(3), 267–276.

McEwan, H., & Egan, K. (Eds.). (1995). *Narrative in teaching, learning, and research.* New York: Teachers College Press.

McGhee, L. (2003). Shaking the foundations of emergent literacy: Book reading vs. phonemic awareness. In J. P. Isenberg & M. R. Jalango (Eds.), *Major trends and issues in early childhood education* (2nd ed., pp. 114–125). New York: Teachers College Press.

McLloyd, V. (1983). The effects of the structure of play objects on the pretend play of low-income preschool children. *Child Development, 54,* 626–635.

McMahon, F. F., Lytle, E. E., & Sutton-Smith, B. (2005). Play, an interdisciplinary synthesis. *Play and Culture Studies* (Vol. 6). Lanham, MD: University Press of America.

Mead, G. H. (1934). *Mind, self, and society.* Chicago: University of Chicago Press.

Meier, D. (2000). *Will standards save public education?* Boston: Beacon Press.

Meier, D. R. (2000). *Scribble scrabble—learning to read and write.* New York: Teachers College Press.

Meisels, S. (1993). Remaking classroom assessment with the work sampling system. *Young Children, 48*(5), 34–40.

Meisels, S. (2000). On the side of the child: Personal reflections on testing, teaching, and early childhood education. *Young Children, 55*(6), 16–19.

Meisels, S. (2005). *Developmental screening in early childhood: A guide.* Washington, DC: National Association for the Education of Young Children.

Melben, L. W. (2000). Nature in the city: Outdoor science projects for urban schools. *Science & Children, 37*(7), 18–21.

Meyers, C., Klein, E., & Genishi, C. (1994). Peer relationships among four preschool second language learners in "small group time." *Early Childhood Research Quarterly, 9,* 61–85.

Milligan, S. A. (2003, November). Assistive technologies: Supporting the participation of children with disabilities. *Young Children Beyond the Journal.* Retrieved September 16, 2005, from www.journal.naeyc.org/btj/200311/assistivetechnology.pdf

Milne, R. (1995, December). Let the children play: Settling in after immigration. *Resource, 85,* 1–2.

Mindes, G. (1998). Can I play too? Reflections on the issues for children with disabilities. In D. Fromberg & D. Bergen (Eds.), *Play from birth to twelve and beyond: Contexts, perspectives, and meanings* (pp. 208–214). New York: Garland.

Mitchell, G. (with Dewsnap, L.) (1993). *Help! What do I do about: Biting, tantrums, and 47 other everyday problems?* New York: Scholastic.

Moll, L. C. (Ed.). (1990). *Vygotsky and education: Instructional implications and applications of sociohistorical psychology.* New York: Cambridge University Press.

Monighan-Nourot, P. (1990). The legacy of play in American early childhood education. In E. Klugman & S. Smilansky (Eds.), *Children's play and learning: Perspectives and policy implications* (pp. 59–85). New York: Teachers College Press.

Monighan-Nourot, P., Scales, B., & Van Hoorn, J., (with Almy, M.). (1987). *Looking at children's play: A bridge between theory and practice.* New York: Teachers College Press.

Montessori, M. (1936). *The secret of childhood.* Bombay, India: Orient Longman.

Moore, R., & Wong, H. (1997). *Natural learning: Creating environments for rediscovering nature's way of teaching.* Berkeley, CA: MIG Communication.

Morrison, H. (1985a). *Learning to see what I saw.* Unpublished report of a research project for the Bay Area Writing Project, Berkeley, CA: University of California.

Morrison, H. (1985b). Workshop for the Bay Area Writing Center at the University of California, Berkeley, CA.

Morrison, H., & Grossman, H. (1985). *Beginnings* [Videotape]. Produced for the Bay Area Writing Project, Berkeley, CA: University of California.

Murphey, D. A., & Burns, C. E. (2002). Development of a comprehensive community assessment of school readiness. *Early Childhood Research and Practice, 4*(2), 1–15.

Murphy, K., DePasquale, R., & McNamara, E. (2003). Meaningful connections: Using technology in primary classrooms. *Young Children, 58*(4), 28–36.

Murray, A. (2001). Ideas on manipulative math for young children. *Young Children, 56*(4), 28–29.

Myers, C., McBride, S., & Peterson, C. (1996). Transdisciplinary, play-based assessment in early childhood special education: An examination of social validity. *Topics in Early Childhood Special Education, 16*(1), 66–87.

Myhre, S. M. (1993). Enhancing your dramatic play area through the use of prop boxes. *Young Children, 48*(5), 6–11.

Nabhan, G. P. (1997). *Cultures of habitat: On nature, culture, and story.* Washington, DC: Counterpoint.

Nabhan, G. P., & Trimble, S. (1994). *The geography of childhood: Why children need wild places.* Boston: Beacon Press.

Nachmanovitch, S. (1990). *Free play: The power of improvisation in life and the arts.* New York: Putnam.

Nacif, V. (2005). The food and restaurant project. *Early Childhood Research and Practice, 7*(1), 1–38.

National Academy of Science. (1995). *National science education standards.* Washington, DC: National Academy Press.

National Art Education Association. (1999). *Purposes, principles, and standards for school art programs.* Reston, VA: Author.

National Association for the Education of Young Children and National Association of Early Childhood Specialists in State Department of Education. (1991). Guidelines for appropriate curriculum content and assessment in programs serving children ages 3 through 8. *Young Children, 46*(3), 21–38.

National Association for the Education of Young Children and National Association of Early Childhood Specialists in State Departments of Education. (2003). *Joint position statement: Early childhood curriculum, assessment, and program evaluation: Building an effective, accountable system in programs for children birth through age 8*. Retrieved September 22, 2005, from www.naeyc.org/resources/position-statements/pscape.asp

National Association for the Education of Young Children and National Association of Early Childhood Specialists in State Departments of Education (NAECS/SDS). (2002). *Joint position statement: Early learning standards: Creating the conditions for success*. Retrieved July 15, 2005, from www.naeyc.org/about/positions/early_learning_standards.asp

National Association for the Education of Young Children and the National Council of Teachers of Mathematics. (2002). *Early childhood mathematics: Promoting good beginnings. A joint position statement of the National Association for the Education of Young children and the National Council of Teachers of Mathematics*. Retrieved October 14, 2005, from www.naeyc.org

National Association for the Education of Young Children. (1996). Position statement: Technology and young children—ages three through eight. *Young Children, 5*(6), 11–16.

National Association of Early Childhood Specialists in State Departments of Education (2002). *Recess and the importance of play: A position statement on young children and recess*. Washington, DC: Author. Retrieved September 25, 2005, from http://naecs.crc.uiuc.edu/position/recessplay.html

National Council of Teachers of Mathematics. (1989). *Curriculum and evaluation standards for school mathematics*. Reston, VA: Author.

National Educational Goals Panel (1998). *Principles and recommendations for early childhood assessments*. Washington, DC: Author.

National Science Education Standards. (1996). Retrieved February 18, 2005, from http://newton.nap.edu/html/nses/6e.html

National Science Resources Center. (1996). *Resources for teaching elementary school science*. Washington, DC: National Academy Press.

National Science Resources Center. (1997). *Science for all children: A guide to improving elementary science education in your school district*. Washington, DC: National Academy Press.

National Science Teachers Association. (1992). Outstanding science books for young children in 1991. *Young Children, 47*(4), 73–75.

Natural Learning Initiative, College of Design, School of Architecture, North Carolina State University. Retrieved October 9, 2005, from http://naturalearning.org

Neeley, P. M., Neeley, R. A., Justen, J. E., III, & Tipton-Sumner, C. (2001). Scripted play as a language intervention strategy for preschoolers with developmental disabilities. *Early Childhood Education Journal, 28*(4), 243–246.

Nel, E. (2000). Academics, literacy, and young children: A plea for a middle ground. *Childhood Education, 76*(3), 136–141.

Neuman, S., & Roskos, K. (1991). Peers as literacy informants: A description of young children's literacy conversations in play. *Early Childhood Research Quarterly, 6*(2), 233–248.

Neuman, S., & Roskos, K. (2005). Whatever happened to developmentally appropriate practice in early literacy? *Young Children, 60*(94), 22–26.

Neves, P., & Reifel, S. (2002). The play of early writing. In J. L. Roopnarine (Ed.), *Conceptual, social-cognitive, and contextual issues in the fields of play* (pp. 149–164). *Play and culture studies* (Vol. 4). Westport, CT: Ablex.

New, R. (2005). The Reggio Emilia approach: Provocation and partnerships with U.S. early childhood educator. In J. P. Roopnarine & J. Johnson (Eds.), *Approaches to early childhood education* (4th ed., pp. 313–335). Upper Saddle River, NJ: Merrill/Prentice Hall.

Newcomer, P. (1993). *Understanding and teaching emotionally disturbed children and adolescents*. Austin, TX: PRO-ED.

Newman, D., Griffin, P., & Cole, M. (1989). *The construction zone: Working for cognitive change in school*. Cambridge, MA: Cambridge University Press.

Newsletter of the Play, Policy, and Practice Interest Forum of the National Association for the Education of Young Children. *Play, policy, and practice connections*. Edinboro, PA: Author.

Nickelsburg, J. (1976). *Nature activities for early childhood*. Menlo Park, CA: Addison-Wesley.

Nicolopoulou, A. (1991). Play, cognitive development and the social world: The research perspective. In B. Scales, M. Almy, A. Nicolopoulou, & S. Ervin-Tripp (Eds.), *The social context of play and development in early care and education* (pp. 129–142). New York: Teachers College Press.

Nicolopoulou, A. (1996b). Narrative development in a social context. In D. Slobin, J. Gearhart, A. Kyratzis, & J. Guo (Eds.), *Social interaction, social context, and language* (pp. 369–390). Mahwah, NJ: Erlbaum.

Nicolopoulou, A. (1997). Worldmaking and identity formation in children's narrative play-acting. In B. D. Cox & C. Lightfoot (Eds.), *Sociogenetic perspectives on internalization* (pp. 157–187). Mahwah, NJ: Erlbaum.

Nicolopoulou, A. (2001). Peer-group culture and narrative development. In S. Blum-Kulka & C. Snow (Eds.), *Talking with adults*. Mahwah, NJ: Erlbaum.

Nicolopoulou, A., & Scales, B. (1990, March). *Teenage Mutant Ninja Turtles vs. the prince and the princess*. Paper presented at 11th Annual Meeting of the Pennsylvania Ethnography and Research Forum, Philadelphia.

Nicolopoulou, A., Scales, B., & Weintraub, J. (1994). Gender differences and symbolic imagination in the stories of 4-year-olds. In A. H. Dyson & C. Genishi (Eds.), *The need for story: Cultural diversity in classroom and community* (pp. 102–123). Urbana, IL: National Council of Teachers of English.

Ninio, A., & Bruner, J. S. (1976). The achievement and antecedents of labeling. *Journal of Child Language, 5*, 1–15.

Nixon, W. (1997). How nature shapes childhood: Personality, play, and a sense of place. *The Amicus Journal, 19*(2), 31–35.

Nourot, P. M. (1997). Playing with play in four dimensions. In J. Isenberg & M. Jalongo (Eds.), *Major trends and issues in early childhood education: Challenges, controversies and insights*. New York: Teachers College Press.

Nourot, P. M. (2005). Historical perspectives on early childhood education. In J. P. Roopnarine & J. Johnson (Eds.), *Approaches to early childhood education* (4th ed.) (pp. 3–43). Upper Saddle River, NJ: Merrill/Prentice Hall.

Nourot, P. M. (in press). Sociodramatic play: Pretending together. In D. Fromberg & D. Bergen (Eds.), *Play from birth to twelve and beyond: Contexts, perspectives, and meaning* (2nd ed.). New York: Routledge.

Nourot, P. M., Henry, J., & Scales, B. (1990, April). *A naturalistic study of story play in preschool and kindergarten*. Paper presented at the Annual Meeting of the American Educational Research Association, Boston.

NSTA/Children's Book Council Joint Book Review Panel. (2001). List of Outstanding Trade Books for Children. *Science & Children, 38*(6), 27–34.

Oaklander, V. (1978). *Windows to our children*. Moab, UT: Real People Press.

Odom, S. (Ed.). (2002). *Widening the circle: Including children with disabilities in preschool programs*. New York: Teachers College Press.

Okagaki, L., & Diamond, K. (2000). Research in review: Responding to cultural and linguistic differences in the beliefs and practices of families with young children. *Young Children, 55*(3), 74–92.

Oravec, J. (2000). Interactive toys and children's education: Strategies for educators and parents. *Childhood Education, 7*(3), 81–85.

Orellana, M. (1994). Appropriating the voice of the superheroes: Three preschoolers' bilingual language uses in play. *Early Childhood Research Quarterly, 9*(2), 171–193.

Osofsky, J. D. (1999). The impact of violence on children. *The Future of Children, 9*(3), 33–49.

Ostrosky, M., Kaiser, A., & Odom, S. (1993). Facilitating children's social-communicative interactions through the use of peer-mediated interventions. In A. Kaiser & D. Gray (Eds.), *Enhancing children's communication* (pp. 159–185). Baltimore: Brookes.

Owacki, G. (2001). *Make way for literacy! Teaching the way young children learn*. Washington, DC: National Association for the Education of Young Children.

Packer, M., & Addison, R. B. (Eds.). (1989). *Entering the circle: Hermeneutic investigation in psychology* (pp. 1–36, 95–117, 275–292). Albany, NY: SUNY Press.

Paley, V. G. (1981). *Wally's stories*. Cambridge, MA: Harvard University Press.

Paley, V. G. (1984). *Boys & girls: Superheroes in the doll corner*. Chicago: University of Chicago Press.

Paley, V. G. (1986). *Mollie is three*. Chicago: University of Chicago Press.

Paley, V. G. (1988). *Bad guys don't have birthdays: Fantasy play at four*. Chicago: University of Chicago Press.

Paley, V. G. (1990). *The boy who would be a helicopter*. Cambridge, MA: Harvard University Press.

Paley, V. G. (1992). *You can't say you can't play.* Cambridge, MA: Harvard University Press.

Paley, V. G. (1994). Princess Annabella and the black girls. In A. H. Dyson & C. Genishi (Eds.), *The need for story: Cultural diversity in classrooms and community* (pp. 145–154). Urbana, IL: National Council of Teachers of English.

Paley, V. G. (1995). *Kwanzaa and me: A teacher's story.* Cambridge, MA: Harvard University Press.

Paley, V. G. (1997). *The girl with the brown crayon.* Cambridge, MA: Harvard University Press.

Paley, V. G. (1999). *The kindness of children.* Cambridge, MA: Harvard University Press.

Paley, V. G. (2004). *A child's work: The importance of fantasy play.* Chicago: University of Chicago Press.

Papert, S. A. (1980). *Mindstorms: Children, computers and powerful ideas.* New York: Basic Books.

Papert, S. A. (1993). *The children's machine: Rethinking school in the age of the computer.* New York: Basic Books.

Parten, M. B. (1932). Social participation among preschool children. *Journal of Abnormal Psychology, 27,* 243–269.

Pellegrini, A. D. (1984). The effects of exploration and play on young children's associative fluency: A review and extension in training studies. In T. D. Yawkey & A. D. Pellegrini (Eds.), *Child's play: Developmental and applied* (pp. 237–253). Hillsdale, NJ: Erlbaum.

Pellegrini, A. D. (1998). Play and the assessment of children. In O. Saracho & B. Spodek (Eds.), *Multiple perspectives on play in early childhood education* (pp. 220–239). Albany, NY: SUNY Press.

Pellegrini, A. D. (2002). Perceptions of play fighting and real fighting: Effects of sex and particpant status. In J. L. Roopnarine (Ed.), Conceptual, social-cognitive, and contextual issues in the fields of play (pp. 223–234). *Play and Culture Studies* (Vol. 4). Westport, CT: Ablex.

Pellegrini, A. D., & Galda, L. (1993). Ten years after: A reexamination of play and literacy research. *Reading Research Quarterly, 28*(2), 163–175.

Pelletier, J., Halewood, C., & Reeve, R. (2005). How knowledge forum contributes to new literacies in kindergarten. *Orbit, 10*(1), 30–33.

Pelo, A., & Davidson, F. (2000). *That's not fair: A teacher's guide to activism with young children.* St. Paul, MN: Redleaf Press.

Perry, J. (2001). *Outdoor play: Teaching strategies with young children.* New York: Teachers College Press.

Perry, J. (2003). Making sense of outdoor pretend play. *Young Children, 58*(3), 26–30.

Phillips, A. (2002). Roundabout we go: A playable moment with a child with autism. In C. R. Brown & C. Marchant (Eds.), *Play in practice: Case studies in young children's play* (pp. 115–122). St Paul, MN: Redleaf Press.

Phyfe-Perkins, E. (1980). Children's behavior in preschool settings—a review of research concerning the influence of the physical environment. In L. G. Katz (Ed.), *Current topics in early childhood education* (Vol. 3, pp. 91–125). Norwood, NJ: Ablex.

Piaget, J. (1954). *The construction of reality in the child.* New York: Ballantine Books.

Piaget, J. (1962a). Comments. In L. S. Vygotsky, *Thought and language.* Cambridge, MA: MIT Press.

Piaget, J. (1962b). *Play, dreams and imitation in childhood.* New York: Norton.

Piaget, J. (1963a). *The origins of intelligence in children.* New York: Norton.

Piaget, J. (1963b). *The psychology of intelligence.* Totowa, NJ: Littlefield, Adams.

Piaget, J. (1965a). *The child's conception of number.* New York: Norton.

Piaget, J. (1965b). *The child's conception of physical causality.* Totowa, NJ: Littlefield, Adams.

Piaget, J. (1965c). *The child's conception of the world.* Totowa, NJ: Littlefield, Adams.

Piaget, J. (1965d). *The moral judgment of the child.* New York: Free Press.

Piaget, J. (1966). *Judgment and reasoning in the child.* Totowa, NJ: Littlefield, Adams.

Piaget, J. (1969a). *The child's conception of time.* New York: Basic Books.

Piaget, J. (1969b). *The language and thought of the child.* New York: World Publishing.

Piaget, J. (1971). *The child's conception of movement and speed.* New York: Ballantine.

Piaget, J. (1977). *The development of thought: Equilibration of cognitive structures.* New York: Viking.

Piaget, J. (1995). *Sociological studies.* New York: Routledge.

Piaget, J., & Inhelder, B. (1967). *The child's conception of space.* New York: Norton.

Piaget, J., & Inhelder, B. (1975). *The origin of the idea of chance in children.* New York: Norton.

Piaget, J., Inhelder, B., & Szeminska, A. (1960). *The child's conception of geometry.* London: Routledge & Kegan Paul.

Piaget, J., & Smith, L. (Eds.). (1995). *Sociological studies.* New York: Routledge.

Pulaski, M. (1970). Play as a function of toy structure and fantasy predisposition. *Child Development, 41,* 531–537.

Pyle, R. M. (1993). *The thunder tree.* New York: Houghton-Mifflin.

Ramsey, P. (1998). Diversity and play: Influences of race, culture, class, and gender. In D. P. Fromberg & D. Bergen (Eds.), *Play from birth to twelve and beyond: Contexts, perspectives, and meanings* (pp. 23–33). New York: Garland.

Ramsey, P. (2004). *Teaching and learning in a diverse world: Multicultural education for young children* (3rd ed.). New York: Teachers College Press.

Ramsey, P., & Reid, R. (1988). Designing play environments for preschool and kindergarten children. In D. Bergen (Ed.), *Play as a medium for learning and development: A handbook of theory and practice* (pp. 213–240). Portsmouth, NH: Heinemann.

Reed, T. L. (2005). A qualitative approach to boys' rough and tumble play: There is more than meets the eye. In F. F. McMahon, E. E., Lytle, & B. Sutton-Smith (Eds.), *Play, an interdisciplinary synthesis. Play and Culture Studies* (Vol. 6). Lanham, MD: University Press of America.

Reifel, S., & Yeatman, J. (1991). Action, talk and thought in block play. In B. Scales, M. Almy, A. Nicolopoulou, & S. Ervin-Tripp (Eds.), *The social context of play and development in early care and education* (pp. 156–172). New York: Teachers College Press.

Reifel, S., & Yeatman, J. (1993). From category to context: Reconsidering classroom play. *Early Childhood Research Quarterly, 8,* 347–367.

Reifel, S., Hoke, P., Pape, D., & Wisneski, D. (2004). From context to texts: DAP, hermeneutics, and reading classroom play. In S. Reifel & M. Brown (Eds.). *Social contexts of early education, and reconceptualizing play (II): Advances in early education and day care* (Vol. 13, pp. 209–220). Oxford, UK: JAI/Elsevier Science.

Reynolds, G. (2002). The welcoming place: Tungasuvvingat Inuit Head Start program. In C. R. Brown & C. Marchant (Eds.) *Play in practice: Case studies in young children's play* (pp. 87–104). St Paul, MN: Redleaf Press.

Reynolds, G., & Jones, E. (1997). *Master players: Learning from children at play.* New York: Teachers College Press.

Richardson, K. (2004). Making sense. In D. H. Clements & A. Sarama (Eds.), *Engaging young children in mathematics: Standards for early childhood mathematics education* (pp. 321–324). Mahwah, NJ: Erlbaum.

Richner, E. S., & Nicolopoulou, A. (2001, April). The narrative construction of differing conceptions of the person in the development of young children's social understanding. *Early Education and Development, 12,* 393–432.

Rideout, V., Vanderwater, E., & Wartella, A. (2003). *Zero to six: Electronic media in the lives of infants, toddlers and preschooler.* Menlo Park, CA: The Kaiser Family Foundation.

Rivkin, M. S. (1995). *The great outdoors: Restoring children's right to play outside.* Washington, DC: National Association for the Education of Young Children.

Robinson, C., Anderson, G. T., Porter, C., Hart, C., Wouden-Miller, M. (2003). Sequential transition patterns of preschoolers' social interactions during child-initiated play: Is parallel-aware play a bidirectional bridge to other play states? *Early Childhood Research Quarterly, 18,* 3–21.

Robinson, T., Wilde, M., Navracruz, L., Haydel, K., & Varady, A. (2001). Effects of reducing children's television and video game use on aggressive behavior: A randomized controlled trial. *Developmental and Behavioral Pediatrics, 22*(3), 179–183.

Robinson, V. B., Ross, G., & Neal, C. (2000). *Emergent literacy in kindergarten: A review of the research and related suggested activities and learning strategies.* San Mateo, CA: California Kindergarten Association.

Roopnarine, J. L., Shin, M., Donovan, B., & Suppal, P. (2000). Sociocultural contexts of dramatic play: Implications for early education. In *Play and literacy in early childhood: Research from multiple perspectives* (pp. 205–220). Mahwah, NJ: Erlbaum.

Rosenkoetter, L., Rosenkoetter, R., Ozretich, R., & Acock, A. (2004). Mitigating the harmful effects of violent television. *Journal of Applied Developmental Psychology*, 25–47.

Roskos, K. (2000). Through the bioecological lens: Some observations of literacy in play as a proximal process. In K. Roskos & J. Christie (Eds.), *Play and literacy in early childhood: Research from multiple perspectives* (pp. 125–138). Mahwah, NJ: Erlbaum.

Roskos, K., & Christie J. (2004). Examining the play-literacy interface: A critical review and future directions. In E. Zigler, D. Singer, & S. Bishop-Josef (Eds.), *Children's play: The roots of reading* (pp. 95–124). Washington, DC: Zero to Three Press.

Roskos, K., & Christie, J. (Eds.). (2000a). Afterword. In *Play and literacy in early childhood: Research from multiple perspectives* (pp. 231–240). Mahwah, NJ: Erlbaum.

Roskos, K., & Christie, J. (Eds.). (2000b). *Play and literacy in early childhood: Research from multiple perspectives*. Mahwah, NJ: Erlbaum.

Roskos, K., & Christie, J. (2001). On not pushing children too hard: A few cautionary remarks about literacy and play. *Young Children, 56*(3), 64–66.

Roskos, K., & Neuman, S. (1998). Play as an opportunity for literacy. In O. Saracho & B. Spodek (Eds.), *Multiple perspectives on play in early childhood education* (pp. 100–115). Albany, NY: SUNY Press.

Rubin, K. H. (1980). Fantasy play: Its role in the development of social skills and social cognition. In K. H. Rubin (Ed.), *Children's play* (pp. 69–84). San Francisco, CA: Jossey-Bass.

Rubin, K. H., & Maioni, T. L. (1975). Play preference and its relationship to egocentrism, popularity, and classification skills in preschoolers. *Merrill-Palmer Quarterly, 21*, 171–179.

Rubin, K. H., Fein, G., & Vandenberg, B. (1983). Play. In E. M. Hetherington (Ed.) & P. H. Mussen (Series Ed.), *Handbook of child psychology: Vol. 4. Socialization, personality, and social development* (pp. 698–774). New York: Wiley.

Rubin, K. H., Maioni, T. L., & Hornung, M. (1976). Free play behaviors in middle- and lower-class preschoolers: Parten & Piaget revisited. *Child Development, 47*, 414–419.

Safechild.net's top 5 toy safety tips. Retrieved September 14, 2005, from www.drtoy.com/tips-on-toys/safechild-nets-toysafety-tips.html

Salmon, M., & Akaran, S. E. (2001). Enrich your kindergarten program with a crosscultural connection. *Young Children, 56*(4), 30–33.

Saltz, E., & Johnson, J. (1974). Training for thematic fantasy play in culturally disadvantaged children: Preliminary results. *Journal of Educational Psychology, 66*, 623–630.

Sandall, S. (2003). Play modifications for children with disabilities. *Young Children, 58*(3), 54–57.

Saracho, O. (2001). Teachers' perceptions of their roles in promoting literacy in the context of play in a Spanish-speaking kindergarten. *International Journal of Early Childhood, 33*(2), 18–32.

Sarama, J. (2004). Technology in early childhood mathematics: Building blocks as an innovative technology-based curriculum. In D. H. Clements & J. Sarama (Eds.), *Engaging young children in mathematics: Standards for early childhood mathematics education* (pp. 361–376). Mahwah, NJ: Erlbaum.

Sarama, J., & Clements, D. H. (2002). Learning and teaching with computers in early childhood education. In O. Saracho & B. Spodek (Eds.), *Contemporary perspectives on early childhood curriculum* (pp. 177–219). Greenwich, CT: Information Age Publishing.

Sawyer, K. (1997). *Pretend play as improvisation: Conversation in the preschool classroom*. Mahwah, NJ: Erlbaum.

Sawyer, K. (2001). *Creating conversations: Performance in everyday life*. Creskill, NJ: Hampton Press.

Saxe, G. B. (1991). *Culture and cognitive development: Studies in mathematical understanding*. Hillsdale, NJ: Erlbaum.

Scales, B. (1970, January). *Word and action: Creating a context for responsible autonomy*. Paper presented at a Drama in Education workshop at the University of Victoria, British Columbia, Canada.

Scales, B. (1989). Whoever gets to the bottom gets the soap, right? In *The Proceedings of the Annual Ethnography in Education Forum*. Philadelphia: University of Pennsylvania.

Scales, B. (1996). Researching the hidden curriculum. In S. Reifel (Ed.), J. Chafel & S. Reifel (Series Eds.), *Advances in early education and day care: Theory and practice in early childhood teaching, Vol. 8* (pp. 237–259). Greenwich, CT: JAI Press.

Scales, B. (1996, April). *Researching play and the hidden curriculum*. Paper presented at the annual meeting of The Association for the Study of Play, Austin, TX.

Scales, B. (1997, April). *Play in the curriculum: A mirror of development and a catalyst for learning*. Paper presented at the annual meeting of The Association for the Study of Play, Washington, DC.

Scales, B. (2000, March). *Math: The missing learning center*. Sacramento, CA: California Association for the Education of Young Children.

Scales, B. (2001, November). *Tales from the classroom: Mapping the social ecology of play sites*. National Association for the Education of Young Children, The Association for the Study of Play, and Play Policy and Practice Joint Seminar, Anaheim, CA.

Scales, B. (2004, November). Standards? Not a problem. Paper presented at the National Association for the Education of Young Children Annual Conference.

Scales, B. (2005, February). *Using technology to track the development of socially isolated child*. Paper presented at the annual meeting of the Association for the Study of Play, Santa Fe, NM.

Scales, B., & Cook-Gumperz, J. (1993). Gender in narrative and play: A view from the frontier. In S. Reifel (Ed.), *Advances in early education and day care: Perspectives on developmentally appropriate practice, Vol. 5* (pp. 167–195). Greenwich, CT: JAI Press.

Scales, B., & Webster, P. (1976). *Interactive cues in children's spontaneous play*. Unpublished manuscript.

Scales, B., Almy, M., Nicolopoulou, A., & Ervin-Tripp, S. (Eds.). (1991). *Play and the social context of development in early care and education. Part II: Language, literacy, and the social worlds of children* (pp. 75–126). New York: Teachers College Press.

Scarlett, W. G., Naudeau, S., Salonius-Pasternak, D., & Ponte, I. (2005). *Children's play*. Thousand Oaks, CA: Sage Publications.

Schor, J. (2004). *Born to buy: The commercialized child and the new consumer culture*. New York: Scribner.

Schrader, C. (1990). Symbolic play as a curricular tool for early literacy development. *Early Childhood Research Quarterly, 5*, 79–103.

Schwartzman, H. B. (1976). Children's play: A sideways glance at make-believe. In D. F. Laney & B. A. Tindall (Eds.), *The anthropological study of play: Problems and prospects* (pp. 208–215). Cornwall, NY: Leisure Press.

Schwartzman, H. B. (1978). *Transformations: The anthropology of children's play*. New York: Plenum Press.

Seefeldt, C. (2005). *How to work with standards in the early childhood classroom*. New York: Teachers College Press.

Seefeldt, C., & Galper, A. (2000). *Active experiences for active children: Social studies*. Upper Saddle River, NJ: Merrill/Prentice Hall.

Seefeldt, C., & Galper, A. (2002). *Active experiences for active children: Science*. Upper Saddle River, NJ: Merrill/Prentice Hall.

Seefeldt, C., & Galper, A. (2004). *Active experiences for active children: Mathematics*. Upper Saddle River, NJ: Merrill/Prentice Hall.

Seefeldt, C., & Galper, A. (2007). *Active experiences for active children: Science* (2nd ed.). Upper Saddle River, NJ: Merrill/Prentice Hall.

Seiter, E. (1995). *Sold separately: Parents and children in consumer culture*. New Brunswick, NJ: Rutgers University Press.

Sheldon, A. (1992). Conflict talk: Sociolinguistic challenges to self-assertion and how young girls meet them. *Merrill-Palmer Quarterly, 38*(1), 95–117.

Shepard, L. (2000). The role of assessment in a learning culture. *Educational Researcher, 29*(7), 4–14.

Shepard, L., Kagan, S. L., & Wurtz, E. (1998). Public policy report: Goal 1, early childhood assessments resources group recommendations. *Young Children, 53*(3), 52–54.

Shepard, L., Kagan, S. L., & Wurtz, E. (Eds.). (1998). *Principles and recommendations for early childhood assessments*. Washington, DC: National Education Goals Panel. (Adaptation). Retrieved July 27, 2005, from www.state.ia.us/educate/ecese/is/ecn/primaryse/tppse08.htm

Sheridan, M., Foley, G., & Radlinski, S. (1995). *Using the supportive play model: Individualized intervention in early childhood practice*. New York: Teachers College Press.

Sigel, I. E. (1993). Educating the young thinker: A distancing model of preschool education.

In J. L. Roopnarine & J. E. Johnson (Eds.), *Approaches to early childhood education* (pp. 179–193, 237–252). Upper Saddle River, NJ: Merrill/Prentice Hall.

Silvern, S., & Chaille, C. (1996). Understanding through play. *Childhood Education, 72*(5), 274–277.

Singer, D. G., & Singer, J. L. (1990). *The house of make-believe.* Cambridge, MA: Harvard University Press.

Singer, D. G., & Singer, J. L. (2005). *Imagination and play in the electronic age.* Cambridge, MA: Harvard University Press.

Singer, D. G., Singer, J. L., Plaskon, S. L., & Schweder, A. E. (2003). The role of play in the preschool curriculum. In S. Olfman (Ed.), *All work and no play: How educational reforms are harming our preschoolers* (pp. 43–70). Westport, CT: Praeger.

Singer, J. L. (1973). *The child's world of make-believe: Experimental studies of imaginative play.* New York: Academic Press.

Singer, J. L., & Lythcott, M. (2004). Fostering school achievement and creativity through sociodramatic play in the classroom. In E. Zigler, D. Singer, & S. Bishop-Josef (Eds.), *Children's play: The roots of reading* (pp. 77–94). Washington, DC: Zero to Three Press.

Skeele, R., & Stefantkiewicz, G. (2002). Blackbox in the sandbox: The decision to use technology with young children with annotated bibliography of Internet resources for teachers of young children. *Educational Technology Review, 10*(2), 79–95. Retrieved August 13, 2005, from www.aace.org/pubs/etr/issue3/skeele.cfm

Sluss, D. J. (2002). Block play complexity in same-sex dyads of preschool children. In J. L. Roopnarine (Ed.), Conceptual, social-cognitive, and contextual issues in the fields of play (pp. 77–92). *Play and Culture Studies* (Vol. 4). Westport, CT: Ablex.

Sluss, D., & Stremmel, A. (2004). A sociocultural investigation of the effects of peer interaction on play. *Journal of Research in Childhood Education, 18*(4), 293–305.

Smilansky, S. (1968). *The effects of sociodramatic play on disadvantaged preschool children.* New York: Wiley.

Smilansky, S. (1990). Sociodramatic play: Its relevance to behavior and achievement in school. In E. Klugman & S. Smilansky (Eds.), *Children's play and learning: Perspectives and policy implications* (pp. 18–42). New York: Teachers College Press.

Smilansky, S., & Shefatya, L. (1990). *Facilitating play: A medium for promoting cognitive, socio-emotional and academic development in young children.* Gaithersburg, MD: Psychosocial and Educational Publications.

Smith, A. F. (2000). Reflective portfolios: Preschool possibilities. *Childhood Education, 76,* 204–208.

Smith, N. R., Fuciano, C., Kennedy, M., & Lord, L. (1993). *Experience and art: Teaching children to paint* (2nd ed.). New York: Teachers College Press.

Smith, P. (1994). Play training: An overview. In J. Hellendoom, R. van der Kooij, & B. Sutton-Smith (Eds.), *Play and intervention* (pp. 185–194). Albany, NY: SUNY Press.

Smith, P. K., & Connolly, K. J. (1980). *The ecology of preschool behavior.* Cambridge, UK: Cambridge University Press.

Snow, C. E., Burns, M. S., & Griffin, P. (1998). *Preventing reading difficulties in young children.* Washington, DC: National Academy Press.

Starbright Foundation. (2005). Retrieved September 25, 2005, from http://starbright.org

Starbuck, S., Olthof, M., & Midden, K. (2002). *Hollyhocks and honeybees: Gardening projects for young children.* St. Paul, MN: Red Leaf Press.

Stegelin, D. (2005). Making the case for play policy: Research-based reasons to support play-based environments. *Young Children, 60*(2), 76–85.

Stein, S. (2001). *Noah's children: Restoring the ecology of children.* New York: North Point Press.

Stewart, D. (2001a). *The kindergarten project, 2001.* Lafayette, CA: Old Firehouse School.

Stewart, D. (2001b). *Sophie the pig project.* Lafayette, CA: Old Firehouse School.

Stewig, J. W., & Buege, C. (1994). *Dramatizing literature in whole language classrooms.* New York: Teachers College Press.

Stomfay-Stitz, A., & Hinitz, B. (1995). *Integration/infusion of peace education into early childhood education programs.* Roundtable presentation at the Annual Meeting of the American Educational Research Association, New Orleans, LA.

Stone, M., & Sagstetter, M. (1998). Simple technology: It's never too early to start. *The Exceptional Parent, 28,* 50–51.

Stone, S. J., & Christie, J. F. (1996). Collaborative literacy during sociodramatic play in a multi-age (K–2) primary classroom. *Journal of Research in Childhood Education, 10*(2), 123–133.

Strickland, K., & Strickland, J. (2000). *Making assessment elementary.* Portsmouth, NJ: Heinemann.

Sutton-Smith, B. (1995). Conclusion: The persuasive rhetorics of play. In A. Pellegrini (Ed.), *The future of play theory: A multidisciplinary inquiry into the contributions of Brian Sutton-Smith* (pp. 275–298). Albany, NY: SUNY Press.

Sutton-Smith, B. (1997). *The ambiguity of play.* Cambridge, MA: Harvard University Press.

Sutton-Smith, B., & Rosenberg, B. G. (1971). Sixty years of historical change in the game preferences of American children. In R. E. Herron & B. Sutton-Smith (Eds.), *Child's play* (pp. 18–50). New York: Wiley.

Swartz, D. (1997). *Culture and power: The sociology of Pierre Bourdieu.* Chicago: University of Chicago Press.

Swartz, M. (2005). Playdough: What's standard about it? *Young Children, 60*(2), 100–109.

Swick, K. (2002). The dynamics of families who are homeless: Implications for early childhood educators. *Childhood Education, 80*(3), 116–120.

Sylva, K., Roy, C., & Painter, M. (1980). *Child watching at play-groups and nursery school, Vol. 2: Oxford preschool research project.* Ypsilanti, MI: The High Scope Press.

Teachers Resisting Unhealthy Children's Entertainment (TRUCE) (2004–2005). *Toys and toy trends to avoid.* Somerville MA: Author.

Tegano, D., Sawyers, J., & Moran, J. (1989). Problem-finding and solving in play: The teacher's role. *Childhood Education, 66*(2), 92–97.

Thatcher, D. H. (2001). Reading in math class: Selecting and using picture books for math investigations. *Young Children, 56*(4) 20–26.

Thomas, K. (2005). Indian Island School, early childhood program, Old Town, Maine: Universal design. In S. Friedman (Ed.), Environments that inspire. *Young Children, 60*(3), 53–54.

Tierney, R., Carter, J., & Desai, L. E. (1991). *Portfolio assessment in the reading-writing classroom.* Norwood, MA: Christopher-Gordon.

Tizard, B., & Hughes, M. (1984). *Young children learning.* Cambridge, MA: Harvard University Press.

Tobin, J. (2000). *"Good guys don't wear hats": Children's talk about the media.* New York: Teachers College Press.

Topal, C. W. (2005). Bring the spirit of the studio into the classroom. In L. Gandini, L. Hill, L. Cadwell, & C. Schwall (Eds.), *In the spirit of the studio: Learning from the Atelier of Reggio Emilia* (pp. 119–124). New York: Teachers College Press.

Torquati, J., & Barber, J. (2005). Dancing with trees: Infants and toddlers in the garden. *Young Children, 60*(3), 40–46.

The toy manufacturers of America guide to toys and play. (2005). Retrieved September 25, 2005, from www.openseason.com/annex/library/cic/X0085-toysply.txt.html

Trawick-Smith, J. (1992). A descriptive study of persuasive preschool children: How they get others to do what they want. *Early Childhood Research Quarterly, 7*(1), 95–114.

Trawick-Smith, J. (1994). *Interactions in the classroom: Facilitating play in the early years.* Upper Saddle River, NJ: Merrill/Prentice Hall.

Trawick-Smith, J. (1998). Why play training works: An integrated model for play intervention. *Journal of Research in Childhood Education, 12,* 117–129.

Trawick-Smith, J. (2001). Play and the curriculum. In J. Frost, S. Wortham, & S. Reifel (Eds.), *Play and child development* (pp. 294–339). Upper Saddle River, NJ: Merrill/Prentice Hall.

Trepanier-Street, M., Bock Hong, S., & Donegan, M. (2001). Constructing the image of the teacher in a Reggio-inspired teacher education program. *Journal of Early Childhood Teacher Education, 22,* 47–52.

Tribble, C. (1996). *Individual differences in children's entrance strategies into preschool peer groups as a function of the quality of the mother-child attachment relationship.* Unpublished dissertation, University of California, Berkeley.

Tyrell, J. (2001). *The power of fantasy in early learning.* London: Routledge Falmer.

United States Consumer Product Safety Commission. (2005). *For kids' sake: Think toy safety* (Document #4281). Retrieved January 25, 2006, from cpsc.gov/cpscpub/pubs/281.html www.liveandlearn.com/toysafe.htmlcpsc.gov/cpscpub/pubs/281.html

United States Consumer Product Safety Commission. *Handbook for public playground safety*. Retrieved September 23, 2005, from www.cpsc.gov/CPSCPUB/PUBS/325.pdf

Uttal, D., Marzolf, D., Pierroutsakos, S., Smith, C., Troseth, G., Scudder, K., & DeLoache, J. (1998). Seeing through symbols: The development of children's understanding of symbolic relations. In O. Saracho & B. Spodek (Eds.), *Multiple perspectives on play in early childhood education* (pp. 59–79). Albany, NY: SUNY Press.

van der Kooij, R. (1989a). Research on children's play. *Play and Culture, 2*(1), 20–34.

van der Kooij, R. (1989b). Play and behavioral disorders in schoolchildren. *Play and Culture, 2*(1), 328–339.

Vandenberg, B. (2004). Real and not real: A vital developmental dichotomy. In E. Zigler, D. Singer, & S. Bishop-Josef (Eds.), *Children's play: The roots of reading* (pp. 49-58). Washington, DC: Zero to Three Press.

Van Hoorn, J. L., & McHargue, T. (1999, July). *Early childhood education for peace and nonviolence*. Paper presented at the International Union of Psychological Science Sixth International Symposium on the Contribution of Psychology to Peace, San Juan, Costa Rica.

Veldhuis, H. A. (1982, May). *Spontaneous songs of preschool children*. Master's thesis, San Francisco State University, San Francisco, CA.

von Blanckensee, L. (1997). *Scale for choosing technology-based activities for young children, ages 3–7*. Unpublished manuscript.

von Blanckensee, L. (1999). *Teaching tools for young learners*. Larchmont, NY: Eye on Education.

Vygotsky, L. S. (1962). *Thought and language*. Cambridge, MA: MIT Press.

Vygotsky, L. S. (1967). Play and its role in the mental development of the child. *Soviet Psychology, 12*, 62–76.

Vygotsky, L. S. (1976). Play and its role in the mental development of the child. In J. S. Bruner, A. Jolly, & K. Sylva (Eds.), *Play: Its role in development and evolution* (pp. 537–544). New York: Basic Books.

Vygotsky, L. S. (1978). *Mind in society: The development of higher psychological processes*. Cambridge, MA: Harvard University Press.

Wadsworth, B. J. (1996). *Piaget's theory of cognitive and affective development: Foundations of constructivism* (5th ed.). White Plains, NY: Longman.

Wagner, B. J. (1990). Dramatic improvisation in the classroom. In S. J. Hynds & E. L. Robin (Eds.), *Perspectives on talk and learning* (pp. 195–211). Urbana, IL: National Council of Teachers of English.

Wagner, B. J. (1999). *Dorothy Heathcote: Drama as a learning medium*. Portsmouth, NH: Heinemann.

Wallach, L. B. (1993). Helping children cope with violence. *Young Children, 48*(4), 4–11.

Wang, X. C., Kedem, Y., & Hertzog, N. (2004) Scaffolding young children's reflections with student-created power point presentations. *Journal of Research in Childhood Education, 19*(2), 159–174.

Wanigarayake, M. (2001). From playing with guns to playing with rice: The challenges of working with refugee children: An Australian perspective. *Childhood Education, 77*(5), 289–294.

Wasik, B. (2001). Phonemic awareness and young children. *Childhood Education, 77*(3), 128–133.

Wasserman, S. (2000). *Serious players in the primary classroom: Empowering children through active learning experiences* (2nd ed.). New York: Teachers College Press.

Wasserman, S., & Ivany, J. W. G. (1996). *The new teaching elementary science: Who's afraid of spiders?* (2nd ed.). New York: Teachers College Press.

Weaver, L. R., & Gaines, C. (1999). What to do when they don't speak English: Teaching mathematics to English-language learners in the early childhood classroom. In J. V. Copley (Ed.), *Mathematics in the early years* (pp. 198–204). Reston, VA: National Council of Teachers of Mathematics; Washington, DC: National Association for the Education of Young Children.

Weber, R. (1978). A conversation with David Bohm—the enfolding-unfolding universe, conducted by Renee Weber. *ReVision, 1*, 3–4.

Wesson, K. (2001). The Volvo effect—questioning standardized tests. *Young Children, 56*(2) 16–18.

Wheeler, L., & Raebeck, L. (1985). *Orff and Kodaly adapted for the elementary school* (3rd ed.). Dubuque, IA: William C. Brown.

White, T. H. (1958). *The once and future king*. New York: Berkeley.

Wien, C. A. (2004). *Negotiating standards in the primary classroom: The teacher's dilemma.* New York: Teachers College Press.

Williams, K. P. (2002). "But are they learning anything?" African American mothers, their children, and their play. In C. R. Brown & C. Marchant (Eds.), *Play in practice: Case studies in young children's play* (pp. 73–86). St Paul, MN: Redleaf Press.

Williamson, P., & Silvern, S. (1990). The effect of play training on the story comprehension of upper primary children. *Journal of Research in Child Education, 4*(2), 130–135.

Winnicott, D. W. (1971). *Playing and reality.* New York: Basic Books.

Wohlwill, J. F. (1984). Relationships between exploration and play. In T. Yawkey & A. Pellegrini (Eds.), *Child's play: Developmental and applied* (pp. 143–201). Hillsdale, NJ: Erlbaum.

Wolfberg, P. (1999). *Play and imagination in children with autism.* New York: Teachers College Press.

Wolfe, C. R., Cummins, R. H., & Myers, C. A. (1998). Dabbling, discovery, and dragonflies: Scientific inquiry and exploratory representational play. In D. Fromberg and D. Bergen (Eds.), *Play from birth to twelve and beyond: Contexts, perspectives, and meanings* (pp. 68–76). New York: Garland Publishing.

Wolfe, J. (2002). *Learning from the past: Historical voices in early childhood education* (2nd ed.). Mayerthorpe, Alberta, Canada: Piney Branch Press.

Woods, J., & Scales, B. (1995, June). *The child's hidden curriculum.* Panel presentation at annual meeting of the Association of Constructivist Teaching, Berkeley, CA.

Wortham, S. (2005). *Assessment in early childhood education* (4th ed.). Upper Saddle River, NJ: Merrill/Prentice Hall.

Wurm, J. P. (2005). *Working in the Reggio way: A beginner's guide for American teachers.* Washington, DC: National Association for the Education of Young Children.

Wyver, S. R., & Spence, S. H. (1999). Play and divergent problem solving: Evidence supporting a reciprocal relationship. *Early Education and Development, 10*(4), 419–444.

Yang, H., & McMullen, M. B. (2003). Understanding the relationships among American primary-grade teachers and Korean mothers: The role of communication and cultural sensitivity in the linguistically diverse classroom. *Early Childhood Research and Practice, 5*(1), 1–20.

Yopp, H. K. (1992). Developing phonemic awareness in young children. *The Reading Teacher, 45,* 696–703.

Yopp, H. K. (1995). Read-aloud books for developing phonemic awareness: An annotated bibliography. *The Reading Teacher, 49,* 20–29.

Youngblade, L. M., & Dunn, J. (1995). Individual differences in young children's pretend play with mother and sibling: Links to relationships and understanding of other people's feelings and beliefs. *Child Development, 66,* 1472–1492.

Zakakai, J. D. (1997). *Dance as a way of knowing.* New York: Stenhouse Publishers.

Zan, B. (1996). Interpersonal understanding among friends: A case study of two young boys playing checkers. *Journal of Research in Childhood Education, 10,* 114–122.

Zimmerman, E., & Zimmerman, L. (2000). Art education and early childhood education: The young child as creator and meaning maker within a community context. *Young Children, 56*(6), 87–92.

Name Index

Subject Index